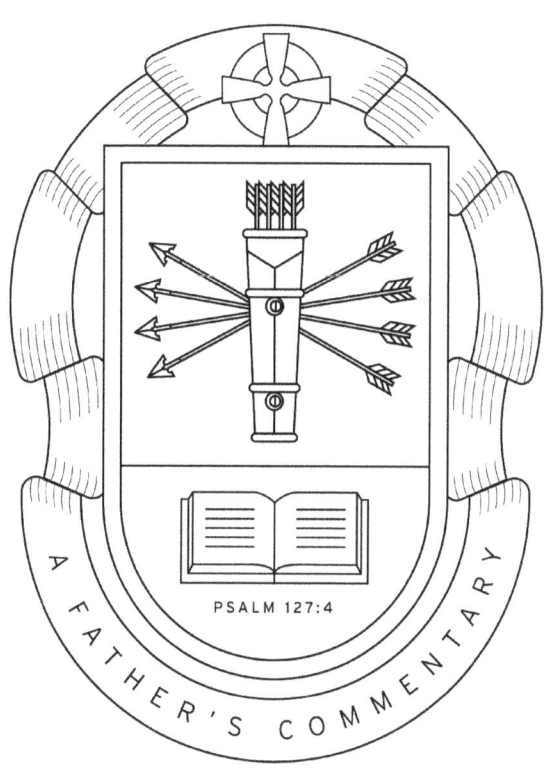

PSALM 127:4

A FATHER'S COMMENTARY

SOLOMON KAFOURE

Copyright © 2022 by Solomon Kafoure

All rights reserved. No part of this publication may be reproduced, distributed, or transmitted in any form or by any means, including photocopying, recording, or other electronic or mechanical methods, without the prior written permission of the author. For permission requests, see www.afatherscommentary.com.

All Scripture quotations are taken from The Holy Bible, English Standard Version, copyright © 2001 by Crossway, a publishing ministry of Good News Publishers Used by permission. All rights reserved.

Printed in the United States of America

Edited by Anna Floit, The Peacock Quill; Nashville, Tennessee

ISBN 978-0-578-38481-8

*For the Glory of God:
to my loving bride Katie
and my four sons:
Nolan, Micah, Titus,
and Caleb*

foreword

A DAD'S DOXOLOGY

At one level, this book is a love letter from a father to his sons. At another level it is a declaration of war against all the disintegrating forces that surround us in these modern days in which we live. But, at the deepest level, it is a heartfelt doxology.

A doxology is a short chorus of praise to the Lord, often sung as a stand-alone piece or as a coda at the conclusion of psalms, hymns, or canticles. The word comes from the Greek doxa, meaning, "appearance" or "glory," and logia, meaning, "study" or "declaration." Common doxologies include the *Gloria in Excelsis Deo* and the *Gloria Patri*. But of course, the most common of all is taken from Psalm 100, and sung to the tune of the Genevan Psalter's Old Hundredth:

> *Praise God from whom all blessings flow; Praise Him,*
> *all creatures here below; Praise him above, ye heavenly host:*
> *Praise Father, Son, and Holy Ghost.*

This treasured doxology is sung every Sunday all around the globe in untold dozens of languages. It was composed by Thomas Ken, a fellow of Winchester College, a prebend of Winchester Cathedral, and later, the Bishop of Bath and Wells during the reigns of Charles II and James II.

Ken was tragically orphaned in childhood. So, his older sister, Ann, and her husband, Izaak Walton, raised him, Walton is celebrated to this day for his classic book, *The Compleat Angler*, as well as for his short biographies of John Donne, Richard Hooker, and George Herbert.

In 1674, Ken published *A Manual of Prayers for the Use of the Scholars of Winchester College*. In it, he gave instructions for the devotional use of his compositions of *Morning and Evening Hymns*. What we now commonly sing as the "Doxology," was actually the closing stanza of each of these long hymns.

According to tradition, Ken may have learned the text and tune from his adoptive father while fly-fishing together in the rivers and streams of Staffordshire. Quite apt, don't you think? A father and son singing praise to God amidst the glories of creation—a doxology so beautiful that it is no longer just a part of their story, but now, it is part of ours.

Reading these practical yet substantial, accessible yet theological devotions, I am reminded of that story. What Solomon Kafoure initially intended to be a simple and systematic habit of opening the Word of God to his boys has now become a means for all of us to open the Scriptures to our own families. That is a fine doxology indeed.

George Grant, Pastor, Parish Presbyterian Church, Franklin, TN

introduction

I wrote this book, by God's grace, for fathers and their children. I wrote it so fathers could show their children how to read God's Word, to pray and apply God's Word, and then live and act accordingly. As fathers teach their children, I pray this book offers godly advice for fathers to show their children how to walk in a godly way,[I] the way that they should go so, when they are old they will not depart from it.[II]

My desire was to write a commentary that would transcend time and circumstance, in which truth and the character of God would illuminate throughout any and every situation. Since there is nothing new under the sun,[III] everything happening today has already happened before. Societies fall when they deny the objective truth—that truth being the Word of God. The act of looking to one's self for the definition of truth makes it so a society will actually turn upon itself. We see this throughout the Greek Empire, the Roman Empire, the French Revolution, and in today's time as well. A culture that gazes at itself is parasitic and will eventually destroy itself.

But for the believer, their hope is in Christ and Christ alone. The Christian knows that though the grass withers and the flowers fade, that the Word of the Lord will stand forever![IV] Christ is firmly and victorious sitting on the throne, and He is even now ruling and reigning according to His will.[V]

[I]Proverbs 5:7, [II]Proverbs 22:6, [III]Ecclesiastes 1:9, [IV]Isaiah 40:8, [V]Hebrews 1:2-3

I wrote this book with a structure that I hope benefits the reader. First is a passage of Scripture. We are to look at every aspect of Scripture as that which is spoken from the very mouth of God[VI] for the edification His people. So when you read the passage, acknowledge that it is God's voice speaking to us. Secondly, I have written out for the reader both truths that God's Word declares in the passage, and practical applications of those truths seen in the believer's life when walking according to His Word. The application is not exhaustive, but is meant to guide the reader toward practical applications in their own life through the Word of God.

Lastly, when we read God's Word, we must be careful to acknowledge that it is not in our own power that our hearts are changed, but only by the power of the Holy Spirit are our hearts truly changed.[VII] Whenever one reads God's Word, they are to pray God's Word back to Him, for His glory and our good. With each devotion, I offer a prayer from my heart as I meditated on the Scriptures on that page.

It is my prayer that this book be a catalyst to reading, studying, and praying God's Word in your life. I pray it be a small model for fathers to lead devotions with their families, and to help them instruct their children in the way they should go. My hope is that God will use this book in whatever way He will, for His glory and the good of His people.

[VI] 2 Timothy 3:16, [VII] Ezekiel 36:26

01

1 Samuel 14:6

Jonathan said to the young man who carried his armor, "Come, let us go over to the garrison of these uncircumcised. It may be that the Lord will work for us, for nothing can hinder the Lord from saving by many or by few."

1. The Lord is in the heavens, and He does whatever He pleases.[1] The Lord is perfect in all His ways and keeps nothing from us that is for our good.[2]

2. In these two truths we must hold fast. For we see that Jonathan neither knew what the Lord would do nor how He would do it, but He knew that nothing could stop the plans and the will of God. For what is impossible with man is possible with God.[3]

3. Many times we go to the Lord and share with Him the desired outcome we choose rather than going to the Lord to know God and His will. We look to our desired outcomes and our own will rather than looking to the Lord.

4. In this, our focus becomes the blessing rather than the Giver of the blessing. We turn the blessing into an idol, and by doing so, either diminish the calling of God based upon our perceived ability, or we seek a desire apart from God because we see the desire as greater than God.

[1]Psalm 115:3, [2]Psalm 84:11, [3]Luke 18:27

Father, who is like You in the heavens? Who is all powerful, all mighty, all glorious? There is none like You! Yet, I so easily am overwhelmed by circumstances, probabilities, and perceptions. I idolize the things of this world rather than looking to You. Forgive me! Help me to walk in accordance with Your will. Lead me on level ground, that I may know You and make You known. In Christ's name.

02

1 Samuel 10:19

But today you have rejected your God, who saves you from all your calamities and your distresses, and you have said to him, "Set a king over us." Now therefore present yourselves before the Lord by your tribes and by your thousands.

1. Ever since sin entered the world through the fall of man,[4] we have been separated from God. We still, in our sin and depravity, desire to hide from God like Adam and Eve did in the garden of Eden.[5]

2. We strive in our hearts and minds for self-lordship and autonomy; we reject the Lord and His work yet never take responsibility before a holy God. There is nothing we can do to stand before a holy God, for all our actions are like filthy rags.[6]

3. We long for someone or something to save us and bring us back to that from which our sin has removed us. We attempt to build up man, money, experiences—anything that gives us hope. We reject God and attempt to find joy in what we can do, rather than in who God is and in trusting His perfect goodness.

4. Yet God, being rich in mercy, gave us the perfect King. He sent His Son to pay the penalty for our sin,[7] that we might be united with God, that we might be a people of God, for God's own pleasure and our good.[8]

[4] Genesis 3, [5] Genesis 3:8, [6] Isaiah 64:6, [7] 2 Corinthians 5:21, [8] 1 Peter 2:9

Father, You are good and perfect in all Your ways. Your love is boundless, for I have rejected You and Your Lordship time after time after time. Forgive me. Forgive me for not submitting to or resting in Your love. Grant me hope in being known and loved by You. Help me to do Your will, for Christ's sake, and for His sake alone. Thank You for Jesus!

1 Samuel 27:1

Then David said in his heart, "Now I shall perish one day by the hand of Saul. There is nothing better for me than that I should escape to the land of the Philistines. Then Saul will despair of seeking me any longer within the borders of Israel, and I shall escape out of his hand."

1. David experienced two incredible acts of providence by the hand of God. For twice, the Lord had placed Saul next to David, and in both instances the Lord protected David and strengthened him to speak boldly in front of Saul. David declared the greatness of the Lord and His faithfulness and protection.

2. Yet, in this verse we see David grow weary and doubt the Lord's faithfulness. He seemed to completely forget the protection and deliverance of God. He doubted the Lord's nearness and preferred to be in the land of his enemies rather than continue running away from Saul. Instead of running to the Lord, he desired to run away and take matters into his own hands.

3. We must remember our strength is in the Lord and in the power of His might.[9] There are times when the Lord removes His presence to test us and to reveal to us our self-reliance, our idolatrous views of our circumstances, and where we trust ourselves rather than trusting Him. David wrote in Psalm 11, "His eyelids test the children of man. The Lord tests the righteous."[10]

4. We must not look at the circumstances of our lives based upon ourselves but in light of who God is. Let us look to Jesus, our Savior and our King, who in the garden of Gethsemane sought the Father and prayed, submitting Himself to the Lord by crying out, "Not my will, but Yours be done." And then let us rise to do that which God has ordained for us; trusting His Word, resting in the comforts of the Holy Spirit, and pressing on toward the goal, which God has prepared in advance for us to do.[11]

[9]Ephesians 6:10, [10]Psalm 11:4–5, [11]Ephesians 2:10

Father, You are strong and mighty and there is none like You. So many times I look at the circumstances of my life and enlarge them to be bigger than You in my heart and mind. I am tempted to not believe Your Word and Your promises, and instead, I make idols out of my circumstances. Forgive me. Help me to know Your strength. Help me to walk in Your strength. Help me to know the joy of the Lord that I may gladly and with my whole heart serve You all my days. Thank You, Lord. In Jesus' name.

04

1 Samuel 30:6

But David strengthened himself in the Lord.

1. Nothing reflects the heart of man more than how we react when difficult situations arise. For those who live according to the flesh set their mind on the things of the flesh. They turn to themselves and turn inward. But those who live according to the Spirit set their minds on the things of the Spirit.[12]

2. In this instance, David had returned from battle, and when he arrived to the city where he'd left his family, he found they had been kidnapped along with all the families of those in his army. He was greatly distressed, and the people threatened to stone him because of the horrific circumstances.

3. However, David did not attempt to justify himself but set his mind on the Lord. He reflected upon the promises of God and strengthened himself on the truths of who God is, rather than defining his circumstances based upon what he saw. He took hold of who God is, the sovereign and holy God, slow to anger and abounding in steadfast love and mercy, and acted in accordance with that truth.

4. In the same way, we must hold fast to the promises of our God in faith and patience and not be sluggish in our affirmation of who God is in all circumstances.[13] For we know that if God is for us, who can be against us?[14] We must draw near to God, knowing with all confidence that He will draw near to us,[15] and that He will lead us and guide us and bring us to victory in accordance with His will.

[12]Romans 8:5, [13]Hebrews 6:12, [14]Romans 8:3, [15]James 4:8

Father, You are strong and mighty. There is nothing that surprises You or deviates from Your plans or Your will. I confess the many times I begin with me rather than beginning with You. I define my circumstances strategically and according to my flesh rather than according to who You are. The pride of my heart wrestles within me to steal Your glory. Forgive me. Humble me with the truth of who You are. May my aim and my strength be defined not by my humanity but by who You are and what You have done through the redemption of Your Son. In Christ's name I pray.

05

1 *Chronicles* 15:26

And because God helped the Levites who were carrying the ark of the covenant of the Lord, they sacrificed seven bulls and seven rams.

1. The ark of the covenant was not a heavy object the Levites carried to Jerusalem, for it contained the tablets of the Law given to Moses by God for God's people.

2. Yet, we see how the author of Chronicles acknowledged that even in this little act, the only reason the Levites could accomplish it was with God's help. This is an acknowledgment of God's providence in our everyday life. Apart from God we can do nothing.[16]

3. We are to depend, seek, and acknowledge God in all circumstances. We are to trust Him in all we do and offer up to Him thanksgiving in every circumstance. By acknowledging His presence, His providence, His blessing in every circumstance, we acknowledge our humanity and depravity and live a life under the full dependence of our God. We will either reflect self-lordship or lordship under a sovereign, holy, and righteous God. For Scripture says even when we lie down at night, the only reason we awake in the morning is because the God of the universe sustains us in our sleep.[17]

4. Every good and perfect gift comes from the Father of lights.[18] The ability to see color; the ability to know things of beauty; the ability to accomplish what He has ordained for the day; and the ability to walk, talk, and understand language are all gifts from the Lord. We depend upon our God for all things, and our thanksgiving and praise should be in direct proportion to our acknowledgment of His greatness and our complete dependence upon Him.

[16] John 15:5, [17] Psalm 41:3, [18] James 1:17

Father, how great You are, and how majestic is Your name in all the earth. In You, I live and move and have my being. Even the ability to write out my prayers and to come before You is a gift from You. The ability to wake in the morning is not a right I have because I am human, but a grace I have been given because of Your greatness. Praise You, Lord. Forgive me for my lack of gratitude and for the temptation to believe I am autonomous from Your grace. Lead me according to Your will. Lead me not into temptation, but deliver me from evil. For Christ's sake.

Psalm 39:9

*I AM MUTE; I DO NOT OPEN MY MOUTH,
FOR IT IS YOU WHO HAVE DONE IT.*

1. David, as he reflected upon all the trials and troubles he experienced, declared to God that he was mute. David resolved in his heart that he would never utter a word in his defense to present his case before man to justify his actions.

2. For David recognized the sovereignty of God over all things. Nothing in life occurs that is not under God's sovereign decree. This does not mean life will be easy or fair in the way humanity measures fairness. But David realized that if he complained in his circumstances, he was accusing God of evil.

3. In a world that denies the sovereignty of God, we feel compelled to not live according to the Word of God but according to our own self-justified word. We gossip and slander; we lie and stir up self-justification because we do not trust God's Word that says, "Vengeance is mine; I will repay."[19] We, in our sinful and depraved hearts, deny that God is orchestrating all things for our good and His glory.[20]

4. Instead of praying and seeking God, we proclaim our own justification and seek our own glory. But let us instead look to Christ, for when He stood before the high priest, He did not need to defend Himself and remained silent.[21] And Peter declared that all that happened to Christ was according to the definite plan and foreknowledge of God.[22] We can then take comfort that our Heavenly Father knows our weaknesses, that He remembers we are dust, and that even in trials He conforms us to the image of His Son. Let us worship our great God and remain silent in humble submission to His will.

[19]Romans 12:19, [20]Romans 8:28, [21]Matthew 26:63, [22]Acts 2:22–24

Father, You are sovereign over all. This is not just a sovereignty over the greatest events in my life but over all things. Even the smallest detail of my life You have ordained and are working for Your glory and my good. Forgive my complaining and griping against You, for it is a heart of unbelief and pride that rages against You. Make me aware of my sin and the completeness of Your sovereign grace in Christ alone. In His name I pray this.

Psalm 56:3-4

When I am afraid, I put my trust in you. In God, whose word I praise, in God I trust; I shall not be afraid. What can flesh do to me?

1. What we do when we are afraid reflects the trust in our hearts and what our hearts seek. Fear is an indicator of that which we worship and what we depend upon when all seems lost.

2. We will either depend upon God and seek Him with all our hearts, or we will seek that which is created. Our hearts are so easily manipulated to deny the nearness, the sovereignty, and the power of God that we are many times seduced by the life we perceive rather than living life according to the Word of God.

3. For God has said in His Word, "I am the one who comforts you; who are you that you are afraid of man? Of the son of man who is made like grass, and have forgotten the Lord your Maker?"[23]

4. We must go to the Lord and meditate on His Word, trusting in Him with all our hearts. For nothing can happen to you that God does not allow. He will withhold nothing for your good.[24] This does not mean He will not bring us through trials or discipline us in ways that cause us pain, but we say with Job, "Shall we receive good from God, and shall we not receive evil?"[25]

5. Our aim is not to understand or define our lives by our circumstances; our aim is to know God. We are to look to God and trust His goodness. In the midst of pain and sorrow we are to look to the Lord and trust His Word, knowing He is good. Nothing can add to or take away from His goodness, and in light of this we say along with our King, "Nevertheless, not my will, but Yours be done."[26]

[23]Isaiah 51:12, [24]Psalm 84:11, [25]Job 2:10, [26]Luke 22:42

Father, You are good and I trust You. Your goodness does not change; Your purposes and ways are sure and true, and in You I trust and will not be moved. Lord, forgive me, for I have not always stood on Your Word. Instead, I have stood on my emotions or perceptions; I have ceased to praise You and I have not trusted in Your Word. Please hide Your Word in my heart that I might not sin against You! Guard my heart from stoicism and allow me to know Your goodness regardless of what You ordain. Thank You for Christ.

Amen

08

Psalm 56:8

You have kept count of my tossings; put my tears in your bottle. Are they not in your book?

1. The Lord is near. He is mindful and near to the brokenhearted and saves the crushed in spirit.[27] He knows our frame and remembers that we are dust.[28]

2. The Lord knows every tossing and every tear we shed. He counts every one of them. There is not one He does not count, or ignores, or deems unworthy of remembering! He knows every tear that falls from pain and sorrow! Our God is not only mindful of them, but He captures every tear in His bottle. They are counted and they are known. There is not one aspect of our lives that the Lord neglects or deems unimportant.

3. He not only captures all our tears but is mindful of every tossing in our bed from the fears and worries, the pain and doubts, and each is recorded in His Book. Our lives are written down; they have purpose and meaning and are known by our Creator. He does not forget them, and He uses all for His glory and our good. He does not waste a moment and uses all things together for the good of those who love Him and are called according to His purpose.[29]

4. Let us then, in light of this knowledge, draw near to the throne of grace with confidence that we might receive mercy and find grace in time of need.[30]

---

[27]Psalm 34:18, [28]Psalm 103:14, [29]Romans 8:28, [30]Hebrews 4:16

Father, how easy it is for me to forget that You know me. I am tempted so often to trust what I see with my eyes and what I feel in my emotions and to deny Your Word. I am tempted so often to believe I am not good enough to be known or that I am not worthy of Your mindfulness of me. Yet You sent Your Son into the world to pay the price of humanity's sin, that I might know You. Jesus took the cup of wrath that I may glorify You. Grant my heart to know You not only in the times of joy but in the times You have ordained when I toss and turn and when tears flood my soul. Grant me the grace of knowing You are near. For the sake of Christ I ask this.

Psalm 59:1-2

Deliver me from my enemies, O my God; protect me from those who rise up against me; deliver me from those who work evil, and save me from bloodthirsty men.

1. Where our hearts go when the Lord ordains trials and temptations reflects our hearts and that which they worship. We must ask ourselves, "When we are delivered over to our enemies, do we seek God or do we seek what is wise in our own eyes?"

2. We see in this instance that David immediately stopped and asked the Lord to protect him from his enemies. He asked Him to deliver him from those who "work evil" and to save him from "bloodthirsty men." David thought not only of the circumstances but of specific people who sought to destroy his life.

3. We must be mindful of our own view of God, for everything we think, say, and do is in direct reflection of where our hearts rest in who God is and who we are. Do we view Him as Lord over all in which we live and move and have our being, where[31] not even a sparrow falls from the sky unless He ordains it?[32] Does He work all things for His glory? Does He know our inmost thoughts, and is He aware of the words in our hearts before they even come out of our mouths?[33]

4. We must look to Christ, who looked to the Father and said, "My Father, if it be possible, let this cup pass from me; nevertheless, not as I will, but as you will."[34] For He knew what was coming and who was coming; but He looked to the Father and prayed and sought God's will in all things. We must, as well be specific in our trials, lay them before the Lord, trust that He will work, and rest in knowing that whatever He ordains is right.

[31]Acts 17:28, [32]Matthew 10:29-31, [33]Psalm 139:4, [34]Matthew 26:39

Father, You are Lord. There is none who can stand before You, none who can defeat You, none who can compare to You. I confess that in the trials and the turmoil, many times I attempt to act wise in my own eyes rather than seek You. I worry and fret because the depravity of my unbelief in Your goodness overwhelms me. Forgive me. Allow me to see Your might. Go before me and help me to think of Your working, of Your glory, of Your beauty, and Your goodness in Christ. Incline my heart to seek and rest in You for the sake of Christ.

Psalm 51:5

BEHOLD, I WAS BROUGHT FORTH IN INIQUITY,
AND IN SIN DID MY MOTHER CONCEIVE ME.

1. We are sinners from birth, and sin corrupts every aspect of our lives. Our thoughts, intentions, motivations, desires, everything is cursed by sin. As the apostle Paul states in Romans 7, sin is a law that is working in the members of our bodies.

2. This sin separates us from a holy God. We are born apart from God and cannot draw near to Him, for God cannot even be around sin. God is perfect, holy, radiant, lovely, and glorious, and we are not. All that we are and all that we bring before the Lord is nothing more than a filthy rag.[35]

3. How do we know all this to be true? It is the very Word of God. God's Law condemns us before a holy God. God's Word, and God's Word alone, makes known to us who God is and who we are. We can never on our own justify anything from the Lord. We can never come before a holy God with anything less than perfection. Paul, in thinking through this, said, "Wretched man that I am! Who will deliver me from this body of death?"[36]

4. "But God, being rich in mercy because of the great love with which He loved us, even while we were dead in our trespasses, made us alive together with Christ Jesus—by grace you have been saved."[37] God the Father sent His only Son to take the wrath that our sinful nature fully deserves. He bore the wrath of God in His body on the cross for those who are His. What beauty, what glory, what grace, and what mercy.

---

[35] Isaiah 64:6, [36] Romans 7:24, [37] Ephesians 2:4–5

Father, You have sent Your only Son into the world! Jesus, who is fully God and fully man, came into the world and took the wrath that my sin so deserves. Who am I that You would do such a thing? Who am I that You would do this for me? I was conceived and brought forth in sin. I have nothing I can stand on or justify myself, and yet You knew me and sent Your Son. I praise You, Father, for Your redemptive work. Help me to know my sin in light of Christ's redemption that I may see the beauty, truth, and goodness of Christ and glorify You, my Father who is in heaven! In Christ's name I ask this.

John 19:11

Jesus answered him, "You would have no authority over me at all unless it had been given you from above. Therefore he who delivered me over to you has the greater sin."

1. All things are ordained by God. All levels of leadership are given by God. There is no king, president, parliament, senate, congressman, or leader, for that matter, who was not ordained and given by God.[38]

2. This does not remove the responsibility of acting just, good, and faithful from those in leadership. This is not a gift that voids or removes that requirement; in fact, because it is given, it will be judged by God in how it is stewarded.

3. This concept does not only apply to politics. All things of leadership, all federal headship, are given by God. Fatherhood is given by God. Management is given by God. Marriage is given by God. Friendship is given by God. All these are gifts from God to be stewarded well and will be judged by God.

4. Prayerfully seek the Lord to help you steward that which the Lord has ordained in your life for His glory. Marriage, fatherhood, friendship, or leadership, for whoever knows the right thing to do and fails to do it, for him, it is sin.[39]

[38]Romans 13:1–5, [39]James 4:17

Father, how easily I let my mind wander. I deny Your Lordship and Your sovereignty and complain and shake my fists at You when things don't go my way. Forgive me. Father, will You open my eyes and my heart, with thanksgiving, that I may praise You and glorify You? Help me to recognize Your sovereignty and love for me, and strengthen me to steward well according to Your will. In Christ's name.

John 15:5

I AM THE VINE; YOU ARE THE BRANCHES. WHOEVER ABIDES IN ME AND I IN HIM, HE IT IS THAT BEARS MUCH FRUIT, FOR APART FROM ME YOU CAN DO NOTHING.

1. Apart from Christ you cannot do anything, and apart from Christ you cannot draw near to the throne of grace.[40] To Jesus Christ be glory, majesty, dominion, and authority before all time, and now and forever. Amen.[41]

2. One might ask, "What does this mean that I cannot do anything? For I do things all the time, and so can the atheist." We must remember that man looks at the outward appearance, but the Lord looks at the heart.[42] Anything that does not come through faith is a sin.[43] That means even our best intentions are sinful if not done by faith in the finished work of Christ.

3. So then, how are we to proceed? We are to acknowledge our dependency on Christ in all things. We are to seek Him and then step forward in a way that reflects and is affirmed by Scripture and is to the glory of God and not ourselves.

4. This can only be because of the redemptive work of Christ and can only be done by the power of God. Even the act of writing this commentary cannot be done in a way that glorifies God apart from the work of Christ, for apart from Him, I can do nothing.

[40]Hebrews 4:16, [41]Jude 25, [42]1 Samuel 16:7, [43]Romans 14:23

Jesus, You are King of kings and Lord of lords. When I read this verse, I confess that my flesh wants to deny its truth and rationalize its way out of it. But that is wrong. Instead, I come to You to repent of my unbelief and plead for mercy in helping me to know You and the power of Christ in my life. Help my heart not to settle on human constructs but to instead flourish in accordance with Your will. I ask this in Christ's name.

John 17:3

And this is eternal life, that they know you, the only true God, and Jesus Christ whom you have sent.

1. You cannot truly know God unless you truly know Christ Jesus.

2. Eternal life is not the strumming of harps while we lounge on clouds. Eternal life is knowing God, being with God, dwelling with God, and glorifying Him in all our thoughts, words, actions, and deeds!

3. The only way to know who God truly is, is to know Jesus Christ. For there is no other name under heaven, given among men, by which we must be saved.[44]

4. There are other religions (Judaism, Islam, Mormonism) that believe they know God but still deny Christ. There is only one God, and He has revealed Himself in the Person of Christ Jesus, who is fully God and fully man. Since all other religions deny Christ Jesus, they deny God.

5. The goal of the Christian is to know God and to make Him known in every thought, word, action, and deed—all to the glory of God. We can only come to know God through His Son, who came according to the Father's will, lived a perfect life, was crucified on a cross, placed in a tomb, raised on the third day, and ascended to the right hand of the Father, still fully God and fully man, and is our great High Priest before the throne of grace.[45]

[44]Acts 4:12, [45]Hebrews 8:1

Father, help me to know You intimately and purposefully through Christ Jesus! Forgive me for how often I walk, talk, and act in unbelief rather than acknowledging Your sovereignty over all things. Help me to walk in accordance with Your Word, by the power of the Holy Spirit, through Christ Jesus, for Your glory. In Jesus' name I ask this.

14

John 11:16

SO THOMAS, CALLED THE TWIN, SAID TO HIS FELLOW DISCIPLES, "LET US ALSO GO, THAT WE MAY DIE WITH HIM."

1. As Jesus went to raise Lazarus from the dead, He told the disciples that Lazarus was dead. They were going to see a dead man.

2. Not only that, but people sought to put Jesus to death. To the extent that Christ walked around in public, the likelihood that death would occur was high.

3. Thomas looked at the situation not in light of who Christ is but by what he perceived with his human eyes. Instead of repenting the unbelieving thought, he voiced that thought to those around him.

4. This unbelief was sin, and by voicing it aloud, he caused those around him to agree with him, and therefore to sin as well. For none of it was true in light of the very Word of God leading them.

Oh Father, how I so easily sin. I whine and complain, I fear and tremble, and yet I open my mouth and tell others what to fear rather than trusting in You. Forgive me! Help me to walk in the truth of who You are! In Jesus' name,

Acts 8:22

Repent, therefore, of this wickedness of yours, and pray to the Lord that, if possible, the intent of your heart may be forgiven you.

1. We cannot cleanse ourselves from our sin. For there is none righteous, no not one. There is none who seek God, and all have turned aside and follow their own ways.[46]

2. Our hearts continually attempt to justify ourselves by our own actions and compare our actions against the world rather than looking to God. We constantly blame our circumstances, our situations as the reason for our actions rather than humbling ourselves before God.

3. With every attempt to fix ourselves, we reject Christ. Our hearts become hardened, and we justify our depravity before a holy God. God sent His Son into the world[47] to pay the penalty for our sins. He has called us to a life of repentance and of seeking the Lord with all our hearts and asking Him to change them. He desires to give us new hearts and new spirits[48] that reflect Christ and Christ alone. Let us look to Christ, for in Him all things are made new, and in Him we have life.

[46]Romans 3:10-12, [47]John 3:16, [48]Ezekiel 36:26

Father, You have made a way for me to know You and to be known by You! Yet, my hardened heart so easily desires to make my own way. Forgive me. Thank You for Your goodness, mercy, and for working all things together. Give me a new heart and a new spirit, and change the intent of my heart for Your glory. For Christ's sake.

Amen

16

Acts 16:25

About midnight Paul and Silas were praying and singing hymns to God, and the prisoners were listening to them.

1. What a man reveals through his trials is the most clear indication of his heart and intimacy with Christ. Paul and Silas, after proclaiming the truth and healing a young woman of her possession from an evil spirit, were beaten and thrown into prison.

2. The Lord uses difficult circumstances and situations to reveal the deepest thoughts, feelings, and emotions within our hearts. It is not in times of peace when the depth of our love of God is reflected but in the trials He brings us through, reflecting our hearts. For how we respond during trials is the greatest witness to the world.

3. Just as grapes, when trampled on, produce sweet wine, so the heart of the believer when trampled on produces prayers and the singing of hymns to our God.[49] This is a glorious witness to the power and work of the Holy Spirit in our lives. We must rejoice in our hope in Christ, be patient in the tribulation God has ordained, and be fervent in prayer. This is the most glorious and sweet reflection of our Lord Jesus Christ that the Holy Spirit works in our hearts! For when dying on the cross, after being falsely accused, beaten, and whipped, Christ pleaded, "Father, forgive them for they know not what they do."[50]

4. Let us then be mindful of our hearts and how we respond to those who persecute us. Let us be mindful of the Lord's sovereignty and rejoice that we are not forgotten and that He uses all things for His glory. And let us bear witness of the truth of our God before the world by the power of the Holy Spirit, that others may see our good works and praise our Father, who is in heaven.[51]

[49]Romans 12:12, [50]Luke 23:34, [51]Matthew 5:16

Father, You have saved me. You have saved me and You know. Who am I? I confess the many times I have not reflected the truth of You in the trials You allow. I succumb so easily to my flesh and desire to justify my griping rather than trust in Your providential hand. Help me to know Your joy and place a new song in my heart, that I may sing Your praises and proclaim the excellencies of You who has called me out of darkness and into Your marvelous light. In Christ's name.

Amen

Romans 1:16

*I AM NOT ASHAMED OF THE GOSPEL,
FOR IT IS THE POWER OF GOD FOR SALVATION TO EVERYONE
WHO BELIEVES, TO THE JEW FIRST AND ALSO TO THE GREEK.*

1. What a glorious exaltation from the apostle Paul! For Paul declared that it is not man's reason, or the force of his words, or the flare of his demeanor that will save a person and bring him into a knowledge of God. But instead, it is a proclamation that the preaching of the Word of God is the power of God for salvation.

2. This power is brought by the Holy Spirit through the Word of God. The Word of God, when it penetrates our hearts and minds, judges our thoughts and intentions of our hearts, and convicts us of our sin, brings us to a saving knowledge of our God. God has given us the Word, the Word came in flesh and dwelt among us, and the Spirit of God uses the Word to bring us from death to life.

3. Though this be contrary to the way the world would have us believe, we are unashamed of this. This is the means by which God has chosen and deemed to build and redeem a people for Himself. Who are we to argue against such a great God or deem Him foolish for choosing His own way? For the wisdom of this world is folly to God.

4. We can finally rest in the sovereignty of God and in His perfect working in this world. If the world's salvation is not achieved by human power but by the power of the gospel, then what we are called to do is to live our lives to reflect and rest in the power of the gospel, trusting the Lord to do His great work in His great way.

Father, Your gospel is glorious and powerful. I confess the many times I have not considered the gospel as powerful. I have been tempted to think it is lacking, but it isn't, according to Your Word. Forgive my unbelief and help me to bear witness to the truth, beauty, and goodness of the power of Your gospel. Use me as a vessel and place Your words in my mouth for Your glory. In Christ's name.

Romans 3:10-11

None is righteous, no, not one;
no one understands; no one seeks for God.

1. The heart of man is desperately wicked and deceitful above all things.[52] It does everything it can to compare itself to anyone and anything other than God. We deceive ourselves by believing that compared to others, we are good and justified. Yet in doing so, we prove the word of God true, for our means of measurement is not ourselves, but God Himself.

2. If we were to truly seek God, we would see our depravity and desperate need for Him. Seeking God would give us an understanding of our sinfulness and the utter darkness of our souls. To seek God would cause us not only to humble ourselves under the mighty hand of God but also cause us to realize that we are not like God and we deserve death.

3. Since the beginning of time, our hearts have desired to be like God and to be His equal.[53] All of humanity has been tempted and failed before Him. For all have sinned and fallen short of the glory of God.[54] We deserve death, for there is no fear of God before our eyes[55] apart from the work of the Holy Spirit.

4. But even in the light of this, God, who is rich in mercy, because of the great love with which He has loved us,[56] sent His only Son into the world to pay the penalty for our sins before a holy, righteous, and just God. The Lord has provided a way that if we confess our sins, He is faithful and just to purify and cleanse us from all unrighteousness.[57] So, seek the Lord while He may be found; call upon His name and He will answer.[58]

---

[52]Jeremiah 17:9, [53]Genesis 3:5, [54]Romans 3:23, [55]Romans 3:18, [56]Ephesians 2:4, [57]1 John 1:9, [58]Isaiah 55:6

Father, You are holy and just, and there is no one who can stand before You. I confess the many times I think I'm a good person, and then I realize I feel this way because I am comparing myself against other sinners rather than looking to You. Forgive me and save me from my sin. Help me to know Christ as my King and my Savior. Soften my heart to adore You and to be more mindful of my sin that I may confess it and lay it at the foot of the cross. Make my heart to know Christ that I may glorify You all my days and to do Your will. In Christ's name.

19

Romans 4:3

For what does the Scripture say?
"Abraham believed God,
and it was counted to him as righteousness."

1. How do we come to know God and be His child? Believe on the Lord Jesus Christ and you will be saved![59] What a simple thing to think and say that even a child can understand it. Yet many a man has faltered at these sayings, for they are difficult and even impossible apart from the work of the Holy Spirit.

2. There was nothing special about Abraham or anything he did to warrant his position as the patriarch of God's chosen people. He was not more righteous, he was not wiser, and he was not more perfect than everyone else. He did one thing and one thing only: he believed God at His Word.

3. The people of God are called to believe Him and walk according to His Word. The righteous shall live by faith![60] So what is faith? Faith is the assurance of things hoped for and the conviction of things not seen.[61] So the people of God do not hope in an idea or philosophy; we hope in a risen Savior, a living God. Our hope is in Christ.

4. As people of God, we are called to believe Him just as Abraham did. We look to God's Word and trust His promises, knowing that in Christ and His atonement for our sins, we are the people of God. We are called to live victoriously in Christ by grace through faith, knowing God works together all things for His glory and our good. He holds nothing back from us that is for our good.[62] We walk with boldness, knowing nothing can separate us from His love.[63] All of this is the work of God so that no one may boast. Our calling, then, is to believe not in our circumstances or observations but in Christ alone and be saved.

[59]Acts 16:31, [60]Romans 1:17, [61]Hebrews 11:1, [62]Psalm 84:11, [63]Romans 8:35

Father, Your Word says I am to believe and be saved; that if I believe, I am a child of Yours. So many words and things loudly call for my attention to believe in them rather than in You. I long to believe You, Lord. I long to walk in accordance with Your will and to walk in the hope of Christ. I believe, Lord; help my unbelief. Help me to walk in strength and boldness in the assurance of Christ in all circumstances, to reflect His Lordship in all things. In Christ's name I ask this.

Romans 6:16

Do you not know that if you present yourselves to anyone as obedient slaves, you are slaves of the one whom you obey, either of sin, which leads to death, or of obedience, which leads to righteousness?

1. There is never a moment in time when we are not serving someone or something. Everything we do is in line with how we view life, how we react to life, what we think is happening in the world—everything. In fact, nothing we ever do is because of something that previously affected our thoughts. The idea of autonomy apart from outside forces is utterly a false notion.

2. Thus Paul, inspired by the Holy Spirit, wrote in his letter to the Romans that we are all slaves to whatever thoughts we have in our hearts and minds. If our hearts are rooted in man and in line with who man is, we are enslaved to do all man would do. We cannot help ourselves, for we will reflect our nature. On the other hand, if the Spirit of God is working in our hearts and minds and we bear fruit in keeping with repentance[64] and dependence on the Holy Spirit, then we are slaves to righteousness.

3. So, we are slaves to whom we obey. There is no moralism, legalism, or coercion that can set us free to live a life of righteousness under the glory of God. All our best-laid plans are filthy rags in light of the holiness of God. But for those who are truly in Christ, the price has been paid, and we now have freedom in Christ and are slaves to righteousness. We obey and act in accordance with whomever we serve.

4. So for the believer, we are to look to Christ and cry out to the Lord for mercy. And God, being rich in mercy because of the great love with which He loves us, will give us a new heart and a new mind to be slaves to Christ. He has promised to send His Holy Spirit to lead and guide and direct us, His people, to do His will, and this all to the glory of God and our good.

---

[64] Matthew 3:8

Father, I have not thought about being a slave to anyone or anything. I have not thought of my mind as being under the servitude of anyone but myself. But I now see that apart from Your Holy Spirit giving me life through the redemption that was paid by Christ, I am bound to a life of slavery for destruction. Forgive me and have mercy on me. Help me to walk under the Lordship of Christ in every moment of every day. Humble me in whatever way You deem best to more truly know You and serve You with all my heart. I ask this in Christ's name.

Amen

Romans 7:18

FOR I KNOW THAT NOTHING GOOD DWELLS IN ME, THAT IS, IN MY FLESH. FOR I HAVE THE DESIRE TO DO WHAT IS RIGHT, BUT NOT THE ABILITY TO CARRY IT OUT.

1. Paul declared that there is nothing good in him whatsoever, apart from the work of the Holy Spirit. If there were anything good in Paul, it was only because of God, through Christ Jesus, by the power of the Spirit guiding and directing him.

2. This belief is contrary to how the heart so desperately tries to deceive us. Our hearts constantly compare ourselves to other people and other situations, blinding us from a holy God. We justify our actions based upon the actions of others and justify our thoughts and intentions and our motives.

3. We must be mindful, though, that we are not held accountable to people but to a Person: Christ Jesus. He is the Word made flesh who dwelt among us.[65] He is the radiance of the glory of God and the exact imprint of His nature.[66] Jesus Christ was born to the world, lived a sinless life, was crucified, resurrected on the third day, and is now seated at the right hand of the Father. All of the Law and all of the perfection of God is reflected and seen through Him. He is our standard.

4. In gazing at Christ, our hearts affirm that we do not have the ability in any aspect or form of our nature or being to reflect Christ. This we must affirm and know with all assurance, for if we do not, then we diminish our need and dependency on Christ and the power of the Holy Spirit. Apart from Him, we can do nothing.[67] For the Scripture even judges the thoughts and intentions of the heart, and we are held to that standard, rather than our own.[68]

5. So let us come to the Lord and seek Him only. Let us repent and trust in Christ, knowing that in Him we have all assurance and fullness of joy, for He has promised to never leave us nor forsake us.

---

[65]John 1:14, [66]Hebrews 1:2–3, [67]John 15:5, [68]Hebrews 4:12

Father, I thank You for Christ. I thank You for the Holy Spirit who opens my eyes and my heart to the knowledge and the need for Christ. I thank You that the Holy Spirit makes known to me my inability and my dependency in Christ. Forgive me of my moralism and legalism, and grant me to know Christ and Christ alone. Grant me joy and freedom in Christ to do His will in all things and everything, for Your glory and my good. In His name I ask this.

22

John 11:35

JESUS WEPT.

1. This is the shortest verse in the entire Bible and yet one of the most profound in the Word's entirety.

2. This verse is used by man in the world to show how people's pain causes the Lord to hurt as well. It is a comforting verse when viewed in that context—but what if there is more?

3. So many people surrounded Jesus but did not believe the words He spoke, particularly that He would raise Lazarus. They did not believe Jesus is the resurrection. They wept based upon what they saw and not trusting in who Christ proclaims He is.

4. D. A. Carson, in his commentary of John, says:

The one who always does what pleases his Father (8:29) is indignant when faced with attitudes that are not governed by the truths the Father has revealed. If sin, illness, and death, all devastating features of this fallen world, excite his wrath, it is hard to see how unbelief is excluded. But the world that is at enmity with God is also the object of God's love [cf. notes on 3:16], so it is not surprising that when he was shown the tomb where the body lay, Jesus wept. The verb wept (dakryō) is different from that describing the weeping of Mary and the Jews (klaiō): it means to shed tears, but usually in lament before some calamity. It is unreasonable to think that Jesus' tears were shed for Lazarus, since he knew he was about to raise him from the dead (v. 11). Rather, the same sin and death, the same unbelief, that prompted his outrage, also generated his grief. Those who follow Jesus as his disciples today do well to learn the same tension—that grief and compassion without outrage reduce to mere sentiment, while outrage without grief hardens into self-righteous arrogance and irascibility.[69]

[69]Carson, D. A. (1991). *The Gospel according to John* (p. 416). Leicester, England; Grand Rapids, MI: Inter-Varsity Press; W.B. Eerdmans.

Father, have mercy on me—a sinner. I am so often filled with unbelief. Fears surround me, and I spend most of my time whining and complaining instead of seeking You and thanking You for who You are. Help me to walk in Spirit and in truth. In Jesus' name.

Romans 8:8

Those who are in the flesh cannot please God.

1. There is nothing apart from the grace of God that pleases Him. There is no amount of self-righteousness, legalism, acts of goodness, or work we could ever do that justifies us standing before a holy God. To think for a second that anything we do warrants our ability to please God is a lack of a right view of His holiness. For to know God's holiness is to know our depravity.

2. God's love for us is entirely an act of grace on His part. His love for us is unwarranted, undeserved, incomprehensible, and unearned in any way. It is a free gift of grace to those who believe. The only way we can offer anything to the Lord that pleases Him is to do so through the finished work of His perfect Son. For the only person God the Father has ever said He is "well pleased" with is His Son.[70]

3. Christ came and died for our sins that we might know God and be known by God. We are His people because of who Christ is. Christ bore the wrath of God on our behalf, that we might come before the throne of grace as a child of God. There is absolutely nothing we can do in our flesh to merit any of this grace; it's all through Christ.

4. So our aim is to seek Christ. Our goal is to know Christ and the redemption and freedom found in Him. To please God is to know His only Son and to rest in His finished work. For He bore our sins on the cross that we might die to sin and live in righteousness. By His wounds we have been healed.[71]

---

[70] Mathew 3:17, [71] 1 Peter 2:24

Father, thank You for Christ. I have often thought myself worthy of Your pleasure, worthy of deserving Your grace, worthy of knowing You, and yet all that is in my flesh and none of it honors and glorifies You. For nothing I do in my flesh pleases You; in fact, I cannot. My "goodness" adds nothing to You, nor does it warrant any pleasure from You; it is only Christ and Christ alone. Help me to know Christ, rest in Christ, seek Christ, and glorify Christ all the days of my life. Thank You for who You are and what Christ has done. In His name I pray.

Amen

Romans 10:4

For Christ is the end of the law
for righteousness to everyone who believes.

1. What is the aim for the believer? Are the sons and daughters of God called to be good just for the sake of being good? Is it our aim to be good and righteous for the sake of moralism or for personal gain? Should our aim to be good be grounded in our desire for peace and love and fulfillment? The answer to all is a resounding *no!*

2. The aim of the believer is Christ and Christ alone. For Christ is the Word of God incarnate, and all Scripture points to Him. The apostle John wrote, "In the beginning was the Word and the Word was with God, and the Word was God. He was with God in the beginning."[72] Also, "The Word became flesh and dwelt among us, and we have seen His glory, glory as of the only Son from the Father, full of grace and truth."[73] We are to be "conformed to the image of Christ"[74] in all things.

3. All creation points toward Christ. The Word is fulfilled and made manifest in Christ. There is no other name under heaven given among men by which we must be saved![75] Christ is now seated at the right hand of the Father, and the Father is now working all things under His subjection. As Christ rules, the Father is bringing all the enemies of Christ under Him as a footstool.[76]

4. Our prayer every morning is that God the Father would orchestrate the day to glorify His Son. We must ask for strength, wisdom, guidance, and love to reflect His Son in all that we think, do, say, and act. We must lay down all our self-righteousness and ask the Lord to do whatever it takes to make us most into the image of His Son. For the end of all things is the glory of Christ, and the Word of God conforms us into the image of Christ, and this is the aim for all who believe and are His.

---

[72]John 1:1-2, [73]John 1:14, [74]Romans 8:29, [75]Acts 4:12, [76]Hebrews 1:13

Father, how easily I forget that all things are for Christ. I many times stand self-righteously on my podium and believe Your will is for me is about what I can get and what I can hold on to. What a fool I have been. Here is all I am and all You have given me. Use them for Your glory. Change my heart and mind to reflect You and You alone. I praise You for who You are. In Christ's name.

Romans 11:36

For from him and through him and to him are all things. To him be glory forever. Amen.

1. From God come all things. What a glorious promise for the believer, and yet what a truth that our flesh so desperately wants to avoid. We don't want to believe that all comes from God because in our depravity and selfishness we want to define for ourselves what is good and true and beautiful. We long to be like God[77] and are tempted to think God is like us.

2. We race to fashion a god in our own minds and bow down to our subjective tendencies to feel better about ourselves. Our hearts seek to dethrone the Lord of all and place our self-righteousness and our self-worth on the throne of grace. Every person, apart from the grace of God, longs to ignore God's Word when He says, "Every man is stupid and without knowledge; every goldsmith is put to shame by his idols, for his images are false, and there is no breath in them. They are worthless, a work of delusion; at the time of their punishment they shall perish."[78]

3. But let us look not to ourselves and only to our blessed Savior. He has promised He will withhold nothing that is for our good.[79] "The Lord is near to the brokenhearted and saves the crushed in spirit."[80] "The Lord disciplines those he loves as a father the son in whom he delights."[81] So let us remember, "in the day of prosperity be joyful, and in the day of adversity consider: God has made the one as well as the other, so that man may not find out anything that will be after him."[82]

4. To God and God alone be the glory forever and ever. Amen.

---

[77]Genesis 3:5, [78]Jeremiah 51:17–18, [79]Psalm 84:11, [80]Psalm 34:18, [81]Proverbs 3:12, [82]Ecclesiastes 7:14

Father, how easily I attempt to avoid Your sovereignty. I pay it lip service when it is convenient and then deny and gnash my teeth at You when it does not fit what I in my depravity desire. Help me to rest in the truth of who You are and to think rightly about You regardless of what the world says. Bring to my mind and my heart the truthfulness of Your Word and lead me in Your way everlasting. Help me to walk humbly before You with the certainty of who You are and who I am in all situations. I praise You, Lord, that You have made known to us that from You and through You and to You are all things. To You be the glory forever and ever.

26

Romans 12:2

Do not be conformed to this world,
but be transformed by the renewal of your mind,
that by testing you may discern what is the will
of God, what is good and acceptable and perfect.

1. The believer is not to conform to the world, think like the world, act like the world, or regard the world as the measurement of any truth whatsoever. For the world, and all that is in it, is evil and exists antithetical to God. There is none righteous apart from Christ. For Christ is our King; He is our aim, He is the One to whom all things are drawn until all His enemies are placed under His feet as a footstool.[83]

2. If we do not keep this truth central in our thinking, we will be tossed around like the waves on the sea and will believe whatever we hear.[84] Our aim should be Christ alone, and the truth of how we live our lives is Scripture alone. As believers, we accept this by faith alone, realizing it is only by God's grace alone, to the glory of God alone. These *alones* are the creeds of the truth that hold us fast. They anchor our hearts to the objective truth of Scripture in Christ.

3. This is battle, then, of the heart and the mind. Though the believer is completely justified before the living God, he is now at odds with the world. We are to daily, moment by moment, take every thought captive and test it before the objective word of our King. We are to look at the thoughts, feelings, and emotions of our hearts and place them at the foot of the cross, that we discern what we do, not according to the world's standards, but against that which is the Word of God. For it is only the Word of our God and nothing else that is good and acceptable and perfect.

[83]Hebrews 1:13, [84]James 1:6

Father, Your Word is true! I praise You, for You have given us Your Word and it is pleasing to my soul. You have opened my heart; You have poured out Your love. You have given me a standard and have given Your Holy Spirit to me to seek and know You with all my heart. Please open my eyes to the sin in my heart, that I may turn from my sin and walk according to Your ways. Lead me, Lord, for the sake of Christ and Christ alone. In Christ's name I ask this.

Romans 13:1

LET EVERY PERSON BE SUBJECT TO THE GOVERNING AUTHORITIES.
FOR THERE IS NO AUTHORITY EXCEPT FROM GOD,
AND THOSE THAT EXIST HAVE BEEN INSTITUTED BY GOD.

1. All authority and all leadership are ordained and orchestrated by the sovereignty of our God. The believer rests in knowing that God is the One who builds up, and He is the One who lays low.[85] The Lord "changes times and seasons; he removes kings and sets up kings; he gives wisdom to the wise and knowledge to those who have understanding."[86]

2. So let us be mindful to guard our hearts and minds from speaking against those the Lord, in His infinite wisdom, has ordained to lead. For when we speak against those in leadership, we speak against the Lord's servant and against the One who has ordained all things. So far as the servant of the Lord does not keep the believer from pursuing and following the Lord, or set him against the command of the Lord, then we are to humbly submit under his authority. We are not to rise against or demean in any way that which the Lord has ordained. The Lord blesses and judges the people according to those whom He has in leadership.

3. Guard your heart against murmuring, and pray. Flee from gossip of those in authority and do not play the fool. Thank the Lord for His perfect sovereignty and pray for those whose leadership is ordained by God. "Pay to all what is owed to them: taxes to whom taxes are owed, revenue to whom revenue is owed, respect to whom respect is owed, honor to whom honor is owed."[87] Do this for the Lord's glory and honor, for by doing this, we bear testimony to the world that the Lord is our king and His Kingdom rules over all.

---

[85]Psalm 75:7, [86]Daniel 2:21, [87]Romans 13:7

Father, You have sent Your Son to us, and He is King over all. How easily I neglect this thought. I am so quickly seduced into believing autonomy and democracy rule the world rather than Your sovereign hand. Forgive and soften my heart. Help me to pray for those in leadership and for those whom You have established according to Your will. Guard my heart from slander, malice, and gossip against those whom You have ordained. Thank You for Christ. In His name I ask this.

Exodus 32:4

And he received the gold from their hand and fashioned it with a graving tool and made a golden calf. And they said, "These are your gods, O Israel, who brought you up out of the land of Egypt!"

1. How corrupt and depraved is the heart of man? God has shown His awesome power to the children of Israel. He sent the plagues on the land of Egypt, He parted the Red Sea and brought the Israelites to Mount Sinai, and they still turned from God.

2. In their turning from God, they denied His power, His sovereignty, His holiness, and His providence, and constructed an idol made of gold. The depravity of the heart even denies its stupidity in that human hands are what created the golden calf.

3. Though we laugh, we do the same thing—but far worse. We may not have lifted a golden calf, but we have lifted ourselves. We have denied the Lord. We shake our hands at the Lord, determined that we can do all things in our own will, in our own way, based upon our own strength. We do not ponder who God is and instead construct things that seem powerful in the human mind, thus denying the Lord. We have lost sight of who God is and fashioned Him from our own minds how we want to see Him. In our arrogance, we have replaced the golden idols with ourselves. We grandstand and declare ourselves good and righteous, denying the holiness and perfection of who God is.

4. We intellectualize who God is rather than humbly walking before Him.[88] Let us turn and repent; let us kneel before the Lord our God, our Maker.[89] For, "The LORD is merciful and gracious, slow to anger and abounding in steadfast love. He will not always chide, nor will he keep his anger forever."[90]

---

[88]Micah 6:8, [89]Psalm 95:6, [90]Psalm 103:8–9

Father, You are holy.
You are so gracious, and You have given us Your Word; You have given us the Holy Spirit, You have given us Your Son, and yet we deny You.
We are caught up in the sensationalized and minimize the beauty of Your common grace. Forgive us.
Father, please grant me a mindfulness of Your love, grace, and holiness, that I may worship You and serve You with all of my heart. In Jesus' name.

Luke 12:2

NOTHING IS COVERED UP THAT WILL NOT BE REVEALED,
OR HIDDEN THAT WILL NOT BE KNOWN.

1. The foolishness of many and the depravity of their hearts is to deny the omniscience and sovereignty of God. Our hearts, apart from the grace of God, feverishly work to deceive and keep us from a holy God.

2. Yet, we must know that all sin is apparent before the Lord. For even darkness is not dark to the Lord; to Him, it is as bright as the day.[91] We cannot hide our sin; our Lord and Savior has said all our sin will be made known.

3. Let us not harden our hearts, but go to the Lord and confess, for there is nothing that is too great, too deep, too depraved that His mercy will not cover. There is no sin that the cross of Christ cannot overcome, but let us make haste, for the time is now!

4. The devil has been defeated, and we are in Christ, so let us seek Him and let us live victoriously in repentance and for His glory. Let us turn and walk in the light of His truth for the glory and the honor of Christ. Sin crouches at the door of our thoughts, in our words, and in our actions, and even now it plots to deceive us and deny our King, but we are free through Christ by the power of His Word to live in spirit and in truth.

[91] Psalm 139:12

Father, You know all things. You know my heart. You have saved it and have brought me to a saving grace with You. Lord, so many times I've willed my heart to live in unbelief. Forgive me and renew a right spirit within me. Bless me in walking in Your truth that I may know You and make You known. Restore to me an intimacy of the fear of You, and embolden and bless my steps for Your glory. I ask this in the name of my Savior, Jesus Christ.

Deuteronomy 30:14

But the word is very near you.
It is in your mouth and in your heart,
so that you can do it.

1. God is near, and He has written His Word upon our hearts. He has removed the heart of stone and has given us a heart of flesh that is engraved with His Word and His commands.[92]

2. All of humanity knows the truth of God. Those who claim they do not know the truth of God are lying and are suppressing the truth—and God's wrath burns against them.[93] All of creation declares the glory of God, and the skies proclaim the work of His hands![94] We must plead with God that His Word be present in our hearts and minds.

3. Let us come to the Lord humbly and meditate on it day and night.[95] Let us seek the Lord while He may be found[96] and call upon Him for mercy and grace. For the Lord is near to the brokenhearted and saves the crushed in spirit.[97]

4. The glorious promise is true in every aspect of our lives, for we can look to the Lord and call upon Him, and by the power of His Holy Spirit, He will bring to our minds His precious Word, that we may reflect our Lord and Savior. Christ is our aim; Christ is our King; Christ is our Savior.

---

[92]Ezekiel 11:19, [93]Romans 1:18, [94]Psalm 19:1, [95]Psalm 1:2, [96]Isaiah 55:6, [97]Psalm 34:18

Lord, Your promises are glorious. Here, You have spoken that Your Word is near; it is in our mouths and hearts. Lord, I have so many times supposed Your Word and denied Your truth and placed my own truth in my heart and mind. Forgive me and have mercy on me. Let the objective truth of Your Word lead me and guide me in all that I do, that You alone receive all the praise, glory, and honor. In Jesus' most precious name I ask this.

Luke 17:5

THE APOSTLES SAID TO THE LORD,
"INCREASE OUR FAITH!"

1. Human nature hasn't changed since the fall of man and is not evolving into better people, for the same sins plague the heart of man today as they have since the time of Adam.

2. When listening to our Lord Jesus, the apostles assumed it was their faith that kept them from doing the things of the Lord. This is untruth, and it's the same heresy the prosperity gospel heretics preach in their churches and organizations across the world today.

3. The things the Lord calls us to do have nothing to do with the size of our faith but rather a knowledge of the greatness of who God is. When churches cease to know God and pursue a right view of who He is, when they cease to behold their God,[98] we instead reconstruct theological words to strive for what our sinful hearts think we desire rather than Him we need most.

4. Our aim should be to know God and make Him known in all of His grandeur, glory, and holiness. We should have a courage that parallels none and is assured in the truth and objectivity of God's Word. We must press, we must press on to know the Lord![99]

---

[98]Isaiah 40:9, [99]Hosea 6:3

Father, You sit enthroned in the heavens and You do whatever You please. So many times I have attempted to dethrone You in my moralistic, therapeutic deism rather than know You as a Person. Father, please make Yourself known, that by Your grace, I may boldly make You known. Help me to know You, personally, humbly, for Your glory and my good. In Christ's name.

Psalm 14:1

The fool says in his heart, "There is no God."
They are corrupt, they do abominable deeds;
there is none who does good.

1. Who says there is no God? A fool! It is the fool who denies the existence and the truth of the Lord.

2. The fool says, "There is no God," but everyone knows there is a God. For the fool surpasses the truth in unrighteousness.[100] The fool desires abominable deeds rather than the beauty and glory of Christ! He would rather be a fool than to acknowledge the one true God.

3. All of creation bears witness to the existence of God,[101] and the heavens declare His glory![102] Every man knows there is a God, but in our sin and rebellion against God we suppress and deny the radiant truth of Him.

4. We must also recognize, "there is none who does good." Even the knowledge we have of the Lord is a gift from Him so that no one can boast.[103] Our hope in the Lord, our knowledge of God, our ability to worship Him are all gifts from the Lord, who brought us out of death and into His marvelous light![104]

---

[100]Romans 1:18, [101]Romans 1:19–20, [102]Romans 19:1, [103]Ephesians 2:9, [104]1 Peter 2:9

Father, my heart rejoices in You. It longs to abide in You, and this is a gift of Your Holy Spirit, through Christ Jesus, my Lord. I confess the circumstances in my life when I have thought, "There is no God," and have taken a practical, atheistic view of those circumstances. Forgive me. Draw near to me and help me to walk in Your way. Help me to know Your Lordship and Kingship in my life. In Jesus' name.

Psalm 143:5

I REMEMBER THE DAYS OF OLD;
I MEDITATE ON ALL THAT YOU HAVE DONE;
I PONDER THE WORK OF YOUR HANDS.

1. Nothing that occurs in our lives happens without purpose. For all things are ordained by God. There is no such thing as luck, chance, or circumstance, for all are held and orchestrated by the providence of God.

2. This we must be mindful of, for our carnal minds apart from this application of truth will attempt to wrestle God's glory from Him. We will seek to take all praise, all glory, all worship from our God and place it on ourselves when we do not think about Him.

3. Be mindful of all things in accordance with the Lord's attributes. For as man plans his way, the Lord directs his steps.[105] The Lord is sovereign over all; His goodness never fades; His mercies are new every morning. Great is His faithfulness![106] Let us look to all of creation and with the Psalmist declare, "The heavens declare the glory of God, and the skies above proclaim His handiwork!"[107]

4. This does not happen in *some* circumstances but in every circumstance in all aspects of life. We are to look, to ponder, to act, and to praise the Lord in all things. For our God is in the, and He does whatever He pleases.[108]

---

[105]Proverbs 16:9, [106]Lamentations 3:23, [107]Psalm 19:1, [108]Psalm 115:3

Father, when I think on Your acts and Your Word and all that you orchestrate and work for Your glory, who is man that You are mindful of him? How little my mind thinks about You and is tempted into unbelief and deism rather than praise. Forgive me, Lord! You give the flower its beauty; You make sure that the sparrow is well fed; You know every hair on my head, and yet so many times I live with my head down rather than lifting my voice in praise! Oh Lord, You are glorious! Place Your Word in my heart, that I may ponder and praise You all my days. In Christ's name.

… 34 …

Deuteronomy 32:18

You were unmindful of the Rock that bore you, and you forgot the God who gave you birth.

1. The heart of man is deceitful above all things, and desperately sick; who can understand it?[109] It does everything it can to forget God and to place itself on the throne of our lives. It whispers in our ears that we do not need the Lord and that all we have is because of our work and not from the Lord.

2. The question the serpent asked in the garden of Eden, "Did God really say…?"[110] is still the question of our hearts. Our hearts seek to worship anything and everything other than the Lord God Almighty. It is our unbelief in the Word of God that threw us out of the garden, and it is unbelief in God that keeps us from knowing and trusting in Him.

3. For God is holy and we are not. Our hearts and our flesh desire to flee a holy God. For in the moment when we see ourselves as we truly are, we realize we are deserving of complete and utter damnation and eternity in hell apart from the grace of God.

4. But the Father, who loved us before the foundation of the world,[111] chose us in Him and sent His only Son into the world to redeem us from our sins. We are to look to Christ and not to the world; we are to trust in Christ and not our own flesh; we are to walk by faith and not by sight.

[109]Jeremiah 17:9, [110]Genesis 3:1, [111]Ephesians 1:4

Father, You are in heaven. You are high and lifted up; You are above all things, yet my mind so often desperately wants to make myself above all things. Unbelief seeps in, and many times I listen to its whispering, deceiving myself by its perceived innocence rather than Your Word. Grant my heart to rest in You; grant my heart to see You working all things together for Your glory. Grant my heart to rest in the hope of Your Kingdom. In Jesus' name.

Deuteronomy 32:4

> THE ROCK, HIS WORK IS PERFECT,
> FOR ALL HIS WAYS ARE JUSTICE.
> A GOD OF FAITHFULNESS AND WITHOUT
> INIQUITY, JUST AND UPRIGHT IS HE.

1. God is the rock of our salvation. Our confidence is never in ourselves but in who God is. He cannot be moved, and nothing can deter Him. All things are done by His will, and nothing can come against Him.

2. His work is perfect and flawless. Though we see a dim portion, we will one day see it fully in its perfection.[112] All of His workings are perfect, and there is nothing outside of His sovereign grace that is not working together for His glory and His people's good.

3. There is not one thing to be said against the Lord, for all of His ways are just and righteous. For what does man deserve but death? But God is rich in mercy because of the great love with which He loved us. Even while we were dead in our trespasses, He made us alive together with Christ—by grace you have been saved through faith.[113]

4. The Lord is faithful and His faithfulness is without error. We are to run to the Lord in all things. We are to cast all our cares upon Him because He cares for His people.[114] Though we are tempted to look to our circumstances for our identity and purpose, they all become corruptible idols. Let us turn our eyes to the Lord and seek the rock of our salvation.[115]

---

[112]1 Corinthians 13:12, [113]Ephesians 2:4–5, [114]1 Peter 5:7, [115]Psalm 95:1

Father, You are the Rock. What hope and peace there is in that. So many times my flesh deceives me and makes me think my identity is in my circumstances rather than in who You are. You are in heaven and I am on earth. You sent Your Son into the world so that I may know You and spend all eternity with You. Forgive my unbelief and open my eyes and my heart to rest in the truth of who You are. In Christ's name I ask this.

Amen

Luke 12:28

But if God so clothes the grass, which is alive in the field today, and tomorrow is thrown into the oven, how much more will he clothe you, O you of little faith!

1. What a glorious promise and grace. For the Lord Himself not only tells us to not be anxious but to look to the providence of God in all His creation to remind us of His goodness.

2. For is God bound to make all flowers beautiful? Is He obligated to make the flower petals bloom and flourish on the hills? Is our God forced to allow us to know beauty and to recognize and enjoy it? Not at all! Yet in His goodness and grace, He has allowed us to know and see and experience objective beauty—those things He deems beautiful.

3. Let us study and see the beauty of God and know the Lord cares more about us than the flowers of the field. Let us remind ourselves of the sovereignty of God and rest in His providence. Let us see with hope the beauty of God in and throughout every day as we call upon Him and ask Him to open the eyes of our hearts and give us an understanding of all that is good.

4. This is all because of the love the Father has lavished upon us. The only reason we are children of the Most High God is because of His great love for us.[116] Let us rest in this; let us flourish in this; let us hope in this, for His glory and our good.

[116] 1 John 3:1

Father, You are radiant and beautiful. You know the days before me and the days behind me. You even know the trials and all You have prepared for me this week and in the days and years to come. Guard my heart against nihilism and hopelessness, and help me to run in the assurance of Your grace. Give me wisdom to do Your will and grace to flourish for Your Kingdom. I ask this in Christ's name.

Joshua 24:19

But Joshua said to the people, "You are not able to serve the Lord, for he is a holy God. He is a jealous God; he will not forgive your transgressions or your sins."

1. Apart from the grace of God, we are unable to serve the Lord. The motivations of the heart are not toward holiness and righteousness, but they are deceitful and filled with pride, selfishness, and unbelief.[117]

2. In our longing to justify ourselves, we deny God's holiness; we reconstruct God in our own image rather than looking to Him and acknowledging His Lordship. We compare ourselves to those around us rather than to Christ. We long to make and create idols rather than beholding God and His awesome glory![118] Instead of looking to God and humbly requesting, "Show us Your glory!"[119] we scream to the Lord from our Tower of Babel, "See my glory!"

3. Look to the cross. Gaze upon Christ. He who knew no sin became sin for us so that in Him we might have the righteousness of God.[120] God has given us His Son so that we may come before Him, and Christ has sent the Holy Spirit by the will of the Father to His people to change their hearts.

4. God, apart from any work of man, has established for Himself a chosen race, a holy nation, a people for His own possession, that we may proclaim the excellencies of Him who called us out of darkness and into His marvelous light.[121] We are not able to do anything apart from God,[122] but in Christ, we are more than conquerors for His glory and our good.[123]

---

[117]Romans 3:10, [118]Isaiah 40:9, [119]Exodus 33:18, [120]2 Corinthians 5:21, [121]1 Peter 2:9, [122]John 15:5, [123]Romans 8:37

Father, You have given me everything;
You have given me Your only Son.
Who am I? Why would You choose me
and be mindful of me and think of me?
I am unable to serve You apart from Your
Holy Spirit. I have tried. I have worked
to show my righteous deeds, and they
are but filthy rags. Help me rest in
Your grace and Your goodness, and
strengthen me to do Your will all the
days of my life. Help my heart to rest
in Christ alone. In Christ's name.

Psalm 15:1

O LORD, WHO SHALL SOJOURN IN YOUR TENT?
WHO SHALL DWELL ON YOUR HOLY HILL?

1. What a glorious question, and yet what a convicting question. The heart of God's people should be able to look at this and know there is only One who can do this.

2. There is no humanistic glory, wisdom, or righteousness that can do anything to earn the right to know God and to dwell in His presence. For there is none who are righteous, and we all deserve judgment.[124]

3. For our God is a consuming fire,[125] holy and just. There are none who can stand before Him.[126] He will not share His glory with any other, for to share it with a created being on that person's own merit is to taint and diminish His glory. It is to lower His own perfection.

4. "But God, being rich in mercy, because of the great love with which he loved us, even when we were dead in our trespasses, made us alive together with Christ—by grace you have been saved."[127] It is by Christ and through His sacrifice that we may sojourn in the tent of our God and dwell on His holy hill.

---

[124]Psalm 143:2, [125]Hebrews 12:29, [126]Ezra 9:15, [127]Ephesians 2:4–5

Father, Your glory outshines the sun, and Your radiance brings me to my knees. Father, I am so tempted to believe the world and my flesh that I am "good enough" to know You. That I am capable of standing before You on my own merit. How foolish and prideful—who am I? Yet, who am I that You would send Your only Son into the world to pay the penalty for my sin? To take Your wrath and Your holy justice, that I may be a child of Yours! Thank You, Father. Open my eyes to this truth more and more, that I may praise You with all my heart! In Christ's name.

Joshua 21:45

Not one word of all the good promises that the Lord had made to the house of Israel had failed; all came to pass.

1. Our God is a covenantal God. There is none like Him, and all that He says, He does. We are not to look to our lives and our circumstances to define who God is, but we are to look to His Word and His Promises.

2. For the promises of God are sure and true. He works together all things for His glory and our good.[128] As God's people, we are to walk by faith and not by sight.[129] We are to walk and pursue all things in light of the promises of God.

3. This is not a foolish demand of God for the inclinations of our hearts. Our God is not a genie in a bottle we should attempt to manipulate, for "our God is in the heavens, and He does whatever He pleases!"[130] But we must walk in a way that *does justly, loves mercy, and walks humbly with our God.*[131] For the "friendship of the Lord is for those who fear Him, and He makes known to them His covenant."

4. So in light of who God is, we can boldly and confidently approach the throne of grace through the finished work of Christ.[132] We can lay our anxieties and burdens before the Lord and rest in His promises, for all of God's promises come to pass. He is good, and His steadfast love endures forever.

---

[128]Romans 8:28, [129]2 Corinthians 5:7, [130]Psalm 115:3, [131]Micah 6:8, [132]Hebrews 4:16

Father, Your promises are sure and true. They are eternal and limitless, yet personal and intimate. Through Christ, I am to hold fast to Your promises; I am to cling to Your Word and to rest in Your truth. Yet I confess that many times Your promises don't come to mind, or I find myself demanding that You answer Your promises how I want You to. Forgive me! Who am I that I should demand anything from You? Will You grant my heart to rest on Your promises based on who You are? In Christ's name.

Genesis 32:11

Please deliver me from the hand of my brother, from the hand of Esau, for I fear him, that he may come and attack me, the mothers with the children.

1. What an incredible prayer. Jacob confessed the fear he had of his brother. He searched his heart and recognized the fear, and he recognized the fear he had was not comparable to the fear he should have of the Lord.

2. Many a heart will attempt to squash fear for fear's sake, then become exasperated when it returns time and again. This is not a matter of nerves but a matter of the heart. Our eyes must be on God, through His Son, and we must acknowledge, repent, and lay before the Lord our fears, trusting the promises of God.

3. Many people acknowledge their fear, but few people acknowledge God in the midst of their fear. The Psalmist writes, "The Lord is on my side; I will not fear. What can man do to me?"[133] Also, "In God I trust; I shall not be afraid. What can man do to me?"

4. Many a fear is left unchecked against the Word of God because we deny God in every aspect of our lives except on Sunday mornings. We do not lay our fears and our worries before the Lord, but stuff them in our hearts and become paralyzed by them. "Draw near to God, and He will draw near to you."[134]

[133] Psalm 118:6, [134] James 4:8

Father, who is there to fear if we have a right and true fear of You? There is none like You, none in heaven above or earth below. But we so easily deny You and fear man rather than You. Forgive me. Lord, grant me to know You and to beautifully fear You in all things, that I may glorify You, worship You, and adore You. Strengthen me by Your promises, as water to a thirsting soul. Make me mindful of the things I have not placed before You, and grant me repentance, faith, and boldness in Your Word. Strengthen me to do Your will—regardless of what the world says—laying down the sins of my heart and taking up Your promises. In Jesus' name.

Psalm 115:3

OUR GOD IS IN THE HEAVENS;
HE DOES ALL THAT HE PLEASES.

1. We must ask ourselves this question: "Is God mainly about *my* glory or *His* glory?" The world and our flesh battle against the God of the heavens. We desire for Him to do what we please, what we desire, what we want. Yet who are we in comparison with who God is?

2. Our God is perfect and holy! Our God has never made a mistake, nor does He ever waiver from His perfection. His throne is in the heavens, and He rules over all. Everything He does is good, perfect, and true. The only reason a person would not trust in the Lord is because he does not know the Lord.

3. Our entire aim is to know God. It is to know God and to make Him known to all the world. We are to seek, His Kingdom come, and His will be done on earth as it is in heaven![135]

4. Even the Lord's discipline is an act of grace. For the Lord disciplines those He loves.[136] Our God is not deistic, but instead, He is near. In Him, we live and move and have our being![137] So as the Lord does whatever He pleases, we must humble our hearts and bow before Him, trusting Him in all things.

---

[135]Matthew 6:10, [136]Hebrews 12:6, [137]Acts 17:28

Father, You do whatever You please. I confess at my first glimpse this seems selfish—until I gaze upon Your perfection and know that all the things You do are right and true and good. I have wrestled many times with the wretched sin of unbelief. Forgive me for not declaring in my heart how much I trust You. Do what You please in my life. Give me wisdom and lead me for Your glory, for I trust You, my God and my King. In Christ's name I ask this.

Deuteronomy 15:10

You shall give to him freely, and your heart shall not be grudging when you give to him, because for this the LORD your God will bless you in all your work and in all that you undertake.

1. Everything we have comes from the Lord. What He gives us are blessings He bestows upon His people. He is not begrudging but freely gives to everyone and to all.

2. The Lord commands His people to reflect to others what the Lord does and gives in our lives. We are to give our time, talent, and resources, all for the glory of God. *"Whether we are at home or away, our aim is to please Him."*[138]

3. When we have a wrong view of the blessings from the Lord, we turn them into idols, ceasing to give and serve and bless others. When our hearts harden toward God, we pridefully believe we bless ourselves rather than all things coming from Him.[139]

4. This command is not without a promise. The more we are willing to surrender what the Lord gives to us for His glory, the more He will bless us in all our work and undertakings. As we serve the Lord, He blesses our work. Beautifully and gloriously, the more He blesses, the more we can give back for His glory and His pleasure and our good.

---

[138] 2 Corinthians 5:9, [139] Romans 11:36

Father, You give us our daily bread. You are the Provider of all things. It is You who should be our aim and our focus. Forgive me. Lord, will You bless me in proportion to the way You would call me to bless others? I confess the many times I've been leery of asking for Your blessing, for I do not want to be blinded by idols. Yet, I ask that You bless my work and the vocation You have given me, that I may bless others more richly for Your Kingdom. In Christ's name.

Amen

Deuteronomy 10:14

Behold, to the Lord your God belong heaven and the heaven of heavens, the earth with all that is in it.

1. All things belong to God. There is nothing that happens, nothing throughout the day that the Lord does not ordain and orchestrate.

2. Not only does what we see belong to the Lord, but all that we don't see—every infinitesimal atom that is in the furthest part of the universe—is under His Lordship, authority, and direction. All that is in heaven above and the earth below, and all things are ordained and orchestrated by God.

3. In this we find refuge, and in this we find our hope. Our aim is to know God: to know Him, worship Him, and glorify Him. We are to seek Him with all our hearts and give to Him all we have, for His glory and our good.

4. To not give Him an aspect of our heart is to deny His Lordship. It is to harden our hearts, and it is to lean on our own understanding. It is to attempt toward self-lordship and to deny the cross of Christ.

5. We are to trust the Lord and know His Word and to strive to live according to His Word by the power of the Holy Spirit. For all things belong to Him and to Him alone.

Father, You are in heaven, and You are establishing Your Kingdom on earth. I don't understand how I am to think and act in this truth. I confess I am unable to in my own strength and flesh. But You, Oh Lord, have sent Your Holy Spirit to help me and lead me and guide me. Please help me to know You, that I may make You known. Grant me to flourish under Your Lordship, for Your glory. In Jesus' name I ask this.

Deuteronomy 9:4

Do not say in your heart, after the Lord your God has thrust them out before you, "It is because of my righteousness that the Lord has brought me in to possess this land," whereas it is because of the wickedness of these nations that the Lord is driving them out before you.

1. All we have is from the Lord, and none of what we have is because of any goodness in our hearts. All of what the Lord does is a beautiful act of mercy, glorious to the Lord, radiating His love and mercy.

2. We are to take every thought captive[140] and guard ourselves against thinking we deserve anything. For anything we think we deserve becomes an idol.

3. Even in our sinful wretchedness, we can glorify and even idolize ourselves. We can say, "Did God really say?"[141] and begin to worship our self-perceived goodness.

4. Let us look to Christ; let us glorify Christ; let us seek Christ; let us hope in Christ, not in ourselves. For all things are under the Lordship of Christ, and in Him we rest for all things.

5. Lastly, let us heed the warning that goes with this. It is because of the wickedness of the nations that God is driving out the people before Israel. Let us seek the Lord and guard our hearts, by the Word of God and the Holy Spirit, from the very same wickedness, lest God drive us out and keep us from knowing Himself.

[140]2 Corinthians 10:5, [141]Genesis 3:1

Father, You are so merciful in allowing us to know You. You are continually and mercifully growing and establishing Your Kingdom. Forgive me for doubting You, and for even thinking it is because of anything I have done, rather than looking to You. Please guide my heart and my steps according to Your grace, and for Your glory, to do Your will, in love. In Jesus' name.

Deuteronomy 8:5

Know then in your heart that, as a man disciplines his son, the LORD your God disciplines you.

1. All things come from the Lord. There is nothing that happens to us that is not from His hand.

2. Many people think of God as a genie in a bottle who only gives what is deemed good by those around us rather than trusting the Lord in every moment, looking to Him, and trusting Him.

3. The Lord's blessing is not only that which we deem a blessing but also the discipline of the Lord to conform us to the image of His Son. He uses all things for the good of those who love Him and are called according to His purpose.

4. Our hearts and minds desire to make God deistic rather than present because our flesh is terrified of submitting to a holy God. This is sin and the opposite of God's Word. The Lord is present, and in Him we live and move and have our being.[142]

5. The Lord disciplines those He loves,[143] so let us humble ourselves before Him. Let us submit to His leading and teaching, and let us walk by grace through faith for His glory and our good, trusting Him with all of our hearts and souls and might.

[142] Acts 17:28, [143] Hebrews 12:6

Father, You are good. I confess that I have not humbled myself under Your discipline. I have shaken my fist at You, I have yelled at You, I have screamed at You. Forgive me. How do I submit joyfully? How do I receive Your discipline with thanksgiving? Teach me Your ways, Oh Lord, that I may walk according to Your Word, that I may praise You with my whole heart. Thank You for Your discipline. In Jesus' name I pray.

Acts 2:21

AND IT SHALL COME TO PASS THAT EVERYONE WHO CALLS UPON THE NAME OF THE LORD SHALL BE SAVED.

1. What a glorious gift God has given us in His Word. Until this point, to be a people of God meant to be a part of the Jewish nation. This all changed when Christ paid the price of our redemption on the cross.

2. Now, all who call upon the name of the Lord shall be saved! Christ has established a new covenant with a people of His own choosing![144] The old covenant is abolished, and a new covenant is springing forward for a people of God![145]

3. Everyone who calls upon the name of the Lord is a part of the church of Christ. They are under the Lordship of Christ and under His sovereign rule. All God's promises in His Word find their "amen" in Christ and are given to the people of God.[146]

4. How do we know this to be true? Because even in this verse from God's Word, it is a promise. It is a declaration! For it declares, "It shall come to pass." This is not human conjecture; this is holy Scripture. This is a promise to God's people for the glory of God and our own good.

---

[144] Hebrews 31:31, [145] Hebrews 8:13, [146] 2 Corinthians 1:20

Father, how little I think upon Your Lordship. How little I take seriously Your gift of being a child of Yours. I confess the many times I fight for autonomy rather than humble submission and a seeking of You. Help me to live and rejoice in being Yours. Restore to me the joy of Your salvation. Embolden my heart in the truth of Your Word, that I may walk as a man who is Christ's and Christ's alone! For Christ's glory I ask this.

Psalm 21:8

Your hand will find out all your enemies;
your right hand will find out those who hate you.

1. The aim for the people of God is Christ—Christ alone and no one else. The aim is to seek the Lord with all our hearts and with all our souls and with all our might.[147] This is the first and the greatest commandment.

2. In doing this, we are to place before the Lord all those things in which the world and all its hate attacks us, leaving everything to the Lord. For the Lord has commanded and promised, "Never avenge yourselves, for I have promised, 'Vengeance is mine, I will repay,' says the Lord."[148]

3. So we are to be a people who look and give an account to the Lord, leaving everything else to the Lord. If we pursue the Lord and people hate us, then we are to leave that in the hands of God; we need only give an account for ourselves.

4. If we seek to avenge ourselves first, we say we do not trust the Lord or believe His Word. Secondly, we don't obey a command of the Lord to leave it to Him. Lastly, we are not believing His promises, His strength, or His love for us. It is in this that we should be scared of our own souls, for it is a terrifying thing to fall into the hands of the living God.[149]

---

[147]Deuteronomy 6:5, [148]Romans 12:19, [149]Hebrews 10:31

Father, I do not think of Your wrath or meditate on Your goodness in Your wrath. I have rarely thought of You defending me or of You giving Yourself fully in working and defeating Your enemies. But I have realized that in not doing so, I have many times placed myself as Your enemy because I have not believed and trusted in You. Forgive me. Go before me, Lord, and lead me in Your path. Destroy the strongholds and the enemies who keep me from doing Your will. Open my eyes to see Your will and fear You with all my heart. In Christ's name.

Luke 22:20

AND LIKEWISE THE CUP AFTER THEY HAD EATEN, SAYING, "THIS CUP THAT IS POURED OUT FOR YOU IS THE NEW COVENANT IN MY BLOOD."

1. This is the turning point of all time, for it is at this moment Christ references a new covenant purchased by His blood for His people.

2. The old covenant of the Law written on stone and given to the Jewish nation has been replaced. God has created a new covenant.[150] Instead of a law written on stone,[151] He is putting His Law into the hearts of His chosen people.[152] Christ is fulfilling the prophecies of the Old Testament. He is removing hearts of stone and replacing them with hearts of flesh.[153]

3. Peter looked back upon and reflected that it was no longer the Jewish nation who are the people of God, but that God's people are a *"chosen race, a royal priesthood, a holy nation, a people for His own possession, that we may proclaim the excellencies of Him who called us out of darkness and into his marvelous light."*[154]

4. The people of Christ are rooted in this covenant and are a part of the Kingdom of God, with Christ as the cornerstone. *"Let us hold fast the confession of our hope without wavering, for he who promised is faithful."*[155]

---

[150] Jeremiah 31:31, [151] Exodus 20, [152] Jeremiah 31:33, [153] Ezekiel 36:26, [154] 1 Peter 2:9, [155] Hebrews 10:23

Father, You have made all things new and are making all things to be under the feet of Christ Your Son who sits on the throne today. These truths are beyond my ability to comprehend, for they are great and glorious but impossible to know apart from Your grace. So many times I act opposite of Your Kingdom. So many times I pridefully declare self-lordship rather than bow my knee. Forgive me. Grant me that I may know You and the freedom of Christ in Your glorious covenant with Your people. In Christ's name I pray.

Judges 7:2

The Lord said to Gideon, "The people with you are too many for me to give the Midianites into their hand, lest Israel boast over me, saying, 'My own hand has saved me.'"

1. All things come from the Lord, and nothing occurs that is not orchestrated by His providence and under His sovereign decree.

2. God in His grace protected Gideon from pride, for it is the power of God that causes all things to work. We are tempted with a practical atheism to not look at all things under the providence of God. We seek to hold in our minds that we are "like God" rather than bowing our knee and acknowledging His grace.

3. The Lord has called us to walk by faith and not by sight. We should walk in a way that moves forward and says to the world, "If the Lord wills, we will do [such and such a thing]."[156]

4. Christ should be the believer's aim. Our focus and our entire being should be to and for Him, to proclaim the excellencies of Him who called us out of darkness and into His marvelous light,[157] and then whatever the Lord ordains is right.

[156] James 4:15, [157] 1 Peter 2:9

Father, You are near and You are present, for in You we live and move and have our being. You are also in heaven. I confess the many times I look at You from a deistic perspective rather than a theistic perspective. In my pride, I am tempted to think I am the one who makes things happen, and in my unbelief, I don't seek or acknowledge Your work. I feel lost many times because Your truth says You are near. Guard my heart from pride, and help me to rejoice in Your salvation through Christ Jesus. In Christ's name.

Amen

Luke 1:78-79

BECAUSE OF THE TENDER MERCY OF OUR GOD,
WHEREBY THE SUNRISE SHALL VISIT US FROM ON HIGH
TO GIVE LIGHT TO THOSE WHO SIT IN DARKNESS
AND IN THE SHADOW OF DEATH,
TO GUIDE OUR FEET INTO THE WAY OF PEACE.

1. Everything we have, we have received from the Lord. There is nothing not given to us, and this is a mercy and grace from God.

2. To see a sunrise is a mercy, and to see the stars at night is a gracious gift. To taste food and enjoy meals together is a mercy from the Lord.

3. Most importantly, the knowledge of God and of His Son is a mercy that is incomparable to anything else. For God is not obligated to allow us to know Him. God is not bound to take us as sinners and to make known to us His loving grace. God was not bound to send His only Son into the world to pay the penalty of our sins and to take the wrath of God that we so deeply deserved.

4. But He did because of His great love with which He loved us.[158] We who have sinned and turned from Him, the Lord has mercifully redeemed a people for Himself. He has given us His Word, that it may be a lamp unto our feet and a light unto our path,[159] and His Holy Spirit has led us through the valley of the shadow of death.[160] All these things God has done and is doing for His glory and our good.

[158]Ephesians 2:4, [159]Psalm 119:105, [160]Psalm 23:4

Father, who am I that You have given me light? Who am I that You have made known to me Your will and Your goodness and Your mercy? Who am I that You have shown me mercy? I confess the many times I have hardened my heart toward the acknowledgment of Your grace and Your mercy. My heart is so dark apart from Your Word and Your grace. Thank You for sending Your Son, and thank You for making known to me Your salvation. Grant my heart to boldly walk in the way of peace according to Your Word for the glory of Christ. In Jesus' name I ask this.

Numbers 23:19

*God is not man, that he should lie,
or a son of man, that he should change his mind.
Has he said, and will he not do it?
Or has he spoken, and will he not fulfill it?*

1. Let us remember that God is not a man. He is not fickle, nor does He change His mind. God never learns anything new, for in Him is all wisdom, sovereignty, and knowledge. Nothing can be added to or taken away from Him, for in Him are all things.

2. God's thoughts and ways are above our thoughts and our ways.[161] He ordains all things, and all that He ordains is perfect. All His ways are good, and they are purposeful in their aim.

3. The Lord's promises are sure and are given to His people. What He says, He will do. God's people are to boldly stand on the promises of God in every and in all circumstances because of the assurance of who God is.

4. God's Word is true,[162] and in this truth we are to boldly rest, prayerfully watchful, with thanksgiving in all circumstances, because God does not lie.[163] Our God is a covenantal God, and He brings to completion all He has ordained for His glory and our good.

---

[161] Isaiah 55:8, [162] John 17:17, [163] Colossians 4:2

Father, Your thoughts and Your ways are far above my thoughts and my ways. Forgive my unbelief and doubt in the dispensations You bring us through. Forgive me for doubting Your Word and instead trusting my thoughts and emotions rather than faithfully resting in Your Word. Please grant me to know You more fully. Please grant me rest in Your sovereign grace. Help me to walk boldly in Your promises. Do not forsake the work of Your hands, Lord, and help me to have a more right view of You. In Christ's name I ask this.

Numbers 20:12

And the Lord said to Moses and Aaron, "Because you did not believe in me, to uphold me as holy in the eyes of the people of Israel, therefore you shall not bring this assembly into the land that I have given them."

1. The Lord told Moses to speak to the rock and water would come out from it. This was a direct command from the Lord. Moses, in turn, came to the rock, and instead of obeying the Word of God, he struck the rock, and water came out.

2. The Word of the Lord is true,[164] and there is no excuse that will ever justify against it, for it is holy. We can never hide behind our frustrations or our self-perceived victimization, for the Word of God is living and active, sharper than any two-edged sword, piercing to the division of soul and of spirit, of joints and of marrow, and discerning the thoughts and intentions of the heart.[165] God is the judge of our hearts; we are not!

3. Our sinful hearts will attempt to find an excuse for why we do not trust the Lord. In the same way, Adam blamed Eve for eating from the tree of the knowledge of good and evil.[166] But God is holy, and He shows no partiality.[167]

4. But God the Father sent His Son into the world to pay the penalty for our sins, pride, selfishness, and unbelief. None of us deserve to be with God; in the same way, Moses had no right to enter the promised land because of his unbelief. But Christ made a way for us to come to know God, and in turn, make Him known for His glory and our good.

[164] John 17:17, [165] Hebrews 4:12, [166] Genesis 3:12, [167] Romans 2:11

Father, You are glorious! Who am I that You would send Your Son into the world to pay the penalty for my sin? Unbelief is so rampant in my heart. It steals my joy and robs my hope, but in Christ we have all things. Grant me to know Christ. Grant me to walk by faith in the assurance of Your Word. For You are the joy of my salvation. In Jesus' name.

Amen

Colossians 1:15–16

He is the image of the invisible God, the firstborn of all creation. For by him all things were created, in heaven and on earth, visible and invisible, whether thrones or dominions or rulers or authorities—all things were created through him and for him.

1. Christ is from all eternity. He is alive, and He is seated at the right hand of the Father.

2. Christ has been from the beginning. He is both eternal and yet was also born into this world. All that ever was created, and will be created, is created by Him. This is both what we live in the world and in all the universe. He is over the clouds of the sky, the weather, the seasons that we go through year by year. He is Lord of every molecule. Every infinitesimal atom in all the universe is held together by the power of the Son of God.

3. There is no ruler, no authority, no leadership that He does not establish. Kingdoms are established by Him, and kingdoms are destroyed by Him. There is no authority that has authority that was not given to Him by Christ.

4. All those who are in Christ are under His Lordship and are under His Kingdom today and now. This is a Kingdom only Christ fully knows from all eternity and is bringing to Himself. All those who are His will be with Him for all eternity, and there is no one who is able to snatch them from His hand.[168]

---

[168] John 10:28

Jesus, You are King. I acknowledge that, and yet I do not understand it. I long to live in that truth and am also bombarded by what I see in it. I believe; help my unbelief. Lord, grant me the peace that passes all understanding and a faith that is rooted in You. Grant me freedom in Christ and to seek You with all my heart. Thank You, Jesus.

Numbers 11:23

AND THE LORD SAID TO MOSES,
"IS THE LORD'S HAND SHORTENED?
NOW YOU SHALL SEE WHETHER MY WORD
WILL COME TRUE FOR YOU OR NOT."

1. Nothing is impossible for the Lord. Time, circumstances, wisdom, knowledge are all in His hands. He commands all things, and all things obey Him. There is nothing He cannot do.

2. We are to come before Him in all things. We are to approach the throne of grace with confidence, through the redemption of Christ Jesus, and lay our burdens at His feet. But we must ask without doubt, for the man who doubts is like a wave of the sea tossed to and fro.[169]

3. We are to do this in everything we do. We are to look to Christ as King, Lord, Provider, and Sustainer of all and to trust in His providence. We are to ask, knowing that He always gives perfectly in accordance with His will.

4. We must be mindful that His thoughts and His ways are not our thoughts and our ways. For there are times where the Lord will say no, but we must not complain, for we know He will never withhold anything that is for our good.[170]

---

[169] James 1:6, [170] Psalm 84:11

Father, You are infinite and You are sovereign. Forgive me, for my mind operates so many times in an aspect of fear: fear of being ridiculed, fear of prosperity gospel, fear of over assuming Your love for me in Christ, fear of speaking my heart and being judged. I confess these fears and repent this pride. Grant me a boldness to bring all things to You, that You may be glorified. Open my eyes to see the goodness of the Lord in the land of the living. Grant Your blessing to remove this humanistic and deistic veil and walk in the truth of who You are. In Jesus' name.

Hebrews 7:25

Consequently, he is able to save to the uttermost those who draw near to God through him, since he always lives to make intercession for them.

1. Christ has saved to the uttermost. There is nothing beyond His saving grace. There is nothing anyone has ever done or could do that Christ cannot and has not redeemed for those who are His.

2. What a glorious truth! His Kingdom for His people will be complete, and there will not be a single soul belonging to Him who is beyond His redemption. The price He paid was infinite and paid to a holy and infinite God. What glory!

3. Yet, our Lord and King does far, far more. Not only does He save His people and bring us into His Kingdom, but He prays for us. He brings our needs and our anxieties before the throne of grace. He is the perfect high priest, interceding for His people. Jesus Christ's death and resurrection were not a one-time act He completed and walked away from; but He is right now interceding on behalf of His people for all eternity. Who are we that our King intercedes for us? We are those whom the Father has loved. We are loved; we are known by God the Father for all eternity, and He sent His Son into the world for His people. Let us know, let us come, and let us worship the Lord our God and our Maker.

Father, what glory and what beauty You have lavished upon us, that we should be called children of God—and so we are! The truth and reality of Your love are overwhelming, and I see but only a glimpse. Open my eyes and my heart that I may know You and see You and that I may worship You and live and strive with all my heart in Your Kingdom. Use me for Your glory in Your Kingdom for all eternity. Grant me success for Your Kingdom in Christ's name.

Leviticus 20:26

*You shall be holy to me,
for I the Lord am holy and have separated
you from the peoples, that you should be mine.*

1. Christians, those called out by God and as a chosen people, royal priesthood, and holy nation,[171] are to be in the world and not of it.

2. There is a clear line of delineation between those who are Christ's and those who are not in Christ. That line is holiness. It is the Kingdom of God the Lord is building, as He is bringing all who are His to Himself.

3. In a world where a moralism continually redefined is now the standard, holiness is marginalized and replaced. It is terrifying to stand before a holy God, so humanity would rather define what is true and good and beautiful based upon their depravity rather than who God is.

4. There is only One who is holy, and He is God. Nothing of human construct or entity is holy. Only God is holy and only when we are mindful of His holiness can we walk in the fear of the Lord. The fear of the Lord diminishes to the extent we deny the truth of God's holiness in every part of our lives. The fear of the Lord is the beginning of wisdom, and the knowledge of the Holy One is insight.[172]

---

[171] 1 Peter 2:9, [172] Proverbs 9:10

Father, the fear of You is the beginning of wisdom, but apart from the knowledge of Your holiness, I in my pride do not fear. My sin stifles the fear and the reverence I should have for You. I know this to be true, but I also realize I cannot conjure this up in my heart and mind. Lord, I need You to grant me the fear of the Lord and the knowledge and mindfulness of Your holiness, that I may worship and adore You all the days of my life. In Jesus' name.

Leviticus 19:15

YOU SHALL DO NO INJUSTICE IN COURT. YOU SHALL
NOT BE PARTIAL TO THE POOR OR DEFER TO THE GREAT,
BUT IN RIGHTEOUSNESS SHALL YOU JUDGE YOUR NEIGHBOR.

1. No one is righteous; no, not one.[173] In the sight of God there are none who, because of wealth or lack of wealth, because of prestige or lack of prestige, makes one person more righteous than any other person. Each individual is accountable before God on the basis of his nature.

2. No one will stand before God and say, "If this person had [done this or that], I would have acted or behaved differently." Any and every way you act is not caused by anyone else but is because of who you are. We are sinful and deserve the wrath of God.

3. Our standard is the Lord God Almighty; we all stand convicted in light of His holiness. For this reason, the Father sent His only Son into the world to pay the penalty for our sin, that we may know God and make Him known.

4. We are to stand on the finished work of Christ, and in Him and Him alone, we are reconciled to the Lord.

---

[173] Romans 3:10

Father, holy be Your name. Let it be known in the heavens and on the earth. Let Your glory abound in all the earth. Father, I confess that my pride diminishes my knowledge of Your holiness. Grant me to be mindful and to know Your holiness, that I may rest in Christ and not in myself. In Jesus' name.

Amen

Psalm 111:2

GREAT ARE THE WORKS OF THE LORD, STUDIED BY ALL WHO DELIGHT IN THEM.

1. All of the works of the Lord are great. There is nothing the Lord does that is mundane or not worthy of praise. Awesome are His works.

2. Yet the heart of man apart from the grace of God is hardened against the Lord. The human heart desires to rationalize and diminish the works of God in all and in every area of life—to take God off His throne and place ourselves on it.

3. The Lord calls us to be mindful of who He is and to study the works of His hands, to acknowledge that He is the One who ordains all things. The more we look at all the areas in our lives in light of who God is, the more radiant we see Christ. For it is Christ who holds all things together; it is Christ who is with us through the valley of the shadow of death; it is Christ who calls, who sustains, who upholds.

4. As we draw near to God, He will draw near to us.[174] As we see a more right view of who He is, we will see how the heavens declare the glory of God and the skies above proclaim His handiwork![175]

---

[174] James 4:8, [175] Psalm 19:1

Father, the heavens declare Your glory! The sunrise bears witness to Your faithfulness. Oh Father, how easy it is for my mind to make idols out of situations rather than to trust Your sovereignty. My heart so easily attempts to rationalize my day rather than to trust and seek Your grace. Will You please stir in my heart a passion for Your glory? Will You open my eyes that I may worship You? Will You restore to me the joy of my salvation, that I may praise You and be in awe and wonder of who You are? In Jesus' name.

Leviticus 11:45

For I am the LORD who brought you up out of the land of Egypt to be your God. You shall therefore be holy, for I am holy.

1. What is the standard God would have for His people? To be holy as He is holy. The people of Israel were to walk in all the ways of God. They were to reflect the holiness of God to all the people of the land and to be completely set apart from the rest of the world.

2. In Hebrew literature, when a writer wanted to be sure the reader understood a point, he would repeat that point. When Christ wanted to make a point to those around Him, He would say, "Truly, truly, I say to you."[176] This doubling of the word would ensure the people around Him would know to listen. If the Hebrew writer really wanted someone's attention, he would take the word to the third degree. There is only one attribute that God, in His Word, has declared to the third degree, and that is His holiness. For in the heavens it is declared, "Holy, Holy, Holy, is the Lord God Almighty."[177]

3. No one can stand before a holy God. Our sin is our conviction and is also the verdict against us. But God, being rich in mercy, sent His Son into the world to pay the penalty for our sins, that we might die to sin and live to Christ. The reality and the truth of God's holiness are not diminished but instead are rooted in Christ, the founder and perfecter of our faith.[178]

[176]John 6:26, [177]Revelation 4:8, [178]Revelation 4:8

Father, Your holiness is true. I know Your holiness intellectually, but so many times I deny it quickly and readily. I am many times antinomian in my heart rather than worshipful toward You. Thank You for Christ, and thank You for redeeming a people of Your own. Grant me to know You and to know and rest in Your holiness, in Christ alone. Guide my steps, my thoughts, and my actions, and give me clarity of Your holiness. May it penetrate deep into my heart that I may know You and worship and glorify You as I ought to. In Jesus' name I ask this.

Leviticus 10:1–2

Now Nadab and Abihu, the sons of Aaron, each took his censer and put fire in it and laid incense on it and offered unauthorized fire before the Lord, which he had not commanded them. And fire came out from before the Lord and consumed them, and they died before the Lord.

1. All that we do, we do before the Lord. Every thought, word, action, and deed is done before the Lord and is weighed in accordance with a holy God.

2. Nadab and Abihu, although instructed by the Lord in what to place in the incense and how to offer right praise before God, did not heed the Word of the Lord but instead acted in accordance with their own will.

3. "God will not be mocked. For whatever one sows, that will he reap."[179] We must be mindful in how we come to the Lord. We are not to justify our actions based upon status or tenure, for these things are meaningless. God is eternal, His glory does not diminish, nothing will keep back His Kingdom, and not even the gates of hell can stand against Him![180]

4. Let us repent and seek the Lord while He may be found; call upon Him while He is near.[181] Let us ask the Lord for wisdom, and let us be mindful of all we do before Him. Let us glory in Christ. For the Lord will not chide us forever, nor will He keep His anger forever.[182]

---

[179]Galatians 6:7, [180]Matthew 16:18, [181]Isaiah 55:6, [182]Psalm 103:9

Father, You are holy. I cannot comprehend Your holiness in the way Your Word describes it. I confess that many times I think of holiness as a "church" word rather than a reality in my heart and mind. I have hardened my heart many times against You and have done a "church" act to check it off a list rather than being mindful of Your holiness. You have been so merciful to me. Grant my heart to know Your holiness. Grant my heart the ability to worship You, in light of Your glory, in light of Christ. I ask this In Jesus' name.

Leviticus 8:29

And Moses took the breast and waved it for a wave offering before the Lord. It was Moses' portion of the ram of ordination, as the Lord commanded Moses.

1. As Moses set up the priesthood for the Israelites, he was commanded by the Lord to offer sacrifices before God to atone for the sins of the priest and also for the children of Israel.

2. This is not a ritual, however, performed far away from God. We do not conjure God up like the worthless idols of others' religions. God is near, and in Him we live, and move, and have our being. Everything we do, all our actions, are done before a holy God.

3. Moses waved his sacrificed offering before the Lord. The Lord saw it; the Lord acknowledged it. The Hebrew word for *before* means "face." The face of God saw the sacrifice Moses offered before Him.

4. Everything we do is seen, weighed, and held accountable by a holy God. We must be mindful that even before a word is on our lips, the Lord knows it altogether.[183] As we go throughout our day, we must seek the Lord; we ask Him to help us recognize that we stand before a holy God. And let us pray with the psalmist when he cries, "Search me, O God, and know my heart! Try me and know my thoughts! And see if there be any grievous way in me, and lead me in your way everlasting!"[184]

[183]Psalm 139:4, [184]Psalm 139:23–24

Father, You are over all, and in all, and through all. You are high and lifted up and are still acquainted with all my ways. Who am I that You are mindful of me? I confess the many times I deny Your nearness, Your intimacy. I walk in a state of unbelief; forgive me. Help me to know Your nearness, search my heart, try my thoughts, and lead me in Your way everlasting. For You are my God and my King. To You be the glory, in Jesus' name.

Proverbs 3:3-4

Let not steadfast love and faithfulness forsake you; bind them around your neck; write them on the tablet of your heart. So you will find favor and good success in the sight of God and man.

1. Our aim is to reflect Christ and to know Him in all aspects of life. For He is Lord, and His rule is over all things. Christ did all things out of love for the Father and completed all that the Father gave Him to do faithfully and to the glory of the Father.[185]

2. Love and faithfulness are attributes of the character of the Father. Our hearts' aim at all times, by the power of the Holy Spirit, is to reflect His character to Him. For this pleases the Lord. We are to be prayerful, mindful of the Word of God, and working and acting in accordance with His Word.

3. We must be mindful that if we are to bind love and faithfulness, which reflect the character of God around our neck, then we must realize that these character traits are not innate to us. Apart from the grace of God, and apart from the power of God, they are contrary to our flesh. This is why we are to bind them, to tie them around our neck. God's attributes are to be so meditated on that they are written on the tablet of our hearts.

---

[185] John 17:4

Father, You are so faithful, and Your love endures forever. My heart is so fickle, so prone to wander, so prone to do things contrary to love and faithfulness. Help me to reflect Your Son. Make my heart rest in Your assurance and grace. Grant my heart to know Your faithfulness and Your love. I praise You, Lord, for who You are. In Jesus' precious name I pray this.

Amen

Hebrews 3:4

FOR EVERY HOUSE IS BUILT BY SOMEONE,
BUT THE BUILDER OF ALL THINGS IS GOD.

1. Everything we see has a beginning, and that beginning is rooted and founded in God alone. Though He uses the means of grace to accomplish His work, it all comes through God.

2. The heresy of deism has placed in the heart of man the idea that God created and walked away from His world, much like a watchmaker who builds a watch, and then that watch just ticks by itself. This is a deplorable deception of reality.

3. For God is sovereign over all things and omnipresent at all times. In Him, we live and move and have our being,[186] and from Him, through Him, and to Him are all things.[187]

4. Every morning, He creates and orchestrates, and every evening He directs and sustains. Every heartbeat in every creature He sovereignly upholds, and every cloud in the sky He designs and moves where He desires.

5. This then is our hope: not to go to Him with our plans and tell the Lord what we can and cannot do. For we do not determine what is within our power or not within our power. Instead, we are to go to Him and to seek Him in all things. This includes wisdom and confidence, hope, assurance, joy, and conviction. For He is the builder and the sustainer of all things.

---

[186]Acts 17:28, [187]Romans 11:36

Father, You are God. Forgive me and have mercy on me for using the humanity You have given me as an excuse not to do Your will. Grant me wisdom to rest and to flourish according to Your will. Forgive my pride when I come to You and tell You what I can and cannot do. Restore to me the joy of the salvation You've granted me, and renew a right spirit within me. In Jesus' name.

Amen

Leviticus 4:1–3

AND THE LORD SPOKE TO MOSES, SAYING, "SPEAK TO THE PEOPLE OF ISRAEL, SAYING, IF ANYONE SINS UNINTENTIONALLY IN ANY OF THE LORD'S COMMANDMENTS ABOUT THINGS NOT TO BE DONE, AND DOES ANY ONE OF THEM, IF IT IS THE ANOINTED PRIEST WHO SINS, THUS BRINGING GUILT ON THE PEOPLE, THEN HE SHALL OFFER FOR THE SIN THAT HE HAS COMMITTED A BULL FROM THE HERD WITHOUT BLEMISH TO THE LORD FOR A SIN OFFERING."

1. The essence of mankind, by nature, is sinful. Apart from the Holy Spirit we can do nothing that is good, true, or beautiful. For even our actions, if our intentions are not done by faith, are sin.[188]

2. There is no one outside of sin. Every human—even pastors—has a sinful nature apart from the work of Christ. Every human being is born with a sinful heart and does not seek after God. For there is none who is righteous, no not one.[189]

3. Since sin is our nature apart from the work of God, we not only sin intentionally, we sin unintentionally as well. The apostle Paul says that everything that does not proceed from faith is a sin![190] The unintentional sin is not any less serious. When the Lord reveals that sin to us, we are still guilty and deserving of death.

4. But God the Father has sent His Son into the world to pay the penalty for our sins, that we might rest in the assurance of Christ, before a Holy God. For the wages of sin is death, but the free gift of God is eternal life in Christ Jesus our Lord.[191]

---

[188]Romans 14:23, [189]Romans 3:12, [190]Romans 14:23, [191]Romans 6:23

Father, You are holy and righteous. There are so many times that I justify my actions and thoughts instead of confessing them before You. There are even sins I am unaware of. Forgive me. Please make known to me my sin, that I may repent and walk by Your grace, through faith, through Christ Jesus. In His name I ask this.

Psalm 27:13-14

I BELIEVE THAT I SHALL LOOK UPON THE GOODNESS OF THE LORD IN THE LAND OF THE LIVING! WAIT FOR THE LORD; BE STRONG, AND LET YOUR HEART TAKE COURAGE; WAIT FOR THE LORD!

1. We are to walk in the assurance and truth of knowing we will see the goodness of the Lord in the land of the living. We will not just see and know God in heaven, but we are to see and know God now. He is making all things new![192] He is redeeming the world and making a people of His own possession.[193]

2. Our prayer is that His Kingdom come, His will be done, on earth as it is in heaven.[194] That means now. That means to expectantly see the work and beauty and majesty of God, who is at work now in our lives.

3. This is not a sensationalized view of the world. This is watching the Lord change lives, renew friendships, bless His people, govern all things, and work all things together for good for those who love Him and are called according to His purpose.[195]

4. But in this truth we are to wait. We shouldn't go to God and chastise the Almighty because He does not work in accordance with our timeline, but we are to patiently and by faith wait on His perfect timing. *"The Lord is not slow to fulfill his promise as some count slowness, but is patient toward you, not wishing that any should perish, but that all should reach repentance."*[196]

---

[192]Revelation 21:5, [193]1 Peter 2:9, [194]Matthew 6:10, [195]Psalm 8:28, [196]2 Peter 3:9

Father, You are working all things together perfectly for Your Kingdom and at Your perfect timing. Many times, when I'm not good at waiting, I almost deny any goodness that occurs and deny You the thanksgiving You deserve. Forgive me. Grant my heart thanksgiving in who You are. Grant me the faith and hope to love those around me. Give me a vision for Christ, and give me the strength to do Your will, for Your glory, by Your grace. In Jesus' name I ask this.

Amen

Psalm 27:1

The Lord is my light and my salvation; whom shall I fear? The Lord is the stronghold of my life; of whom shall I be afraid?

1. Our view of God affects every aspect of our lives. When we sin and fear man, we have a bigger view of man than we do of God.

2. God is not a gnostic idea or a golden ticket into heaven. He is the Lord of all; in Him we live and move and have our being.[197]

3. The Lord reveals those things that He would have us do, that He would have us pray for, that He would have us be mindful of. The Lord is our protector and defender, a very present help in trouble.[198] In light of a right and true view of God, there is absolutely nothing to fear—not politics, or sickness, or finances, or evil, because God and God alone is our light and our salvation.

4. In God, we have our refuge. This goes against the world in every circumstance. What causes fear in every instance of news and media is not that what we see is scary, but that in the midst of the uncertainty, we tend to deny the sovereignty and love of God and elevate the perceived autonomy of man. A perceived universe with a loving Heavenly Father is a terrifying life.

[197] Acts 17:28, [198] Psalm 46:1

Father, You are near and You are present. In every circumstance, the world declares that it is autonomous and that it is foolish to think You are near. Forgive how many instances I have acted in unbelief. Grant me to know Your nearness and Your goodness. Grant me to know You as my light and my salvation. Grant my heart to rest in the peace of Your sovereign grace. In Jesus' name.

Hebrews 1:3-4

HE IS THE RADIANCE OF THE GLORY OF GOD AND THE EXACT IMPRINT OF HIS NATURE, AND HE UPHOLDS THE UNIVERSE BY THE WORD OF HIS POWER. AFTER MAKING PURIFICATION FOR SINS, HE SAT DOWN AT THE RIGHT HAND OF THE MAJESTY ON HIGH, HAVING BECOME AS MUCH SUPERIOR TO ANGELS AS THE NAME HE HAS INHERITED IS MORE EXCELLENT THAN THEIRS.

1. Jesus Christ is God. He is not just a good person or a nice guy; He is God made flesh who dwelt among us. We have seen His glory, the glory of the One and only.[199]

2. Jesus Christ upholds the universe by the word of His power. He is sitting on the throne, and all things are orchestrated, ordained, and bound by Him. There is nothing that does not happen outside of His decree.

3. Christ is seated today, right now, fully God and fully man, at the right hand of the Father, and He is greater than all things. He is the Uncreated Eternal, birthed to Mary and Joseph, and in Him all creation exalts and magnifies Him.

4. The angels rejoice over Him, and His beauty is without parallel. There is none who can compare to His power, His glory, His perfection, and His rule. He strikes fear in the heart of man, yet humbled Himself and paid the penalty for our sins. He is the Alpha and Omega, the Beginning and the End.[200]

5. It is only through Christ that we can draw near to God. Whoever does not know Christ does not know God. There is no amount of knowing about God, for Satan knows about God. There is no recognizing angels, for Satan is the "angel of light;"[201] there is no being mindful of Scripture, for Satan uses Scripture; there is no acknowledgment of a supernatural world, for Satan dwells in the supernatural world—that can save you. It is Christ and Christ alone. For He and He alone is the radiance of the glory of God.

[199]John 1:14, [200]Revelation 22:13, [201]2 Corinthians 11:14

Jesus, I praise You, for You are glorious. I confess that many times I have viewed You as a felt-board character. I have viewed You as a good person or a golden ticket rather than as God. Will You please grant me to know You and to know Your glory? Will You please place my hope in Your Lordship? Give me wisdom and knowledge and strength to serve You, as You would have me serve You. In Jesus' name, I ask this.

Exodus 38:22-23

BEZALEL THE SON OF URI, SON OF HUR, OF THE TRIBE OF JUDAH, MADE ALL THAT THE LORD COMMANDED MOSES; AND WITH HIM WAS OHOLIAB THE SON OF AHISAMACH, OF THE TRIBE OF DAN, AN ENGRAVER AND DESIGNER AND EMBROIDERER IN BLUE AND PURPLE AND SCARLET YARNS AND FINE TWINED LINEN.

1. God is objectively beautiful, and all creation declares His glory and beauty![202] As the children of Israel passed through the wilderness, the Lord commanded them to build a tabernacle in which to worship Him. He designed every square inch of the tabernacle and all corresponding items and tools to serve in the worship of Him.

2. Beauty is a grace. The Lord is glorified and magnified in objectively beautiful creations. Beauty reflects intentionality and thought and glorifies the Creator. It reflects the Lord, who spoke mindfully of each created being, down to its most microscopic detail. From the smallest molecular atom to the greatest star in the universe, all these first were in the mind of God. They were thought of and rejoiced over in all creation[203] and created to display God's glory.

3. The Lord is glorified in beauty because it reflects Him. The Lord placed in the hearts of Uri, Hur, and Oholiab the design of the Tabernacle and supplied the material, design, heart, and will to complete the building. The Lord provides all things.

4. Sin has corrupted beauty. We diminish the idea and hope of beauty and define it by the lust of our hearts rather than the glory of God. We desire beauty to reflect who we are rather than display the majesty and holiness of God. We declare beauty meaningless and measure our ability by what we see rather than trusting by faith in the providence and the love of our God.

5. Yet God redeems beauty. The Lord took the most horrific man-made device, the cross, and placed His only Son on it, crucifying Him by the hand of the people, that we might be saved from our sins and know who God is. The cross is the beauty of God's redemption of His people for all of eternity.

[202] Psalm 19:1, [203] Psalm 19:1

Father, You are beautiful. What an incredible truth, what hope, what joy. Father, I confess that I have many times defined truth based upon what I can see and what I perceive can happen, rather than seeking You. Forgive me. I have denied Your sovereignty and love and have instead been pragmatic. Forgive me. Grant me the freedom to know Your beauty, to reflect Your beauty, and to be a beacon to those whom You would have me share who You are. In Jesus' name.

Amen

Galatians 5:2

Look: I, Paul, say to you that if you accept circumcision, Christ will be of no advantage to you.

1. Christ and Christ alone. There is nothing anyone can add or take away from Him. For to add anything to Christ is to diminish Him, and to take away anything from Him is to take all of Him.

2. Neither baptism, nor pietism, nor Gnosticism, nor liberalism, nor any other man-made institution can add to Christ. He is complete. Yet, here is also a promise the apostle warns us about. If we add anything to Christ, He will be of no advantage to us. Our worship adds nothing, our words add nothing, our prayers add nothing. Christ and Christ alone!

3. The power of God needs nothing added. The power of God is complete, and to add anything to it is to deny the power of God and remove His power from that with which He has called you. Who are we as mere men to think we can add anything to the Creator? God has always been complete, and not even the creation of the world added anything to Him! He was perfectly content before anything was, and yet He still created us.

4. Let us search our hearts prayerfully, asking the Holy Spirit to reveal to us by His Word the things we so needlessly add to Christ. Let us cling to His Word boldly and without apology, trusting in His purposes. Let us deny the world with all its lies and seek first the Kingdom of God and His righteousness, and all these things will be added.[204]

---

[204]Matthew 6:33, [205]Acts 17:28

Father, You are complete! There is nothing that can be added to or taken away from You, for in You, we live, move, and have our being.[205] *Father, I confess that in my pride I have attempted to add to You. I have attempted to think my life is not complete without certain things. Forgive me and have mercy on me. Help me to know Christ, to be satisfied in Christ, to walk according to Christ. Keep all those who ridicule me at bay, and grant my heart peace in Christ and Christ alone. In Jesus' name.*

Exodus 9:16–17

But for this purpose I have raised you up, to show you my power, so that my name may be proclaimed in all the earth. You are still exalting yourself against my people and will not let them go.

1. There is a purpose and reason that God does anything and everything. There is nothing that does not fulfill the plans of the Lord in His own way. God has predestined every human according to the purpose of His will.[206]

2. God will be proclaimed, and He will not be hidden. This is a mercy and a grace. For the Lord is not bound by any requirements that others see His power, or that His name be proclaimed on the earth, or that He is even known. But the Lord graciously makes Himself known to the world. The heavens declare the glory of God, and the skies above proclaim His handiwork.[207] The more we know God, the more we must humble ourselves and declare His glory.

3. But in our humanity, we fight against the Lord. We attempt to exalt ourselves rather than humble ourselves before a holy God. In our depravity, we demand that we sit on the throne of grace rather than God. We gaze at our navels in wonder, proclaiming to the world how mighty we are. In Scripture, the word *exalt* means "to build up as a highway, or as a ramp as when you placed a city under siege."[208] Apart from the grace of God, our hearts attempt to do everything they can to deny the Lordship of Christ and to build up against a holy God.

4. Do not be deceived: God is not mocked, for whatever one sows, that will he also reap.[209] If we deny the Lord, the Lord will deny us.[210] Seek the Lord and plead for His mercy. Ask the Lord to reveal to you those places where you do not submit to His ways, where you resist Him in the same way Pharaoh resisted Moses.

---

[206]Ephesians 1:5, [207]Psalm 19:1, [208]Brown, F., Driver, S. R., & Briggs, C. A. (1977). Enhanced Brown-Driver-Briggs Hebrew and English Lexicon (p. 699). Oxford: Clarendon Press. [209]Galatians 6:7, [210]2 Timothy 2:12

Father, I come to You and acknowledge that You are on the throne. Who am I? Father, I know I have attempted so often to impress others with what I have accomplished and done. I have believed the lie that I caused my own accomplishments. Forgive me. Remove from me the desire to justify myself. Grant me Your nearness and give me wisdom, that I may behold Your glory and worship You in heaven above. Use me for Your glory and Yours alone, for You are God and I am not. In Jesus' name.

Amen

Exodus 13:17

When Pharaoh let the people go, God did not lead them by way of the land of the Philistines, although that was near. For God said, "Lest the people change their minds when they see war and return to Egypt."

1. God's thoughts and ways are not our thoughts or our ways.[211] For the Lord is sovereign and omniscient. The Lord knows our hearts; He knows where each of us is at; all these things the Lord intimately and fully knows.

2. In this we rest. We are not to complain to God about His leading, for He knows where and how to perfectly lead us. The Lord will fulfill His purposes for me.[212]

3. The Lord also knows our frame. He knows our needs, our dependency, our timidity, and our weaknesses. He does not tempt us beyond what we can bear.

4. God is leading us in Christ to Himself. Ever pressing on. He does not want us to go back to Egypt—from where we came—but to press on to know Christ and fulfill the mission He has ordained for us. We are to walk by faith in the assurance of the infinite wisdom of God. For from Him and through Him and to Him are all things.[213]

---

[211]Isaiah 55:8, [212]Psalm 138:8, [213]Romans 11:36

Father, I love You and Your wisdom. You know my coming in and going out and are acquainted with all my ways. Forgive me for the many times my heart has raged against You rather than trusting You. Forgive my unbelief. Grant me hope and joy to rest in humble dependence on You and You alone in all things. In Jesus' name.

Amen

Galatians 2:20

I HAVE BEEN CRUCIFIED WITH CHRIST. IT IS NO LONGER I WHO LIVE, BUT CHRIST WHO LIVES IN ME. AND THE LIFE I NOW LIVE IN THE FLESH I LIVE BY FAITH IN THE SON OF GOD, WHO LOVED ME AND GAVE HIMSELF FOR ME.

1. Paul proclaimed the gospel! Until this point, the belief was that the blood of a sacrifice made you a child of God. Thus, if you were a relative of Abraham, Isaac, and Jacob, then you were covered. The blood of the patriarchs was the golden ticket. Paul destroyed this argument with the truth rooted in Christ.

2. There is not DNA, bloodline, work, act, circumstance, or anything that can bring you before a holy God. The sin of Adam permeates every and all aspects of our lives. Our thoughts, words, actions, and emotions are rooted in sin, and there is no escaping this.

3. God the Father sent His only Son into the world to pay the price of our sin and to take the wrath of God His people deserve, along with full judgment, so that in Christ and His finished work alone, we can stand before a holy God.

4. So the logical question is, "Who are His people"? Everyone who calls on the name of the Lord, for it is they alone who are saved from the damning and eternal wrath of God.[214] Once we have called out to God to save us, we now have, by faith in Christ, a new life. Our lives are now in Christ, and it is Christ in us and the assurance of Christ who lives in us that we walk boldly for His glory and our good. All the promises of God are fulfilled in Christ,[215] and we live under the Lordship and freedom of Christ, as we seek first the Kingdom of God and His righteousness, and everything else the Lord will work for His glory and our good.[216]

---

[214]Romans 10:13, [215]2 Corinthians 1:20, [216]Matthew 6:33

Father, what freedom in Christ, what glory in Christ, what beauty and wisdom in Christ! Many times I do not recognize nor am I mindful of Christ. Many times I am more mindful of the world and what I see rather than Your Word! Forgive my unbelief and grant that I walk by Christ, the truth of Christ, the assurance of Christ, the hope of Christ. I ask this in Jesus' name.

1 Samuel 4:3

And when the people came to the camp, the elders of Israel said, "Why has the Lord defeated us today before the Philistines? Let us bring the ark of the covenant of the Lord here from Shiloh, that it may come among us and save us from the power of our enemies."

1. The people of Israel had just gone to war with the Philistine army and were defeated on the field of battle. Even though Israel had not turned to the Lord, they did acknowledge Him by stating how it wasn't the Philistines who had defeated them in battle but the Lord Himself.

2. We must be mindful that the Lord is the sovereign One over all things. It is the Lord who gives and the Lord who takes away,[217] and it is His name and not our own that must be praised.

3. The Lord disciplines those He loves,[218] and He orchestrates all things to lead us to repentance and grace in Christ. Yet many times we deny the Lordship of Christ, and instead of seeking Him, we fall back on pragmatic acts to achieve our desired outcome rather than glorify God. We attempt, just like the Israelites, to control God through our duties and self-righteousness rather than humble ourselves before the mighty hand of God.[219]

4. Let us at all times seek the Lord while He may be found.[220] Let us repent and come before Him and seek His will, trusting Him with all our hearts and leaning not on our own understanding. Whatever He ordains is right and deserving of all worship and honor and praise.

---

[217] Job 1:21, [218] Proverbs 3:12, [219] 1 Peter 5:6, [220] Isaiah 55:6

Lord, You are Lord!
You have created the heavens and the earth, and all of creation cries glory! When I look at my life, I see I have placed a heavy emphasis on self-lordship. I have declared You Lord with my mouth, but in my heart, I have sat upon my perceived autonomous throne. Forgive me, Lord, and have Your way. Be glorified and magnified, and open my eyes that I may see You as Lord and myself Your humble servant.
In Christ's name.

Amen

Acts 4:10

Let it be known to all of you and to all the people of Israel that by the name of Jesus Christ of Nazareth, whom you crucified, whom God raised from the dead—by him this man is standing before you well.

1. What is in a name? The identity of that person, who that person is, what that person represents, how that person lives his or her life—is what makes a name.

2. All of life points toward Christ. It is His name that must be exalted. It is His glory that must be praised. It is Christ and Christ alone, for in Him we live and move and have our being.[221] Christ is the One who upholds the universe and by whom the entire world was created.[222]

3. Yet, since the Garden of Eden, our desire is to be equal to Him.[223] We desire to share God's glory rather than rest in His love for us. We want to make ourselves someone to be feared and praised, rather than fearing and praising Christ.

4. God does not give His glory to any other.[224] It is in Christ alone, who upholds the universe this very day, that all things are done. The Father has placed Christ on the throne, so at the name of Jesus, every knee should bow, in heaven and on earth and under the earth, and every tongue confess that Jesus Christ is Lord, to the glory of the Father.[225]

---

[221]Acts 17:28, [222]Hebrews 1:2–3, [223]Genesis 3:5, [224]Isaiah 48:11, [225]Philippians 2:10–11

Father, I praise You for Christ. I praise You for His Lordship, for His Kingship, for His Kingdom. Father, I confess the many times I desire and attempt to make a name for myself. I am tempted to believe if I don't do this for myself, who will? Forgive my pride and unbelief in Your love for me. Grant my heart rest and confidence, boasting and hope in Christ and Christ alone. In His name I ask this.

Ruth 4:14

Then the women said to Naomi, "Blessed be the Lord, who has not left you this day without a redeemer, and may his name be renowned in Israel!"

1. Blessed be God who has saved us and redeemed our life from the pit![226] We must praise the Lord, for He has not left us to our sin and our depravity, and He has not given us what we deserve, which is separation from Him.[227]

2. Our God, who is complete and without need, who is perfect in all His ways and needs nothing to add to Him or take away from Him, created us out of the abundance of His love. And though we have sinned against Him, He did not give us the death we so richly deserve.[228]

3. Our God is also just, for though He is loving, He is also holy.[229] He demands that all who are His to be holy. When we sin against the Lord, a price must be paid. There must be redemption for the sin that goes against the holiness of God.

4. But God the Father sent His only Son into the world to redeem a people for Himself.[230] Christ paid the ultimate price as the perfect redeemer. "For our sake he made him to be sin who knew no sin, so that in him we might become the righteousness of God."[231] Now God has exalted Him and given Him a name above every other name, so that at the name of Jesus, every knee shall bow and every tongue confess that Jesus Christ is Lord![232]

---

[226]Psalm 103:4, [227]Psalm 103:10, [228]Genesis 2:17, [229]Leviticus 11:44, [230]John 3:16, [231]2 Corinthians 5:21, [232]Philippians 2:10–11

Father, You have redeemed a people for Yourself. You have exalted Your Son, and His throne shall be established for all eternity! How glorious and how marvelous. Who am I that You know me? Who am I that You would redeem me? Who am I that You have called me by name? Lead me in Your way, Father, in accordance with Your will, to the glory of Your Son. In Christ's name I ask this.

Acts 3:19-20

Repent therefore, and turn back, that your sins may be blotted out, that times of refreshing may come from the presence of the Lord, and that he may send the Christ appointed for you, Jesus.

1. Our hearts and minds long to be refreshed and feel complete. Ever since Adam sinned against God in the Garden of Eden, our hearts have longed and groaned inwardly to go back to where we originally came from in the presence of God.[233]

2. Even all of creation groans with the pains of childbirth for the redemption of the Sons of God![234] For all of creation has been subjected to futility until the Lord's return.

3. But we cannot work ourselves to completion. For we are dead in our trespasses and sins, in which apart from God's grace we walk.[235] We follow the prince of the power of air, the spirit that is at work in the sons of disobedience.[236]

4. But "If we confess our sins, the Lord is faithful and just to forgive us our sins, and to cleanse us from all unrighteousness!"[237] If we come to the Lord, and repent, and lay before Him our self-lordship, and look to Christ as our King through repentance, we will know the refreshment of the presence of God. Repentance through the redemption of Christ leads to peace.

[233]Romans 8:23, [234]Romans 8:22, [235]Ephesians 2:1, [236]Ephesians 2:2, [237]1 John 1:9

Father, You have prepared a way for me. I have worked and strived in my own perceived strength to make myself whole. I have denied Your Lordship and tried all things to bring joy and happiness, and apart from You I have nothing. All things are like filthy rags, like gravel in the mouth, rather than peace and refreshment. Grant me repentance and the nearness of You. Grant me freedom in Christ and boldness in His finished work for Your glory. Grant me hope for Christ's sake and for Your glory. In His name I pray.

77

Exodus 15:9

The enemy said, "I will pursue, I will overtake, I will divide the spoil, my desire shall have its fill of them. I will draw my sword; my hand shall destroy them."

1. Notice how the enemy says what he will do. "I will pursue," "I will overtake," "I will divide," "my desire," "I will draw my sword," "my hand shall destroy." This entire chapter is about the awesome power of God, and the only part that discusses the individualized viewpoint is the enemies of God.

2. The enemies of God only know themselves, and they do not look to the Lord. Their sole focus is on themselves. They are individualistic in their thoughts, words, actions, and deeds.

3. Who are we to go before God and demand our justice? On what grounds do we stand that give us any right to proclaim our lordship? Our God is in the heavens, and He does whatever He pleases![238]

4. This is also terrifying because the church has denied the sovereignty and Lordship of Christ in our lives. We have relegated Him to a morality, an ideal, rather than the reigning King. We have made Him into a golden ticket to get into heaven rather than the One from whom all things are orchestrated. We are to look to God, we are to know God, and we are to meditate on the goodness of the Lord and to be mindful of His awesome power. We are to rest in the hands of the Lord at all times and look to Him for all things. For the scariest thing in the world is when we look to ourselves rather than to God. We become like an enemy of God.

[238] Psalm 115:3

Father, the repetitions of "I" in this verse knock the breath out of me. For I now see my own pride and arrogance in my undertaking over the years. I have believed the tickling of my ears in the world, where the temptation is to believe the individual and self-help, rather than trust the living God. Rather than come to You and to seek Your will. Forgive me, Lord. Teach me Your ways and go before me. Help me to walk in Your truth. For You are my God, and I will forever praise You. Help me to not think too small in prideful piety, and guard me from selfish ambition. Glorify Your name in and through my life. In Jesus' name.

Exodus 15:18

The LORD will reign forever and ever.

1. The Lord reigns. He is sitting on his throne. He is coordinating, ordering, decreeing, and working all things together. The very words of this verse captivate and inspire awe. There is no time outside forever and ever.

2. Forever and ever is for all eternity. This does not apply only to the Israelites or to an Old Testament reality that ever ends. This is now. Christ is seated on the throne of heaven![239]

3. Many times, our hearts desire to place God on His throne in the past and then think He will one day reign. Our hearts lash out at God if, for a millisecond, we acknowledge Him on His throne at any moment. When we take our eyes off of God's Word and place them on the circumstances of life, defining our experience by what the enemies of God declare them to be, we lose the eyes of faith.

4. We are to walk by faith, not by sight.[240] For the righteous shall live by faith.[241]

5. This is not a blind faith, a leap-in-the-dark faith. This absurd thought is foolish and denies the truth and authority of Scripture. This faith is a faith rooted in truth, rooted in the Word of God, and empowered by the Spirit of God through the redemption of Christ and to the glory of God the Father. This faith is rooted in a Person who came to earth in the form of a baby, grew in wisdom and stature, was crucified, raised on the third day, ascended into heaven, and is seated at the right hand of the Father. This Person is Christ, and His Kingdom is established forever and ever.

---

[239]Revelation 4:2–6, [240]2 Corinthians 5:7, [241]Romans 1:17

Father, Your Kingdom is established. What hope and joy! I confess the many times I have not walked in the reality of Your Kingdom and instead walked in the depravity of my kingdom. How do I live in Your Kingdom, and how do I seek to serve You in Your Kingdom? How do I live with You as my King in a nation that proclaims autonomy? Help me to walk in a way that glorifies You and that does Your will by grace through faith. In Jesus' name.

Exodus 30:22-25

THE LORD SAID TO MOSES, "TAKE THE FINEST SPICES: OF LIQUID MYRRH 500 SHEKELS, AND OF SWEET-SMELLING CINNAMON HALF AS MUCH, THAT IS, 250, AND 250 OF AROMATIC CANE, AND 500 OF CASSIA, ACCORDING TO THE SHEKEL OF THE SANCTUARY, AND A HIN OF OLIVE OIL. AND YOU SHALL MAKE OF THESE A SACRED ANOINTING OIL BLENDED AS BY THE PERFUMER; IT SHALL BE A HOLY ANOINTING OIL.

1. God is perfect in all His ways, and even in the worship of Himself, He made known to Moses exactly what to do to bring Him glory. The Lord shared with Moses the exact spices, amounts of spices, and how to blend each for the perfumer. What a grace! For did God have to do this? Was He bound to do this? Did having a human worship Him add anything to God whatsoever? No!

2. This is opposite of every other worldview, for all other religions have to wonder if they are working enough, doing enough, striving enough to warrant recognition or earn their salvation by their presumed god.

3. The Church then must never go to the Lord with their own worship but must look to Scripture to see how the Lord commands His worship. We must cease all attempts to add to or take away from Scripture and instead seek and read His Word both day and night, all to know God more.

4. For God sent His Son, and no one can come to the Father except through Him.[242] There is only one name under heaven, given among men, by which we must be saved.[243] So let us come to Christ, by grace through faith, and let us approach the throne of grace with confidence, in the finished work of Christ, to worship and magnify the Lord God Almighty.

[242] John 14:6, [243] Acts 4:12

Father, You are so merciful, for You did not have to share anything with us; we add nothing to You at all. But because of Your love for us, You sent Your only Son to pay the ultimate price in our place, that we may know You and live with You forever. Who are we? Please make known to me those things in which I justify my worship and adoration of You apart from Christ. Lead me to repentance of those untrue thoughts that are not reflective of Your Son, that I may know You and make You known. In Jesus' name.

Psalm 90:8

YOU HAVE SET OUR INIQUITIES BEFORE YOU,
OUR SECRET SINS IN THE LIGHT OF YOUR PRESENCE.

1. The Lord knows all things and everything. There is nothing He does not know. We will not and cannot hide our sin from Him, for He is the One who set our iniquities before Himself. This is done apart from anything we attempt to conceal in our hearts.

2. Our sins will be made known in light of who God is. The greatest travesty in the church is we do not know who God is because we compare our morals to other people rather than looking to God. Our darkness is concealed in the darkness of our comparison.

3. When we all stand before Christ, all our sins will be exposed. All our nothingness will be seen, and all that we are will be on display.

4. At that time, two things will be seen. First, we will see all our sins, both our iniquities and our secret sins, and we will also see this in light of the glory of Christ.[244] Our depravity will be on display, and Christ's glory will be on display as well.

5. Those who are in Christ will be under that radiance of Christ. For Christ has taken our sins and made Himself a propitiation for them,[245] that we might dwell with Him for all eternity in His Kingdom.

[244]Hebrews 1:3, [245]Romans 3:25

Father, thank You for Jesus. Help me to see Jesus and to know Him. Grant me to rest in His assurance, in His glory You gave Him before the creation of the world. Remove from me all gnostic, mystic, and human constructs, and help me to know Christ and be strengthened by Him. Help me rest assured in Christ and strive in Christ and Christ alone. In Jesus' name I ask this.

Genesis 16:13

So she called the name of the Lord who spoke to her, "You are a God of seeing," for she said, "Truly here I have seen him who looks after me."

1. This is the only place in all of Scripture where someone uses the name *El Roi* (לְאֵ֣ל יֳאִ֔י), the "God of seeing."

2. Hagar, an Egyptian maidservant and single, pregnant mother, fled into the wilderness. God saw her; God knew her, and God was with her.

3. As Christians, we are to walk by faith and not by sight.[246] This is not a blind walk or a step into the abyss; this is a step toward the objective truth of who God is.

4. The Lord searches us and knows us. He knows when we sit down and when we rise, and He knows every one of our thoughts from afar.[247] There is nowhere we can go from His presence, and even before a word is in our mouths, He knows it completely.[248] There is nowhere we can flee from His Spirit.[249] He is near.

5. Yet, no way exists for us to conjure this up. Go to Christ. Ask Christ to make Himself known. Repent and turn and seek the Lord with all your heart, and with all your mind, and with all your soul, and He will answer.

[246]2 Corinthians 5:7, [247]Psalm 139:1, [248]Psalm 139:2–4, [249]Psalm 139:7

Jesus, I praise You that You see me and know me. I confess the many times I do not seek You and do not walk in a way that reflects Your Word. I am tempted to doubt and not believe. Forgive me. Please give me a boldness and be gracious to me, and help me to know You are near. Help me to walk in accordance with Your will. In Jesus' name I pray this.

Amen

Mark 9:32

BUT THEY DID NOT UNDERSTAND THE SAYING, AND WERE AFRAID TO ASK HIM.

1. How sad. The disciples "were afraid to ask" Jesus about what they didn't understand. What would make a disciple of Christ afraid to ask Christ any question? For Christ is both the power and the wisdom of God![250]

2. God knows our hearts and knows our words before they even leave our mouths,[251] and He calls for all of us who labor and are heavy laden to come to Christ, who will give us rest![252]

3. We fear going to Christ when we don't trust Him. We don't trust His goodness and His gentle kindness. We are afraid He will not give us the desires of our hearts when He is the desire of our hearts. As we seek first the Kingdom of God and His righteousness, we can rest assured that all these other things will be added to us,[253] and we also forget the words of the psalmist, who prays, He will grant you the desires of your heart, and fulfill all your plans.[254]

4. So, in the midst of being afraid to ask Christ and not trusting Him with the desires of our hearts, to answer us in a way that is good, true, and beautiful, God's Word chastises us and reminds us that we have not, because we ask not.[255] Instead of asking Christ and trusting His sovereign grace to give us what we need and truly desire, we become timid, afraid, and we deny the love of Christ in our hearts and exchange it for self-pity and self-gratification rather than the glory of Christ.

---

[250]1 Corinthians 1:24, [251]Psalm 139:4, [252]Matthew 11:28, [253]Matthew 6:33, [254]Psalm 20:4, [255]James 4:2

Jesus, stir in my heart a courage and a tenderness to come to You with all things. Help me to know Your love for me and Your willingness and desire for me to come to You as a child. So many times I stifle my prayer to You, deeming it so little worth Your time. Yet, You command me to come to You as a child. Please help me to know You and adore You, to trust You, to serve You, and to do all for Your glory. In Your name I ask this.

2 Peter 3:9

The Lord is not slow to fulfill his promise as some count slowness, but is patient toward you, not wishing that any should perish, but that all should reach repentance.

1. The Lord is personal. He is sovereign, strong, and mighty! He does not forget what He is doing, and His plans are not run by luck, chance, or circumstance. Everything is the Lord's and the fullness of it![256]

2. Since the Lord has not come yet, we know He is still calling those He has chosen and elected for His good pleasure.[257] The moment all are in Christ who are His, Christ will return. We can rest in that. We can also fight in that and be confident in it. One day the Lord will return, but it will not be until every person He chooses is brought into His fold.

[256] Psalm 24:1, [257] John 6:39

Jesus, You are the Good Shepherd. You gather all the Father has given You, and You know them by name. They are not a mass of humanity You know only generally, but a people of Your own choosing. You have made me a part of a royal priesthood, a holy nation, a special race that You have elected and called. Who am I? Send me to do Your will, for the glory of the Father by the power of the Holy Spirit!

1 *Chronicles* 29:18

O LORD, THE GOD OF ABRAHAM, ISAAC, AND ISRAEL, OUR FATHERS, KEEP FOREVER SUCH PURPOSES AND THOUGHTS IN THE HEARTS OF YOUR PEOPLE, AND DIRECT THEIR HEARTS TOWARD YOU.

1. Our hearts are directed like a watercourse and are under the mercy and grace of God.[258]

2. God is the One, the only One, who is sovereign above all things. He knows, leads, guides, and directs according to His sovereign pleasure. All things from Him are a mercy and a grace. The ability to know God is only by His grace; there is no intellectual ability to work myself up, for apart from the grace of God and His loving-kindness, I am a dead man. I can no more see God and know the finished work of Christ apart from His sovereign grace than Adam could know God as a lump of clay before God breathed life into him.[259]

3. This is a work of God so that no one may boast.[260]

---

[258] Proverbs 16:8, [259] Genesis 2:7, [260] Ephesians 2:9

Lord, do not let my heart go.
My heart has wrestled with You in
the same way Jacob wrestled with You.
By Your grace, lead my heart to rest
in You, to serve You, to know You.
In Jesus' name.

Amen

1 Samuel 12:24

Only fear the Lord and serve him faithfully with all your heart. For consider what great things he has done for you.

1. The only One we are to fear is God and God alone. There is none other. For it is the Lord who works all things for our good,[261] and it is the Lord who ordains all things.[262] His thoughts and His ways are not our thoughts and our ways,[263] and in Him alone do we live and move and have our being.[264]

2. Yet our prideful hearts are constantly at war with the fear of the Lord. We forget the Word of the Lord, we cease to be thankful in all circumstances, we doubt that the Lord listens to our prayers, and we deny His providence in the moment-by-moment He has ordained.

3. We must repent and ask the Lord to soften our hearts. As long as it is today, let us not harden our hearts, but let us worship the Lord.[265] Let us look in every dispensation of our day and ask the Lord to make us mindful of Himself, to trust in Him, and not to look to our prideful and arrogant thoughts.

4. Let us *only* fear God. Let us *only* worship Him. Let us *only* repent to Him and come before him only with our worship and our gratitude. For to Him belongs all things.

---

[261] Romans 8:28, [262] Romans 11:36, [263] Isaiah 55:8, [264] Acts 17:28, [265] Hebrews 3:7–8

Father, I praise You, for You are God. I praise You, for You have sent Your Son into the world to save my soul. Who am I? Yet You have done it. Father, I confess that I have had a high and prideful view of myself and a low view of You throughout my day. Will You draw near to me, Lord? Will You open my eyes to the truth of Your Word? Will You lead me and guide me according to Your ways? Praise You, Lord.

Mark 3:5

And he looked around at them with anger, grieved at their hardness of heart, and said to the man, "Stretch out your hand." He stretched it out, and his hand was restored.

1. We must not look at Jesus as a felt-board Jesus, but as God in the flesh, the very Son of God, who has been from all eternity, yet began His life in an animal manger.

2. Why does this matter? Because when we see how Jesus reacts, we should also know how God the Father reacts. God is not dismissive of our thoughts and actions but is angered by our pride and unbelief. To deny the Word and truth of God—these are sins.

3. Many Scripture passages express God's anger, sorrow,[266] and even delight.[267] Christ reflects the holiness of God and the anger of God at the sin of man. Jesus is the Son of God.

4. So what should we do? We should stretch our hearts out to God and repent, asking Him to make us new in Christ. We are not to recreate Jesus or fashion Him in the likeness we desire of Him, but we are to humble ourselves, trust His sovereignty and His ways, and to know God, right where He has us, for His glory.

[266] Genesis 6:6, [267] Psalm 149:4

Father, so many times I minimize Christ in my life. Forgive me. Heal me from my sin and make me new in You. Help me to know Your joy. Make the things that break Your heart to break my heart too, and those things that bring You joy, bring me joy as well. In Jesus' name.

Amen

Psalm 104:31

*May the glory of the LORD endure forever;
may the LORD rejoice in his works.*

1. What are the works of God? Read Psalm 104! Every season is a work of God, and every drop of rain is because of His decree. Every creature that walks on the earth looks to God for its food. The sky stretching from horizon to horizon is held together by the glory of God, and the blowing winds of earth are messengers that do God's bidding. Who set the foundation of the earth and suspended it in space in the most perfect detail? God did, and He holds and sustains it in this very moment! Who has handcrafted the detail of the mountains reaching skyward and the valleys sinking below? It was God's hand. All things point to the glory of God!

2. All creatures know this, but only one denies it: the one made in His image—man. Humanity denies God. We want to not think of Him but of ourselves. We want to rely on our own wisdom and deny the sovereignty and providence of God. Even Christians take credit for this small minutia and only credit God with cosmic miracles.

3. How truly sad when we insist that the power of God is seen only in the charismatic, miraculous ways we as humans decide, rather than looking to God's Word and seeing how He orchestrates and holds every detail, act, creature, hour, minute, second, and aspect of time, by His power and by His work.

Father, how great and awesome You are! You are glorious! You uphold all things by Your Word, and You created everything by it as well! Who am I, then? You sent the Word into the world to draw Your people to Yourself, that we might know You, glorify You, be redeemed by You, and spend all eternity with You! Who are we? Lord, we believe; help our unbelief.[268] In Jesus' name.

---

[268] Mark 9:24

Ephesians 2:16

AND MIGHT RECONCILE US BOTH TO GOD IN ONE BODY THROUGH THE CROSS, THEREBY KILLING THE HOSTILITY.

1. All of God's people are found, rooted, and established in One Person. That is the Person of Christ Jesus. There is no distinction and no superior person. Those who are in Christ Jesus are grounded in Christ and nothing else. For God has said in His Word, "There is neither Jew nor Greek, there is neither slave nor free, there is no male and female, for you are all one in Christ Jesus."[269]

2. As Paul looked to the church, he saw Christ and Christ alone in all things. In Christ, God destroyed the hostilities between the ethnicities of the Jew and the Gentile and bringing into view His church—His Bride—He made the cornerstone of that church Christ Jesus Himself.[270]

3. We must be mindful to remember that Christ does not have multiple Brides; He has one Bride. Christ does not have multiple Kingdoms; He has one. Christ does not have multiple Laws; He has one. The aim of the believer is not to raise himself up above his brother but to serve his brother, as Christ came not to be served but to serve and to give His life as a ransom for many.[271] We are to grow together into Christ's church and to forgive each other as God in Christ Jesus has forgiven us.[272]

4. The bonds of forgiveness are what make the church so formidable. It brings us under one Kingdom with only one King. It allows us to wake up in the morning looking to Christ, walk throughout the day with Christ as our aim, and lying down with dependence on Christ's sustaining grace to lead us to the next day for His glory. We are to forget at the cross what lies behind us and strain with everything in our being for what lies before us. Those who are mature in their thinking must press on toward the goal for the prize of the upward call of God in Christ Jesus.[273]

---

[269]Galatians 3:28, [270]Ephesians 2:20, [271]Mathew 20:28, [272]Ephesians 4:32, [273]Philippians 3:13–15

Father, You have sent Your Son, You have redeemed a people for Your own, and You are bringing us to full completion within Your perfect timing. Who are we, Lord, that You would redeem us? Yet, Lord, there are so many times when we are tempted to take our eyes off Christ and to place them on philosophy, emotions, and the things of this world. Forgive me. Please help me to have a greater view of Your Son. Help me to walk humbly with boldness in the assurance of who He is and what He has done for His people. In Christ's name.

Psalm 19:1-3

*THE HEAVENS DECLARE THE GLORY OF GOD,
AND THE SKY ABOVE PROCLAIMS HIS HANDIWORK.
DAY TO DAY POURS OUT SPEECH, AND NIGHT TO NIGHT
REVEALS KNOWLEDGE. THERE IS NO SPEECH,
NOR ARE THERE WORDS, WHOSE VOICE IS NOT HEARD.*

1. Objective beauty declares the intentionality and purpose behind that which is created. Beauty, truth, and goodness are all objectives the human heart sees, recognizes, and bears witness to, as they bear witness to someone beyond them.

2. The most glorious beauty of every day is that of the heavens in the morning and the sunset at night. These sights are objectively deemed beautiful by every human. Why? Because we were created in the image of God, and therefore recognize His creation as beauty.[274] God has written on our hearts what shows His objective glory, "For what can be known about God is plain to them, because God has shown it to them. For his invisible attributes, namely, his eternal power and divine nature, have been clearly perceived, ever since the creation of the world, in the things that have been made. So they are without excuse."[275]

3. How does this encourage the believer? We can know that regardless of our circumstances, God, who has purposefully created all things for His glory, whose creation declares His glory, rules over all. For beauty reminds us of purpose, and God's purposes are perfect.

[274]Genesis 1:26-27, [275]Romans 1:19-20

Father, thank You for allowing me to recognize Your beauty; to see Your handiwork and how it declares Your majesty is truly humbling. Forgive me for the many times I take my eyes off You and turn them to myself. Please lift my eyes to You, that I may see the testimony of Your creation and join with all creation in singing Your praises! In Jesus' name.

Genesis 1:1

In the beginning, God created the heavens and the earth.

1. "In the beginning, God…" Before time began, before the beginning, before all things. Before heaven was created, and before the angels and time were created, before all things, *God*. In perfect unity, the triune God, total and complete and without want, need, or any lack, created the heavens and the earth.

2. The Lord created "creating." He created the ability to work. He sanctified work and let it be the first thing He revealed to us about Himself. He created! He created time and space and did this all for His glory.

3. How easy it is for us to look at the world and our circumstances, at our lives, and to diminish the beauty of who God is and what He has done and still is doing. Everything we experience was intentionally planned by a loving God who works all things together for good for those who love Him and are called according to His purpose.[276]

4. All creation obeys the voice of God. For all things, created and uncreated, burst into existence by God's command. From the color of the sky to a butterfly's fragile wing; from the balance of oxygen in the air to the fragrance of a flower, all things obey the voice of God and were created by the command of God Most High.

---

[276] Romans 8:28

Father, You are the great I Am. How glorious that You have allowed us to know You. How glorious that You have made known to us that You are the Creator of all. Everything we know, everything we experience, everything that happens, was first thought of by You. Thank You for grace; thank You for Christ Jesus; thank You for who You are.

Malachi 4:6

And he will turn the hearts of fathers to their children and the hearts of children to their fathers, lest I come and strike the land with a decree of utter destruction.

1. Relationships are not a human construct, nor are they something that evolved over time. Man, however, wants to declare we came together for the sake of survival. This is utterly false and is an affront to the Lord. Relationships are reflective of God because God is One God made up of three Persons, and He alone created the construct of relationships.

2. In light of this, our relationships on earth and how we view them are a direct reflection of how we view God. We are to look at our parents and our children each as gifts from God, ordained by God, sovereignly decreed by God, for His glory and our good. If we deny the covenant and the holiness of those relationships, our view of relationships will become man-centered rather than centered on God.

3. This is seen most intimately in the family and the roles and purpose of each family member: Husbands loving their wives, wives submitting to their husbands' love, and children honoring their parents are all a part of God's covenantal relationship with His people. If our view of God crumbles, the covenant of family will crumble.

Father, You are the One who has ordained relationships, for You are a triune God: Father, Son, and Holy Spirit, who have existed together perfectly for all eternity. You did not have to create us, but You did for Your glory, and You created us in Your image! Lord, open our eyes and our hearts to behold You and to know You in light of our family. Bless our family in accordance with Your grace. We praise You.

Amen

Revelation 19:11–16

THEN I SAW HEAVEN OPENED, AND BEHOLD, A WHITE HORSE! THE ONE SITTING ON IT IS CALLED FAITHFUL AND TRUE, AND IN RIGHTEOUSNESS HE JUDGES AND MAKES WAR. HIS EYES ARE LIKE A FLAME OF FIRE, AND ON HIS HEAD ARE MANY DIADEMS, AND HE HAS A NAME WRITTEN THAT NO ONE KNOWS BUT HIMSELF. HE IS CLOTHED IN A ROBE DIPPED IN BLOOD, AND THE NAME BY WHICH HE IS CALLED IS THE WORD OF GOD. AND THE ARMIES OF HEAVEN, ARRAYED IN FINE LINEN, WHITE AND PURE, WERE FOLLOWING HIM ON WHITE HORSES. FROM HIS MOUTH COMES A SHARP SWORD WITH WHICH TO STRIKE DOWN THE NATIONS, AND HE WILL RULE THEM WITH A ROD OF IRON. HE WILL TREAD THE WINEPRESS OF THE FURY OF THE WRATH OF GOD THE ALMIGHTY. ON HIS ROBE AND ON HIS THIGH HE HAS A NAME WRITTEN, KING OF KINGS AND LORD OF LORDS.

1. What a glorious view of Jesus Christ! We see here that Christ is not a felt-board puppet on Sunday morning. He is not a storybook Bible character representing a good person. Christ is King of kings and Lord of lords. He has conquered death, and He is fully alive now!

2. Meditate on all the descriptions of Christ: He comes riding on a white horse; He is called Faithful and True; He judges and makes war. He has eyes of fire; He is called the Word of God; He leads the hosts of heaven; He strikes down nations and rules with a rod of iron. He treads the winepress of fury of the wrath of God. This is Christ Jesus now.

3. Christ is a Person. He is not an idea. He is a Person, and He is coming. He has conquered death,[277] and He will return.

4. He is our King; He is our Lord. We are to walk in light of who Christ is now, what He has done, and what He will do. Christ will right every wrong; He will wipe away every tear.[278] He will bring justice; but until He is completely finished, we are to do the work of our Lord in all places and at all times for His glory, according to His Word!

---

[277] 1 Corinthians 15:55, [278] Revelation 21:4

Jesus, You are King of kings and Lord of lords! I confess the many times I have such a low view of You. I worry and am fearful when the media tempts me to believe their stories of doom and nihilism, all in an attempt to steal the reality and truth and victory of what You have done, what You are doing, and what You will do. Forgive me, and help me to know You as King and as Lord over my life. Help me to know Your Word, that I may serve You with all my heart and with all my soul and with all my might. In Jesus' name.

Amen

1 Samuel 15:23

For rebellion is as the sin of divination, and presumption is as iniquity and idolatry. Because you have rejected the word of the LORD, he has also rejected you from being king.

1. Sin permeates all that we do, and there is nothing righteous within us. We do no good apart from the grace of God, for even the intentions of why we do things are measured by the very Word of God.[279]

2. In this dialogue, Samuel shared with Saul that even rebellion against the Word of God is the equivalent of the sin of divination, and presuming what we should and should not do is equal to idolatry. The sin we commit in our hearts every day is not the act alone but its contradiction to the Word of God.

3. When we deny the Lord and the goodness of His Word, we sin against a holy God. No circumstances, excuses, or situations can pardon or defend us against the righteous judgment of a holy God. When we stand before the Lord, no other person can take the blame for our lives. We will each be accountable as we stand before the seat of judgment.

4. But God, being rich in mercy because of the great love with which He has loved us, sent His Son to be that Person who takes the wrath of God on Himself.[280] For as God's people, we will be able to stand though we have no merit of our own, for we have all sinned and fallen short of the glory of God.[281] We will see the Person of Christ, who has taken our guilt and shame and paid the penalty of death for our sin.

---

[279]Hebrews 4:13, [280]Ephesians 2:4–5, [281]Romans 3:23

Father, You are holy. I so easily justify my actions and approach You with excuses that I deem worthy of being less holy than I ought to. This is wrong. My sin is ever before me, and there is nothing I can do in my own strength. Forgive my sin and my pride. Please strengthen me in Christ, for I am a wretch and in need of Your grace. Help me to be alive in Christ, for His glory. In Jesus' name.

Acts 17:11

Now these Jews were more noble than those in Thessalonica; they received the word with all eagerness, examining the Scriptures daily to see if these things were so.

1. How glorious that these Jews, who were noble in character, did not accept just any word given to them but examined them in light of the Word of God. The Bereans are to be looked to as models of how the body of Christ should receive any word proclaimed as truth.

2. We are to read the Word of God, "precept upon precept, precept upon precept, line upon line, line upon line, here a little, there a little."[282] This process guards our hearts and minds from the doctrine and careless words of the day that change like the direction of the wind.

3. Our basis of truth is not what we feel or our emotions or desires. We must be skeptical of these, for their basis is our humanity, and every atom and every aspect come from a deceptive heart that's deceitful above all things.[283]

4. Let us be Berean in our walk with the Lord. When we hear a sermon, let us search the Scriptures. When we read a book, let us reflect on the Word of God. When we are told that reality is based upon an opinion, let us weigh it against the truthfulness of God's Word, that we may walk in truth and glorify God in every aspect of life.

---

[282] Isaiah 28:10, [283] Jeremiah 17:9

Father, Your Word is truth! Your Word is the foundation and supremacy of truth in all and in every aspect of life. Lord, how easily I forget and how easily I am persuaded to find truth in things other than Your Word. Open my eyes and my heart to seek and to walk in accordance with Your Word. Inscribe Your Word on my heart, that I may see the richness of Your mercy and goodness in all of life. In Christ's name.

Exodus 36:2

And Moses called Bezalel and Oholiab and every craftsman in whose mind the Lord had put skill, everyone whose heart stirred him up to come to do the work.

1. Every good and perfect gift comes from the Father of lights.[284] Everything we have we have been given, and the Lord uses it all for our good and His glory.

2. In the creation of the Tabernacle of God, the Lord gave Bezalel and Oholiab skill, knowledge, wisdom, and craftsmanship.[285] There is nothing God leaves to chance, circumstance, luck, or even IQ. The Lord is the giver of all things.

3. So we are to go to Him. If anyone lacks wisdom, let him ask God, who gives generously to all without reproach, and it will be given to him![286] This wisdom is not a gnostic wisdom but a wisdom in all areas of life.

4. Then in all vocations, as we seek the Lord and His wisdom, we are to *"Only let each person lead the life that the Lord has assigned to him, and to which God has called him."*[287] Trust in the Lord with all our hearts and lean not on our own understanding. In all of our ways acknowledge Him, and trust that He will make our paths straight.[288]

5. The Lord uses this for His Kingdom—which is not our kingdom, but the Lord's He is establishing. He uses every one of our vocations, places of work, homes, and communities to establish His Kingdom for His glory and our good.

[284]James 1:17, [285]Exodus 35:31, [286]James 1:5, [287]1 Corinthians 7:17, [288]Proverbs 3:5–6

Father, You are wise and omniscient. There is nothing You do not know in its most infinitesimal detail. Many times I haven't sought You first. I begin with my perceived intellect and deny Your Lordship. Forgive me. Lord, help me to see You and to know Your wisdom in my life, in leading my family, in working within the community, that Your Kingdom come and Your will be done, on earth as it is in heaven. In Jesus' name.

Exodus 32:16

The tablets were the work of God,
and the writing was the writing of God,
engraved on the tablets.

1. The Law of God is not a human construct. It was not written by a human committee that decided what the Law of God should be. The Law of God is His character, the very essence of who He is. The Law of God declares the holiness of God and is the standard by which we are all held.[289]

2. The Law was spoken by God.[290] The tablets given to Moses were the work of God, and the engraving was done by the hand of God. None of what the Law contained was created by man but out of the heart of God.

3. This Law is written on the hearts of man,[291] and all of creation bears testimony to the Law and to the Lordship of God.[292]

4. But the church has devalued the Word of God. It has grabbed onto heresies of antinomianism and declared that we are free to be whoever we desire. This is a heresy. Christ did not come into the world to abolish the Law but to fulfill it.[293] The Law shows us our sin that all have sinned and fallen short of the glory of God.[294] It declares our need for Christ. To remove the Law is to remove the need for Christ.

5. We must repent and seek the Lord while He may be found. We must call upon Him while He is near.[295] The Law of the Lord is perfect, reviving the soul.[296] It points us to the One who has saved us and given His life, that we may glorify and praise the Father for all eternity.

---

[289] 1 Peter 1:16; Leviticus 11:44–45, [290] Exodus 20:1, [291] Romans 2:15, [292] Romans 1:20, [293] Matthew 5:17, [294] Romans 3:23, [295] Isaiah 55:6, [296] Psalm 19:7

Father, You are holy. Your Law is perfect in every way. Regrettably, I have spurned Your Law and diminished it in my heart and mind so many times. I have hardened my heart to You and have denied Your love. Forgive me and have mercy on me. Soften my heart to Your Law; send Your Holy Spirit to renew a right spirit within me and help me to walk according to Your precepts. Help me to be mindful of who You are, of who I am, and of who I am in Christ—all for Your glory.

Joshua 18:2

THERE REMAINED AMONG THE PEOPLE OF ISRAEL SEVEN TRIBES WHOSE INHERITANCE HAD NOT YET BEEN APPORTIONED.

1. The people of Israel had come into the land of Canaan. They had fought and conquered some of the cities and people of the land, but there were seven of the twelve tribes who had not taken over the land they had inherited from the Lord their God.

2. We, in our unbelieving hearts, do the exact same thing. For God has said in His Word, *"In him we have obtained an inheritance, having been predestined according to the purpose of him who works all things according to the counsel of his will, so that we who were the first to hope in Christ might be to the praise of his glory."* [297]

3. Yet how many people see Christ but do not cling to Him? Who do not hold fast to Christ nor seek Him? In their unbelief, they look to Christ as a golden ticket to gaining what they want, or they see Him as merely a good person, rather than God incarnate, who gave His Son in order that we might know God and make Him known!

4. In Christ, all the promises of God are an amen for those who are His![298] We have an inheritance in Christ under His Lordship in His Kingdom. Let us not sit around in some sort of moralistic therapeutic deism, but *let us press on toward the goal, for the prize of the upward call of God in Christ Jesus!* [299]

---

[297] Ephesians 1:11–12, [298] 2 Corinthians 1:20, [299] Philippians 3:14

Father, You have sent us Your Son. Apart from Him I have nothing, and in Him I have everything. For in Christ I am a new creation, and in Him and Him alone I am known by You. Oh, how easily I am deceived to think that You know me and love me because of my own goodness. How foolish, for You love me because I am Your creation. In Christ, I have been purchased by His blood to know You and to make You known. What a glorious inheritance. In Christ's name.

Judges 17:6

IN THOSE DAYS THERE WAS NO KING IN ISRAEL.
EVERYONE DID WHAT WAS RIGHT IN HIS OWN EYES.

1. There is a truth by which we are all held accountable: the very Word and commands of God. They are not to be taken lightly. Every thought, word, action, and deed will be measured by God according to His objective Word.

2. Man in his heart fights against this.[300] For to be held accountable means I am responsible, and to be responsible means I need to be disciplined and mindful of who God is and who I am. It is to test everything with an objective truth in my heart and mind.[301] The more I know God, the more I know myself; the more I know myself, the more I need and depend on God.

3. To need and depend on someone else means I must look to and pursue that Person rather than myself. I must deny my nature and measure every desire I have against the nature of the other Person, seeking Him with all my heart.

4. That Person is Christ and Christ alone. Just as Paul said, *"But whatever gain I had, I counted as loss for the sake of Christ. Indeed, I count everything as loss because of the surpassing worth of knowing Christ Jesus my Lord."*[302]

---

[300]Romans 3:10, [301]1 Thessalonians 5:21, [302]Philippians 3:7–8

Father, thank You for Christ. I have worked so hard to keep myself, my identity, and my desires that I have denied Your Lordship. I have trusted myself more than I have trusted in You. Forgive me. I do not know how to die to myself and live to and for You. In fact, apart from Your grace I cannot. So here I am; use me in Your Kingdom according to Your will and Your purpose, all for Christ's sake.

Exodus 1:8

Now there arose a new king over Egypt, who did not know Joseph.

1. History is extremely important, for it allows us to look back on the things God has done and to look at the different dispensations of our lives.

2. We must be mindful, though, of history because if we aren't, we will forget where the Lord has brought us, and we will lose hope as to where He is leading us. Joseph had saved the people of Egypt, and the Lord had even used Him to grow the wealth of the land of Egypt, but because the new Pharaoh did not know his history, he did not see the providence of God in those events.

3. It has been said numerous times that Christianity is only one generation from passing away from the world. This could be true if Christianity were left in the hands of humanity. The Lord sent a Helper to draw His people to Himself and to bear witness about Christ.[303]

4. History truly is His story. If we are so tunnel-visioned to look only at our own lives, we will miss Christ. We will forget our entire dependency is on Christ alone, and we will have a higher view of ourselves rather than a high view of God.

---

[303] John 15:26

Father, You are the One who organizes and orchestrates all things and for Your own good. It is You who has predestined us according to the purpose of Him who works all things according to the counsel of Your will.[304] *So many times, Lord, when I look upon life, when I look upon the past, my heart and mind stop at the human actions rather than acknowledging Your sovereign hand. Help me be mindful of Your sovereignty throughout all of time. Help my heart to be bold as it clings to Your grace. Help me be mindful of where I have been and how Your Holy Spirit has brought me to this place. In Jesus' name.*

[304]Ephesians 1:11

Galatians 3:7

Know then that it is those of faith who are the sons of Abraham.

1. This passage from the Word of God is a command from God that we are to accept by faith. We must not look at it as a mere suggestion or a good idea, but a command directly from the mouth of God that all the elect are sons of Abraham by faith and faith alone.

2. We must remain mindful of what Christ has done for us. Up to this point, God had set apart for Himself a chosen people, the Jewish nation, to be His. We can watch, see, and observe all His providences, but most importantly, we can know the Savior of the world would come through these people. But Christ's coming was not to save an ethnicity; Christ came to save a chosen people.

3. So who are the sons of Abraham, if not the people of Israel? "Those of faith" in Christ Jesus are the sons of Abraham.[305] Christ Jesus turned it away from bloodlines, from an ethnic people group, and rooted His people by grace through faith as children of Israel.

4. We who believe in and trust the redemptive work of Christ have been grafted in, by faith, and now share in the nourishing truth of Christ Jesus, and are sons and daughters of God the Father![306] All those who are redeemed are now God's chosen people. *"There is neither Jew nor Greek, there is neither slave nor free, there is no male and female, for you are all one in Christ Jesus. And if you are Christ's, then you are Abraham's offspring, heirs according to promise."*[307]

---

[305]Galatians 3:7, [306]Romans 11:17, [307]Galatians 3:28–29

Father, the truth of this and the redemptive work of Christ is beyond my comprehension. Apart from the work of the Holy Spirit, I do not have any ability or capacity to know, understand, accept, or walk in the light of this truth. Even now, as my heart sees a glimmer of light about it, it almost desires to deny it because of how beautiful it is. Forgive my unbelief. Please send Your Holy Spirit to root this Scripture, this truth deep, deep, deep into my heart, that I may walk according to it. In Jesus' name.

Genesis 41:16

Joseph answered Pharaoh, "It is not in me; God will give Pharaoh a favorable answer."

1. Pharaoh had troubling dreams throughout the night, and when he awoke, he sought all the "wise men" of the land to interpret this dream. No one on Pharaoh's court could interpret the dream, but the cupbearer remembered Joseph, whom he'd met when he was in prison.[308]

2. Joseph acknowledged and declared that it is not himself who would accomplish the wish of Pharaoh, but that God Himself would. Joseph is the vessel of grace God used, but it was God who gave Pharaoh the dream, and it was God alone who knew the dream.

3. This belief is opposite of the world we live in. The world and our flesh are tempted to believe we embody truth, that what we experience is right, that what is in us can accomplish anything, and all of this is a narcissistic lie and the epitome of practical atheism. Christ said, *"For from within, out of the heart of man, come evil thoughts, sexual immorality, theft, murder, adultery, coveting, wickedness, deceit, sensuality, envy, slander, pride, foolishness. All these evil things come from within, and they defile a person."*[309] There is no one righteous, no not one.[310]

4. Apart from Christ, we can do no good,[311] and it is only through Him, by the power of the Holy Spirit, that we bear any good fruit. Every good and perfect gift comes from God alone,[312] and we are to walk in accordance with the truth of His Word.

---

[308]Genesis 40, [309]Mark 7:20, [310]Romans 3:10–11, [311]John 15:5, [312]James 1:17

Father, You are truth, and You have sent Your Son who is truth, and You have sent the Holy Spirit to conform our hearts to the truth. How glorious! Father, I am tempted to easily despair and think what I am experiencing is true or desire to say I am true apart from Your Word. Forgive me. Help me to know Your truth and to trust Your Word. Incline my heart to Your testimony that I may glorify You![313] In Jesus' name.

Genesis 43:8–9

And Judah said to Israel his father, "Send the boy with me, and we will arise and go, that we may live and not die, both we and you and also our little ones. I will be a pledge of his safety. From my hand you shall require him. If I do not bring him back to you and set him before you, then let me bear the blame forever.

1. The famine was severe within the land of Canaan, and the sons of Israel needed to go back to Joseph to get more food. They informed their father, though, that they were not allowed to go back unless they brought Benjamin with them, for this is what Joseph required.

2. Judah took responsibility for Benjamin and told their father he would fulfill Israel's desire to keep him safe. In fact, Judah pledged that Israel should look to him and him alone for the safety of Benjamin. If this didn't happen, he would carry the blame for all eternity. In the same chapter, Judah presented himself before Joseph, pleading that he take him rather than Benjamin, who deserved the punishment. Judah said, *"Now therefore, please let your servant remain instead of the boy as a servant to my lord, and let the boy go back with his brothers. For how can I go back to my father if the boy is not with me? I fear to see the evil that would find my father."*[314]

3. Judah is the father of the tribe of Judah, and out of the tribe of Judah came the Messiah, Jesus Christ. Christ looks to the Father and all He has given Him, no one could snatch from His hand.[315] Christ does the will of the Father to bring His children to completion.[316]

4. Not only does Christ do all the Father sent Him to do, but He also goes beyond Judah and takes the blame for all who are His. Therefore, we who are in Christ have no condemnation who are in Christ Jesus![317] For He who knew no sin, became sin for us so that we might become the righteousness of God.[318] He has finished this work so we might be with Him for all eternity.

[314]Genesis 44:33–34, [315]John 10:28–29, [316]John 5:30, [317]Romans 8:1, [318]2 Corinthians 5:21

Father, You have sent Your Son! You have sent Your only Son to come to earth and die, paying the penalty for our sins. Who am I? Father, forgive me for having such a small, shallow view of this redemption from Your Son on my behalf. Help me to walk in the joy of Your salvation, for Your glory and my good. In Christ's name I pray this.

Genesis 45:7-8

And God sent me before you to preserve for you a remnant on earth, and to keep alive for you many survivors. So it was not you who sent me here, but God. He has made me a father to Pharaoh, and lord of all his house and ruler over all the land of Egypt.

1. Joseph did not have a high view of himself when he revealed his identity to his brother. Rather, he had a high view of God's sovereignty and providence.

2. We must never measure our circumstances separate from the sovereignty and providence of God. When we go through trials, we must remember, "the Lord disciplines those He loves,"[319] and "for from Him and through Him and to Him are all things. To Him be the glory forever and ever amen."[320] Also, "In Him we live and move and have our being."[321]

3. The Lord is ever near, in all things and in everything. Joseph was not strong-willed or even an incredibly intellectual man; his view of God was strong, and the fear of the Lord was the means of grace to give him wisdom.[322] The truth of God is what made Joseph strong and wise. Joseph realized he was not a self-made man, but he was a man who walked humbly with his God.[323]

4. Let us not look at our circumstances apart from the providence of God. This does not mean we will understand everything the Lord is doing, for His thoughts and His ways are not our thoughts or our ways.[324] By faith, may your courage and strength be rooted by the Holy Spirit in the finished work of Christ, holding fast to the promises of our God and Father.

---

[319]Hebrews 12:6, [320]Romans 11:36, [321]Acts 17:28, [322]Proverbs 1:7, [323]Micah 6:8, [324]Isaiah 55:8

Father, You are sovereign, and You work all things together for the good of those who love God and are called according to His purpose. Lord, I confess I have many times in my pride been distressed and angry because my eyes have been upon my circumstances, rather than holding fast to You. Forgive me, Lord. Open my eyes that I may behold You. Help me to walk by faith and let the joy of You, my Lord, be my strength. In Jesus' name.

Genesis 49:10

The scepter shall not depart from Judah, nor the ruler's staff from between his feet, until tribute comes to him; and to him shall be the obedience of the peoples.

1. All of Scripture points toward Christ: the hope of Christ, the fulfillment of Christ, the assurance of Christ, the coming of Christ.

2. The blessing Jacob gives to Judah tells of a scepter, which is royalty that will not depart from Judah. This is reflective of the kingship of David, which sets up the Davidic Covenant, which points toward Christ.

3. In our world, we are tempted to question whether Christ sits on His throne. The temptation is subtle because we want to fit into the world rather than seek the holiness of God. Our faith is tested because of what we see rather than be rooted in the Word of God. Our emotions want to overwhelm us and rule our lives rather than submitting to the Lordship of Christ.

4. Christ knew we could not keep this in our hearts and minds apart from His grace. This is why He sent the Holy Spirit. For Christ said, *"But the Helper, the Holy Spirit, whom the Father will send in my name, he will teach you all things and bring to your remembrance all that I have said to you."*[325]

5. So pray and seek the Lord by faith. Ask the Lord to help your heart to rest and meditate on the Lordship of Christ. For the scepter has not departed from Christ. Paul writes of Christ in the book of Colossians, *"He is the image of the invisible God, the firstborn of all creation. For by him all things were created, in heaven and on earth, visible and invisible, whether thrones or dominions or rulers or authorities—all things were created through him and for him. And he is before all things, and in him all things hold together."*[326]

---

[325] John 14:26, [326] Colossians 1:15–20

Father, thank You for sending Your Son and making known to us His dominion over all things. Father, so many things tempt my unbelief to almost lose hope that Christ is King and that the scepter has not departed from Him. Help me to know the complete, all-encompassing dominion of the Lordship of Christ. Help me to know personally and intimately that I may be bold and serve Him for His glory by the power of the Holy Spirit. In Jesus' name.

Ruth 1:15

And she said, "See, your sister-in-law has gone back to her people and to her gods; return after your sister-in-law."

1. In the book of Ruth, we read about Naomi and her two daughters-in-law: Ruth and Orpah. After both of Naomi's sons passed away, she began her journey back to Judah. She encouraged her daughters-in-law to stay in the land of the Moabites rather than return with her to her homeland. Orpah agreed and returned to her own land and her gods, but Ruth stayed with Naomi.

2. Notice how God's Word makes clear Orpah's choice to not only return geographically but theologically as well. Every choice we make and every word we utter reflects our view of God—or our lack of view of God.

3. We must search our own hearts as well, for "the heart is desperately wicked and deceitful above all things, who can understand it?"[327] We cannot trust our emotions, or whatever it is that makes us feel comfortable, for pursuing and following Christ is not comfortable. For Christ said, "I did not come to bring peace, but to bring a sword!"[328]

4. We are to leave everyone and everything to pursue the Lord[329] and seek His face. We are to recognize that all we do or say is either an act of worship before the Lord or an action of unbelief.

---

[327]Jeremiah 17:9, [328]Matthew 10:34, [329]Mark 10:29–30

Father, You are omniscient over all things. There is none like You. I confess the many times I have acted as though You were a good idea, but not God. Forgive me. Help me to be mindful of Your nearness. Help me to be mindful of my heart and my actions. I pray that regardless of the cost, You will give me confidence and boldness in the hope of Christ so that others may see my good works and praise You in heaven. In Christ's name I pray this.

Exodus 20:6

But showing steadfast love to thousands of those who love me and keep my commandments.

1. One of the worst things to plague the church is the heresy of antinomianism—the idea that we are all under grace, and that all things are covered by grace, and that we are totally and completely free of all law.

2. For in the Law of Moses, the greatest way we can show the Lord we love Him is to keep His commandments. We are to know the Word of the Lord. We are to meditate on it day and night![330]

3. There is also a promise given. To those who keep the Law of God out of love for Him, God shows steadfast love. What glory and mercy! Who are we that God would love us, and He has made known His love!

4. This points us to Christ. For it is God the Father who, out of His love for us, sent His only Son into the world to pay the penalty for our sin,[331] that we should be called children of God. And so we are![332]

5. The more we grow in the knowledge of who God is and what He has done through His Son, by grace through faith, the more we will have a heart and passion to follow and love the Lord! We will desire to know His Word; we will hunger and thirst for God. We will desire to walk according to His Word, for His glory, because of our love for Him and for our good.

---

[330] Joshua 1:8, [331] John 3:16, [332] 1 John 3:1

Father, thank You for Your Law! Thank You for revealing to us how to love You. I confess my nature, apart from Your grace, is against Your Law, but I know Your Spirit is working within me. My heart delights in You and Your Word. Lord, grant me to hide Your Word in my heart, that I might not sin against You! In Jesus' name.

Amen

Exodus 28:3

You shall speak to all the skillful, whom I have filled with a spirit of skill, that they make Aaron's garments to consecrate him for my priesthood.

1. This is the first time Scripture declares an individual was filled with the Spirit.

2. In so many instances, we attempt to make a secular-sacred divide between what we do spiritually and what we do in the real world, but this is an atheistic worldview, for apart from Christ, we can do nothing.[333]

3. This is why we are to *"Rejoice always, pray continuously, and give thanks in all circumstances,"*[334] because everything granted us we have received from the Lord Most High.

4. In this we have hope, which is antithetical to the world. For if the Lord gives us His Spirit to work, then He is working through us now as a means of grace to build His Kingdom. We can rest assured that He is working at this very moment and in this very time to bring together His plan, His purposes, His will, His Kingdom—and Christ is sitting on His throne, working all things together for His glory and our good.

---

[333] John 15:5, [334] 1 Thessalonians 5:15–17

Father, You are the giver of all wisdom, of all knowledge, of all skill. You lack nothing. Lord, within my vocation, will You please give me the will, and the skill, for Your Kingdom? Guard my heart from selfish ambition, and keep an idle heart far away. Help me to know the joy of the Lord, for You are my strength. I humbly ask this, for Your glory and my good, in Jesus' name.

Genesis 24:12

And he said, "O Lord, God of my master Abraham, please grant me success today and show steadfast love to my master Abraham."

1. Abraham's servant had traveled many miles by the command of Abraham to find Isaac a wife. He had made an oath to Abraham that he would do everything he could to fulfill his mission.

2. When he arrived, though, he did not first do everything in his power to find a wife; instead, He went to the Lord in prayer. He acknowledged God's sovereignty and beseeched His grace and mercy in His endeavor.

3. All things are from the Lord, for from Him, and through Him, and to Him are all things.[325] In Him, we live and move and have our being.[326] Christ has said that apart from Him we can do nothing.[327]

4. So as we go about our day, as we do the fantastic and the mundane, seek the Lord. Ask Him to work all things together for the love of Christ, His Son, and then move forward by grace through faith. Ask the Lord for particulars; ask for strength, for His glory and your good. Then step forward by faith, with boldness and assurance, that whatever the Lord ordains is right.

---

[325]Romans 11:36, [326]Acts 17:28, [327]John 15:5

Father, I thank You that You have made known to us Your love, through Your Son Jesus. I thank You that You have said we are to pray continuously and to give thanks in all circumstances.[338] Father, I confess the many times I do not pray and do not even expect You to work; forgive me, and change my heart. Help my heart to rest and rejoice in Your sovereign grace. Open my eyes to behold Your work in all and in every aspect of life. In Jesus' name.

Genesis 10:8–10

Cush fathered Nimrod; he was the first on earth to be a mighty man. He was a mighty hunter before the Lord. Therefore it is said, "Like Nimrod a mighty hunter before the Lord." The beginning of his kingdom was Babel, Erech, Accad, and Calneh, in the land of Shinar.

1. Everything we have, everything good and true and beautiful, is from God. For *"Every good gift and every perfect gift is from above, coming down from the Father of lights, with whom there is no variation or shadow due to change."*[339] And "From Him, and through Him, and to Him, are all things!"[340] Our strength, joy, hope, vocations, wealth, and wisdom are from God for His glory.

2. Yet, with each blessing comes the temptation to turn our eyes away from the Lord and onto ourselves. Nimrod was the first "mighty man" on earth. *Nimrod* means, "We shall rebel," and in the very next verse we see that out of the family of Nimrod came the city of Babel, from which came the Tower of Babel.[341] The city of Babel became the world power of Babylon that eventually conquered the land of Judah.

3. In the book of Revelation, Babylon is not only a geographical location and world power, but it reflects a heart that has rebelled against the Lord and drinks the cup of wrath from God.[342]

4. In each of these instances, the lust and allure of power, strength, and might allure the heart and mind to rebel against God. To deny our need for a Savior, we must daily depend upon Christ in all circumstances. Let us hold fast to Christ. Let us plead with the Lord to give us His Spirit to lead and guide and steward His gifts everywhere He has us, for His glory and our good, and may our hearts be filled with thankfulness for all the Lord has done and continues to do for His glory.

[339]James 1:17, [340]Romans 11:36, [341]Genesis 11:1–9, [342]Revelation 17:5

Father, You are the giver of all good things. There is not one thing I have that was not given to me by You. I am tempted day after day to think I can do things apart from You or that I am to work apart from You. But even the ability to breathe is a grace You give moment by moment. Help me to recognize and see Your power and grace at work in the moment-by-moment aspects of my life, that I give You thanks and praise in all and every aspect of life. In Jesus' name I ask this.

Amen

1 Samuel 18:14

And David had success in all his undertakings, for the Lord was with him.

1. All that David did and all that he accomplished was because of the grace and power of God. There is no such thing as a self-made man, for everything we have, we have received from the Lord.[343]

2. The Lord is the One who goes before us. It is the Lord who has prepared work for us in advance for His glory and our good. For we are God's workmanship, created in Christ Jesus for good works, which God prepared beforehand, that we should walk in them.[344]

3. It is the fool who says there is no God.[345] It is the wicked who think in their hearts, "The Lord does not see; the God of Jacob does not perceive."[346] For they deny that God is sovereign and that He is near. They harden their hearts and suppress the truth that they know to be true to justify their evil hearts.[347]

4. But for those who love the Lord and are called according to His purpose, we can boldly say that we are more than conquerors through Christ Jesus to do His will for His glory and our good.[348] We can trust that nothing can separate us from the love of God in Christ Jesus![349] Our God is good, and His steadfast love endures forever.[350] Though we may go through the valley of the shadow of death, we will not fear that God will be overwhelmed. His goodness will not be diminished, His glory will never be abated, and we in Christ and Christ alone can trust Him as He works all things perfectly for His glory and our good.

---

[343]1 Corinthians 4:7, [344]Ephesians 2:10, [345]Psalm 14:1, [346]Psalm 94:7, [347]Romans 1:18, [348]Romans 8:37, [349]Romans 8:39, [350]Psalm 100:5

Father, Your will is perfect and can never be deterred in its direction and its goal. Your aim for all creation is Your glory, for there is none other like You. I confess, Lord, when circumstances in my life become idols and I make them bigger than Your plans and Your will, I am overwhelmed by fear. When I desire more for my comfort rather than Your glory, I become overwhelmed with paralyzing fear and unbelief. Forgive me. Grant me a boldness and a courage rooted in the knowledge of who You are and who I am in Christ. Bless the work of my hands and lead me to do Your will. For I praise You, my God and my King. In Christ's name.

Genesis 3:1

Now the serpent was more crafty than any other beast of the field that the Lord God had made. He said to the woman, "Did God actually say, 'You shall not eat of any tree in the garden'?"

1. Sin has never changed; it has stayed constant since the fall of man, and temptation has remained since Satan was cast down from heaven. The temptation is to question the very will of God. "Did God actually say…"

2. This question is not a sympathetic question or one of intellect, but it drives a wedge of doubt into the sufficiency and authority of Scripture in all and every aspect of life. Notice how this particular Law from God was not one regarding the day of rest; it is a Law God gave regarding the eating of a piece of fruit.

3. God's will pertains to every aspect of all God is Lord over. Dutch theologian Abraham Kuyper wrote, "There is not a square inch in the whole domain of our human existence over which Christ, who is Sovereign over all, does not cry, Mine!"[351] Lordship constitutes the relinquishing of wills at the foot of the cross and declaring, "Speak Lord, for your servant is listening."[352]

4. Every act, every moment, reflects the answer to a question we are faced with in every aspect of life. Who is God, and what does He demand of my life? If God is a golden ticket to heaven, we will deny His Lordship and eat the fruit. But, if He is Lord and Savior, then we will seek His Word, pray to Him, and by faith walk by grace, for His glory.

---

[351] Abraham Kuyper, "Sphere Sovereignty: Inaugural Address at the Free University, Amsterdam," Abraham Kuyper: A Centennial Reader, ed. and trans. James D. Bratt (Grand Rapids, MI: Eerdmans and Carlisle: Paternoster Press, 1988), 488. [352] 1 Samuel 3:9-10

Father, may Your Kingdom come, may Your will be done. In today's culture, we scream and continue to scream, "May our kingdom come, may our will be done." Forgive us. Lord, Your will and Your plan are perfect. Please change my heart to seek and know You, and to desire to do Your will above all, for Your glory and my good. In Jesus' name.

Amen

Job 19:25

FOR I KNOW THAT MY REDEEMER LIVES,
AND AT THE LAST HE WILL STAND UPON THE EARTH.

1. It is the truth of who God is that brings the believer, by faith, through the most difficult circumstances of his or her life. Preceding this passage, Job experienced a family far and estranged from him;[353] close friends had forgotten and left him;[354] his employees and guests treated him as a stranger and gave him no answer;[355] his wife and mother were estranged to him; the community, even the children, despised him and talked about him; and everyone he loved turned away from him.[356] Lastly, his health failed and he became completely void of everything.[357]

2. Though Job experienced these tragedies, he reminded himself of the ultimate truth: that he had a Person, an advocate, and that regardless of what happened in life, the Lord truly rules and will stand on the earth as King.

3. This is to be the aim of all believers in all circumstances. We are not to be darkened in our thinking as those who do not know Christ and how we also once walked.[358] For to do so is to act like children and to be tossed around like the waves of the sea, believing every little circumstance and experience that we hear and see.[359]

4. Our aim and focus are to be Christ and Christ alone. Regardless of what we perceive, experience, feel, or think, our aim is to grow up in every way into Christ.[360] This is the life of the mature believer. The mature believer guards his heart and renews his mind daily in the Word of God, so as not to be taken captive by the ways of the world.[361] It is our relationship and walk with Christ that brings us into mature manhood, for the glory of God and for the good of others.[362]

---

[353]Job 19:13, [354]Job 19:20, [355]Job 19:15–16, [356]Job 19:18–19, [357]Job 19:20, [358]Ephesians 4:17–18, [359]Ephesians 4:14, [360]Ephesians 4:15, [361]Ephesians 4:23, [362]Ephesians 4:13

O H L ORD, HOW EASILY I AM TOSSED TO AND FRO BY THE THOUGHTS AND IDEAS OF THE WORLD. I SO EASILY FORGET THAT MY R EDEEMER LIVES AND THAT Y OU ARE L ORD OVER ALL. M Y HEART, MIND, AND AFFECTIONS ARE SO EASILY MANIPULATED AND DRAWN AWAY FROM Y OUR W ORD THAT I AM TEMPTED TO BELIEVE THE WORLD AND THE PEOPLE CLOSE TO ME WHO DENY Y OUR TRUTH. F ORGIVE ME. R OOT MY HEART IN THE TRUTH AND REALITY OF Y OUR W ORD. G IVE ME COURAGE TO BOLDLY, WITH JOY, LIVE FOR Y OUR GLORY AND THE GOOD OF OTHERS. I N C HRIST'S NAME I ASK THIS.

2 Chronicles 7:13-16

When I shut up the heavens so that there is no rain or command the locust to devour the land, or send pestilence among my people, if my people who are called by my name humble themselves, and pray and seek my face and turn from their wicked ways, then I will hear from heaven and will forgive their sin and heal their land. Now my eyes will be open and my ears attentive to the prayer that is made in this place. For now I have chosen and consecrated this house that my name may be there forever. My eyes and my heart will be there for all time.

1. First, God does not presuppose His people would be sinless.

2. Second, the Lord tells Solomon He will cause times of no rain, or will command the locusts to devour the land, or will even send pestilence among the people of Israel. He is not a deistic God. He is not bound by global warming, and no amount of anything in the air above, or the earth below, or the water beneath the earth can snatch the control of all things from God's hand.[363]

3. Third, luck, chance, and circumstance do not exist; all things are held together and commanded by a personal God.

4. Fourth, God is merciful. Even as He will do anything to punish or discipline His people, He also makes a covenant with His people that if they "humble themselves, and pray and seek His face and turn from their wicked ways, then He will hear them from heaven, He will heal their land, and He will forgive their sins."[364]

5. Notice, no sin is too big that God, in His mercy and grace, will not forgive. Today, Christ's death, burial, and resurrection are sufficient!

6. Lastly, see how God says He is listening to the prayers of His people. No circumstance can cause God to remove His eyes and ears from the believer. For in Christ, the cornerstone, we ourselves are God's temple, where His Holy Spirit dwells and He lives among His people![365]

[363] Exodus 20:4, [364] 2 Chronicles 7:14, [365] Ephesians 2:21; 1 Peter 2:5

Father, You are so merciful and gracious. Who are we that You love us, and who are we that You come among us? For our sin, apart from Christ, is ever before us. But You sent Your only Son to come and pay the penalty for our sins, that we might know freedom and life in You. Your Word states that Your eyes and ears are toward Your temple, toward Your people; who are we that You should listen and be mindful of us? Thank You for Your grace and mercy. Thank You for Christ! Strengthen our hearts to seek You and to do Your will, and bless us according to Your will. In Jesus' name.

Amen

Genesis 22:1

After these things God tested Abraham and said to him, "Abraham!" And he said, "Here I am."

1. Regardless of what the world screams, we are not autonomous. We do not have a deistic God who stands outside space and time. God orchestrates all things for His glory, and all things are under His dominion.[366]

2. In this truth, then, we see the Lord test the heart of man.[367] One reason the Lord does this is to see if there are any who understand, who seek after God.[368]

3. Therefore, every trial, every moment, every detail is ordained by God and is used to draw us into a closer relationship with and dependency upon Christ and His finished work. He opens our eyes to the idols in our hearts, the pride that so easily blinds us, and leads us to repentance and trust in the Lord and His Word.

4. Our response should be the same as Abraham when he responded, "Here I am," in all and in every circumstance. We are to cry out to the Lord, "Here I am! I trust your Word; I trust your promises; and I resolve to say with Christ, 'Not my will but yours be done.'"[369]

5. In this, we can cling to His Word that promises, "After you have suffered a little while, the God of all grace, who has called you to his eternal glory in Christ, will himself restore, confirm, strengthen, and establish you. To him be the dominion forever and ever. Amen."[370]

---

[366]Colossians 1:15–20, [367]Proverbs 17:3; Jeremiah 17:10; Psalm 11:5, [368]Psalm 14:2, [369]Luke 22:42, [370]1 Peter 5:11

Father, in all of life, and in every moment, help me to know You are near. Bring Your promises to my heart and mind that I may walk in accordance with Your way, for Your glory.

Psalm 33:10-11

THE LORD BRINGS THE COUNSEL OF THE NATIONS TO NOTHING; HE FRUSTRATES THE PLANS OF THE PEOPLES. THE COUNSEL OF THE LORD STANDS FOREVER, THE PLANS OF HIS HEART TO ALL GENERATIONS.

1. There is no amount of planning, from the smallest person to the greatest kingdom, that can thwart the sovereignty of God. No well-constructed plan can contradict the commands and directions of the Lord Most High!

2. The Lord Himself brings plans and counsel to nothing. It is God who frustrates the plans of the people. We are to seek the Lord and ask that His Kingdom come and His will be done.

3. Look to Christ! For He only did what the Father commanded Him to do![371] The entire aim of Christ is to do the will of the Father.[372] Christ did not have to build a platform or to create a following. Only those who God drew to Himself followed Him.[373]

4. What comfort to the believer, that regardless of what the world declares, there is no such thing as a self-made man. Everything we know and experience—the wars and rumors of wars—are all ordained and planned by God. What a witness, what a comfort to the world, that we are not to live in fear, but to walk humbly with our God.[374]

[371] John 5:19, [372] John 5:30, [373] John 6:37, [374] Micah 6:8

Father, Your will is perfect. So many times I have become frustrated because of my circumstances. How do I walk in the truth of Your perfect will? How do I set goals, then place them at Your feet? How do I strive in hope, and yet only seek Your will? I ask this out of love, not anger or frustration, but a desire to know You and to make You known! In Jesus' name.

Amen

Isaiah 14:24

The Lord of hosts has sworn: "As I have planned, so shall it be, and as I have purposed, so shall it stand."

1. The Lord never speaks an idle word. Every word He speaks is a promise and a command, a judgment and a truth. His words are always relevant and always work to bring all glory to Him. In light of this, we must always behold the Lord within His Word and proclaim only that which is true according to His Word—for His Word is the truth of all things.[375] All things are under the Lordship of Christ, for all authority in heaven and on earth has been given to Him and Him alone.[376]

2. The world, when denying the Lordship of Christ, regards the dispensations of the world in terms such as *luck, chance,* or *circumstance.* They drop their eyes from God and suppress the truth in unrighteousness[377] so as to deceive themselves to avoid accountability before a holy God.

3. But all the Lord has proclaimed will come to pass. He prepared work for us to do for His Kingdom before even creating the world.[378] He has purposefully thought out every detail of our lives for His glory. None of God's words will ever return void, but shall return to Him and shall accomplish all He has commanded successfully in every situation.[379]

4. In this truth, we are not to worry about tomorrow, for tomorrow has enough troubles of its own.[380] We are instead in this moment to press on to know God. To know who He is and to remain confident in His providence over every infinitesimal detail of our lives.[381] By looking to God and trusting His Word, we are not like the wicked who flee at every discomfort or fear that tempts us, but instead, we are as bold as lions, going forth in spirit and in truth.[382]

---

[375]John 17:17, [376]Matthew 28:18, [377]Romans 1:18, [378]Ephesians 2:10, [379]Isaiah 55:11, [380]Matthew 6:34, [381]Hosea 6:3, [382]Proverbs 28:1

Oh Lord, how glorious is Your Word! Every Word that comes from Your mouth is true, and all of it brings to fruition Your plans and purpose for all our lives. I confess how my flesh attempts to wrestle against this, or how I shake my fist at You in this, but help me to rest in the truth. Forgive me for my pride and strengthen me in the truth of You, and reign over all of my life. In Christ's name.

Revelation 20:2-3

And he seized the dragon, that ancient serpent, who is the devil and Satan, and bound him for a thousand years, and threw him into the pit, and shut it and sealed it over him, so that he might not deceive the nations any longer, until the thousand years were ended. After that he must be released for a little while.

1. God has always had a plan of redemption from the very beginning of time. There has never been plan B, but a beautiful story of redemption from the beginning of time and for all eternity. Since Adam and Eve's sin in the garden of Eden, He promised there would come from Eve a Person who would crush the head of the great serpent.[383]

2. Since Creation, God has had a people for Himself. He chose the Jewish nation as His chosen people to lead and to be an example of a people under God. This made it so Satan had the freedom to make the rest of the world *his* people.

3. When Christ conquered Satan, the power of Satan over the world was diminished, and Satan's power to influence the nations was suppressed. God's sovereign plan is coming to fruition in His perfect timing, and there is nothing that can inhibit it.

4. Christ is now bringing His people, from every tribe, people group, language, and nation, to Himself. Satan cannot stop Him or suppress His all-pervading truth.[384] The gates of hell cannot hold back the truth of the gospel that is proclaimed![385] This does not mean it will be easy, but we are not to measure our advancement by what we see—only by what Scripture proclaims.

5. What glorious hope, what power of God, and the time is now. Satan has been defeated; Christ commands us with all authority in heaven and on earth to "Go therefore and make disciples of all nations, baptizing them in the name of the Father and of the Son and of the Holy Spirit, teaching them to observe all that I have commanded you. And behold, I am with you always, to the end of the age."[386]

---

[383]Genesis 3:15, [384]Revelation 14:6, [385]Matthew 16:18, [386]Matthew 28:19-20

Father, your way is perfect! You have brought a people to Yourself and have defeated Satan. He has no claim on any of your plans. In Christ there is victory, and in that victory we praise you. I confess the many times my mind is pulled to and fro with doubts and temptations of this victory. I am prone to act as though it's a cosmic war between good and evil, rather than abide in the truth of Christ's victory. Forgive me, and help me to walk in the beauty, goodness, and truth of Christ reigning over all things and bringing all things under His lordship for His glory and my good. In Christ's name.

Malachi 1:2

"I have loved you," says the Lord.
But you say, "How have you loved us?"

1. How many times do we experience the love of God and then shake our hands at Him, declaring that He does not love us?

2. We complain about our life, we complain about our circumstances, we complain about His sovereignty, and we complain about all of His means of grace. Our human nature compares with others what the Lord gives us and envies what our neighbors have. We demand better, we demand more, we demand different life experiences, and we forget that all we have are gifts from God. What do we have that we did not receive?[387]

3. In our demands, we show our hearts have no desire for Him and His Kingdom. We want Him to bless our kingdoms and to give us what we think we deserve. But our heavenly Father has given us everything in sending His Son. Did He have to send Christ? Did He have to pay the penalty for our sins, so those who believe may spend all eternity with Him?

4. The question we should ask is not, "How have You loved us?" But instead, in light of all the evil we do, "Why do You love us?" We who deserve death, who deserve to not even exist—and actually deserve damnation, have been given the greatest gift the world has ever known. God's Son.

[387] I Corinthians 4:7

Father, You have loved me; this I know. Who am I, Lord, that You would send Your only Son into the world to die for a wretch like me? Father, I walk in my pride day in and day out. It clings to my heart and my soul, and it clings to my very being like a disease—yet You love me. Have mercy on me. Open my heart and my mind to more fully know and to more fully understand Your love, that I may glorify You all the more! In Jesus' name.

2 *Chronicles* 29:16

The priests went into the inner part of the house of the Lord to cleanse it, and they brought out all the uncleanness that they found in the temple of the Lord into the court of the house of the Lord. And the Levites took it and carried it out to the brook Kidron.

1. The priests went into the temple to pull out all the uncleanness, everything not holy before the Lord.

2. To do so requires a mindfulness of who God is and who we are. His commandments, His precepts, His holiness, and His Word pour light into the believers' hearts, so we can see and repent of those things not of Him and what we must turn from.

3. Our bodies are a temple of the Holy Spirit.[388] We are to look at our hearts, our minds, and our lives and measure them against the Word of God. We are to not uphold a human standard, or a human measuring line, or a man-made list of moralism, but we are to look to Christ and gaze upon Him in His Word, asking the Lord to reveal to us the sin in our lives.

4. As the Lord reveals to us the sin so grievous to Him, we are to go to the cross and repent. In the same way the priests took the uncleanness of the temple to the brook Kidron, we are to take our sin to the river of blood that flowed from Christ and to wash ourselves in His righteousness.

---

[388] 1 Corinthians 3:16; 1 Corinthians 6:19

Father, what a high view of man I have. I confess that one of the scariest prayers I am to pray all the time is for You to reveal to me my sin. I confess the many times I am terrified to pray this because I am scared of what You will show me. The reason I am scared is many times I do not have a right view of You. I am tempted to think You will be harsh rather than forgiving, that You will be critical rather than merciful. But none of this is true! Forgive me, and help me to have a right view of You. Reveal the uncleanness in my heart that I may glorify You. In Jesus' name.

2 *Chronicles* 29:10

Now it is in my heart to make a covenant with the Lord, the God of Israel, in order that His fierce anger may turn away from us.

1. It was in Hezekiah's heart to make a covenant with the Lord, to make a promise to God to follow the Lord and to do His will. In light of who God is, we are to do the very same things with our lives in light of the covenant He has made with us.

2. This covenant is not a flippant process or idea but an oath to the Lord, to seek the Lord, and to call upon Him in all aspects of life.

3. This is opposite of the two church heresies of man-made moralism or legalism. This covenant is between two persons: the Person of God and the person of man.

4. Christ Jesus came as a covenant between God the Father and His people. He came to pay the penalty for our sins, to take on the wrath we deserve, and to give us His righteousness. This covenant cannot be broken for God's elect. God has promised it, and it will be fulfilled.

Father, Your Word is true and Your covenant is eternal. There are so many times I have been flippant toward You. I have not been mindful of Christ and the price He paid. I have been prideful in my actions, thinking You did not know them. I have broken covenant with You, though You have never done the same to me. Who am I? Forgive me, and help me to be mindful of the truth of Your covenant and what Christ has done for me. Help me to be mindful of what the Holy Spirit is doing even now, for Your glory. In Jesus' name I ask this.

John 12:24–26

Truly, truly, I say to you, unless a grain of wheat falls into the earth and dies, it remains alone; but if it dies, it bears much fruit. Whoever loves his life loses it, and whoever hates his life in this world will keep it for eternal life. If anyone serves me, he must follow me; and where I am, there will my servant be also. If anyone serves me, the Father will honor him.

1. The only way for a fruit or a grain to flourish is to die. It must pass through death, and in that death it will bear much fruit.

2. Christ has called each of us to die to ourselves, to take our hopes, dreams, and desires and give them to Christ as we say, "Yet, not my will, but Yours be done."[389]

3. Those places in our hearts that we guard, protect, deny repentance of, and hold fast to do not flourish in whatever way He deems best. In not handing these things over to the Lord, we tell Christ that we know better than He does.

4. This is also a way for Satan to tempt us. If there are things we hold onto, rather than giving over to Christ, these become our idols and fears that we worship. Yet, if Satan comes to attack us and we tell him, "All that I have is Christ, even my very life," then what can Satan do? You are a terrifying opponent if you are not afraid of anything… even death.[390]

[389]Luke 22:42, [390]Philippians 1:21

Father, I long to serve Your Son, yet I have not acted this way very often. Many times I tell You how important things are to me and how much I cling to them rather than to Christ. Forgive me. Father, please help me to follow Christ and guard my steps from selfish ambition and vain conceit. You know the desires of my heart; please help these desires to reflect Your will and help me to think rightly about all You call me to. Help me to do Your will. In Jesus' name.

Deuteronomy 31:6

Be strong and courageous. Do not fear or be in dread of them, for it is the LORD your God who goes with you. He will not leave you or forsake you.

1. How merciful that our God gives us commands and promises. We are a people of the Word, and the Lord speaks to us through His Word.

2. In the things of God we are commanded to be strong and courageous. We are not to fear or dread anything the Lord has for us. These are commands, not suggestions. These are things to pray through as we face our day and what the Lord has set before us.

3. The beautiful part of this command is not the command itself but the foundation of the command. It is foolish for man to be strong and courageous for man's sake, for who is man? But the Lord God Himself has commanded us to be strong and courageous because of who He is.

4. Our God never sends us out to battle without going before us. He does not send us out without first making known to us that He is our shield and our God. We are never apart from the truth that it is His saving strength that is winning the battle for His glory and our good. Let us never separate the commands of God from His promises, and let us hold fast to the truth of our God by grace through faith.

Father, Your commands and promises are holy. They are all-encompassing and perfect in all their ways. Father, I confess that many of these I have read in unbelief. I have read as suggestions rather than as truth. Forgive me and strengthen my heart in Your truth. Let me know You are near. Go before me and defend for Your glory. Let me not be put to shame, but may Your name be blessed from the highest mountain, and in Your grace use me for Your Kingdom this week and forevermore. In Christ's precious name I pray.

Galatians 6:9

AND LET US NOT GROW WEARY OF DOING GOOD,
FOR IN DUE SEASON WE WILL REAP,
IF WE DO NOT GIVE UP.

1. We are not to look to ourselves for strength or compare our lives to others, but we are to look to God. For it is God who ordains everything we do in every moment of our lives.

2. This verse is both a command and a promise. The command is to not grow weary of doing good. This command is in all things and in everything the Lord has set before us. We are not to give excuses on external circumstances, but to seek the Lord, trust the Lord, press on in doing what is good. Let us look to God and trust His sovereign grace, pressing on toward the goal.

3. Graciously, by the Holy Spirit, Paul does not leave us with a command. But he gives us a beautiful promise from God, the promise that what we are doing will yield a crop we will reap in due season. Let us not put our human expectations on God. It is the Lord who ordains the seasons and the times. He orchestrates all things. Let us rest in His perfect providence. Let us not grow weary by comparing ourselves to others, but keep our eyes focused on Christ, walking by grace through faith.

4. In doing this, the joy of the Lord will be our strength. Not the results, though; they are in God's hands. Not the timing; that is in God's hands. Let us move forward, let us press on, let us fight the good fight in joy and with thanksgiving, trusting in the goodness and the sovereignty of our great God.

Father, You are the One who ordains the seasons. Thank You for who You are. Father, You have been so merciful to me, for I have complained and whined and denied Your grace in so many aspects of my life. Thank You for Christ, for apart from Him I could not even know You. Grant me hope and strength to not grow weary. Guard me against a faint heart. Help me to know You, in all my life, and let me be like a tree planted by streams of water that yields fruit in season, for Your glory, and my good. In Jesus' name.

Exodus 4:13-14

BUT HE SAID, "OH, MY LORD, PLEASE SEND SOMEONE ELSE."
THEN THE ANGER OF THE LORD WAS KINDLED AGAINST
MOSES AND HE SAID, "IS THERE NOT AARON, YOUR BROTHER,
THE LEVITE? I KNOW THAT HE CAN SPEAK WELL.
BEHOLD, HE IS COMING OUT TO MEET YOU, AND WHEN HE
SEES YOU, HE WILL BE GLAD IN HIS HEART."

1. Until this point, Moses had given God objections, and the Lord mercifully answered each one. We must remember the Lord knows our frame and remembers that we are but dust.[391]

2. But when Moses asked God to send someone else, the anger of the Lord was kindled against Moses. We must remember the Lord is the One who orchestrates all things. We are to obey and follow the Lord by faith in everything and in all things. For whatever does not proceed from faith is a sin.[392]

3. In all of life we are to do the will of the Lord. The anger of the Lord rose against Moses because he did not walk by faith in the command of God. We are to walk by faith in every thought, word, action, and deed, regardless of our circumstances. God is not bound in any way, by our circumstances, by our infirmities, by our history, or by our lives. Our God is in the heavens, and He does whatever he pleases.[393]

4. Let us know God and make Him known. Let us not only talk about the goodness of God but act in accordance with who God is. Let us step forward in faith, to whatever the Lord has called us, and trust His sovereign grace to carry us through. Let us not pridefully make excuses, but let us walk humbly with our God.[394]

---

[391]Psalm 103:14, [392]Romans 14:23, [393]Psalm 115:3, [394]Micah 6:8

Father, I come to You this morning to praise and worship You, acknowledging Your goodness and power! Father, I confess the many times I have looked at my lot in life and have defined it by those circumstances, rather than seeking first Your Kingdom and Your righteousness.[395] Grant me the strength, conviction, joy, and hope to boldly walk by Your grace. Teach me Your ways and help me to walk in truth. For Your glory and for Christ.

Galatians 4:8–9

Formerly, when you did not know God, you were enslaved to those that by nature are not gods. But now that you have come to know God, or rather to be known by God, how can you turn back again to the weak and worthless elementary principles of the world, whose slaves you want to be once more?

1. Pragmatism, nihilism, Darwinism, existentialism—all these philosophies are from the minds of those who are enslaved by nature and have no control in one's life, despite their beliefs. These are man-made constructs to allow humans to deny the sovereignty of God and the Lordship of Christ over all things.

2. But be careful because the more we look to Scripture, the more we will become opposite of the world. We will be judged, ridiculed, and persecuted because we do not measure what happens in our lives in the same way the world does. But in this persecution, we will affirm the words of Christ who said, "Blessed are those who are persecuted for righteousness' sake, for theirs is the Kingdom of heaven."[396]

3. The way the world measures life's circumstances compared with the truth of God's Word is "worthless elementary principles." They mean nothing, yet our hearts are easily allured and desire to believe them because the world, not God's Word, declares them to be true.

4. Those who do not know Christ are enslaved to this way of thinking. Just in the same way that we used to be![397]

5. Press in to know God, now that you are known by God. Prayerfully lay everything at the foot of the cross, and trust Him, and pursue the knowledge of knowing Him, in all, and let everything else be cast off while you seek first the Kingdom of God and His righteousness, and all these things will be added unto you.[398]

---

[396]Matthew 5:10, [397]Ephesians 2:1–3, [398]Matthew 6:33

Father, I am known by You. What glory! The truth of this many times is belittled in my mind. Father, I confess to You that the elementary things of this world so easily entangle my mind. They sneak in so subtly and cause me to doubt Your Word; forgive my unbelief. Teach me Your ways, free my heart, and help me to walk by faith in the finished work of Christ, by the power of the Holy Spirit and to the glory and praise of God our Father. In Jesus' name.

Genesis 46:3–4

Then he said, "I am God, the God of your father. Do not be afraid to go down to Egypt, for there I will make you into a great nation. I myself will go down with you to Egypt, and I will also bring you up again, and Joseph's hand shall close your eyes."

1. What a beautiful verse God has spoken to us. As Jacob headed into Egypt, the Lord came to him in a dream to encourage and command him in the promise of His Word.

2. First, the Lord declared who He is. He is God! We must always look to this truth and press in to know this God.[399] We must seek Him, praise Him, know Him, glorify Him, worship Him, and adore Him for one reason: He is God!

3. After declaring to Jacob, God spoke from His authority, "Do not be afraid to go down to Egypt." This was not a suggestion, and God did not speak to Jacob as a mentor. He is God, and His Word was a command. Jacob was not to fear.

4. In addition to commanding Jacob not to fear, God gave him a beautiful promise. God commanded Jacob to not fear and then declared the command's blessing would come from who God is, and not from anything Jacob would do. God would go to Egypt with him, and God would bring him up again. All things are rooted in who God is.

5. We must, by God's grace through the power of the Holy Spirit, not base our hearts on our circumstances, but look to God always. We must press on to know Him. We must trust His Word and press forward. We do not know what the results will be; we do not know what trials the Lord will providentially lead us through, but we know He will be with us, and that if God is for us, who can be against us?[400]

[399] Hosea 6:3, [400] Romans 8:31

Father, so many times I take my eyes off You and Your Word and place them on my circumstances. What unbelief, what lack of faith; for You uphold all things. So, if I am "feeling" a certain weight, it's because I have a wrong view of You. Help me to seek You with all my heart, soul, and mind, and grant me the strength and wisdom to walk boldly in repentance and faith for Your glory, Your will, and Your Kingdom. In Jesus' name.

Ephesians 6:10

FINALLY, BE STRONG IN THE LORD AND IN THE STRENGTH OF HIS MIGHT.

1. How glorious is the strength of God, and how mighty are His ways! All His ways are wise and perfect. He is merciful and kind, slow to anger, and abounding in steadfast love and mercy!

2. Our strength is not in our intellect or physicality. Our hope is not in our ability to reason or in our influence on others. All things are rooted in the Lord. Our strength is God's strength, for His Kingdom come and His will be done. God's will is and will be accomplished, thoroughly and completely. Let us then strive in His grace and strength!

3. God's children are to be rooted in the strength of God. We are to think, meditate, be mindful of, and hope in the strength of God. The fears of man arise when our view of God diminishes and we begin to define God by who man is rather than by who God is.

4. Let us approach the throne of grace daily. Seek His gracious strength and do all He has ordained for us that day. Let us repent of our excuses, our human reasonings, and let us worship before His throne, trusting that His mercies are new every morning![401] Let us do this by faith in who God is, and not in who we are.

---

[401] Lamentations 3:23

Father, grant me the conviction of faith to do Your will. Keep anything from my heart and mind that would plant any doubt or questioning, and let my heart humbly soar in the faith that only You provide. Guard my steps, silence my mouth, and fill my heart with the joy of the Lord, for Your joy is my strength, Your hope is my nourishment, Your peace is my guide, and Your contentment is my desire. Grant me the faith to do Your will. In Jesus' name.

Amen

Philippians 1:28

[You are] not frightened in anything by your opponents. This is a clear sign to them of their destruction, but of your salvation, and that from God.

1. Fear of man is a subtle sin that sneaks into the hearts of man. It is inflamed by the sin of unbelief and denial of the Lord. The darkness in the world does everything in its power to quench the light, for it screams in terror of the light as it grows, and it cannot overcome it.[402]

2. Our hope is not to be in our own strength but in God's. We are to seek first His Kingdom and His righteousness, and all these things will be added unto you.[403]

3. The more our hope is in God and the less we look to ourselves, the more our confidence, hope, and assurances rise, for they are in the hands of the Lord. Then we can say with Daniel's friends who were to be thrown in the fiery furnace when they denied worshiping King Nebuchadnezzar, *"We have no need to answer you in this matter. If this be so, our God whom we serve is able to deliver us from the burning fiery furnace, and he will deliver us out of your hand, O king. But if not, be it known to you, O king, that we will not serve your gods or worship the golden image that you have set up."*[404]

4. Nothing is impossible with God,[405] and death has lost its sting;[406] for us, to live is Christ and to die is gain![407] This boldness is the assurance of the defeat of darkness, the defeat of sin, and to encourage the believer to walk in the salvation of God. Let us not fear man; but let us, in love and by grace through faith, fear the Lord!

---

[402]John 1:4, [403]Matthew 6:33, [404]Daniel 3:16–18, [405]Luke 1:37, [406]1 Corinthians 15:55, [407]Philippians 1:21

Father, there are so many times all people, those who call themselves Christians, and those who are not believers, fear the unknown. They fear opposition. Lord, I have feared opposition and feared man. Forgive me. Help me know Your strength and Your assurance. Give me a boldness for the gospel; help me to speak in truth and in love, with a holy conviction. Humbly by the power of the Holy Spirit, in the name of Jesus.

1 Samuel 22:3

And David went from there to Mizpeh of Moab. And he said to the king of Moab, "Please let my father and my mother stay with you, till I know what God will do for me."

1. In the life of David, we see a man not only practical in his actions but one who sought the Lord. David recognized that Saul's heart was turned against him, and he acted with haste to flee from his anger. But he did not forget God.

2. The believer must saturate his life with prayer. Every step must be sought after by the grace of God. For Scripture states, "Be joyful always, pray continuously, and give thanks in all circumstances for this is the will of God in Christ Jesus for you."[408] We must look to God, who orchestrates all things for His glory, fully expecting He will make known to us what to do.

3. With prayer, though, must come decisive action. That action might be the act of waiting on the Lord, or changing direction completely, or taking the one step forward we see placed before us and acknowledge before the Lord that all things are in His hands. Our God is good, and He does whatever He pleases.[409] Whatever the Lord ordains is right. Our calling is not to know the outcome but to know the One who orchestrates all things and to trust His goodness and mercy.

4. In the tension between his own actions and the actions of God, David placed himself under the authority of God, desiring to take decisive action and knowing that unless God moves first, he could do nothing. All that we do must come from the knowledge that God must work first.

---

[408]1 Thessalonians 5:16–18, [409]Psalm 115:3

Father, You are good, and Your love endures forever. I recognize the many times I see Your goodness in light of what You give me, and in light of what I receive, rather than in who You are. Forgive me. Will You open my eyes to see You? Will You soften my heart and forgive me of my unbelief? Will You lead me on Your path for Your name's sake? Apart from You I am lost; apart from You I can do nothing; but in You I have fullness of joy. In Christ's name.

1 *Chronicles* 4:10

JABEZ CALLED UPON THE GOD OF ISRAEL, SAYING,
"OH THAT YOU WOULD BLESS ME AND ENLARGE MY BORDER,
AND THAT YOUR HAND MIGHT BE WITH ME, AND THAT YOU WOULD
KEEP ME FROM HARM SO THAT IT MIGHT NOT BRING ME PAIN!"
AND GOD GRANTED WHAT HE ASKED.

1. Prayer is a means of grace the Lord has given us to come before Him, worship Him, and lay our hearts before Him. We are to come to the Lord with everything and lay before Him our hearts and our lives, sharing with Him the desires of our hearts because He cares for us.[410]

2. Jabez rightfully went before the Lord and acknowledged that God and God alone could bless him. It is God and God alone who keeps us from harm and guards us from pain. This does not mean the Lord will not lead us through the valley of the shadow of death or that we will not experience painful circumstances, but as we seek the Lord, He will lead us and guide us, and the joy of the Lord will be our strength.[411]

3. As we lay our hearts before the Lord and make known to Him our thoughts and desires, the Lord answers our prayers. We must not be scared to share with Him all our thoughts, feelings, and emotions and to trust Him with the cares and anxieties of our hearts. For Christ has said that if He cares for the lilies of the valley, will He not also cloth and keep us?[412]

4. Let us guard against a pragmatic, practical atheism that deceives us in thinking we cannot share our hearts with the Lord. Let us be more prayerful than we are strategic and trust the Lord in His sovereign grace with the cares of our hearts, knowing He will answer every prayer according to His will and in His perfect time.

---

[410] 1 Peter 5:7, [411] Nehemiah 8:10, [412] Matthew 6:28–30

Father, I come to You, for You are the giver of all things. I confess the many times I do not share my heart with You. I suppress the idea that You care about me or believe that what I think or feel is beneath what You truly care about. I become afraid of my emotions and deny coming to You. Forgive my pride. Will You loosen my tongue and my heart to share with You the desires of my heart? Will You open my eyes to see You working and orchestrating all things for Your glory? Will You reveal to me the sins of my heart and direct and guide my path for Your glory? I ask this in the name of Your precious Son.

Psalm 60:12

*With God we shall do valiantly;
it is He who will tread down our foes.*

1. The Lord is before all things. We are not to look at our circumstances and decisions in light of what we perceive we can and cannot do but in light of who God is. Our God is strong and mighty. He is omniscient and sovereign over all. Our God hears and draws near to the brokenhearted, and He rewards those who seek Him.

2. So we are to present the things He allows in our day back to Him for His glory. Be mindful of the different dispensations of circumstances and opportunities, and come to the Lord and seek His will. Stop for a moment and pray and seek the Lord. Seek godly counsel and pray that you have wisdom in each step and in each moment, and then act for God's glory.

3. Many a man forfeits the blessing of doing God's will because he measures the work and the calling in light of his humanity rather than in who God is. They look to science and to the achievements of other men rather than seek the Lord and His will. All the plans of the Lord work together, not because of our own strength but because of who God is.

4. We can be assured that everything the Lord calls us to, He will bring it to completion in His perfect timing and in His perfect way. With God, we will do valiantly, for we know that He brings all things to completion, and it is He who will fight and win our battles and accomplish His perfect will in and for His Kingdom and our good.

Father, You are strong and mighty! Who is like You in the heavens? Who can compare to Your glory? Who can thwart You in any way? Father, I confess the many times I look at the circumstances in my life and perceive their success in light of who I am rather than in who You are. I measure my perceived ability rather than seeking Your will and trusting Your plan. I see that Christ desired above all things to do Your will, and I confess that my unbelief hedges my will rather than Yours. Forgive me. Strengthen me and help me resolve to do all of Your will for all of Your glory, with all of Your strength. In Christ's name.

Proverbs 3:25–26

Do not be afraid of sudden terror or of the ruin of the wicked, when it comes, for the LORD will be your confidence and will keep your foot from being caught.

1. Our confidence is not to be in anything or anyone other than the Lord, for God is our refuge and strength, a very present help in trouble. Therefore, we will not fear.[413]

2. Our God is never not in control of all things. Regardless of what the world may say, regardless of what the world points to, the people of God are to look to the Word of God. We are a people who live by faith and not by sight.[414] We are not to look at the world and define our lives by what we see.

3. The Lord is our confidence; He has promised to keep our feet from being caught in the traps and the destruction of the wicked. Let us look to God, know God, walk humbly before our God. Let us trust God at His Word, knowing that He works all things together for good for those who love Him and are called according to His purpose.[415]

4. The Lord allows fears in our lives and anxiety in our hearts for us to see the idols we cling to and to see where we have depended on someone or something other than Christ. Let us repent of these things and hold fast to Christ. Let us ask God in His mercy to show us what we have more confidence in other than Him and turn to Him, seeking His mercy and grace.

---

[413]Psalm 46:1–2, [414]2 Corinthians 5:7, [415]Romans 8:28

Father, I so easily look at things of the world to define my life and how I feel about it. You, in Your awesome wonder, never fret, never worry, never regret, and never second guess. Not one thing takes You by surprise, and You seek no one for counsel. Yet, we depend fully on You in all things and in everything. Bring to my mind Your promises and Your truth, that I may hold fast to it and praise You all the more. Help me to walk in integrity and boldness, that I may honor You with my whole life. Send Your Spirit to show me my depravity and my need and to lead me in accordance with Your will for the glory of Christ. In His name I ask this.

John 4:34

Jesus said to them, "My food is to do the will of Him who sent me and to accomplish his work.

1. Jesus did need sustenance, but that which sustained Him was not food of this world. It was not entertainment nor relaxation. It was not even the knowledge that He was God and can do whatever He pleases, even to the point of aimlessness.

2. Christ's sustenance, His life, was to do the will of God. This was the mission of Christ, to do that which the Father had commanded Him and to accomplish the work of the Father.

3. We as Christians are to do the will of Him who called us out of darkness and into His marvelous light,[416] and to live on mission.

4. We are to repent and to seek the Lord and His will. Our aim is His Kingdom come, His will be done, on earth as it is in heaven."[417]

---

[416]1 Peter 2:9, [417]Matthew 6:10

Father, Your Kingdom is perfect. There is not defect or imperfection; there is no enemy that can withstand. There is nothing that can prevail against it, and I praise You! Yet, Father, I confess I have not looked to that Kingdom but instead have looked to my own. I have sought to build my own kingdom, pridefully and for my glory, rather than for Yours. Forgive me. Help me to serve You. Bless me to serve You. Give me wisdom to do Your will. Give me strength and zeal for Your glory! I ask this in Jesus' name.

John 16:7–11

Nevertheless, I tell you the truth: it is to your advantage that I go away, for if I do not go away, the Helper will not come to you. But if I go, I will send Him to you. And when He comes, He will convict the world concerning sin and righteousness and judgment: concerning sin, because they do not believe in me; concerning righteousness, because I go to the Father, and you will see me no longer; concerning judgment, because the ruler of this world is judged.

1. Jesus Christ's leaving earth and returning to heaven did not leave us alone, nor did He send back an impersonal "force" with which to live our lives.

2. Jesus Christ sent the Holy Spirit to help us walk in accordance with the will of God. The Holy Spirit is a Person. The true believer detests the heretical presence of luck, chance, and circumstance because he knows the Holy Spirit is the One who orchestrates all things to the will of the Father, through the Son. The Holy Spirit is with those whom God the Father has brought to Himself. He brings conviction of sin, and He prays for us in accordance with the will of God, even when we don't know what to pray for.[418]

3. We can walk by faith and have a personal relationship with the Holy Spirit as we go in and through our lives.

4. We must also be careful, though, because if we do not acknowledge God and instead deny His sovereignty, if we are not thankful for what the Lord does in all and every circumstance of our lives, and pray and seek Him continually, then we quench the Holy Spirit.[419]

5. We are to seek the Holy Spirit and trust that, as we are faithful to the Lord, He will lead and guide us in all truth.[420]

[418]Romans 8:26–27, [419]1 Thessalonians 5:16–19, [420]John 16:12

Holy Spirit, we thank You for who You are and for working through us in accordance with the will of the Father, to the glory of Christ. I confess the many times I have been thankless and walked in unbelief. I have acted in a way not glorifying to God and have hardened my heart to You. Forgive me. Work in my heart and mind a truthfulness, a nearness, a hope, a certainty, a glorious beauty of the reality of You in my life, and a working of You in my life for the glory of God, and my good. In Jesus' name.

Amen

Deuteronomy 29:4

But to this day the Lord has not given you a heart to understand or eyes to see or ears to hear.

1. All knowledge of God is a gift and a grace. God cannot be known by intellect or measured by any of man's standards. For we are dead in our trespasses and sins apart from the grace of God.[421]

2. Unless the Lord opens the eyes of our hearts and minds to know Him, we are unable to know the true God. All who are His are claimed by the grace of God, and there are none who He will leave behind. None of God's people will ever be snatched from the hand of the Father.[422]

3. This is only by the grace of God. The gospel is the power of God unto salvation.[423] It is the gospel alone that works in our hearts and minds to open us to the saving knowledge of God so that no one can boast![424]

4. Our prayer should always be that God would open the eyes of our hearts that we might know the surpassing goodness of His grace for us. That we might walk in accordance with His truth, and that we should know Him who is sovereign over all things. To this end, may we praise and adore Him, bless Him in all things, and worship the Lord our God who made heaven and earth.

---

[421]Ephesians 2:1, [422]John 10:29, [423]Romans 1:16, [424]Ephesians 2:9

Father who can know You apart from Your grace? What pride and selfishness we have to think there is anything we can do apart from You. Lord, I confess that in my pride, I have many times thought of You intellectually or conjured You in my mind; not done so according to Your Word. I have brought false worship and "strange fire"[425] before You rather than Your Word. Lord, have mercy on me and open my eyes that I may behold Your glory. Help me to walk in accordance with Your ways, that You may be praised and lifted up. In Jesus' name!

[425]Leviticus 10:1

Psalm 28:7

The Lord is my strength and my shield; in him my heart trusts, and I am helped; my heart exults, and with my song I give thanks to him.

1. One of the most important aspects of prayer is expressing thankfulness to God. This is not a virtuous or absent-minded, obligatory thankfulness, but a thankfulness for what the Lord is specifically doing in our lives moment by moment, day by day.

2. The thankfulness of a heart toward God in the moments of our lives is an outward witness to what we proclaim to be theological truth. For if we say that God is sovereign over all things, yet harden our hearts and remain mindless in the moment-by-moment aspects of our lives, then we are not living out the truth of what we proclaim to the world.

3. The proper response to the Lord working in our lives in all things is thanksgiving. But if we are not prayerful, we cannot be thankful. If we do not trust that the Lord will answer, we will not be thankful. If we believe ourselves to be capable of doing things apart from God's grace, we will not be thankful. Lastly, we must be mindful that if we are not thankful to God, we are not different than the wicked, than those who are damned to hell.

4. Let us, as the people of God, rejoice in His great works. Let us be mindful of all circumstances—those we understand and those we do not—and present our thanksgiving before God for the specific instances that He is bringing us through. Let us be mindful of His protection, His Word, and let us exclaim, proclaim, and sing His praises—for His glory and our good!

Father, I thank You for allowing me to be mindful of You in all aspects of my life, for that which You allow me to be part of, for the people You brought into my life even this week, the sun You cause to rise, and the beauty You allowed me to behold. I confess that my selfishness and pride focus more on my acts rather than Your providence. I confess that my pride many times desires to take credit for Your daily graces. Forgive me and soften me to praise You. In Jesus' name.

Psalm 28:1

*To you, O LORD, I call; my rock,
be not deaf to me, lest, if you be silent to me,
I become like those who go down to the pit.*

1. We must seek the Lord, and pray, and call upon Him in all situations. For David cries out to the Lord and pleads with Him to not only hear his prayer but also to speak to him and not be silent in His answers to prayer.

2. We must search our hearts and see what unbelief has gripped our hearts in the expectations of the Lord speaking to us. Do we plead that the Lord speak with us, or do we view prayer as a form of therapeutic self-talk? Many people do not hear the voice of God because they do not know or recognize it in every area of their lives.

3. We are to take everything in our lives and present it before the Lord. Then we are to plead with Him to speak to us and to be our God. As David did, we are to remind the Lord that if He does not answer and remains silent instead, we are tempted to think as the atheist who denies the truth of God.

4. We are to cast all our anxieties, hopes, and fears before the Lord and listen for Him, expectantly waiting and asking Him to open the eyes of our hearts and give us wisdom, understanding, and confidence that He will hear and answer our prayers, according to His sovereign, perfect, and good will.

Oh Father, You speak, and You answer prayers. From the very beginning You spoke, and from Your very Word, You created all things![426] *Then You sent Your very Son into the world, for He is the very Word of God, the embodiment of the very Word!*[427] *I confess that I act many times as a practical atheist and deny that You speak and answer prayers. Forgive my hard heartedness and open my ears and my heart to pray, to listen, and to look for You in all aspects of my life for Your glory and my good. In Jesus' name.*

[426]Genesis 1, [427]John 1:1–2

Joshua 9:14

So the men took some of their provisions but did not ask counsel from the LORD.

1. In our humanity, we often depend on what we see rather than going to the Lord. We deny the Lordship and love that God has for us and deem ourselves like God Himself, knowing good from evil.[428] This is an egregious sin against the Lord, for it acts in a way of the fool. We deem that we are like God and that we know all things. It is a practical atheism that subtly deceives the heart.

2. For in this instance, the men of Israel depended upon their senses and trusted their eyes to make a covenant with a people of the land of Canaan. Instead of going to the Lord, they were wise in their own eyes.

3. There is nothing in our lives that the Lord does not desire for us to come to Him about. For the Lord is God over all things and ordains all things for His glory. He knows everything, orchestrates everything, and nothing is out of His sovereign decree.

4. We are to cast all our cares upon Him because He cares for us.[429] We are to pray continually and give thanks in all circumstances.[430] Let us repent of our unbelief and seek the Lord while He may be found.

---

[428]Genesis 3:5, [429]1 Peter 5:7, [430]1 Thessalonians 5:17–18

Father, I praise You for You know all things, and You love me. How glorious and beautiful that You love me. I confess the many times I act in practical atheism rather than seeking You. My heart, at times, does not believe that You will answer me; forgive me. Grant my heart to trust and to seek You in all my decisions and for Your glory. I praise You, Lord.

Psalm 34:4

I SOUGHT THE LORD, AND HE ANSWERED ME AND DELIVERED ME FROM ALL MY FEARS.

1. The psalmist does not pray mindlessly and without direction to the Lord concerning his fears about life. He is not only mindful of what he feels but of his exact circumstances in which the Lord has placed him.

2. Many times our prayers are filled with unbelief and psychological babble rather than aimed at the Lord, who sits upon His throne. We speak into the air, not expecting the Lord to answer and work a solution for our good and His glory.[431] A moralistic, therapeutic deism subtly whispers in our hearts, "Did God really say…?"[432] so we check our prayers off our list and move ahead in our lives, rather than trusting in God.

3. But God's people are to confess these things before the Lord, and we are to seek Him in all things, trusting and mindful of His goodness. We are to take every fear, doubt, and situation and look to the Lord. We are to be mindful of His sovereignty and works. We are to rest in His grace and depend upon the Lord.

4. Let the believer then look to the promises of God in all situations. Let him remind himself and the body of Christ of the Lord's goodness, His truth, His covenant, His purposes, and His sovereignty, for His glory and our good.

[431]Romans 8:28, [432]Genesis 3:1

Father, You are a God who answers all our fears. An idol does not talk back. An idol is truly worthless. We erect idols in our hearts all the time, in every circumstance. We depend upon wealth, intellect, and self-perceived power, rather than looking to and trusting in You. Forgive me. Grant my heart to seek and to hear Your answers in my life based upon Your wisdom, Your sovereign grace, and Your goodness. In Christ's name I ask this.

Amen

Mark 11:24

Therefore I tell you, whatever you ask in prayer, believe that you have received it, and it will be yours.

1. Prayer is a grace given by God and is used by Him in extraordinary ways. We are commanded repeatedly within Scripture to pray continually[433] and to make our requests known before God.[434]

2. We must be extremely careful with our expectations. Many people look at this verse and see God as a genie in a bottle who should give us exactly what we ask of Him. This idea is heresy. We must first look at the object and the desire of our hearts before we take a request to God.

3. The greatest thing God has called us to is to *"Go into all the world and proclaim the gospel to the whole creation. Whoever believes and is baptized will be saved, but whoever does not believe will be condemned."*[435] He has not called us to do this apart from Him, but in Him, and by the power of the Holy Spirit.[436]

4. Our hope is not in our own worth, strength, wisdom, power, or might, but in God and God alone. We proclaim this truth by seeking the will of our Father, seeking His kingdom, and prayerfully asking Him to grant us His hope, wisdom, and strength while walking by faith in a manner that glorifies the truth of who He is.

---

[433]1 Thessalonians 5:17, [434]Philippians 4:6, [435]Mark 16:15–16, [436]Romans 15:13

Father, thank You for the grace of prayer. Please forgive me for not being prayerful enough, and also for not seeking You in my prayer but seeking my will. Lord, grant me the faith to pray boldly for Your will, the strength to be steadfast, and the hope to persevere regardless of what others say. In Jesus' name.

Amen

Mark 14:38

WATCH AND PRAY THAT YOU MAY NOT ENTER INTO TEMPTATION. THE SPIRIT INDEED IS WILLING, BUT THE FLESH IS WEAK.

1. The command from our Lord is to not only pray but to watch as well. We are not to pray mindlessly, as a way to merely process our thoughts, but we must be mind*ful* of who God is and that He is working together all things for His glory and our good.

2. In watching, we must also guard our hearts. Our eyes must not be on the desire but on the Lord. We present our desires to Him and trust His sovereign goodness—that His will is perfectly done. If our eyes are on and hope is in the desire rather than the Lord, then the desire could become the idol rather than the beholding of God's glory.

3. The Lord is always at work. He has brought to life our spirits.[437] Our flesh is still sinful within us,[438] and it does everything it can to not come in contact with a holy God. Our thoughts, feelings, and emotions are at enmity against Him. For the mind that is set on the flesh is hostile toward God, for it does not submit to His Law; indeed, it cannot. Those who are in the flesh cannot please God.[439]

4. We must seek the Lord and His strength continually.[440] When you pray, ask the Lord for strength; when you speak with a friend, ask the Lord for wisdom; when you walk about your day, ask the Lord to lead and guide you; when you worry about the future, ask the Lord to give you peace that passes all understanding. All our circumstances must be placed before the throne of grace, as we trust in His strength at all times.

---

[437]Romans 8:4, [438]Romans 8:3, [439]Romans 8:7, [440]Psalm 105:4

Father, You are good. I praise You for making Yourself known. Lord, many times I believe the lies of the world, thinking I can do things apart from You. I am tempted to believe I am good or wise apart from You, and pride sneaks in to steal Your glory. Forgive me. Lord, will You strengthen me? Will You please help me to walk and to know Your strength and Your wisdom? Will You guard my heart and emotions from man-made excuses and help me to walk in the truth of Your Son according to Your Word? Thank You, Father. In Your Son's name.

Amen

Genesis 32:9

And Jacob said, "O God of my father Abraham and God of my father Isaac, O LORD who said to me, 'Return to your country and to your kindred, that I may do you good.'"

1. Prayer is the means of grace by which God has ordained we are to approach Him. In this, we are to be mindful of prayer and of who God is and who we are.

2. Jacob approached God under the promises of God. He reminded himself of and humbly approached the Lord with the Lord's promises of, *"Return to your country and to your kindred, that I may do you good."*[441]

3. Jacob left Laban because the Lord had called him out from that land and back to the land the Lord had given to Abraham and Isaac.[442] So, the initial act was based on the promises of God.

4. We are to do the same thing. We are not to approach the Lord absentmindedly or with a double mind; we are not to approach Him superstitiously or as though we depended more upon the stupidity of luck. But we are to approach Him with the boldness of His promises! The Lord said, "I will never leave you nor forsake you."[443] He said, "The Lord your God is with you wherever you go!"[444] Also, "Fear not, for I am with you. I will strengthen you, I will help you, I will uphold you with my righteous right hand."[445] Let us approach the throne of grace with confidence,[446] not on our merit, but on the merit of Christ, rooted in the promises of God and whatever the Lord ordains is right.

---

[441]Genesis 32:9, [442]Genesis 31:3, [443]Hebrews 13:5, [444]Joshua 1:9, [445]Isaiah 41:10, [446]Hebrews 4:16

Father, thank You for the promises You have given us in Your Word and confirmed in Christ. I confess, Lord, that many times I do not cling to Your promises and instead cling more to what I see or feel. Forgive me. Grant me to rest in Your promises and to be strengthened by them; to be bold, not in myself, but in Your promises, for Your glory and my good. In Jesus' name.

Luke 10:2

AND HE SAID TO THEM, "THE HARVEST IS PLENTIFUL, BUT THE LABORERS ARE FEW." THEREFORE PRAY EARNESTLY TO THE LORD OF THE HARVEST TO SEND OUT LABORERS INTO HIS HARVEST

1. The Lord is establishing His Kingdom on earth and is bringing all nations to Himself for His glory.

2. Notice, we must not have a scarcity mindset as God's people when it comes to the expanding power of God's Kingdom. For the harvest is plentiful; it is bountiful. There is more harvest than there are workers to preach and live out the gospel.

3. Yet, we must not begin the work with a pragmatic and humanistic view. We are to begin the work with prayer to the Lord. Prayer for the Lord's laborers, for His wisdom, for His guidance, for His favor. The preaching of the Word is a means of grace that the Lord has ordained to bring His people to Himself, but it is the power of God unto salvation that saves a sinner from hell.[447]

4. We must be mindful that apart from Christ we can do nothing.[448] Even the devil knows Scripture,[449] and he is the great deceiver who prowls around like a roaring lion, seeking who he may devour.[450]

5. So let us seek the Lord while He may be found.[451] Let us ask Him to send His people out into all the nations and to give us victory for His glory, in His Kingdom, and for our good.

---

[447]Romans 1:16, [448]John 15:5, [449]Matthew 4:4, [450]1 Peter 5:8, [451]Isaiah 55:6

Father, who is like You? There is none in heaven above or earth below! Forgive me for how many times I seek my own wisdom rather than seeking You! Lord, where shall I go, and what shall I do for Your glory? Give me wisdom and lead me according to Your glorious grace for the sake of Your Kingdom. If it be physical action, financial action, or prayerful action, stir in my heart what You command and the will to do Your command. In Jesus' name.

Amen

Acts 1:24

And they prayed and said, "You, Lord, who know the hearts of all, show which one of these two you have chosen."

1. With every decision we make in our lives, our first action should be to pray. We are to seek the Lord in all things; we are to humble ourselves before Him and trust His providence in every situation.

2. The world breathes lies every day, stating that luck, chance, or circumstance are what hold all things together. This belief is opposite of the Word of God. The world attempts to make us believe in a practical atheism rather than in the sovereignty of God.

3. This prayer, though, should be followed by faith. We are to pray, seek the Lord, and act in accordance with where we believe the Lord is leading us. We are not to sit idly but to walk by faith and not by sight.

4. The depth and width of our prayer life overall reflect our submission to the Lord in all things. Let us be in constant prayer, offering up all He has already prepared for us,[452] for His glory and our good.

---

[452]Ephesians 2:10

Father, You are sovereign over all things, and all things You do out of Your abundant love. I confess the many times my mind and heart are hardened to You, rather than seeking You. Help me to know, and to recognize, and to rejoice in You in every moment. Give me Your peace to walk boldly in faith in Christ Jesus. In His name I ask this.

Luke 22:42

"Father, if you are willing, remove this cup from me. Nevertheless, not my will, but yours, be done."

1. Prayer is a beautiful grace the Father has given us, a way to commune and talk with the Lord. We must, though, be mindful of our prayer to the Lord. We must be mindful of who we are praying to and be sure our prayers reflect the glory of God and not the glory of man.

2. Too many times we don't actually pray, but instead we tell the Lord what we are going to do. We declare our kingdom, our will, and our desires but never seek to know the desire of God. We, in our pride and unbelief, cry out to God, "Make Your will my will!"

3. How foolish and arrogant. We are to petition the Lord and desire Him, who knows all things and works all things according to His will in and through the events of our lives. We are to humbly and with thanksgiving accept His mercies and disciplines to conform us to the image of His Son.

4. Let us seek God's will, trust it, rest in it, and place all our fears, worries, doubts, and anxieties before the throne of grace, and rest, saying, "Not my will but Yours be done."

Father, Your will is glorious. It is perfect and without any variance. Please forgive my arrogance and how many times I shake my fist at You, wanting my own will, rather than seeking Your will. So often I want for You to do what I want, rather than walking humbling in faith in You. Forgive me. Soften my heart to Your Word, and lead me in Your way everlasting. For You are my God, and I am Yours through Christ Jesus. In His name I pray.

Luke 1:38

And Mary said, "Behold, I am the servant of the Lord; let it be to me according to your word." And the angel departed from her.

1. The aim for the believer is humble submission to the will of God. We are to bow our knees and to seek His Kingdom to come and His will to be done. For our God is good, and everything that He calls and leads us through is good and perfect.

2. The Lord knows and directs all things for His glory. He does this according to His perfect Word. God ordains all things, knows all things, orchestrates all things, and directs all things. There is nothing He does not direct, and in that our hearts find rest.

3. Mary's response is a submission to the Word of God. She knew His will, and in that, she submitted to God's Word for her life. Thirty-three years later, the Son she gave birth to knelt in the garden of Gethsemane and prayed, "Father, if you are willing, remove this cup from me. Nevertheless, not my will, but yours, be done."[453]

4. Let us repent and come before the Lord God our Maker, and let us bow our knees and our hearts before His throne, for His glory and our good.

---

[453]Luke 22:42

Father, Your will is perfect, and Your will is from Your goodness. Who am I that You have created me? I confess, Father, that I am tempted to grumble and to seek my will rather than to submit to Yours. I many times am tempted to just throw my hands up and give up because of my pride. Forgive me. Grant my heart to know the joy of Your salvation and help my heart and my mind to rest in Your perfect will, trusting You with all my heart and all my soul and with all my might. In Jesus' name.

Colossians 4:2

CONTINUE STEADFASTLY IN PRAYER, BEING WATCHFUL IN IT WITH THANKSGIVING.

1. The Christian's prayer should have three aspects to it. We are to be steadfast, watchful, and filled with thanksgiving.

2. In being steadfast, we are to pray at all times and at every time. We are to pray continuously[454] in all circumstances. Our first call to action when we wake in the morning is to thank the Lord and ask for His strength. The last thing we are to do at night is to thank the Lord for His sustaining grace and to bring before Him the things we have been tempted by or burdened with and lay them at the throne of grace.

3. This is not a mindless prayer but one that is watchful at all times. Watching as to the things the Lord places before us, and watching for those things in how the Lord is answering and glorifying Himself in the prayers of His people. God is working together for good all things, and we are to be mindful and offer up our praises to our Heavenly Father, regardless of His answers.

4. We are to be thankful. All things come from God, and all things are ordained by our Heavenly Father. We are to be mindful to offer thanksgiving to the One who is our Lord and Savior.

---

[454] 1 Thessalonians 5:17

Father, You have given us a beautiful means of grace in prayer. You have allowed us to draw close to You and to seek Your face and lay our burdens down at Your feet. Who are we to come before You like this? We are nothing, but Christ is all. He is our great High Priest, and in His finished work we are able to come to You and give You praise and honor and glory. Grant my heart joy and hope in Christ and Christ alone, in all that You have for me today. In Jesus' name.

Numbers 9:8

And Moses said to them, "Wait, that I may hear what the Lord will command concerning you."

1. In all situations and in all circumstances we are to go the Lord of all and ask Him. We are not to be wise in our own eyes, but instead, we are to fear the Lord.[455]

2. Prayer is a gift from the Lord that He has given us to seek and come before Him continuously and in all circumstances.[456] We are to come to the Lord when the things of life seem insurmountable; we are to come to the Lord when in our pride we believe we can accomplish something apart from Him, for apart from Christ we can do nothing.[457]

3. In prayer, we are to wait. We are to acknowledge our dependency on God, and in faith know that He will work all things together for good for those who love the Lord and are called according to His purpose.[458]

4. So let us be mindful of who God is; let us be mindful of who we are and our dependence upon God. Let us repent of our sin and self-dependency, and let us cast all our cares on Him, for He cares for us.[459]

---

[455]Proverbs 3:7, [456]1 Thessalonians 5:17, [457]John 15:5, [458]Romans 8:28, [459]1 Peter 5:7

FATHER, YOU ARE GOD. WHAT A FOREIGN AND OPPOSITE MINDSET IN A WORLD THAT DEEMS ITSELF "SELF-RELIANT." FATHER, MANY TIMES I HAVE APPROACHED LIFE IN MY PERCEIVED SELF-STRENGTH AND HAVE NOT GLORIFIED YOU BUT GLORIFIED MYSELF. FORGIVE ME, AND GRANT ME FREEDOM AND MINDFULNESS TO COME TO YOU AND BEHOLD YOUR GLORY. IN JESUS' NAME.

Leviticus 14:20

*And the priest shall offer the burnt offering
and the grain offering on the altar.
Thus the priest shall make atonement for him,
and he shall be clean.*

1. In this passage of Leviticus, a person diagnosed with leprosy by the priest has been healed and brought back into the community of Israelites, where he would present himself before the priest. The priest would examine him and would make atonement for him before the Lord.

2. All that we go through, whether health, sickness, joy, or heartache, is ordained by God. These things neither add to nor take away from God's goodness, but they should be seen in light of who God is. For we are to go to God with all things. We are to look to Him and come before Him.

3. Our thankfulness, or lack of thankfulness, in all circumstances reflects our submission, dependence, and view of who God is. It shows us the attitude of our hearts. Do we recognize we do not deserve to be healthy? But the Lord gives us health for His glory. Do we recognize we do not deserve peace? But He is the Prince of Peace.[460]

4. Our thankfulness and mindfulness of who God is, in all and every aspect of our lives, is a direct reflection of the Lordship of Christ in our lives. Let us humble ourselves; let us kneel before the Lord our God, our Maker.[461]

[460]Isaiah 9:6, [461]Psalm 95:6

Father, You are Lord over all things. Our health, our sickness, our joy, our worry—all these things are under Your sovereign control. Who am I that You are mindful of me? Father, I ask Your forgiveness for in my pride. I often walk throughout life as though I deserve to have what I desire—as though I am entitled to peace and joy rather than in humble dependence on You. Forgive me. Grant me to know Your nearness; grant me favor to walk in the light of Your truth. Give me a boldness in Christ and an assurance of Your salvation that I may praise You, my God and my King. In Jesus' name.

Psalm 27:8

You have said, "Seek my face." My heart says to you, "Your face, LORD, do I seek."

1. God has commanded that we seek His face, to seek intimacy and fellowship with Him in all areas and in every area of our lives.

2. This is not a suggestion; this is a command to the believer. In the midst of every circumstance, we are to seek the face of the Lord, to strive to be in intimate relationship with Him, to trust His Word and rest in its promises.

3. Scripture says, "Draw near to God, and He will draw near to you."[462] These are beautiful promises. We are not to think of God existentially but in grace and truth. We are to come to Him by prayer and trust that He will make Himself known.

4. Our hearts are prone to erect idols and many things that steal our hearts from God. The world will lie to us and tell us that if we do not worry about our family, finances, friends, and future, then we have failed. But Scripture tells us to "Seek first the Kingdom of God, and His righteousness and all these things will be added to you."[463]

5. When you read Scripture, ask the Lord to reveal Himself. In difficult situations when you need to make choices, ask the Lord to show Himself. When times seem dire, stop and pray, and ask the Lord to let you "see His face." In every circumstance, pray and seek the Lord, and then press on, expectantly hoping in God, as He fulfills His promises at His perfect time.

---

[462]James 4:8, [463]Matthew 6:33

Father, You are near. You are present. That is why I can be joyful always, pray continuously, and give thanks in all circumstances, because You are near, and You are present, working all things together for Your glory and my good. Yet, how do I seek Your face? How do I keep You at the center of my mind? How do I look for You in and through Your world? Grant me to know You, that I may praise You. Stop every preconception and temptation to tell You what to do, and grant me the peace of watching You place Your glory on display in every circumstance of my life. In Jesus' name.

Psalm 26:2-3

Prove me, O Lord, and try me; test my heart and my mind. For your steadfast love is before my eyes, and I walk in your faithfulness.

1. One of the most beautiful yet terrifying prayers the believer can ask of the Lord is to try our hearts, to test our hearts and minds, that we may radiate our faithfulness to and love for God. Our flesh cringes at the request, not because it's not true, but because it is a terrifying thing to fall in the hands of a living God.[464]

2. But over every mountain and through every valley, we are to keep the steadfast love of our Heavenly Father before us. How do we see His steadfast love for us? We see it in that the Father sent His only Son into the world to pay the ransom for sin, for His children.

3. Our eyes, in every situation, are to remain focused on Christ. Regardless of what the world claims, regardless of any affirmation or persecution, we are to cling to Christ and take each step by grace and through faith.

4. This is not a philosophical stoicism; this is a faith rooted and grounded in a Person. This Person is the way and the truth, and the life, and no one can come to the Father except through Him.[465] Christ promised He will never leave us nor forsake us,[466] so let us press on. Let us ask the Lord to lovingly do what He will to draw us closer to Him, and the more clearly we see Christ, the more boldly we will walk in humble faithfulness.

[464]Hebrews 10:31, [465]John 14:6, [466]Hebrews 13:5

Father, I am scared to pray this, but I ask You to try and test my heart according to Your will. Help me to walk faithfully in all aspects of life, for Your glory. I do not ask this in my own strength but look to Christ, who is before me. May Your will be done. In Jesus' name.

Exodus 14:14

The Lord will fight for you,
and you have only to be silent.

1. In all things and in everything, we are to fear the Lord. We are to check our thoughts, words, actions, and deeds and present them to the Lord. Our God will fight for us! We do not live in an impersonal universe, but in a universe ordained, orchestrated, and working for His glory and our good!

2. Our grumbling and fear arise when we take our eyes off the Lord and turn them on ourselves, defining our lives by what we perceive rather than trusting the Word of God. This is a denial of the Lord; this is a denial of the finished work of Christ; this egregious sin is the sin of unbelief in a loving Heavenly Father. It deceives the believer and reflects that of a practical atheist.

3. Let us look to Christ! For when the Son of God stood before the High Priest, He was silent.[467] He needed not beg for His life. He needed not worry about what His circumstances would hold, for into the Father's hand He committed His spirit.[468]

4. In Christ and Christ alone, we by faith boldly need not worry or fear. For we have a Great High Priest who knows our suffering and has passed through to heaven to intercede for us.[469] Let us keep silent, with thanksgiving, faithfully and prayerfully stewarding that which the Lord places before us, for the Lord will fight for us. Christ has sealed us in Him, and we have only to be silent.

---

[467]Matthew 26:63, [468]Luke 23:46, [469]Hebrews 4:14

Father, You are Alpha and Omega, the beginning and the end. You know me, and You know all that is going on in my life, for You orchestrate all things. Father, forgive me for the times I have murmured, complained, and not trusted You. I have so many times asked You to use someone else. Forgive me. I have never pondered Your anger or Your holiness; I have many times relegated You to a morality rather than a reality and the truth. Forgive me. Grant my heart a boldness in You, to look to You. Place Your praises in my mouth, fill my heart with Your prayers, and open my eyes to see You working all things for Your glory. In Jesus' name.

Psalm 105:4

*Seek the LORD and his strength;
seek his presence continually!*

1. Seek the Lord at all times and in every situation. We, in our foolishness, construct a mindset of a sacred and secular divide. We relegate God to Sunday mornings or when we have an emotional experience. God is not an emotion, nor is He a mystical being. He is Lord over all things.

2. This means that in all and every situation, we should seek the Lord. Call upon His name! Let us not rest in our perceived mind, but in faith let us cry out to God for strength and for the nearness of God.

3. *Continually.* This is an infinite word, defining the never-ending cycle of depending on God's strength and trusting His sovereign grace. We must constantly search our hearts, asking the Lord to reveal those places in our hearts and minds where we depend upon our own strength and will.

4. Confess these things before the Lord! Cease all excuses in the things the Lord places before you. Walk by faith in Christ's finished work to do all the Lord calls you to, and do this at all times.

Father, You are strong and mighty, and there is nothing that isn't from You. Lord, so often I have come to You with excuses and human arguments and have denied Your Lordship. I have thrown my circumstances and attempted to use these as justification to not seek You and Your presence continually. In fact, Lord, I have attempted to hide behind my circumstances, that I may deny Your presence. Forgive me. Grant me Your strength and grant me to know the nearness of You. Make my heart grow in intimacy with You and less with the world. You are God, and Your Word promises that if we draw near to You, You will draw near to us.[470]
Come, Lord Jesus; come.[471]

Amen

---

[470] James 4:8, [471] Revelation 22:20

Galatians 3:11

Now it is evident that no one is justified before God by the law, for "The righteous shall live by faith."

1. "The righteous shall live by faith." Romans 1:17 offers these words as well, and God used this verse to help Martin Luther light the fuse of the Reformation.

2. The implications of this verse are so vast that we could spend a lifetime thinking and meditating on it.

3. This Scripture does not say the righteous shall receive a golden ticket to heaven. It does not say the righteous shall say the sinner's prayer. Faith is not a moment, or a day of the week, or a circumstance, or an instance; we are to live an entire life of faith.

4. Faith must permeate all that we say, do, act, and know. When we wake in the morning, we are to know and believe He sustained us for that moment. When we look at our calendars, we are to acknowledge, by faith, that God has ordained every meeting we have that day. We are to recognize by faith that God is the One who holds all things together. As Christians, we are free from the things of the world and must walk by faith in every aspect of our lives.

5. Lastly, we must ask the Lord to give us wisdom in every circumstance. In light of this truth, God's Word also says "whatever does not proceed from faith, is a sin."[472] We are to humbly acknowledge by faith every thought, word, action, and deed and live out fully the life God has set for us. We are not to hide, blame, worry, fear, or doubt. We are to lay aside every weight and sin, which clings so closely to us, and run with endurance the race that is set before each of us while looking to Jesus Christ, the author and perfecter of our faith, who for the joy set before Him endured the cross, despising the shame, and is seated at the right hand of God the Father.[473]

[472]Romans 14:23, [473]Hebrews 12:1–2

Father, thank You for Christ. The weightiness of this verse is impossible to comprehend apart from Your Holy Spirit. Grant me the freedom to walk in the assurance of this. Grant me to live by faith. Strengthen me to endure the race set before me. Guard my heart from anyone and anything that seeks to slander or ridicule me and the beautiful truth of the redemption You have given me through Your Son. Pour out Your joy and open my eyes to see, know, and pursue all You would have for me to serve You for Your Kingdom. In Jesus' name I pray this.

Amen

Psalm 119:36

*INCLINE MY HEART TO YOUR TESTIMONIES,
AND NOT TO SELFISH GAIN!*

1. This verse is a prayer. This is not a working of one's mind to do good; it is a petition to the Lord to incline one's own heart to the testimonies of the Lord.

2. The Lord works this through His grace and mercy. When we think this way, our hearts may shriek in terror at the thought of asking the Lord to incline our hearts, but we must be mindful of who our Father is. Our Father is loving and caring, and His grace is gentle and true. Trust the Lord with your heart and place your heart in His loving hands.

3. This verse reminds us that our hearts are never idle. They are never neutral. If they aren't pursuing the Lord, they are pursuing the world. They raise idols in our hearts and do whatever they need to do to worship something.

4. Apart from the work of the Holy Spirit, every inclination, desire, hope, and dream is left to our carnal flesh. Seek the Lord; trust Him; trust that He knows you better than you know yourself, for He created you. He knows your frame; He remembers you are dust.[474] The Lord knows what you need and when you need it and will work all things perfectly. So trust Him and ask the Lord to incline your heart to Himself and to His Word.

---

[474] Psalm 103:14

Father, You know me completely! You know the inclinations of my heart. You know my self-justification and even my desire to protect myself from ridicule or self-preservation. You know how easily, apart from Your Word, I worry and fear failing, about letting my family down and not being able to provide. This is all an unbelief of Your Word, thinking from a covetous heart and not trusting Your testimonies. Forgive me! Please incline my heart to Your testimonies. Help me to see, recognize, and rest in Your providence, and place Your assurance, by the Holy Spirit, through the redemptive work of Christ Jesus in my heart. In Jesus' name.

Psalm 24:3–4

Who shall ascend the hill of the Lord?
And who shall stand in his holy place?
He who has clean hands and a pure heart,
who does not lift up his soul to what is false
and does not swear deceitfully.

1. What a beautiful—and terrifying—verse. In verses one and two of this same chapter, the psalmist declares all things are the Lord's, and there is nothing that is not from Him. God has not only created it; He has established it.

2. In light of all of this truth: the sovereignty, the glory, the majesty, the power of God, who can stand before Him? Only those with clean hands and a pure heart, who does not lift his soul to what is false and does not swear deceitfully. This is not only beauty but a condemnation, for there is none righteous, no not one.[475]

3. So, as we read this passage we must not end with ourselves. We must humbly bow our heads and hearts to Christ Jesus. For it is by His grace, through faith in His finished work, that we are saved.[476] We are to look to Christ, the author and perfecter of our faith, who for the joy set before Him endured despising the shame and is now seated at the right hand of the throne of God.[477]

4. In this, let us rejoice! We are not to be nihilistic, but we are to lift our heads and hearts in joyful celebration of the finished work of Christ, by the will of the Father! Lift up your heads, O gates! And lift them up, O ancient doors, that the King of glory may come in. Who is this King of glory? The LORD of hosts! He is the King of glory! Selah.[478]

[475]Romans 3:10, [476]Ephesians 2:8, [477]Hebrews 12:2, [478]Psalm 24: 9–10

Father, I am many times so nihilistic in my thinking. I am so small in my joy of all Christ has done. Christ has won the victory for His people and is bringing all who are His to Himself for Your glory! Father, grant me the joy of the reality of Christ in and through my day. Place Your words in my mouth that speak truth to this, in all and in every aspect of my life, for Your glory. Grant me the strength and the mind to relish in the joy of Your salvation. In Jesus' name I ask this.

Psalm 108:12–13

Oh grant us help against the foe, for vain is the salvation of man! With God we shall do valiantly; it is He who will tread down our foes.

1. "Oh grant us help against the foe." What a beautiful and glorious prayer from the psalmist. He knows the Lord is the One who works all things, and it is in God where our hope, our strength, our work rests. In ourselves, we have nothing, and we are vain to think that we can do anything apart from Him.[479]

2. This goes against everything the world, and even our own flesh, says to be true. Sometimes, to cause us to assess our hearts and cry to the Lord for mercy, God will allow us not to feel and see Him for a time. But He is never far, always working, and always drawing His people to Himself.

3. Fear enters our hearts when we look to ourselves instead of to God. Fear sneaks in when we base our reality on what we see with our eyes rather than on Scripture. Fear and unbelief creep in when we begin to listen to the world and the pragmatic calculations of things that haven't even happened. Fear sneaks in when we replace the Word of God with the word of man.

4. Lastly, we are to look at our circumstances and trust it is God who will triumph over them for His glory. We must be mindful to pray, *"Your Kingdom come, Your will be done, on earth as it is in heaven."*[480] The Kingdom of God is not an epic fight against good and evil; the Kingdom of God has been ordained before the foundations of the world,[481] and it is He who is bringing all things together in His perfect time. Not even one of His elect children will ever be left behind. Amen!

[479]John 15:5, [480]Mathew 6:10, [481]Ephesians 2:4

Father, what glorious strength and power and might and majesty are Yours! I am so humbled and convicted. My flesh and unbelief fight against the truth of this daily. Please, Lord, grant me to strive in Your strength, to rest in Your hope, to run by Your grace, and tread down all that will be in Your way, and make Your way straight before me. Please, Lord, grant this for Your glory. In Christ's name I pray this.

Psalm 25:16-18

TURN TO ME AND BE GRACIOUS TO ME, FOR I AM LONELY AND AFFLICTED. THE TROUBLES OF MY HEART ARE ENLARGED; BRING ME OUT OF MY DISTRESSES. CONSIDER MY AFFLICTION AND MY TROUBLE, AND FORGIVE ALL MY SINS.

1. When we are lonely and afflicted, to what or whom do we turn? For instance, if we are lonely and afflicted, do we turn to the Lord, or do we turn to and justify our inward thoughts? If we are lonely and afflicted, do we turn to God, or do we bury our problems in television or the internet? When the Lord brings us through times of loneliness and affliction, do we turn to the Word of God, or do we turn to anything and everything else?

2. God is not only sovereign over the blessings in our lives but also over the trials and difficulties. He is working on us through it all, drawing us toward Him and molding us into the image of His Son. In this truth we can rest, knowing we submit to the sovereign hand of God and lay before Him our burdens and our sorrows.

3. Sin is the reason for burdens and sorrows, trials and tribulations. God is redeeming people for Himself, and He is making all things new in His time.[482] We, as people of God, are to wait by faith, trusting in God's Word, by the power of the Holy Spirit, for the glory of the Father.

4. In this we see Christ. Our hope is in Christ. For, *"He has borne our griefs and carried our sorrows; yet we esteemed him stricken, smitten by God, and afflicted. But he was pierced for our transgressions; he was crushed for our iniquities; upon him was the chastisement that brought us peace, and with his wounds we are healed."*[483] Christ was abandoned and forsaken on the cross by the Father[484] so that in Him, we may have assurance. And regardless of how or what we feel, we may rest assured knowing we are never abandoned, and our Lord and Savior has conquered death and sin.

[482]Revelation 21:5, [483]Isaiah 53:4–5, [484]Matthew 27:46

Father, You are Lord and sovereign over all things. I confess the many times I go through the trials You lead me through and fall into the temptation of making that trial bigger than You. In fact, I almost make an idol of it. Forgive me. Father, lead me not into temptation and fill me with Your truth. Help me to walk in Your way. Help me to have hope and joy in Christ and Christ alone. Thank You for Jesus. In His name I pray.

Amen

Mark 9:24

I BELIEVE; HELP MY UNBELIEF!

1. What a beautiful prayer! In a culture that celebrates the self-made man, there is no more honest prayer and no more righteous plea than going to the Lord and asking Him to help you believe.

2. The sin of unbelief is a vile and cunning sin that permeates the heart and soul. Apart from the grace of God, our hearts and minds forget the promises of God, His redemption, and our hope in Christ, and we begin to believe in what we perceive in ourselves and in the things around us.

3. The unbelief we have in the promises of God dethrones the Lord in our hearts. We seek to make other things our God and our hope,[485] and in doing that, we begin to worship either ourselves or people and things around us we think of as the source of goodness.[486] As this sin blinds us to the glory of God, we more and more take the name of the Lord in vain[487] and worship the created rather than the Creator, who is blessed forever! Amen![488]

4. Let us approach our merciful Father; let us come in the boldness of Christ. Let us ask Him to reveal our unbelief and help us in our time of need, to lead us in His ways, for His glory and our good!

[485]Exodus 20:3, [486]Exodus 20:4, [487]Exodus 20:7, [488]Romans 1:25

Father, I believe; help my unbelief. Open my eyes to those things I do not trust You with, and grant my heart to rest in Your sovereign peace. Take away my unbelief, and in Your goodness, pour Your Spirit into my heart to walk with boldness and assurance in Christ in all and every aspect of life. Thank You, Jesus!

Amen

Psalm 107:28

Then they cried to the Lord in their trouble, and he delivered them from their distress.

1. Psalm 107 repeats this refrain in verses 6, 13, and 19. In each instance, the Lord sent trials and tribulations to bring low the person the psalmist speaks of; then, at the lowest part, they finally cry to the Lord.

2. In each instance, the Lord saves them. There is nothing too great or too difficult that can even come close to keeping the Lord from saving those who call upon His name.

3. Every hardship is to remind us of the psalm's beginning, "Oh give thanks to the LORD, for he is good, for his steadfast love endures forever!"[489]

4. Yet, how easily we forget Him. Our eyes and our aim wander from God's Word and promises, and we focus on His blessings rather than on the One who blesses. We create idols out of His providence. We worship the created rather than the Creator.

5. But also in that moment, God shows His love the brightest! For He could allow us to stumble and to not know Him. He could allow the hardships of this world to overwhelm us. He could keep us comfortable so we do not call aloud to Him, but He doesn't! In His mercy, He directs all things to bring us to a humble dependence on Him and to observe His awesome power!

6. The psalmist ended this prayer with an incredible exhortation, "Whoever is wise, let him attend to these things; let them consider the steadfast love of the LORD."[490] Do not be blind to what the Lord is doing. Take heed in each moment. Humble yourself under the mighty hand of God, and at the proper time He will exalt you and save you from all things.[491]

---

[489]Psalm 107:1, [490]Psalm 107:43, [491]1 Peter 5:6

Father, You hear me every time I call to You. In Christ, I am Yours, and in Christ and Christ alone I am confident You know me. Will You open my eyes, my heart, and my mind to know You? Help me to rejoice in Your blessing and have peace in the trials, knowing You receive all the glory. I praise You for Your sovereignty. Give me wisdom and help me consider Your steadfast love for me.

Amen

Genesis 18:13-14

Is anything too hard for the Lord?

1. What a beautiful question. Is anything too hard for the Lord? How often do we take the burdens of our hearts and ponder them in our minds, feeling the weight of them, staking our identities on them, and never give them over to Christ?

2. Instead of approaching the Lord prayerfully in all aspects of our lives, we approach our lives strategically, never pondering that Christ is and will establish His Kingdom, and not even the gates of hell will prevail against Him![492]

3. We have not, for Christ's Kingdom, because we ask not.[493] We hang Jesus on a felt board and relegate Him to a moralism for life, rather than as the King of kings who sits on the throne of all Creation with all things under His Lordship. This does not mean He will always give us our hearts' desires, for He knows what is best for us. He knows what will lead us from Him. But we can still trust Him with these desires, pray about these desires, and ask Him to direct the desires of our hearts in accordance with His will. Then we can watch the strength and glory and majesty on display for His glory and our good.

[492]Matthew 16:18, [493]James 4:2

Jesus, what does it mean to pray for big things? I confess, I am tempted not to pray for things on my heart because I am tempted to think of them as a part of a "prosperity gospel." Or I am tempted not to believe because of unbelief and nihilism. Forgive me. Lead me to pray for big things for Your glory, and settle my heart to observe Your majesty on display, in whatever way You deem best. For there is nothing too hard for You. Open my eyes to behold Your glory. In Jesus' name.

Amen

Matthew 27:4

"I HAVE SINNED BY BETRAYING INNOCENT BLOOD."
THEY SAID, "WHAT IS THAT TO US? SEE TO IT YOURSELF."

1. By what standard is evil measured? Is it measured against a culture that deems what is right and wrong? Is it measured against feelings and circumstances? Does a culture have a right to deem what is or is not a sin based upon the depraved heart of each individual?

2. Each of these questions is absurd. For there to be sin, there has to be a standard; and for a standard to exist, it must transcend the human answer to any of the above questions. If that standard does not transcend humanity, then it is all subjective desire based upon society's prerogative that can change moment by moment.

3. Sin is sin because it acts against a holy God, not because it hurts someone's feelings. Sin is sin because it breaks the Law of God, not because it defies what someone arbitrarily deems as right or wrong. As the Scriptures say, the Law of God is written on every person's heart, so that man is without excuse.[494] In this passage, Judas feels guilt for betraying the Lord; but instead of going to God, he goes to the Pharisees to ease his conscience. It's not the Pharisees whom he sinned against, but he sinned against God and God alone—and it is God who will judge him.

4. David, in Psalm 51, wrote a beautiful prayer of repentance for the murder of Uriah: "Against you, and you alone, have I sinned."[495] Our sin is always against God and God alone. Christ is both our standard and our aim. He is the One in whom God the Father is well pleased,[496] and it is He who reigns supreme. And it is Christ alone who took the punishment we deserve. Our "standard" became our sacrifice, and He conquered death, making an atonement for those who believe in Him, that we may live not under the judgment of the Law but by the grace and mercy of God.

---

[494]Romans 1:18–20, [495]Psalm 51:4, [496]Matthew 3:17

Father, You are holy and perfect in all Your ways. How easily I fall into denying Your Lordship, denying Your sovereignty, denying even Your existence at times. I apologize many times not to You, but to people, to just keep the peace. I foolishly attempt to appease humanity rather than walk humbly before You. Forgive me, Lord, and help me to walk in a way that glorifies and reflects Your Son Jesus, who paid a debt I could never pay. In Christ's name.

Amen

Mark 1:12-13

The Spirit immediately drove him out into the wilderness. And he was in the wilderness forty days, being tempted by Satan. And he was with the wild animals, and the angels were ministering to him.

1. Neither the devil nor luck, chance, or circumstance drove Jesus into the wilderness. Only the Holy Spirit. We must remember this throughout our trials. God, who is good and perfect, is in ultimate control, and He is the One who leads us through the valley of the shadow of death, for His good and our glory.

2. Jesus' time in the wilderness came immediately after God the Father declared, "You are my beloved Son; with you I am well pleased."[497] Many times, the Lord allows the most tempting situations after a time of blessing to remind us of our dependency on Him and to bring to light the pride and unbelief that consume our hearts.

3. This affirms that Christ knows our temptations. Our Lord and Savior experienced temptation beyond anything we can imagine, so in our trials we can affirm the Hebrew writer's words, "For we do not have a high priest who is unable to sympathize with our weaknesses, but one who in every respect has been tempted as we are, yet without sin. Let us then with confidence draw near to the throne of grace, that we may receive mercy and find grace to help in time of need."[498]

---

[497]Mark 1:11, [498]Hebrews 4:15–16

Father, grant us to know Your Son and the nearness of Him in our weaknesses and temptations. Help us to remember that Christ knows our weaknesses, He sympathizes with us, and He leads us on paths of righteousness for His name's sake and for our good. Forgive us our unbelief that steals our joy and gratitude in the work of the Holy Spirit, and let Your joy abide in us deeply and richly. In Jesus' name.

Amen

Matthew 23:9

And call no man your father on earth, for you have one Father, who is in heaven.

1. When Christ taught His disciples to pray, He taught them to begin with, "Our Father in heaven, hallowed be Your name."[499] The first Person of the Trinity, who has been before all time, and in whom we all have our being,[500] is the same God who intimately loves us and is working all things together for His glory and our good.

2. As He is our Father, we are to trust Him in all things and in all circumstances. There is no person above Him; there is no one He submits to, and there is none who do not do His bidding. He instructs and guides the hearts of kings[501] and is the defender of the poor.[502] In His infinite wisdom, He is both just and merciful.[503]

3. Yet, many times we deny God as our Father and instead worship the created rather than the Creator.[504] We relegate our Heavenly Father to an ideal or a figment of our imagination. We turn those who are in authority over us into idols, rather than looking beyond what we see to Him who is over all things.

4. Let us look to the Father and see the love He has for us. He has lavished upon us, even calling us His children![505] Our Father sent His only Son into the world to pay the price for our sins so that, in turn, we might know Him as our Heavenly Father. Let us meditate on the truth of God as our Father in all circumstances; let us think on the sacrifice paid for this reality, and let us worship Him who is above all and who gives us all things.

---

[499]Matthew 6:9, [500]Acts 17:28, [501]Proverbs 21:1, [502]Psalm 109:31, [503]Psalm 7:11, Psalm 103:8, [504]Romans 1:25, [505]1 John 3:1

Oh Father, I praise You! You have sent Your Son to pay the penalty for my sins. You have exalted Him and given Him victory over death. You have sent Your Holy Spirit to affirm our hearts and to lead us in Your ways. I do not deserve this. There is nothing I have done to warrant this, and I confess the many times when I diminish the truth and the reality of You as my Father. Guard my heart from unbelief, and help me to walk in the reality of You, through Christ as my Father. In Christ's name.

Mark 9:23–24

And Jesus said to him, "If you can! All things are possible for one who believes." Immediately the father of the child cried out and said, "I believe; help my unbelief!"

1. In verse twenty-two, the father of a boy possessed by evil spirits uttered the words to Christ, "If you can do anything...." This man's faith was almost nonexistent, and in his fear and doubt—instead of going to Christ and declaring what Christ could do—he made his request known based upon "if" Christ could do something.

2. How easy it is for the heart to measure its assurance, hope, and confidence not upon Christ but upon the circumstances surrounding us. Our doubt, fear, and unbelief in who Christ is, is what keeps us from observing and trusting in God's perfect plan.[506]

3. Christ's response was to take the father's words of unbelief and show him his error by uttering, "If you can!" Faith and certainty in Christ are what give us boldness to live freely and with hope. Knowing Christ can do all things and resting in His sovereign grace, through faith in Him, is what breathes life, hope, and freedom in all of life, regardless of our circumstances. The trials the Lord ordains are the tests that open our hearts to the reality of our view of God. It forces us to ask, "Is Christ really ruling over all things,[507] or is He a philosophical ideal that is good morally for the greater good?"

4. Faith has no confidence in itself, but in turn measures itself against the One toward whom the faith is pointed. Faith cries out in all its weakness and frailty to the One who is the object of that faith and begs and pleads that it be rooted in the truth of the object of our faith. The boldness and courage we act upon every day are in direct correlation to the One in whom our faith abides.

5. This cannot be done by anything within ourselves but by asking the One who gives us faith[508] to increase our faith, hope, and our view of Him. The daily prayer of the believer is to pray, "I believe; help my unbelief."

[506]Mark 13:58, [507]Hebrews 1:2-3, [508]Romans 12:3

*Father, I believe;
help my unbelief.*

Amen

Zechariah 10:1

Ask rain from the Lord in the season of the spring rain, from the Lord who makes the storm clouds, and he will give them showers of rain, to everyone the vegetation in the field.

1. Do not boast, whine, or brag about what you have done, and don't complain to those around you about what you have not done. But go to God, who is the One who gives all things!

2. God commands us to commit our work to the Lord, and then He promises that He will act[509] in His perfect timing and in His perfect way. We are not to be wise in our own eyes,[510] but to humble ourselves before the Lord and seek Him in the daily providences of our lives.

3. What will He give you, you ask? Exactly what He knows you need. He will give you your daily bread. He will give you that which gives Him the most glory. You can rest in knowing He will never withhold anything that is for your good,[511] so pray. Ask the Lord for your cares and needs, and then wait for the Lord. Be strong, and let your heart take courage, and wait for the Lord.[512]

---

[509]Psalm 37:5, [510]Proverbs 3:7, [511]Psalm 84:11, [512]Psalm 27:14

Father, You are the provider of all things. Yet my heart is so easily deceived in attempting to seek after other gods, other things they appear to provide. My heart's desire is to be more strategic and less faithful in prayer. Forgive me. Make Yourself great in whatever way brings You the most glory, and place Your praise in my mouth for Your glory and Yours alone! In Jesus' name.

1 Samuel 18:14

And David had success in all his undertakings, for the Lord was with him.

1. All that David accomplished was by the grace and power of God. There is no such thing as a self-made man, for everything we have comes from the Lord.[513]

2. The Lord is the One who goes before us. He prepares work for us in advance, for His glory and our good. For we are God's workmanship, created in Christ Jesus for good works, which God prepared beforehand, that we should walk in them.[514]

3. It is the fool who says there is no God.[515] It is the wicked who think in their hearts, "The Lord does not see; the God of Jacob does not perceive."[516] For they deny God's sovereignty and nearness. They harden their hearts and suppress the truth to justify their evil hearts.[517]

4. But for those who love the Lord and are called according to His purpose, we can boldly say we are more than conquerors through Christ Jesus to do His will for His glory and our good.[518] We can trust that nothing can separate us from the love of God in Christ Jesus![519] Our God is good, and His steadfast love endures forever.[520] Though we may go through the valley of the shadow of death, we will not fear that God will be overwhelmed and His goodness will not be diminished. His glory will never be abated, and we in Christ and Christ alone can trust Him as He works all things perfectly for His glory and our good.

---

[513]1 Corinthians 4:7, [514]Ephesians 2:10, [515]Psalm 14:1, [516]Psalm 94:7, [517]Romans 1:18, [518]Romans 8:37, [519]Romans 8:39, [520]Psalm 100:5

Father, Your will is perfect and can never be deterred in its direction and goal. Your aim for all of creation is Your glory, for there is none like You. I confess, Lord, when circumstances in my life become idols and I make them bigger than Your plans and Your will, I am overwhelmed by fear. When I desire more for my comfort rather than Your glory, I become overwhelmed with paralyzing fear and unbelief. Forgive me. Grant me a boldness and courage rooted in the knowledge of who You are and who I am in Christ. Bless the work of my hands and lead me to do Your will. For I praise You, my God and my King. In Christ's name.

Amen

1 Samuel 25:32

And David said to Abigail, "Blessed be the Lord, the God of Israel, who sent you this day to meet me!

1. David and his mighty men were on a mission to destroy the fool Nabal for holding back food and nourishment from them when they sought his kindness. David, when hearing Nabal had sent his men back empty-handed without even a crust of bread, declared that he would kill every male in Nabal's estate by the end of the day.

2. Nabal's wife, Abigail, described as "beautiful and discerning,"[521] heard about her husband's foolishness and rushed to send food to David and his men before they could destroy Nabal. When she met David, Abigail bowed and blessed the Lord, seeking both His and David's mercy.

3. In response, David did not first acknowledge Abigail's wisdom, but he acknowledged the sovereignty of God in using Abigail to stop his advance. Every circumstance we experience must not have a humanistic view but one that honors the Lord. John Newton, the famous hymn writer, once said, "When I hear a knock at my study door, I hear a message from God. It may be a lesson of instruction; perhaps a lesson of patience; but since it is His message, it must be interesting."

4. The call of God's children is not to be people of the world but people of the Word. We are to walk by faith and not by sight.[522] This doesn't mean we only gather on Sunday mornings, or only talk with God in our quiet times, but to know Him in every moment. God's Word tells us the mature believer is to use his power of discernment, trained by constant practice, to distinguish good from evil in every moment of our lives.[523]

---

[521] 1 Samuel 25:3, [522] 2 Corinthians 5:7, [523] Hebrews 5:14

Father, how Your sovereignty and Your rule is over all creation. You are good and holy, and You are orchestrating every moment and detail of our lives. How easily I forget this. Just like David, I many times react violently to Your grace rather than trusting Your sovereignty. I complain, I moan, and I gossip rather than trusting and praising You. Have mercy on me, and soften my heart that I may see You and praise all You do in every moment of my life. In Christ's name I ask this.

1 *Chronicles* 11:9

*And David became greater and greater,
for the Lord of hosts was with him.*

1. David became "greater and greater" not because of himself or anything he did, but because the Lord was with him. David became greater because God was fulfilling His purpose and His plans for David. We must be careful because we can also slip into error by believing greater material possessions are what we receive when we follow God, rather than everything we receive from the Lord is good because He is great.

2. Everything we have, we receive from the Lord, and the Lord will and does fulfill all His purposes for His people. The reason David grew greater and greater is because God is infinitely great. The greatness David received isn't measured for greatness' sake, but is measured because of the greatness of God—and the focus must be on God rather than on the things of the world.

3. So as people of God, we are to focus and learn to be content with where our God has placed us.[524] We must trust the Lord and know He will keep nothing from us that is for our good.[525] So our aim is God, our hope is in God, our trust is in God, and our peace is in God and His goodness. As God's people, we trust that in His goodness we are who we are and have received what we have because of His goodness, and we give thanks in the circumstances, knowing He is bringing us and conforming us to the image of His Son, purposefully and intentionally in the moments of today.

---

[524]Philippians 4:11, [525]Psalm 84:11

Father, You are so good in every way. In all circumstances You are good. In the trials You bring us through, Your goodness leads us and guides us and is purposefully and intentionally working in every moment of our lives. I confess the many times I have diminished Your goodness in my life based upon how I felt or what I experienced, but I have seen and recognized this is because I have made idols of Your blessings. Forgive me. Make my heart to rest in who You are. Root out of my heart the idols I find satisfaction in other than You, and may Christ be exalted. In His name I pray.

Amen

Psalm 57:2

I CRY OUT TO GOD MOST HIGH,
TO GOD WHO FULFILLS HIS PURPOSE FOR ME.

1. We are to go to the Lord with all the cares and desires, concerns and emotions of our hearts. To Him all things belong. He knows our thoughts and feelings and knows the purpose behind every one of them.

2. He is "God Most High," and we can know with certainty that He is not caught in the mundane or in the moment by moment, for He reigns above all. He is high and lifted up!

3. We are to do this not as an attempt to coerce something from Him but because God is fulfilling His purpose for His people in every moment of every day. He knows the reasons and the direction in which He is leading His people.

4. We are to entrust the Lord with the deepest desires of our hearts, knowing that our lives are not meaningless in Christ, and there is no such thing as luck, chance, or circumstance. We have a king seated on the throne of grace who is intentionally and purposefully orchestrating all things for His purpose and our good.

5. All of our aim, all of our focus should be to reflect God's Son when He said in the garden before His crucifixion, "Yet not my will but Yours be done."[526]

---

[526]Luke 22:42

Father, You are sovereign over all things! You are purposeful with every aspect of each of our lives. There is nothing outside of Your purposes. You can never be thwarted, never be deterred, never be changed. In You, my life is defined by Your grace. In You, my heart rejoices and is glad; in You, I have the light of life and am satisfied. Please open my eyes and soften my heart to rest in You. In Christ's name.

Amen

Psalm 52:7

"See the man who would not make God his refuge, but trusted in the abundance of his riches and sought refuge in his own destruction!"

1. We must be mindful of where we place our confidence and our boasting. The heart of man is desperately wicked, and there is none who can understand it.[527] Those who are not of God do not place their confidence in God but in what they see, what they perceive, what they touch. The hearts of many so desire to be like God that they boast in what is created rather than the Creator.

2. The fear of the Lord is the beginning of wisdom.[528] This is where we must start and end. All things point to the providence of God, and we must rest in His sovereign grace. The moment our confidence is in what we see rather than in who God is, we have sinned against the Most High God.

3. To trust in anyone or anything else is to pursue something that in the end will lead to our destruction. Hope in anything other than Christ and Christ alone will fail in every aspect of our actions. We must seek the Lord, call upon His name, wait for Him, and trust—by grace through faith—that He is bringing all things together in His perfect timing. Our aim must be God; our goal must be God; our hope must be God; our joy must be God. Anything other than God is an idol and thus a stumbling block and will lead to our inevitable destruction.

---

[527]Jeremiah 17:9, [528]Proverbs 1:7

Father, You are God. How easily I forget that You are God and are over all things. I make my god from numbers and data and finances and circumstances rather than acknowledging You as my God. I many times seek outcomes rather than seeking You. I am tempted to think of You as far away rather than close by, working in my life intimately. Forgive me. Grant me hope and peace in who You are. Strengthen me and lead me in Your way. Make my heart to know You are near, that I may rejoice in Your salvation. Guard my heart from idolatry and from those things that would tempt me from You. I ask this in Christ's name.

Proverbs 24:12

*If you say, "Behold, we did not know this,"
does not he who weighs the heart perceive it?
Does not he who keeps watch over your soul know it,
and will he not repay man according to his work?*

1. We do everything before a holy and omniscient God. God knows all things, sees all things, orchestrates all things, and in Him we live and move and have our being.[529] In this truth we should approach all of life, for our eyes should never be on ourselves but on who God is, for it is God who looks at our souls and will repay us according to how we act before Him.

2. In each and every moment in this, then, we are not to look at the circumstances before us and weigh them according to what we perceive about ourselves, but on who God is. The reason this is true is because every moment we encounter is purposefully and intentionally ordained by God for our good and His glory. Thus, we are accountable before the Lord in every moment.

3. The people of God are called to be salt and light in a world of darkness. We are called in every situation to work and strive in such a way that others may see our good works and praise our Father, who is in heaven.[530] The Kingdom of God is made manifest by the people of God on earth as we strive for His glory in all that we do. Our hearts and minds are reformed by the power of God through the work of the Holy Spirit, and we are called to be ever reforming in this world by the power of God.

4. So let us guard ourselves from laziness and from looking to the world. Instead, let us pray in every circumstance that it not be our will, but the Lord's will that is done,[531] trusting that God's Kingdom come and His will be done on earth as it is in heaven.[532]

---

[529]Acts 17:28, [530]Matthew 5:13–16, [531]Luke 22:42, [532]Matthew 6:10

Father, You ordain all things, and in You we live and move and have our being. I confess the many times unbelief tempts my mind to minimize Your sovereignty over all things. I rest in my own strength rather than in Yours. Forgive me and open my eyes and my heart to seek You and to reflect Your Kingdom by the power of the Holy Spirit and to the glory of Christ. Thank You for saving me. In Christ's name.

Proverbs 28:4

THOSE WHO FORSAKE THE LAW PRAISE THE WICKED,
BUT THOSE WHO KEEP THE LAW STRIVE AGAINST THEM.

1. Law is neither a human construct nor something that evolved from the need or necessity of organization and structure. We know this to be true because law is based upon and reflective of absolute truth, and absolute truth is not based upon human experience but comes from outside humanity. The Law was spoken by the voice of God on Mount Sinai[533] and given to Moses, that we may know God and His holiness.

2. The Law shows us the holiness of God and our need for His grace. For the Law of God does not cause us to sin, but in turn shows us the sin and depravity of our hearts. If we do not know the Law of God, then we do not know the truth of who God is and who we are. For it is just as Paul writes in Romans, that if it had not been written that we are not to covet, we would not know that covetousness is sin![534] This does not mean the Law caused us to sin, but because the Law is holy and righteous and good, it in turn reveals our depravity and need for a Savior before a Holy God![535]

3. The wicked, though, strive with everything in their hearts and minds to deny the Law of God. They suppress the truth in unrighteousness[536] and deny the living God. Isaiah writes that God curses them, saying, "Woe to those who call evil good and good evil, who put darkness for light and light for darkness, who put bitter for sweet and sweet for bitter!"[537] The more we deny the Law of God, the more foolish and wicked we become.

4. But the righteous delight in the Law of the Lord, and on His Law they meditate day and night! They are like a tree planted by streams of water that yields fruit in season, and everything they do prospers.[538]

---

[533]Exodus 20:1, [534]Romans 7:7, [535]Romans 7:12, [536]Romans 1:18, [537]Isaiah 5:20, [538]Psalm 1:2–3

Father, thank You for Your Law, for it is holy and righteous and good. I confess I have not meditated on Your Law as I should, and at times I have run from it. In my pride, I created my own law and my own rules, rather than looking to Christ. Forgive me and have mercy on me. Soften my heart and pour into it a longing to know Your Law that I may seek You, repent, and turn and follow Christ in all things. I ask this in Christ's name.

John 11:4

*But when Jesus heard it he said,
"This illness does not lead to death.
It is for the glory of God, so that
the Son of God may be glorified through it."*

1. What we see is but a glimpse of what the Lord sees. There is nothing cosmic that ever moves God or takes Him by surprise, and all things are for His glory.

2. For the believer, this is where his confidence resides—not in what he sees, but his trust is in the One who sees and knows and directs all things for His glory.

3. We are frail and are nothing in comparison to the glory of God, and God has given those whom He loves confidence in Himself.

4. We are to look to Christ. We are to trust in Christ and cast our burdens at the foot of the cross. We are to repent and walk in accordance with His will.

Father, You use and make all things for Your glory. What a fleeting thought that is so easy to say and yet so hard to remember. My pride and my selfishness make me want to even fear at times rather than trusting in You. My flesh actually tempts me and causes me to desire to be fearful because it measures things against the world rather than against Your Word. Help me to see, and walk, and to know You, to stand firm in You. In Jesus' name.

John 6:28–29

Then they said to him, "What must we do, to be doing the works of God?" Jesus answered them, "This is the work of God, that you believe in him whom he has sent."

1. What is the work I am to do for God? There is only one answer: "That you believe in him whom he has sent."[539]

2. But how do I say this and mean it? Only by the grace of God! This is not an intellectual exercise but a fundamental shift in our thinking.

3. This cannot be done by human ingenuity but can only be done by the grace of God.

4. How can I do the work of God that can only be done by a work of God? Jesus flipped it back to a high view of God.

---

[539] John 6:29

Father, I praise You, for You are good and mighty. I cannot ascend into heaven on my thoughts; I can only rest on the finished work of Christ and Christ alone. Holy Spirit, help me to walk in this truth. I can do nothing apart from You. I flounder and I collapse; please help me, strengthen me, empower me, encourage me to do Your will. In Jesus' name.

Mark 2:17

And when Jesus heard it, he said to them, "Those who are well have no need of a physician, but those who are sick. I came not to call the righteous, but sinners."

1. Jesus Christ came for one reason and one reason only: to save sinners from the wrath of God.

2. The most terrifying thing anyone can think is that they are not a sinner. In the mindset of today's culture, we begin by presupposing we are good people. We believe we are good people who mess up sometimes, rather than realizing there is no good in us. "The heart is deceitful above all things, and desperately sick; who can understand it?"[540] To the extent that we think there is a little bit of righteousness in us, and that what we read in Romans, "There is no one that is righteous, no not one,"[541] is just hyperbole, then we will not see or understand our depravity.

3. Christ died to pay the penalty for our sin, but that does not mean we are not sinners needing to daily depend on Christ. It is Christ in us. He is our hope—not ourselves—and apart from Christ we can do nothing.[542]

4. Lastly, our dependency on Christ never ceases. We are all to come to Him. All who, by the power of the Holy Spirit, realize we are heavy laden and labor with the knowledge that we cannot be good apart from Christ, are to go to Him, and He has promised to give us rest in Him.[543]

---

[540]Jeremiah 17:9, [541]Romans 3:23, [542]John 15:5, [543]Matthew 11:28

Father, thank You for Christ. I confess the many times I am tempted and fail because I believe I can do anything apart from Christ's righteousness. I tend to compare myself against the world rather than against Your Word. I tend to read Your Word rather than let Your Word read me, which leads to repentance. Please help me to see, know, and rest in the sufficiency of Christ in all things. Thank You, Father. In Jesus' name.

Romans 14:12

So then each of us will give an account of himself to God.

1. No neutral action comes from the heart of man. Every action of ours either glorifies God or glorifies man and will be held accountable when we stand before Christ.

2. The carnal mind does whatever it can to suppress the truth[544] and deceive itself. We continually blame and accuse others for how we act. We gossip among each other, pointing out the reasons and purposes of our hearts, justifying our actions based upon our circumstances rather than trusting in the Lord. The heart tends to scream, "Did God really say He was sovereign over all?" and "Your situation is unique, so you deserve to think and act differently because of your experience."

3. This is a lie. There is no circumstance, situation, or experience that can justify the believer before a holy God. The Lord has given us His word and has placed before us His commands and precepts, His promises and testimonies so that men are without excuse.[545] When we stand before Christ, we will hear one of two things as we give an account. We will either hear, "Well done, good and faithful servant."[546] Or we will hear, "I never knew you; depart from me, you workers of lawlessness."[547]

4. So let us turn to Christ, plead for His mercy, and call upon His name. Let us trust the Word of the Lord and let us fall on the finished work of Christ, "for all who call upon the name of the Lord will be saved!"[548] We are to "look to Jesus, the founder and perfecter of our faith, who for the joy that was set before him endured the cross, despising the shame, and is seated at the right hand of the throne of God"[549] and trust Him as we stand before our God.

---

[544]Romans 1:18, [545]Romans 1:20, [546]Matthew 25:23, [547]Matthew 7:23, [548]Romans 10:13, [549]Hebrews 12:2

Father, it is terrifying to stand before a holy God. So many circumstances I have thrown before You to justify my thoughts, words, actions, and deeds, and yet none of them justify my sin. Sin can only be justified in one way, and that is in the sacrifice of Your Son, who You sent to pay the price for my sin. Who am I? Thank You for Christ and for sending Your Holy Spirit to strengthen and lead me according to Your will—for His glory and my good. In Christ's name.

1 Thessalonians 2:4

But just as we have been approved by God to be entrusted with the gospel, so we speak, not to please man, but to please God who tests our hearts.

1. One of the greatest sins our hearts can deceive us into committing is the sin of man-pleasing. This sin is a subtle lie that causes our hearts to pridefully yearn for recognition from others and to puff ourselves up. We begin to measure our worth not in the finished work of Christ but instead upon the praise of man.

2. For believers, our lives are not our own; we were bought with a price, and all we are to do is live for the glory of God.[550] Our lives are to be lived for the glory of God, to please God, and to seek His Kingdom. For we have died to this world, and our lives are now hidden with Christ in God![551]

3. As we walk in the Lord, we are not to measure our circumstances according to what we see, but according to God's Word. This does lead to persecution and hardship, but these are blessed gifts from the Lord to test us and draw us to Himself. For Christ said, "Blessed are you when others revile you and persecute you and utter all kinds of evil against you falsely on my account. Rejoice and be glad, for your reward is great in heaven, for so they persecuted the prophets who were before you."[552]

4. So, every moment of our lives is ordained by God as an opportunity to walk by faith according to the Word of our God, or contrarily, to walk according to the world. Each moment is a test from the Lord to either please God or please man. As we walk by faith and not by sight, let us keep our eyes on Christ, "the founder and perfecter of our faith, who for the joy that was set before him endured the cross, despising the shame, and is seated at the right hand of the throne of God."[553]

---

[550]1 Corinthians 6:19–20, [551]Colossians 3:3, [552]Matthew 5:11–12, [553]Hebrews 12:2

Father, how easy it is to desire to please man rather than to seek Your glory. So many times I fear what others think of me rather than walking in the fear of the Lord. Forgive me, and strengthen me to do Your will. Guard my heart from the temptation of this world, and open my eyes to see Your Kingdom. In Christ's name.

Philippians 3:13–14

Brothers, I do not consider that I have made it my own. But one thing I do: forgetting what lies behind and straining forward to what lies ahead, I press on toward the goal for the prize of the upward call of God in Christ Jesus.

1. Our identity is not in our past or our circumstances but in Christ. When we look behind us, we are to see Christ, and as we press forward, we are to do so to know Christ and to be with Him.

2. To the extent that we define ourselves by our circumstances, we will diminish the sovereignty and love of God. For it is God who leads us; it is God who directs us; it is God who knows every word on our tongues before they leave our mouths.

3. This is an act of faith in the Person of Christ and promises of God. This is a look toward Christ, trusting Him in all things, and defining ourselves based upon nothing other than Christ.

4. This way is opposite of the world's way. Those who do not know Christ define themselves by their emotions, circumstances, happiness, and disappointments. The unbeliever has no alternative except to fear man and to fear past choices, for there is no one good who is Lord over all. Their self-lordship drives fear into their hearts.

5. But the mature believer looks to Christ, depends upon Christ, defines all of life in Christ, holds fast to Christ, seeks Christ, and places all their hope in Christ, holding fast to the finished work of Christ, as His own.

Father, You have sent Your Son into the world to save Your people. How glorious! Lord, help me to focus and to know and act in accordance with the truth of Jesus. Help me to fall more deeply in love, more bold, and more confident in who Christ is. Give me strength to press forward to what lies ahead, that I may reach the prize of knowing Christ. In Jesus' name.

Joshua 14:12

So now give me this hill country of which the Lord spoke on that day, for you heard on that day how the Anakim were there, with great fortified cities. It may be that the Lord will be with me, and I shall drive them out just as the Lord said.

1. We must never presuppose the outcome of God's promises but fully walk according to them. Caleb, at eighty years old, did not fear the size of the giants and the cities he faced, for he saw them in light of the assuredness of the promises of God.

2. We must repent of any circumstance that takes away from or makes us distrust the promises of God. We are to go to the Lord, confess our fear and unbelief, and ask Him to send His Holy Spirit to strengthen our hearts according to His Word!

3. The promises of God do not guarantee outcomes based upon our desires, but they assure us of who God is. We are not to fear, for there is nothing that can defeat God—and He is with us.[554] We aren't to worry about money because He has promised to never leave us nor forsake us.[555] He has promised that if we draw near to Him, He will draw near to us.[556] If we ask the Lord for wisdom, for His glory He will give us that wisdom.[557] We are to live courageously in the circumstances the Lord places before us, for He is with us.[558]

4. Caleb did not know what the Lord would do and said, "It may be that the Lord will be with me." In the same way, we are to look at all circumstances and situations in our lives through the promises of God and trust that whatever the Lord ordains is right for His glory and my good.

---

[554]Isaiah 41:10, [555]Hebrews 13:5, [556]James 4:8, [557]James 1:5, [558]Joshua 1:9

Father, thank You for Your promises. Thank You for Your Word! Your Word is true! I confess the many times I have presupposed in my own circumstances my adequacy or inadequacy without even coming to You. Forgive me. Please send Your Holy Spirit and grant my heart to relish and thrive on Your Word and Your promises. Grant that I live a life that honors and magnifies Your Word and Your truth for Christ's sake! In His name and for His glory I ask this.

Joshua 14:10–11

And now, behold, the Lord has kept me alive, just as he said, these forty-five years since the time that the Lord spoke this word to Moses, while Israel walked in the wilderness. And now, behold, I am this day eighty-five years old. I am still as strong today as I was in the day that Moses sent me; my strength now is as my strength was then, for war and for going and coming.

1. The promises of God are sure and true, and they are not bound by age. Caleb, who went into the promised land at the age of forty, still clung to and boldly lived his life in light of those promises at the age of eighty-five.

2. We are never to take our experiences in life and use them as a reason or excuse to live contrary or beneath the promises of God. We must go forward under the certainty of God's promises for His will and His Kingdom.

3. The Lord does not heed age but works according to His Word. Look at Abraham, who had a son at the age of ninety-nine. Moses led the people of Israel out of Egypt at the age of eighty, and Joshua began to lead the people of Israel also at the age of eighty. Daniel was thrown into the lion's den at the age of eighty.

4. Remember, it is not our circumstances that have brought us to these places at this time, but the sovereign hand of God. He ordains all things, orchestrates all things, and uses all things for His glory and our good.

Father, You perfectly ordain all things in Your timing. There is nothing that deviates, speeds up, or changes Your time. Forgive me for so often pridefully shaking my fist at You in the timing of Your providence. I have doubted You so many times and have felt like a failure in my lack of accomplishments, but You are perfectly working together all things. Grant me wisdom and discernment to walk by Your strength, according to Your Word, to do Your will in Your Kingdom and for Your glory. In Jesus' name.

Psalm 29:1-2

Ascribe to the LORD, O heavenly beings,
ascribe to the LORD glory and strength.
Ascribe to the LORD the glory due his name;
worship the LORD in the splendor of holiness.

1. The word *ascribe* is defined as giving. We give accolades and credit to many things in this world, but very rarely apart from God's grace do we desire to give credit to that which is Ultimate.

2. Our hearts and minds only go so far as to what we see rather than what is objectively true. For we see the sun rise in the east and set in the west, and ascribe this to science, but fail to see past it and recognize that the only reason that the sun rises and sets is because the Lord has made a covenant to do so.[559]

3. We ascribe to a king or a leader the choices he makes in instructing his people, yet we must see that the Lord is the One who directs the heart of that king like a stream of water, to turn it wherever He wills.[560]

4. We must seek the Lord and first repent of our unbelief and our practical atheism that so easily permeates our hearts and minds, and ask the Lord to open our eyes that we may see the world through the truth of Holy Scripture and ascribe to Him the glory due His name![561]

---

[559]Jeremiah 33:20–21, [560]Proverbs 21:1, [561]Psalm 119:18

Father, You sit enthroned in the heavens and You do whatever You please! Yet, Lord, my eyes are ever dim toward Your glory, and my mind is closed to the truth of who You are apart from Your grace and mercy. I confess that in my heart and mind I have not had a spirit of thankfulness but instead a heart of unbelief. Many times I walk by sight rather than by faith in Your Word. Forgive me. Soften my heart, and fill it with thankfulness that I may ascribe to You all things. That I may boldly proclaim the truth and the reality of Your sovereign grace. I ask this in the name of Jesus Christ.

Luke 14:11

For everyone who exalts himself will be humbled, and he who humbles himself will be exalted.

1. Our hearts are constantly tempted by the idea of the "self-made man," which is a deceitful and deceptive lie to our sinful hearts. The status of a man, the power of a man, the influence of a man are all given by God, and He uses all things for His glory.

2. The Lord is the One who gives and He takes away; the name of the Lord be praised![562] We aren't to think too highly of ourselves,[563] but in all things, humble ourselves before the Lord.

3. The idols of our hearts' desire and yearn for acknowledgment and praise rather than doing our Lord's will in every aspect of our lives. Let us joyously submit to our God, trusting that whatever He does is right. Let us, "present [our] bodies as a living sacrifice, holy and acceptable to God, which is your spiritual worship. Do not be conformed to this world, but be transformed by the renewal of your mind, that by testing you may discern what is the will of God, what is good and acceptable and perfect."[564]

[562]Job 1:21, [563]Romans 12:3, [564]Romans 12:1–2

Father, You are the One who is glorious; You are radiant in all Your ways! I confess that I have pridefully attempted to build my own life and to do my own will, and You have shown me that in all things You are God, and I am not. Forgive me. Lead me for Your glory. Guard my heart against selfish ambition and ignite my heart to do Your will. In Christ's name I pray.

Luke 21:36

BUT STAY AWAKE AT ALL TIMES, PRAYING THAT YOU MAY HAVE STRENGTH TO ESCAPE ALL THESE THINGS THAT ARE GOING TO TAKE PLACE, AND TO STAND BEFORE THE SON OF MAN.

1. The things of God require the strength of God, and cannot be done by human intuition, strength, will, or assertion. For the Lord is God, and He does whatever He pleases,[565] and we are to be strong in the Lord and in the strength of His might.[566]

2. We are to never in our pride go to the Lord and tell Him what we can and cannot do. We are to never take our likes and dislikes, our presuppositions and tell God we are unable to do His will. For Christ is King, and we are to take His yoke upon ourselves. For His yoke is easy and His burden is light.[567]

3. So we are to seek the Lord with all of our hearts and not lean on our own understanding. As we seek Him, we are to also ask for His strength to do His will, and the Lord will go before us. It is only when we take our eyes off Him and place them upon ourselves that we begin to sink into the depths of our lives in the same way Peter did when our Lord called Him upon the sea.

4. So let us stay awake and look to Christ with a clear mind, asking Him to do His will and to give us wisdom to discern His will. Then let us beg the Lord for His strength and press forward in it. Let us not ask idly with a mind of unbelief, but let us ask boldly in Christ, pressing onward for His glory and our good.

---

[565]Psalm 115:3, [566]Ephesians 6:10, [567]Matthew 11:30

Oh Father, who is mighty like You? Who holds the heavens and the earth and establishes the sun and the moon? For You are God and I am not. Father, I confess that with many things, I look at my circumstances and my life and deem the tasks before me too hard to complete. Then I harden my heart and I do not seek You as I ought, instead denying Your Lordship on the account of my humanity. Forgive me! Strengthen me and refresh me with Your life, Your strength, and Your assurance, to do Your will—boldly and without apology. O God, be my God, in Christ's precious name I ask this.

Psalm 16:4

THE SORROWS OF THOSE WHO RUN AFTER ANOTHER GOD SHALL MULTIPLY; THEIR DRINK OFFERINGS OF BLOOD I WILL NOT POUR OUT OR TAKE THEIR NAMES ON MY LIPS.

1. Idolatry permeates all aspects of our hearts and minds. Idols are what define us that we cling to apart from the truth of who God is and all He does for His glory and our good.

2. We are so prone to wander and to take the goodness of God and ascribe our identity only in the blessings rather than ascribing to God all things.[568]

3. Our default is to find our identity in our finances and things we can purchase. We desire to find our identity in our spouses and in the beauty of marriage. We based our hope on our children and what they accomplish in life. We place our hope in the emotions we feel and seek to do whatever we can to cling to a feeling rather than in the Person of Christ.

4. Everything we cling to that is not Christ multiplies our sorrows. All that we cling to apart from Christ will fail us. Secondly, as we cling to God's blessing rather than to God Himself, the Lord removes His grace and mercy from us. In fact, He ceases to know us and instead hands us over to our idols, and Christ does not even take our names on His lips before the throne of grace.

---

[568] Psalm 29

Father, You are God! I have made my identity in so many idols rather than in You. I have determined my identity based upon what the world deems to be good rather than in You! Please forgive me and change my heart. Bring my heart to know You, to worship You, to trust You, to pursue You, to cling to You, and to rejoice in Your salvation. Draw near to me, God, and know me. In Christ's name.

Psalm 16:2

I say to the LORD, "You are my Lord;
I have no good apart from you."

1. All that is good comes from the Lord, and He does not keep from us anything that is for our good.[569]

2. This does not mean that all we go through is easy or pleasant, but God is always working together all things for our good and His glory.[570] We must be mindful of our definition of good. Is it a feeling, an emotion, or is good a Person? For even Christ said, "Only God is good."[571]

3. The Lord knows us. He knows our frame and remembers that we are but dust.[572] The goodness and lovingkindness of the Lord disciplines those He loves and brings us to a saving knowledge of Himself.[573]

4. Let us not define ourselves by our circumstances or emotions; let us be mindful of that which we use to attempt to define ourselves. The Lordship of Christ is over all things; this is a truth that, as the people of God, we hold by faith. Christ is good and He is ordering all things together as He builds His Kingdom for His people. Let our souls rest in the sovereign grace of our good God, recognizing that we have nothing good apart from Him and that He is bringing all things under His sovereign rule.[574]

---

[569]Psalm 84:11, [570]Romans 8:28, [571]Matthew 19:17, [572]Proverbs 103:14, [573]Hebrews 12:6, [574]1 Corinthians 15:27

Father, You are good. I realize that in the midst of a secular culture, I have defined good by the times rather than by Your Word. I have redefined goodness based on my experiences rather than in Christ. I have looked at goodness practically, rather than objectively in the Person of Christ. Forgive me. Help me to know what true goodness is, objective goodness, that I may worship You and adore You all of my days. In Christ's blessed name I ask this.

Joshua 23:3

AND YOU HAVE SEEN ALL THAT THE LORD YOUR GOD HAS DONE TO ALL THESE NATIONS FOR YOUR SAKE, FOR IT IS THE LORD YOUR GOD WHO HAS FOUGHT FOR YOU.

1. All that we have comes from the hand of God, for it is from His hand that all blessings come, and it is from the hand of the Lord that we have anything at all.[575]

2. In this truth we have no boasting; we have nothing to give to God except our praise, our worship, our everything. For everything is from Him, and through Him, and to Him, to Him be the glory forever and ever! Amen.[576]

3. Yet our hearts so easily want to grab a hold of every opportunity to steal glory from our God. Our flesh longs for acknowledgment of things we have been allowed to do, or recognition for achievements made, but this is taking the very thing of God and making it an idol.

4. It is the Lord who gives and the Lord who takes away, yet in both the name of the Lord is to be praised.[577] "In the day of prosperity be joyful, and in the day of adversity consider: God has made the one as well as the other, so that man may not find out anything that will be after him."[578]

5. We must guard our hearts against vanity, humble ourselves before the Lord, and rest in His sovereign grace. We must seek the Lord while He may be found, and call upon Him while He is near,[579] trusting that it is the Lord who fights for us; it is the Lord who does all things, and we are to worship Him alone.

---

[575] 1 Corinthians 4:7, [576] Romans 11:36, [577] Job 1:21, [578] Ecclesiastes 7:14, [579] Isaiah 55:6

Father, it is by Your strength,
Your sovereignty, Your goodness,
and Your might that all things occur.
Who am I that I can do anything?
I deceive myself in my actions that I am
autonomous from Your grace, and then
when You remove that, I see that I have
erected an idol. Forgive me and have
mercy on me. Help my heart to rest in
humble worship of who You are.
Make me to know Your grace, by Your
grace and mercy. In Christ's name.

Mark 12:24

Jesus said to them, "Is this not the reason you are wrong, because you know neither the Scriptures nor the power of God?"

1. Strength is knowing the promises of God and obeying His Word, regardless of what others think, say, or do. To believe anything else is the sin of unbelief. We know this to be true because this is what our Lord declares.

2. The Word of the Lord is true.[580] What freedom, what hope, what joy, what glory! Christ, when He reasoned with the Sadducees and Pharisees, did not reason with man-made arguments. He only lived and spoke the Word of God. He trusted His Father, whose power is evident. For the power of God conquered death, and nothing can hold Him back.

3. We often attempt to rationalize our thoughts, feelings, and emotions based upon our circumstances rather than acknowledging who God is—and who we are in view of our relationship with Him. Let us humbly repent and submit ourselves to the Word of God, which is the power of God, even unto salvation.

---

[580] John 17:17

Father, Your Word is true. Many times I reason from my sinful flesh, rather than trusting and hoping in Your Word. Many times, I pridefully believe the nihilistic words of the world, rather than hoping in what is before me! Help me to walk in accordance with Your Word. Grant me the strength and faith to joyfully pursue and trust in You, by grace through faith.

Genesis 31:3

Then the LORD said to Jacob, "Return to the land of your fathers and to your kindred, and I will be with you."

1. God's Word spoke to Jacob while he was working for Laban. When God's Word speaks to us, we must act—immediately and without question. The Holy Spirit speaks through the Word of God and convicts us, assures us, and leads us according to the will of God, and we must pursue and walk in the promises of God and trust His Word.

2. With every command the Lord gives us comes a promise. Even in the command God gave Jacob to leave, He immediately followed with the promise that He would be with Him. What hope! What beauty!

3. The more we follow the Word of the Lord, the more we will know God. God commanded Jacob to leave, and promised Himself in return. He has promised that if Jacob leaves what is familiar, God Himself will be with him.

4. What things do our lives and souls cling to that tempt us not to let go of them to follow the Lord?[581] What of our actions go against the very Word of God, as we deny listening to His command and promises because we do not trust the faithfulness of the Lord? Do we act, or do we argue? Do we pursue the Lord, or do we justify our actions? Do we live our lives fearing the Lord, or fearing man?

5. Let us look to Christ, who, for the joy set before Him, endured the cross, despised the shame, and who is now seated at the right hand of God![582] The very Word of God[583] humbled Himself, becoming obedient to the command of God to the point of death, even death on a cross,[584] for the Father's glory and for our good. Let us look to Christ, trust His promises, and walk by faith according to His Word.

---

[581]Hebrews 12:1, [582]Hebrews 12:2, [583]John 1:1, [584]Philippians 2:8

Father, what things do I hold on to that I trust more than I trust You? What things have stopped up my ears, rather than drawing me to Your Word? Your Word is so precious to me. By Your mercy, open my eyes to do Your will, and grant me the strength and the joy to follow You all the days of my life. In Jesus' name.

Amen

Genesis 28:3-4

God Almighty bless you and make you fruitful and multiply you, that you may become a company of peoples. May he give the blessing of Abraham to you and to your offspring with you, that you may take possession of the land of your sojournings that God gave to Abraham!

1. Notice the centrality of God in this blessing Isaac gives to his son Jacob. The blessing is about the greatness of God. He first states God's blessings on Jacob, followed by the Lord making Jacob fruitful and multiplying his family. The blessing continues from Abraham and down through all of Jacob's life, finally passing on to Jacob the land the Lord gave Abraham.

2. This is totally opposite of our hearts. Our hearts want the glory. We—instead of asking the Lord to grant us strength, wisdom, and discernment—instead of asking the Lord to grant us joy, peace, hope, and to bless the work of our hands for His glory—we instead want to be the self-made man. We make idols of ourselves, and then tell God what we can and cannot do based upon our personality profiles.

3. What foolishness and stupidity! Instead of going to the Lord and proclaiming, "Your Kingdom come, Your will be done, on earth as it is in heaven,"[385] we tell God what our kingdom is like and demand that He make it our way. This demand is judgment against our very souls. It denies the perfection of God and demands that He submit Himself to our will.

4. Let us stop and look to the Lord. Let us ask that He grant us wisdom, strength, and the joy of the Lord for our strength,[386] and seek His will. Let us ask Him for His grace to fulfill what He has ordained for our day, and to meditate on the truth of His Word, for His glory and our good.

---

[385]Matthew 6:10, [386]Nehemiah 8:10

Oh Father, You are great and glorious, and You work all things in accordance with Your will, for You do whatever You please.[587] I confess the many times I have looked at situations in my life and attempted to build myself up, or I have shrunk under the immensity of the situation, and have not come to You. Forgive me. You are so gracious and merciful. Grant me a heart that desires and seeks You. Do not forsake the work of Your hands, and strengthen me to accomplish all that You have for me today. Lastly, please grant me to see Your glory in the fantastical and the mundane, that I may praise You, my God and my King.

[587]Psalm 115:3

Genesis 37:1

AND HIS [JOSEPH'S] BROTHERS WERE JEALOUS OF HIM,
BUT HIS FATHER KEPT THE SAYING IN MIND.

1. We must not make too much of the events that go on in our lives, but we must not make too little of them either. The Lord ordains all things, and there is nothing that occurs outside of His sovereign grace.

2. In this we must be mindful of all things. Some make sense in the moment; others do not. But all things happen for the Lord's glory.

3. Let us then guard our hearts and minds from mindlessness and the distractions of the world that so easily captivate our hearts. From the lies that tempt us to think our God is deistic, or that such things as luck, chance, or circumstance even exist. God is always at work, working all things for good for those who love Him and are called according to His purpose.[588]

4. Jacob hid these things in his heart and mind and recalled them later when the Lord brought Joseph to power in Egypt.[589] We also see this with Mary as well, when she treasured up all the Lord had told her pertaining to her son—our Lord and Savior, Jesus Christ.[590]

---

[588]Romans 8:28, [589]Genesis 41, [590]Luke 2:51

Father, You are always at work, and You are always working things in accordance with Your will. Many times I have not been mindful of You. I have not stopped and pondered what You are doing, and I have filled my mind with practical, atheistic thoughts. Lord, grant that I would have a mind of watching You work in every detail. Guard my heart from a low view of Your sovereignty and also from a mystical and prideful view of Your work. Make my heart rest in Your sovereign grace, and place in my heart a song that praises You in all circumstances.

Amen

Genesis 39:9

How then can I do this great wickedness and sin against God?

1. Joseph is approached by Potiphar's wife, who tempts him to sleep with her. The Lord has blessed Joseph in every way pertaining to his work,[591] and everything in Potiphar's house is under Joseph's authority. Potiphar's wife recognizes this and also sees that Joseph is handsome[592] and so desires him.

2. Joseph's response to sin is a focus on who God is. We cannot sin against each other apart from sinning against God. In today's society, we seek to deny God yet at the same time demand justice. Why is this? Because God has written the Law on our hearts so that man is without excuse.[593]

3. All sin, wickedness, and evil are against the Lord. It is a denial of His Lordship and His Word. When we sin, we determine our thoughts and our ways are greater than God's purpose and His ways.

4. So what are we to do? Seek the Lord and His forgiveness. Repent and ask the Lord to soften your heart to His Word. Beg the Lord to conform you to the image of Christ, and the Lord will answer you. He will draw near to you and will bring you to Himself.

5. Let us trust in the Lord with all our hearts and lean not on our own understanding.[594]

---

[591]Genesis 39:2, [592]Genesis 39:6, [593]Romans 2:15, [594]Proverbs 3:5

Father, You are holy and I am not. You have given Your Word to us that we may know You and that we may walk in accordance with Your ways. But so many times we attempt to belittle You and deny Your Lordship. Father, forgive how I have sinned against You. How in my denial of You I have sinned and done great evil against You. Have mercy on me, and create in me a clean heart and renew a right spirit within me.[595] In Jesus' name.

[595] Psalm 51:10

Psalm 11:4-5

THE LORD IS IN HIS HOLY TEMPLE; THE LORD'S THRONE IS IN HEAVEN; HIS EYES SEE, HIS EYELIDS TEST THE CHILDREN OF MAN. THE LORD TESTS THE RIGHTEOUS, BUT HIS SOUL HATES THE WICKED AND THE ONE WHO LOVES VIOLENCE.

1. We do not serve an impersonal God, a deistic God who set up the world and then walked away. We serve a God who works all things together for the good of those who are called according to His purposes.[596] The Lord could stay in His temple and not even look upon us, for the Lord is complete. He does not need us, but He loves us for His glory! He works in every aspect and moment of our lives.

2. Regardless of what the world tells us, there is no such thing as luck, chance, or circumstance in any part of our lives. How we react to what the Lord ordains tells Him the depth in which we fear Him. If we pridefully grumble at our circumstances and selfishly whine about what the Lord is doing, it shows we do not trust Him, His sovereignty, and His grace. If we complain in our envy of not being like those we idolize, we say God is not wise in His dealing with His people and that His plans are not perfect.

3. All things are from Him; through Him and to Him is the glory in all things.[597] The word *test* (חָבַן) in Hebrew means to try, in the same as one "tries" gold[598] to purify it. The Lord is conforming us to the image of His Son;[599] He is purifying us because He disciplines those He loves[600] so we can know Him and reflect His glory. How terrifying to think of our lives without His concern for us.

[596]Romans 8:28, [597]Romans 11:36, [598]Zechariah 13:9, [599]2 Corinthians 3:18, [600]Proverbs 3:12

Father, I read Your Word and am struck by how much of the world has infiltrated my mind. I see how I have not always trusted You in the trials but have grumbled and complained to You. I have feared You are not in control. I have pridefully listened to the world rather than trusting in Your Word. Forgive me. Grant me a peace that passes all understanding to know You love me and are with me, and that You are purposefully orchestrating all things for Your glory. Father, open my eyes to see You working in my heart, and grant to me the assurance of things hoped for, the things not seen.[601] In Jesus' name.

[601] Hebrews 11:1

Psalm 12:7-8

You, O LORD, will keep them; you will guard us from this generation forever. On every side the wicked prowl, as vileness is exalted among the children of man.

1. Let us be mindful of the promises of God and the truthfulness of His Word. Since the fall of man,[602] wickedness has prowled around like a roaring lion,[603] and vileness is exalted in every aspect of the world. For there is none righteous, no not one.[604]

2. But this is not a cosmic war between good and evil. Death has been defeated![605] The Lord is not overthrown; He is working all things according to His purposes.[606]

3. As people of God, we are to set our minds on the things above and not on things going on in this evil world.[607] The world is constantly at work, attempting to deceive us from believing Christ is King and Lord over all things, that God is never out of control, that His purposes are being worked every day and at every moment.

4. The promise God gives to His people is that He will keep His people. Every generation He ordains He will hold fast and will guard them against every temptation, flattering lip, and double heart.[608] Our eyes must not look at the world but to the Lord. Our ears must not listen to the deceitful nihilism of the world but remain attentive to the promises and truth of God's Word.

---

[602]Genesis 3, [603]1 Peter 5:8, [604]Romans 3:10, [605]1 Corinthians 15:55, [606]Romans 11:36, [607]Colossians 3:2, [608]Psalm 12:2

Father, Your Word is true, and there is no other word that is pure, holy, or good for the edification of the saints, except Your Word. Lord, I confess the many times I have grabbed ahold of flattering words, of vain thoughts, or even nihilistic fears because I have not trusted Your Word. Grant my heart to rest and rejoice and walk by grace through faith in the truth and the assurance of Your Word. In Jesus' name.

Deuteronomy 23:23

You shall be careful to do what has passed your lips, for you have voluntarily vowed to the Lord your God what you have promised with your mouth.

1. All words that come out of our mouth are weighed before the Lord, for God is a God of knowledge, and by Him our actions are weighed.[609] Everything we think, act, and say is before the Lord, and He judges everyone.

2. We are to be mindful of our words and the heart in which they come from the mouth. For even though the tongue is a small member of the body, it boasts of great things.[610] Even our thoughts we are to take captive to obey Christ.[611]

3. To speak arrogantly or boastfully, to make vows we cannot keep apart from the grace of God, is to deny Christ Lordship. When we make a promise, when we make a vow, we are making it before the Lord, and unto Him for He is our King. For in Him we live and move and have our being.[612] We must be quick to listen, slow to speak, and slow to become angry.[613]

4. We will give an account for every idle word and thought, for all are voluntarily vowed unto the Lord. We are to seek Christ; we are to seek Christ's Kingdom and righteousness, and all these things will be added unto us.[614]

---

[609] 1 Samuel 2:3, [610] James 3:5, [611] 2 Corinthians 10:5, [612] Acts 17:28, [613] James 1:19, [614] Matthew 6:33

Oh Father, You created the Word with Your Word, and You sent Your Word in the form of man into the world. Who are we? This world, where words are used so idly and superficially, reflects an extreme lack of fear of You. Even myself—I confess many idle words have come from my mouth, and idle thoughts have entered my mind. Forgive me, Lord. Give the fear of You within my words that I may speak in a way that brings You pleasure. May my thoughts be honoring to You, and may I fear You in every thought, word, action, and deed. In Jesus' name.

Amen

Deuteronomy 20:1

When you go out to war against your enemies, and see horses and chariots and an army larger than your own, you shall not be afraid of them, for the LORD your God is with you, who brought you up out of the land of Egypt.

1. There are many instructions the Lord has given the people of Israel, but these must be carried out in light of who God is, not by how they are perceived.

2. First, God tells the Israelites that they will not be the largest army or the most powerful army but that they are commanded not to fear because of who God is.

3. Second, God tells them, "You shall not be afraid." This is not a suggestion; it is a command. That means, if the Israelites are afraid, they are sinning against God. We must go to the Lord and ask Him for strength and assurance in what He has for His Kingdom and our good.

4. Third, the Lord has called each of us to task as He spreads His kingdom across the world. We are not to go to the Lord and give an excuse as to what we can or cannot do based upon our time, talent, or resources, but we are to seek the Lord. We are to be mindful of God and to walk in accordance with His truths. We are to confess our fears and walk in the assurance of who God is.

Father, You are King and Lord!
I am Your servant, Lord. I confess the many times I've told You my will rather than to seek Your will. I look and I see the size of the enemy, and I base my hope in myself rather than You. I do this in my giving, my work, my family, and my circumstances. Forgive me. Grant me a right and true, hopeful view of You. Lift my head to behold Your glory. I ask this in Christ's name.

Luke 9:23–24

And he said to all, "If anyone would come after me, let him deny himself and take up his cross daily and follow me. For whoever would save his life will lose it, but whoever loses his life for my sake will save it."

1. The aim of God's people is Christ and Christ alone. Christ is not a golden ticket or a get-out-of-hell playing card; He is King. Our entire aim and purpose is to serve our King.

2. Yet the only way we can serve Christ is by denying ourselves. We are to deny ourselves and everything we think is more glorious than Christ, and go to and rest in Him.

3. This is not a one-time act but a daily sacrifice. We are to put to death daily the things of the world. *"For all that is in the world, the desires of the flesh and the desires of the eyes and pride of life, is not from the Father but is from the world."*[615]

4. Our desire is for Christ, to trust Christ, to pursue Christ, and to love Christ. In this pursuit we will gain all we need or even hope for, for we will have Christ.

---

[615] 1 John 2:16

Father, what does it mean to deny myself? In a time and culture opposite of denying ourselves and indulging ourselves instead, how do I deny myself? I confess those words terrify me at times because who will look out for me if I deny myself? Does this mean I shouldn't work? No! For You have ordained and created work. Forgive me my selfishness, and lead me in Your way everlasting. Soften my heart to Your will and Your purposes. In Jesus' name.

Deuteronomy 6:24

AND THE LORD COMMANDED US TO DO ALL THESE STATUTES, TO FEAR THE LORD OUR GOD, FOR OUR GOOD ALWAYS, THAT HE MIGHT PRESERVE US ALIVE, AS WE ARE THIS DAY.

1. We are to do all the Lord commands us to do, for we are God's people. We are in His kingdom, under His blessed rule, and under His Lordship.

2. It is not pragmatism or legalism or antinomianism that draws us to the Lord. These are man-made human constructs; they take the Word of God and either add to or take away from it to fit the narrative of our hearts' desires.

3. Our hearts' desire is to know God and to make Him known. We are to seek first the Kingdom of God and His righteousness, and all these things will be added to us.[616] We are to fear the Lord rather than man; we are to trust Him in all circumstances. As we do this, we must remember His promises that He will preserve us, and all things He leads us through are for our good.

4. There is no greater good for our lives and souls than to fear the Lord. For to fear the Lord is the beginning of all wisdom and[617] all understanding; all knowledge begins with God, for God is all wisdom, and all knowledge, and has all understanding.

5. As we seek the Lord and seek Him with our entire being, He has promised to preserve us. Regardless of what our flesh may cry out, the Lord will preserve His people. Let us boldly, and with all diligence, run to God.

[616]Mathew 6:33, [617]Proverbs 1:7

Father, You are holy and good. Your Law is good, and You have written Your Law on our hearts. So often I have denied Your Law, even as You make it known to me. I praise You, for You are glorious! Help me to walk in Your way, for Your glory. Soften my heart to Your nearness; help me to know how to walk, act, think, and work in a way that glorifies You. I ask this in the name of Your Son, Jesus Christ.

Deuteronomy 6:5

You shall love the Lord your God with all your heart and with all your soul and with all your might.

1. This is the first and the greatest commandment;[618] this is the commandment we are to strive for in all aspects of life.

2. We are created for one purpose, and that is to love God and to enjoy Him forever. Our hearts are created to know God; we are created in the image of God, and we are to know Him and to make Him known.

3. There is no aspect of our lives that should not be centered around knowing God. Our hearts, our entire consciences should be to the praise and adoration of the Lord, our soul—which is our thoughts and our being—and our might, which is all of our bodies.

4. This is not just the greatest commandment, but this commandment we fail every day apart from the grace of God. We can easily say it, but our dependence is upon the grace of God Almighty. We are to seek the Lord, to be mindful of His ways, and to ask Him to work in us to love Him with all of our hearts, souls, and might.

---

[618] Mathew 22:36–38

Father, You are God, and You are glorious. I confess the many times my heart feels like stone, and I am tempted to rest in that rather than to seek You. Forgive me. Draw near and grant me Your strength to love You with all of my heart, all of my soul, and all of my strength. Help me to see You working and to rest in Your sovereign grace. In Jesus' name.

Hebrews 2:3

How shall we escape if we neglect such a great salvation?

1. Eternity has been placed into the heart of man.[619] Our hearts are never satisfied, and our desire to fill the longing in them is constant from the day we are born until the present. Yet, if we are not mindful of what Christ has done and live in accordance with His truth, we are not and will not be saved.

2. Apart from the grace of God, we cannot escape this longing. We must know and walk in the truth of the salvation of Christ. For Christ came to earth and made Himself even lower than the angels; He made Himself like us in every way, that He might redeem us as His chosen people.[620]

3. All things now are under His Lordship, and nothing is out of His control—though we fully cannot see how He works all things.[621] The Lord has destroyed Satan, and death has lost its grip on His people.[622] He is now working all things together for His glory and our good,[623] as He is sanctifying His people and bringing us to Himself.[624]

4. God does not do these things mercilessly though, but as a great high priest, faithfully coming before the Father and asking for mercy to pardon our sins.[625] He knows our frame; He remembers that we are dust;[626] for He Himself became like us in every way. As we press on to see Him and know Him, He walks beside us and helps us along the way, leading us through every trial and storm to bring us to Himself.[627]

---

[619]Ecclesiastes 3:11, [620]Hebrews 2:17, [621]Hebrews 2:8, [622]Hebrews 2:14, [623]Romans 8:28, [624]Hebrews 2:11, [625]Hebrews 2:17, [626]Psalm 103:14, [627]Hebrews 2:18

Jesus, You are my King. This is so hard for me to comprehend; it is apart from Your Holy Spirit, opening my eyes and my heart. My sin of unbelief permeates every part of my being, and I have not been mindful of what is Your salvation. Forgive me and have mercy on me. Use my life in whatever way You would deem best. Help me to see, know, adore, and praise You for Your glory. Thank You, Jesus.

Acts 2:23–24

This Jesus, delivered up according to the definite plan and foreknowledge of God, you crucified and killed by the hands of lawless men. God raised him up, loosing the pangs of death, because it was not possible for him to be held by it.

1. All of history is in the hands of God, and all of history points to Christ. All that Christ did, and all that He is doing now, is according to the definite plan and foreknowledge of God.

2. We must be mindful of the tension between God's sovereignty and our responsibility. For even here, all things were done by God's sovereign and foreordained decree, yet at the same time, *"Christ was crucified and killed by the hands of lawless men."*

3. How glorious though, that nothing holds back the sovereignty of God. It is not possible that sin can hold back Christ. It is not possible that circumstances can hold back God's plan. For all things work together for good for those who love God and are called according to His purpose.[628]

4. Christ is King and God is sovereign! He has defeated sin, He has defeated Satan, and He has defeated death. God is working to make all things new; He is bringing His kingdom on earth, and not even the gates of hell will prevail against His advance.[629]

---

[628]Romans 8:28, [629]Matthew 16:18

Father, You are glorious and Your Kingdom rules over all. How easily I am tempted to belittle Your Kingdom and Your sovereignty. I so easily make myself lord rather than thinking on the Lordship of Christ. I believe, Lord; help my unbelief. Help me to see Your Kingdom come, and Your will be done, on earth as it is in heaven! In Jesus' name.

Psalm 146:3

Put not your trust in princes, in a son of man, in whom there is no salvation.

1. Our hope is to be in Christ and Christ alone, for to place our hope and joy in anyone or anything else is idolatry.

2. The heart of man constantly seeks to find justification and purpose in places and things other than God. Since the fall of Adam, we have attempted to fill the depravity of our hearts with the things of earth rather than God Himself.

3. We base our identities on politics, theologians, philosophers, on anyone or anything other than Christ. We desire not to walk by faith, but instead, in our actions we desire to walk by our sight. We presuppose that our thoughts, motivations, and actions are good and start with a view of ourselves rather than Christ.

4. Let us look to Christ for our help, our identity, our hope. Let us be mindful of all He has done and how He has set us free from the law of sin and death. We are now alive in Christ![630] Any boasting we do in ourselves or our intellect is sin and evil.[631] We are to look *"to Jesus, the founder and perfecter of our faith, who for the joy that was set before him endured the cross, despising the shame, and is seated at the right hand of the throne of God."*[632]

---

[630]Romans 8:2, [631]James 4:16, [632]Hebrews 12:2

Father, You are in heaven, and my eyes are to be on You in Christ Jesus! Forgive me for taking my eyes and my hope off You and placing them on others. I have idolized others; forgive me! Grant me the heart of passionately knowing and pursuing You. Help me to keep my eyes on Christ, my hope in Christ, my joy in Christ, my passion in Christ. All things Christ for Christ. In His name I ask this.

Amen

Judges 14:3

But Samson said to his father,
"Get her for me, for she is right in my eyes."

1. Notice the standard by which Sampson measures the desire he has for the Philistine woman, "She is right in my eyes."

2. Each of us measures what we do or don't do by some sort of standard. We act, see, think, and believe based upon a standard we think to be objectively true. Here, Samson denies the truth of Holy Scripture and bases his entire premise upon what he sees with his eyes.

3. As people of God, we are called to be in the world but not of the world. For the desires of the flesh and the eyes, and the pride of life, are not from the Father, but from the world.[633]

4. We are not to walk according to the flesh, which is the path of death. But we are, by the Spirit, who is the Word of God, to put to death the things of the flesh.[634] *"For all who are led by the Spirit of God are sons of God."*[635]

---

[633]1 John 2:16, [634]Romans 8:13, [635]Romans 8:14

Father, You are holy and perfect in all Your ways! Oh, how easily I am swayed by different standards and false doctrine. I so easily cling to idols and things measured by a human standard rather than the Word of God. Forgive me and save me from my pride. Grant me a heart rooted and grounded in Your Word, and may Your Word be the standard that You, by Your Holy Spirit, lead me in all life. For Christ's sake and Your glory.

Judges 13:8

Then Manoah prayed to the Lord and said, "O Lord, please let the man of God whom you sent come again to us and teach us what we are to do with the child who will be born."

1. Manoah, the father of Samson, prayed to the Lord when he did not know what to do or how to raise the promised boy when he was born. He did not question or doubt but instead called upon the Lord for wisdom.

2. In all circumstances, we are never to be wise in our own eyes.[636] We are to come to the Lord, pray continuously,[637] and ask for wisdom in all things from God, who gives generously and without reproach, and it will be given to us.[638]

3. We must also be mindful that all our prayers are to be for God's glory. We are to seek first the Kingdom of God, and all these things will be added to us.[639] So, Manoah not only sought the Lord in how to raise the child, but notice how he asked the Lord how He wanted the child to be raised.

4. This guards our hearts and minds from a practical atheism as we seek the things of God. We are to ask the Lord who is in heaven to help us act in a way that reflects His Kingdom here on earth and trust Him by grace and through faith to give us the wisdom to do His will.

---

[636]Proverbs 3:7, [637]1 Thessalonians 5:17, [638]James 1:5, [639]Matthew 6:33

Father, You are wise in all You do. So many times and in so many ways I have looked at life through a humanistic, practical lens rather than seeking You for Your glory. I have taken a step back and attempted to build or defend my glory rather than humbling myself before You. Forgive me. Give me wisdom and strength to do Your will. Help me to define my actions based upon the truth of who You are, that I may glorify You all my days. In Christ's name I pray.

Psalm 17:15

As for me, I shall behold your face in righteousness; when I awake, I shall be satisfied with your likeness.

1. Many things allure and tempt us to find satisfaction in them. All the world declares, and all our flesh desires is to find and be satisfied by ungodly things.

2. Everything we seek that is not God is an idol. For to find our identity in anything other than God is to worship and adore and serve that thing to find our value. If we find our value in marriage, marriage becomes our idol. If we find our identity in our children, children become our idol. If we find our identity in the idea of being happy, then the pursuit of happiness becomes our idol.

3. But the psalmist states that in the middle of the degenerate and corrupt, he will find complete satisfaction in the likeness of God. He will be complete, and he will be satisfied.

4. When does he do this? When he awakes! The first thing he pursues is seeing and knowing the likeness of God; to be mindful of God, to behold the Word of God, and to be satisfied in God and in God alone.

Father, there is none like You. For who has created the heavens and the earth? Who sustains us every day? Who leads and guides us, and who gives us all things, but You? Lord, I confess there are many temptations to worry and to doubt. I am tempted moment by moment to fall into unbelief and anxiety and worry. Forgive my unbelief. Help me to find my satisfaction in You and You alone. Help me to know You and to rest in the assurance of Your grace, Your providence, Your purpose, and Your will, that I may glorify You, my God and my King! In Christ's name.

Colossians 3:23–24

Whatever you do, work heartily, as for the Lord and not for men, knowing that from the Lord you will receive the inheritance as your reward. You are serving the Lord Christ.

1. Our aim is Christ in every thought, word, action, and deed. The work the Lord has given us, He gives us daily, and that work is to be done for His glory and not ours, and not those for whom we work.

2. Work is that which the Lord has given us to accomplish in each day. It is training up our children in the way they should go;[640] it is to be profitable and to strive to keep that which the Lord has given us;[641] it is to love the Lord our God with all of our hearts, and with all of our souls, and with all of our might.[642]

3. We do this because we know Christ is ordaining all things for His glory and our good.[643] For all things are from Him, and through Him, and to Him![644] In these truths, the righteous shall live by faith![645] Our hope is in Christ; He will give to us according to His will. We can know this and trust in Him.

4. The world and our flesh revolt against this. Our sin seductively attempts to bring us back from submitting to the Lord. But Christ is all, and in all His people, and in Him we live and move, and have our being.[646]

---

[640]Proverbs 22:6, [641]Genesis 2:15, [642]Deuteronomy 6:5, [643]Romans 8:28, [644]Romans 11:36, [645]Romans 1:27, [646]Acts 17:28

Father, thank You for giving us Your Son. Thank You for ordaining our day and for the Holy Spirit, who works in our hearts and conforms us to the image of Your Son. Forgive me for not being mindful of Your Word. For questioning Your truth. Help me to walk, moment by moment, in the assurance of who You are, and for Your glory. Bless the work of my hands. In Jesus' name.

Colossians 3:2

Set your minds on things that are above,
not on things that are on earth.

1. The heart and mind of the believer are to be set on Christ, not on the things of the flesh or the earth.

2. This is not a gnostic mindset or a mindset not fully engaged in the world that the Lord is orchestrating for His glory. But instead, we look to Christ as King in our lives. We are dead to sin, so how can we live in it any longer?[647] For if we live according to the flesh, we will die, but if by the Spirit we put to death the things of the flesh, we will have life and peace.[648]

3. When we wake, we must seek the Lord. When we walk about the day, we are to seek the Lord. When we lie down, we are to know that Christ is watching over us.[649]

4. We must be mindful to walk according to the Word, which is to walk opposite of the world. The more we look to Christ, seek Him, and make Him our aim, the more we will know Christ and the more opposite the world will become.

[647]Romans 6:2, [648]Romans 8:13, [649]Proverbs 6:22

Father, You have made us in Your image. It is You and You alone who has saved us, redeemed us, called us by name, and we are Yours. Lord, so many times my mind wanders from You. Forgive my unbelief in trusting You, my self-reliance in walking according to my flesh instead of by faith in You, in my selfishness in not trusting Your providence. Grant me to know You, that I may make You known. Strengthen my heart, and my mind, and my flesh to walk in accordance with Your will. In Christ's name.

Colossians 2:6–7

Therefore, as you received Christ Jesus the Lord, so walk in Him, rooted and built up in Him and established in the faith, just as you were taught, abounding in thanksgiving.

1. Jesus is the foundation on which we stand. In Him and the finished work upon the cross are we to walk and live our lives.

2. Our faith is rooted and established in Him alone, and there is no other name under heaven given among men by which we must be saved.[650]

3. So how are we to respond in light of being rooted and established in Christ? We are to live abounding in thanksgiving, for we know that Christ is King of all and He is sitting on His throne. He is working all things together for good for those who love Him and are called according to His purpose.[651]

4. We are to know this, teach this, and preach this. This truth leads us, so we know we need not fear, but rejoice, for it is finished in Christ alone.

---

[650]Acts 4:12, [651]Romans 8:28

Father, thank You for Jesus. I confess that apart from Your grace, I am unable to rest in the assurance of Christ. Forgive me for my lack of thankfulness. Forgive me for my grumbling and my lack of faith. Help me to walk in the truth of Christ Jesus for Your glory. Establish my thoughts, words, actions, and deeds in the truthfulness of Christ Jesus. In His name I ask this.

Numbers 14:11

And the LORD said to Moses, "How long will this people despise me? And how long will they not believe in me, in spite of all the signs that I have done among them?"

1. We are to walk by faith in all things, for everything that does not proceed from faith is a sin.[652]

2. Every thought, word, action, and deed reflects our hearts and our views of who God is. To not walk in accordance with the truth of who God is, is to despise God. In all circumstances we are to rejoice, knowing that our God is God over all things. To think otherwise is to despise the Lord.

3. To despise God is to not believe His promises. It is to believe our emotions, thoughts, and perceptions. It is to believe what we see with our eyes rather than to acknowledge God through faith in Him. It is to turn our humanity into an idol and to worship that idol rather than God.

4. This breaks both the second commandment and the first commandment. For if we trust ourselves, and are wise in our own eyes, and do not seek the Lord, that we have worshiped our humanity and have made ourselves God rather than the living and true God.

---

[652]Romans 14:23

Father, there is no one else like You. I praise You, for You are God! I confess that many times I do not know what to do or how to act, and I fall back into what I perceive rather than trusting Your Word. In fact, Lord, many times I have trusted others rather than Your Word because I have perceived they are wise rather than to walk by faith in Your Word. Forgive me. Grant me the faith and strength and conviction to pursue and follow You all the days of my life. In Jesus' name.

Amen

Numbers 13:30

But Caleb quieted the people before Moses and said, "Let us go up at once and occupy it, for we are well able to overcome it."

1. When the Israelites came back from spying out the land God had promised them, they spoke both of its bounty and its fears. Ten of the spies spoke in light of how powerful the people were whom they had seen and observed.

2. Caleb, though, spoke opposite of them, for Caleb spoke in light of who God is. Caleb spoke by faith in accordance with the promises of God.

3. We are to walk by faith and not by sight.[653] We are to walk in accordance with who God is. When we look at our circumstances and situations, we are to seek the Lord and draw near to Him, and He will draw near to us.

4. It's as John Bunyan once wrote, "To fear man is to forget God." We are to look at all of life in light of who God is. We are to seek the Lord while He may be found.[654] Then, we are to step forward in faith because of the truth of who God is. He has promised, "I will never leave you nor forsake you." So we can confidently say, "The Lord is my helper; I will not fear; what can man do to me?"[655]

---

[653]2 Corinthians 5:7, [654]Isaiah 55:6, [655]Hebrews 13:5-6

Father, You are glorious and mighty. There is none like You in all the heavens! Forgive me for having such a small view of You. Forgive me for making things bigger and more powerful than You in my heart and mind. Grant me the faith to walk in the truth of who You are, and open my eyes that I may see You working and praise You, my Father who is in heaven. In Jesus' name.

1 Thessalonians 5:24

HE WHO CALLS YOU IS FAITHFUL;
HE WILL SURELY DO IT.

1. All things are held together by God, and there is nothing that is not under His rule. His Kingdom rules over all.[656] We need not fear any of what God does, and all His promises will come to pass at the proper time because He is faithful.

2. Our fears arrive when instead of looking to God, we define God by our own humanity. When we see our unfaithfulness, or the unfaithfulness of those whom we have placed our trust in who are not God, we, in our depravity, place human attributes on our Father.

3. When we have a sinful and corrupt view of God, we begin to lose our thankfulness, joy, and hope. We cease waiting for the Lord and trusting His promises; we worry and fret and build our anxiety on the foolishness and depravity of our hearts. We do as Martin Luther accused Erasmus of when he said, "Your thoughts of God are too human!"

4. We must go to the Lord and ask Him to open the eyes of our hearts. For *"without faith it is impossible to please Him. But whoever would draw near to God must believe that He exists and that He rewards those who seek him."*[657] When we draw near to God, we truly know Him as He is, and we can rest assured that *"he will surely do it."*

---

[656]Psalm 103:19, [657]Hebrews 11:6

Father, You are faithful beyond all measure. There is none like You in heaven above or in the earth below. All things are held together by You. So many times I presuppose Your faithfulness. I presuppose that You will make the sun rise, my heart beat, my eyes see; I don't deserve any of this, but they reflect Your faithfulness. Thank You for Your faithfulness and Your mercy. Soften my heart that I may rejoice in Your salvation and Your grace and mercy. In Jesus' name.

Leviticus 23:1-2

The Lord spoke to Moses, saying, "Speak to the people of Israel and say to them, 'These are the appointed feasts of the Lord that you shall proclaim as holy convocations; they are my appointed feasts.'"

1. Praise the Lord at all times; keep His praises continually on your lips.[658] The appointed feasts are times the Israelites came together to celebrate one thing: the goodness of God.

2. Let us also be mindful that these feasts are not human constructs, though they are told by Moses. They are God's appointed feasts set apart by Him, for His glory, and by all God's people.

3. God's people are to walk in such a way that we reflect the truth of the Kingdom of God throughout our lives. We are to *"be joyful always, pray continuously, and give thanks in all circumstances."*[659] A thankful heart is a heart fully dependent on God. Everything that happens in our day, from the sun rising to every interaction throughout, whatever the Lord ordains must be accepted in humble gratitude.

4. When we believe our own efforts, and not the Lord's mercy, sustain us through our day, our hearts harden. We must be mindful of Christ's words, *"Apart from me, you can do nothing."*[660]

---

[658]Psalm 34:1, [659]1 Thessalonians 5:16–17, [660]John 15:5

Father, You are the Creator and sustainer of life. From You and through You and to You are all things, and in this knowledge we are to rest and rejoice. For You are our God, and we are Your people! Lord, forgive my selfish pride that so easily hardens my heart, and grant my heart to sing Your praises in all that You do, for Your glory and my good. In Jesus' name.

Amen

Psalm 31:5

INTO YOUR HAND I COMMIT MY SPIRIT;
YOU HAVE REDEEMED ME, O LORD, FAITHFUL GOD.

1. This very psalm our Lord prayed when they raised Him on the cross.[661] Jesus Christ, who knew no sin, became sin for us that in Him we might become the righteousness of God.[662]

2. We as Christians are to do the same thing. We are to take up our cross and follow Christ.[663] We are to take all the Lord has given us: our time, talents, and resources, and give them to the Lord for His Kingdom.

3. We do this out of humble gratitude. For we do not deserve to know God and be His children, but He has redeemed us by the blood of His only Son. Secondly, we do this because we trust that God is a faithful God. For He is faithful and just and works all things together for good for those who love Him and are called according to His purpose.[664]

4. This then allows us to walk with confidence in the assurance of Christ in a world that denies God's existence. Our entire lives are committed to the Lordship of Christ and to His Kingdom, and we can rest by faith in knowing our King is victorious.

---

[661]Luke 23:46, [662]2 Corinthians 5:21, [663]Matthew 16:24, [664]Romans 8:28

Father, I have read this passage and heard these words many times. I confess, though, that I have rarely lived out this truth. I have not committed all of myself to You for Your Kingdom. I have many times attempted to commit my morality on Sundays but not saturated my life with it. Please change my heart to walk in the assurance of Your Kingdom for Your glory. In Jesus' name.

Leviticus 18:1–5

And the Lord spoke to Moses, saying, "Speak to the people of Israel and say to them, I am the Lord your God. You shall not do as they do in the land of Egypt, where you lived, and you shall not do as they do in the land of Canaan, to which I am bringing you. You shall not walk in their statutes. You shall follow my rules and keep my statutes and walk in them. I am the Lord your God. You shall therefore keep my statutes and my rules; if a person does them, he shall live by them: I am the Lord."

1. God declared to Israel that He is their God, and no person, region, or future could change that truth. They were to be set apart and not walk in any of the laws, rules, or customs of their past or of the people to where they were going. They were to be totally set apart to and for their God.

2. The Israelites were to do everything according to the rules and statues the Lord had given them. The Lord reminded them that Moses was not the imposer of His rules but that Moses dictated those very rules and statues of the Most High God.

3. In the New Testament, Peter writes, *"But you are a chosen race, a royal priesthood, a holy nation, a people for his own possession, that you may proclaim the excellencies of him who called you out of darkness into his marvelous light. Once you were not a people, but now you are God's people; once you had not received mercy, but now you have received mercy."*[665] So for the Christian, our aim is the same—we are to know God by His Word and to live according to His Word, for the Lord is God.

4. We must be mindful, then, of what the world wants us to worship and what God has called us to worship. We are not to worship good deeds or people; we are not to worship status or body image; we are not to worship emotions or self-identity. We are to know God and make God known under His Lordship for His glory in His Kingdom at all times.

[665] Peter 2:9–10

Father, You are God. How easy it is for me to fall into the mindset of the culture and to relegate You to morning devotions and Sunday morning. The culture berates and fights against the idea of being under Your Lordship and being under God. Satan still whispers in our ears, "Did God really say?" and we listen to him and fall prey to "goodness" rather than holiness. Forgive me and my unbelief and open my heart and mind to walk in accordance with Your will, by Your Word, for Your Kingdom and glory. In Jesus' name I ask this.

Hebrews 4:7

Again he appoints a certain day, "Today," saying through David so long afterward, in the words already quoted, "Today, if you hear his voice, do not harden your hearts."

1. When are we to act upon the promises of God, and when are we to repent? "Today!" We are to change now and to seek the Lord while He may be found.[666]

2. When we hear the voice of the Lord, we are to seek Him. We are not to harden our hearts. We are not to presuppose that we will hear His voice again; we are to act upon it immediately by faith. For everything that does not come from faith is a sin.[667]

3. Each of the Lord's callings is specific. They are intentional for that specific day. They are perfect as they are heard in our hearts and minds. We are to seek the Lord in prayer; we are to ask for wisdom[668] and believe He will give it.

4. Run to Christ, repent, and seek the Lord at all times and at every time, as long as it is today, so we will not fall back into the sin of unbelief.[669]

5. It is sin that entangles our hearts and whispers in our ears and causes us to question the very Word of God. We are to stand on the promises of God; we are to walk by faith and not by sight,[670] trusting in the Lord with all our hearts and leaning not on our own understanding.[671]

---

[666]Isaiah 55:6, [667]Romans 14:23, [668]James 1:5, [669]Hebrews 3:13, [670]2 Corinthians 5:7, [671]Proverbs 3:5

Father, Your Word is perfect and holy. You never utter a meaningless or unintentional word. Your Word creates and sparks action to progress forward. Your Word can also harden an unrepentant heart. Soften my heart to Your Word. Grant my heart to be nourished by Your Word alone, that I may repent and walk in Your ways. Restore to me the joy of Your salvation. In Jesus' name I ask this.

Hebrews 3:12-14

Take care, brothers, lest there be in any of you an evil, unbelieving heart, leading you to fall away from the living God. But exhort one another every day, as long as it is called "today," that none of you may be hardened by the deceitfulness of sin. For we have come to share in Christ, if indeed we hold our original confidence firm to the end.

1. We are to trust in the Lord with all our hearts and lean not on our own understanding. To not trust the Lord is to not believe in His promises, His power, His goodness, and His love. This unbelief then turns into mindless drivel, and we fall away from the living God.

2. Our God desires that we encourage each other and lift each other up as long as there is a "today." He doesn't mean one specific time or place, but the Lord has redeemed all things, and He has done it "today." For sin is deceitful and hardens the heart to the things of God. Sin removes the joy of Christ and replaces it with the pride, selfishness, and unbelief of sin.

3. Our confidence must be in Christ and in His finished work, His hope, His truth, His goodness, and His righteousness. We must seek the Lord always and trust in His grace and mercy. For the Lord is gracious and merciful, slow to anger and abounding in steadfast love and righteousness.[672]

---

[672] Psalm 103:8

Father, You are truth. Everything apart from You is not truth. You have given us Your Word and have loved me with an everlasting love. Lord, what does it look like to have an unshaken confidence in You? So many times I lay my humanity before You as an excuse. Forgive my unbelief and pride. Grant me a confidence and boldness in Your nearness, in Your providence, in Your love, and for Your glory. In Jesus' name,

Amen

Hebrews 2:8

Now in putting everything in subjection to him, he left nothing outside his control. At present, we do not yet see everything in subjection to him.

1. Everything is under the Lordship of Christ. Regardless of what the world says, regardless of what every secular television show portrays, regardless of what our flesh feels, all things are under the Lordship of Christ.

2. There is nothing outside of Christ's control. There is no government outside of His sovereignty, no news story beyond His control, and no situation outside of His grasp. Christ is seated at the right hand of the Father and is working all things together.

3. Yet, we must be mindful that the Scriptures say, "we do not see everything in subjection to him." Does this mean something is not in subjection? No! Just because we cannot see it does not mean it is not true. Truth goes beyond all evidence of sight, which is why we walk by faith![673]

4. Let us encourage each other, and exhort each other, and remind each other that Christ is King. That we are His, and in that freedom, we boldly press on toward the goal.

---

[673] 2 Corinthians 5:7

Jesus, You are King! You are Lord, You are Sovereign! Knowing this renders me speechless and places such joy in my heart. Who am I that You would allow me to be Yours? For I have sinned so many times. Grant me boldness, favor, hope, and peace to do Your will. Not my will, but Yours be done. In Your name, which is above every name, I ask this.

Psalm 27:10

For my father and my mother have forsaken me, but the Lord will take me in.

1. One of the greatest forms of idolatry in the world today is *family*. This is not to say family is evil in any way, for family is a God-ordained grace!

2. But the family becomes an idol when we worry about what our family thinks and does more than we seek the Lord. This happens when the emotions of our hearts deceive us and make us stop our pursuit of the Lord so we can feel closer to the world.

3. Our fathers and mothers are not absolute truth, and all things must be measured and weighed against the Word of God. Our standard must be God, not our parents. If our parents are not pursuing the Lord, we must not pursue our parents. But we can rest, knowing God's Word promises that God will take us in. The God of the universe, through Christ Jesus, will take us to Himself.

4. A word of warning. Even if our parents abandon us because of our pursuit of God, we must still honor them, for this is right and is commanded by God.[674] We honor God by honoring our parents, but we are not to pursue them or their affections outside of or contrary to our pursuit of God.

---

[674] Exodus 20:12

Father, You are my Father through Christ Jesus. You are my Father! How glorious; how awesome. Lord, I have been tempted to put my head down and weep or to raise other humans up to be a "father" to me, and in doing so have denied You many times. Forgive me. Grant me to know You as my Father. Grant me to know You and to walk in the truth of You as my Heavenly Father. Help me to walk in this truth and in reality, in peace and assurance, rooted in Christ, for Your glory, and my good. Help me to please You in every thought word, action, and deed. In Jesus' name.

Philippians 4:1

And my God will supply every need of yours according to his riches in glory in Christ Jesus.

1. What a glorious promise from our God! He will provide for every need. We must cling to this promise. On the top of the mountain, we must recognize that it's not the mountain itself but God who supplied us with providence. When we are in the valley, we must be mindful that the Lord is sovereign over the valley, and we must humbly accept His providence, trusting in Him, and Him alone.

2. We must guard our hearts against making idols of our perceived needs. For our identity is not in the gift, but in the One who gives all things. We must look to the Lord, trusting Him that He will give in a way that shows His love.

3. Our greatest need is to know God. Let us praise God the Father, who sent His Son to us out of love for us. The Father has never diminished His love; His love has been perfect since before time began.[675] But because of our sin, we could not draw near to Him. For those who are bought by the blood of His Son, to pay the penalty for our sins, He made Him to be sin who knew no sin, that we might become children of God.[676]

---

[675] Ephesians 1:4, [676] 2 Corinthians 5:21

Father, Your love is perfect. There is no change or deviation in it. Lord, I come to You and confess that I have made my idols, selfish ambition, envy, pride, and all the things of the world my identity. I confess that I have feared at times that You do not know me and that You would not provide for me. Yet You have lavished Your love on me. Who am I? Grant me, Lord, to rest in Christ, to serve Christ, to hope in Christ, and to press on in Christ, by Your strength and Your grace. In Jesus' name.

Philippians 4:4–5

Rejoice in the Lord always; again I will say, rejoice. Let your reasonableness be known to everyone. The Lord is at hand.

1. Christians are to rejoice at all times. The word always is what I consider an *infinite* word. We cannot get outside of it; it encompasses all circumstances. There is no time, no situation, no occurrence, and no joy or sorrow that is outside of *always*.

2. This is not a suggestion from the Word of God but a direct command. Christians are to rejoice. This is not a reaction based upon circumstances, but this is a joy in knowing who God is and trusting His promises and sovereignty. The Christian must know that what the Lord ordains is right, even though we might not understand it.

3. God's perfection, sovereignty, goodness, and purposes are never diminished by our circumstantial experiences. He never deviates nor wanes in His perfection. His plan is always good and must be measured by who He is, not by what we feel.

4. In being mindful of this truth, we must not be stoic when it comes to the chastening of the Lord. We must not deny our emotions but instead accept the different dispensations of the Lord by faith. Not begrudgingly but with joy, knowing that the Lord works all things together for those who love God and are called according to His purpose.[677]

---

[677] Romans 8:28

Father, You are in heaven, and You are high and lifted up. The heavens declare Your glory, and the skies proclaim Your handiwork.[678] Father, so many times have I made circumstances my idol or fear my companion, rather than seeking You, trusting in You, and hoping in You. Forgive me. Grant me to know You, that I may rejoice in You. Soften my heart to rejoice in Your salvation. Guard my heart from a gnostic view of You, and let me see the goodness of the Lord in the land of the living. In Jesus' name.

[678] Psalm 19:1–2

Exodus 1:17

But the midwives feared God and did not do as the king of Egypt commanded them, but let the male children live.

1. The fear of the Lord is the beginning of wisdom.[679] This is true in every aspect of our lives. We must search our hearts and ask the Lord to reveal where we fear man more than we fear Him.

2. The midwives, even under command from the King, knew aborting a baby—murdering a child—would be an abomination to the Lord because such an action went against God. And they'd rather fear the Lord than man. Many times the Lord puts us in places in our lives to test us and to bring us to a greater knowledge and fear of Him. How fickle our hearts are, and how quickly we are consumed with worry, doubt, fear, suspicion, skepticism, and the desire to please man rather than trust in the Lord. Our pride creeps into our hearts and we go by what we see and feel rather than trusting in the Lord.

3. Let us search our hearts and our minds and ask the Lord to reveal to us where we are clinging to the world, or to a certain group of people, or even to our pride rather than trusting and clinging to the Lord Most High. Let us ask Him to keep us from listening to the deceit of the world and accumulating teachers and thoughts for our sinful passions rather than trusting in Him.[680]

---

[679] Proverbs 1:7, [680] 2 Timothy 4:3

Father, You are God, and there is none other like You. I confess the many times my sinful desires tempt me to place myself on Your throne rather than submit to Your Lordship. Many times I act and do and think in a way that gives me temporary satisfaction rather than coming to Christ, who is the bread of life. Forgive me. Open my eyes and teach me Your ways, that I may walk in Your truth! I am captive to my pride, apart from Your grace. I long to be under Your Lordship; please renew a right spirit within me. In Jesus' name.

Exodus 2:15

When Pharaoh heard of it, he sought to kill Moses. But Moses fled from Pharaoh and stayed in the land of Midian. And he sat down by a well.

1. Moses killed an Egyptian when he saw he was beating an Israelite to death.[681] The next day, Moses saw two Hebrews doing the same thing and confronted them. They, in turn, challenged him and asked if he would kill them in the same way he had killed the Egyptian.[682]

2. Moses then fled to the land of Midian. Notice, as John Calvin wrote in his commentary on Exodus, *"He is not ashamed of what he had done, so as to endeavor to appease the king, but he betakes himself to exile; nor is he so alarmed in this critical time as to sink down in helplessness or despair, but he departs into the land of Midian, and prefers wandering in the Desert, to a reconciliation with the enemies of the chosen people."* [683]

3. There are a few things to reflect on. First, are we so consumed with the fear of the Lord that we will abandon what is familiar to draw near to God? Moses, in his act, was more concerned with the people than he was with his adopted family. Secondly, are we decisive in our action, or do we play and coddle our thoughts and emotions when pursuing the Lord?

4. When Moses fled Egypt for the wilderness, he was more content being with God in that place than in the comfort of the palace. The things of this world are secondary to the things of the Lord. He would rather sleep under the stars than to gain power at the hand of man.

5. We must search our hearts and ask ourselves what passions hold our hearts in bondage. Do we let go in our hearts and minds of everything and trust the Lord in His dealing with us, or do we attempt to control and manipulate our circumstances for the sake and deception of personal comfort?

---

[681] Exodus 2:11–12, [682] Exodus 2:13–14, [683] Calvin, J., & Bingham, C. W. (2010). Commentaries on the Four Last Books of Moses Arranged in the Form of a Harmony (Vol. 1, pp. 50–51). Bellingham, WA: Logos Bible Software.

Father, You are holy, and I am not. You are above all; Your Word proves true. Forgive me for clinging to the world rather than clinging to You. Forgive me for clinging to my emotions rather than trusting in Your sovereign grace. Forgive me for whining and complaining about my trials rather than offering You thanksgiving and trusting You in all aspects of life. Grant me strength and conviction, with Your peace to follow You. I praise You, Jesus, and seek You in all things. In Jesus' name.

Exodus 3:11–12

But Moses said to God, "Who am I that I should go to Pharaoh and bring the children of Israel out of Egypt?" He said, "But I will be with you, and this shall be the sign for you, that I have sent you: when you have brought the people out of Egypt, you shall serve God on this mountain."

1. Moses, when he heard the Lord's voice while standing on holy ground, asked an incredibly honest question of the Lord without taking to completion in rooting it in who the Lord is. We must remember it was not a suggestion the Lord gave Moses but a command.[684]

2. The commandments of the Lord are pure enlightenment to the eyes.[685] When God commands us to do something, we are to look with enlightened eyes to the One who declares the command and walk in accordance with who He is, not who we perceive ourselves to be. We must be mindful of His goodness, faithfulness, love, mercy—all His attributes—and walk in accordance with who He is.

3. When God gives His commands, He not only gives them and then sends us, but He goes with us. All His commands are sure, and all His promises are true. He will bring to fruition all He commands, and we are to walk in faith of who God is.

4. When we cling to the world rather than trust in the Lord, we deny the Lordship of God in our lives. We begin to look like the world rather than followers of Christ. We must look to Christ; we must trust His Word; we must walk in accordance with His Holy Spirit; and regardless of what we perceive to be true, we must acknowledge that nothing is impossible with God.[686] We are only to obey.

[684]Exodus 3:10, [685]Psalm 19:8, [686]Luke 1:37

Father, Your commands are pure. Help me to know and walk according to Your Word. Grant me to draw near to You and to trust You, wherever You lead me. I confess my spirit of unbelief in many things. I have looked at losses and shaken my fist at You rather than holding and clinging to Your promises. Forgive me. Grant me the joy of the Lord as my strength. Forgive my man-centeredness and lead me in Your way everlasting. In Jesus' name.

Exodus 4:1

Then Moses answered, "But behold, they will not believe me or listen to my voice, for they will say, 'The Lord did not appear to you.'"

1. Notice Moses, when he heard what God called him to do, did not step forward. Instead, he shared with God a problem he foresaw in God calling him to go back to Egypt.

2. Thankfully, this was not a bold rejection. Moses didn't declare to God that he wouldn't do it, but he was not bold in his trusting of God either. When we know what the Lord would have us do next, we must be careful to never place our circumstances or experiences before following the Lord. We can present before Him our concerns, but we are to walk forward by faith in who God is.

3. So many times we place excuses, situations, physical well-being, or even time before God, rather than taking our burdens to Him and laying them before the Lord. Nothing is impossible with God,[687] and He is working together for the good of all who love Him and are called according to His purpose.[688]

4. This is why we are to know God. We are to pursue Him with all of our hearts, souls, and might. Our actions and deeds should be in direct correlation with who God is and His glory. God is not a God of excuses but a God of covenant. Present to the Lord your anxieties and fears, then boldly step forward in the truth of who He is. For whatever the Lord ordains is right.

---

[687]Luke 1:37, [688]Romans 8:28

Father, You are wise, and You work all things together for Your glory. Forgive me for coming up with man-made excuses and not seeking You in everything. Worrying about that which You are orchestrating is foolish. Grant me strength and wisdom to do Your will. Give me clarity of mind to work in a way that reflects Your glory. That others may see my good work and praise You in heaven. In Jesus' name.

Exodus 6:1

But the LORD said to Moses, "Now you shall see what I will do to Pharaoh; for with a strong hand he will send them out, and with a strong hand he will drive them out of his land."

1. It is God who orchestrates all things. All things! Let us not look to our circumstances or to our trials and tribulations the Lord leads us through, but let us look to God, for He is the founder and perfecter of our faith![689] We are to look at every circumstance in our lives, not apart from the gospel, but through the gospel.

2. When we gripe and moan, we declare to God that He is not wise. We proclaim His thoughts and ways are beneath ours. What sinning unbelief!

3. Let us trust the Lord with all our hearts and lean not on our own understanding. In all our ways acknowledge Him, and He will make straight our paths.[690] Let us cling to the promises of God and stand boldly and firmly on who He is.

4. We must acknowledge that apart from God's grace we are unable to do this. So we are to pray without ceasing and give thanks in all circumstances, for this is the will of God in Christ Jesus for us.[691] Let us call to Him, and let us rest by faith in knowing He will answer us when we call.[692]

5. When we humbly do this, when we stop our navel-gazing and look to God, trusting His Word, then in His perfect timing, we feel the strength of the Lord. We see the power of God. We see the goodness of the Lord in the land of the living. Let us wait for the Lord; be strong, and let our hearts take courage and wait for the Lord.[693]

---

[689]Hebrews 12:2, [690]Proverbs 3:5–6, [691]1 Thessalonians 5:15–18, [692]Psalm 91:15, [693]Psalm 27:13–14

Father, Your thoughts and Your ways are perfect. Forgive me, Lord, for so many times I have sought to strive in my strength, to push for immediate gratification, or to deny Your love for me. Yet Your mercies are new every morning; great is Your faithfulness. Grant me Your joy and Your strength, by Your wisdom, to do Your will, for Your glory. In Jesus' name I ask this.

Galatians 1:10

For am I now seeking the approval of man, or of God? Or am I trying to please man? If I were still trying to please man, I would not be a servant of Christ.

1. Our aim is not to please man or to strive for our own pleasure. For the gospel does not need anything added to bring or enhance beauty in any way, shape, or form.

2. When we diminish the beauty, truth, and goodness of the gospel by adding what we think it needs for improvement, we condemn ourselves, for if we truly knew the gospel we would know there is nothing we could ever add to improve it.

3. The gospel works by the power of God. The gospel is not about numbers, it is not about people liking you, it is not about impact; it is about the power of God, by the Spirit of God, through the Son of God, to the glory of the Father. Anything we think we add to God's power actually detracts from the beauty of God, for it is taking the perceived power of man (an oxymoron) and attempts to do what only God can do.

4. Let us cease in our striving to be liked by man, and let us relish in the love of the Father. In doing this, we will love people more—and better—for we will speak truth in love through our thoughts, words, actions, and deeds because they will not be for man's glory but for the glory of God Himself.

Father, how glorious is Your gospel! Father, so many times I am fearful of man rather than trusting Your Word. I fear the aimless words of little man rather than the voice of the Lord, whose very voice holds up, sustains, and establishes the entire universe. Lord, grant me to know Your voice through Your Word. Bring to mind Your promises and remove the fear of man. Let others see my good works and praise You in heaven. In Jesus' name.

Galatians 3:3

Are you so foolish? Having begun by the Spirit, are you now being perfected by the flesh?

1. Let us be mindful and remain on guard against every form of deceit the devil whispers to us. There is a subtle and destructive temptation to think once we are reconciled to Christ, we have received a golden ticket into heaven, and the need for God is over. The aim of heresy is to get into heaven, not to know God.

2. All of life should be lived under the power of God. There are no good works that can earn the blessing of the Lord, but the blessing of the Lord is shown through His work through us. Our works must not be man-centered, but God-centered. They must be rooted in the Word of God and walked out by faith.

3. The inclination of the heart of man, apart from the work of the Holy Spirit, is to whisper to ourselves, "Did God really say…"[694] We must hold fast to the Word of God and make our salvation sure, by faith in the finished work of Christ.

4. This is the life of the Christian. It is an everyday, moment-by-moment, second-by-second step. Pray continuously, and give thanks in all circumstances.[695] The power of God is shown in the common means of grace. It is our waking in the morning and giving thanks to the Lord for sustaining us through the night. We experience this common grace when we pray before meeting with a friend that God would bless the conversation. In the evening, we spend time thanking the Lord for all the dispensations of grace He worked through us that day, for His glory and our good.

[694] Genesis 3:1, [695] 1 Thessalonians 5:17–18

Father, You are Lord over every moment. There is no moment You are not Lord over. I am tempted to walk in the wretched sin of unbelief and to be man-centered, to fear man and the future rather than trusting in Your receptive strength. Forgive me. Make me walk in the joy of Your salvation, by the power of the Spirit, in every thought, word, action, and deed, for Your glory. In Jesus' name.

Amen

Galatians 48:9

Joseph said to his father,
"They are my sons, whom God has given me here."

1. Man was not created by chance, and he is not a glob of proteins and atoms randomly arranged and come to life through the absence of nothing. Think about this. How can something that doesn't exist, exist if nothing exists? It can't.

2. Man is created in the image of God.[696] In that truth, we give all the praise, honor, and glory to God, for from Him, and through Him, and to Him are all things.[697]

3. Children, then, are a gift from the Lord. They too are born in the *Imago Dei*. Every child conceived is a heritage from the Lord.[698] Each child is unique; no two children on the face of the planet are alike since the creation of the world—even those with the same parents. All are fearfully and wonderfully made![699]

4. In light of this, we must acknowledge the Lord's sovereignty; we must train up our children in the way they should go, so when they are older they will not depart from it.[700] We must pray for our children, pray the Lord gives them hearts for Him, and pray they fear the Lord. Lastly, we must entrust our children to the Lord, for it is He who gives them to us, and it is He who will finish the work he has for them, for His glory.

---

[696]Genesis 1:26, [697]Romans 11:36, [698]Psalm 127:3, [699]Psalm 139:14, [700]Proverbs 22:6

Father, thank You for the gift of children. They are such a blessing and delight. You have taught me so much about You as a Heavenly Father by giving me sons of my own. So many times, Father, I do not look at them in the truth of Your creation. Help me to see You working in their lives, and give me wisdom to train them up in the way they should go. In Jesus' name.

Genesis 50:19–20

But Joseph said to them, "Do not fear, for am I in the place of God? As for you, you meant evil against me, but God meant it for good, to bring it about that many people should be kept alive, as they are today.

1. Joseph's brothers grew terrified because their father Jacob passed away. Their fear is that since he passed, Joseph would seek vengeance on them for what they did to him. Once again, they looked at the situation pragmatically and not in truth of who God is.

2. Joseph spoke to them in light of who God is. Joseph acknowledged straightforwardly that God is who orchestrates all things, and God is in complete control. God would revenge that which needed to be done.

3. Joseph did not brush under the rug what his brothers did to him. He acknowledged it was evil, but he also acknowledged the intent of his brothers was not the plan of God, who is good in all things.

4. When we take our eyes off God and place them on ourselves, we create a victim mentality and deny the sovereignty of God. We use human terms such as "wound" or "emotional scars" to describe our circumstances and justify our thoughts, words, and emotions. The danger in this mentality is the denying of the sovereignty of God. For the Scriptures say, "And have you forgotten the exhortation that addresses you as sons? "My son, do not regard lightly the discipline of the Lord, nor be weary when reproved by him. For the Lord disciplines the one he loves, and chastises every son whom he receives." It is for discipline that you have to endure. God is treating you as sons. For what son is there whom his father does not discipline?"[701]

5. The Father uses discipline to conform us to the image of Christ. It is the Father's hands that lead us through the valley of the shadow of death, not victimization. Let us look to and trust the Lord. Even though evil occurs, let us by faith humbly acknowledge God, who uses everything for His glory and our good.

[701] Hebrews 12:5–7

Father, You work all things in accordance with Your will. The world so quickly desires that we look at ourselves. To begin with ourselves, to justify ourselves, and to deny Your power and Your timing. We have done this since the garden of Eden, attempting at all times to "be like God." Forgive us, Lord. Have mercy on us. Help us to walk by faith humbly before You. In Jesus' name I ask this.

Psalm 119:34

"Give me understanding, that I may keep your law and observe it with my whole heart."

1. We depend upon the Lord for understanding. Truth is not something we find inside ourselves; truth is outside of us. Truth is only in One: the Lord Jesus Christ. For Christ said, *"For I am the way, and the truth, and the life. No one comes to the Father, except through me."*[702]

2. We must go to the Lord prayerfully. Man, in his flesh and apart from the work of the Holy Spirit, presupposes that he is good and knows how to work his way to goodness. But as Scripture says, *"Can the Ethiopian change his skin or the leopard his spots? Then also you can do good who are accustomed to do evil."*[703]

3. We must humble ourselves and seek the Lord, depending upon the promises of God. We must trust the work of the Holy Spirit and seek Him with our whole hearts. We must realize that apart from Christ, we can do nothing.[704] But in Christ, all the promises of God say amen.[705]

4. This is not a matter of morality or a veneer of manipulative piety we are trying to accomplish, but the desire is for the whole heart to change. For apart from the work of the Holy Spirit, *"Out of the heart come evil thoughts, murder, adultery, sexual immorality, theft, false witness, slander."*[706]

---

[702]John 14:6, [703]Jeremiah 13:23, [704]John 15:5, [705]2 Corinthians 1:20, [706]Matthew 15:19

Father, You are holy. Your ways are holy. When I meditate on Your Word and am mindful of Your holiness, I am overwhelmed. For I have to look at my heart and see that apart from the work of the Holy Spirit, my nature is completely depraved. My heart even attempts to deceive itself by saying it is good and does not need to change. Lord, change my heart. This is a terrifying prayer for me because I don't know what all You will do in changing my heart. Help me to know Your love for me, and help me to know Christ, and may Your will be done, that I may know You more, and observe Your Word and Your Law with my whole heart.

1 Samuel 7:3

If you are returning to the Lord with all your heart, then put away the foreign gods and the Ashtaroth from among you and direct your heart to the Lord and serve him only, and he will deliver you out of the hand of the Philistines.

1. The believer's aim is to know God and to make Him known in every thought, word, action, and deed.

2. Yet we do not do this, for we are tempted to think we are like God.[707] In this subtle, vile temptation, we start to think God does not know us, that He forgot us, and if we establish freedom from the catastrophe and the circumstances in our lives, it is our own work and deeds that save us. We cease to look at the sovereign God, who is doing all things for His glory and our good, and look at the circumstances as gods instead.

3. We allow the idols of comfort, ease, self-preservation, material blessings, and companionship to become our focus, rather than putting them away and returning to the Lord. When times are difficult, instead of entering into repentance and acknowledging the sovereign God who ordains these very situations, we puff up our chests and fight off and deny the tender touch of our Father. We harden our hearts against Him.

4. Our deceitful and wretched hearts spew theological truths as a philosophy, rather than humbly looking to the Lord and saying, "Whatever the Lord ordains is right; may Your Kingdom come, may Your will be done on earth as it is in heaven."[708] The Lord will fight for His people, and He will do what is right, and true, and good.

---

[707]Genesis 3:5, [708]Matthew 6:10

Father, how gracious You are, and holy. Forgive me for holding on to the things of this world and not seeking You. I have sought self-preservation rather than Christ and Christ alone. Forgive me, for I am a wretch apart from Your grace. Please free me from my sin and pride in whatever way You deem the most glorifying to You, that I may praise You all my days. To You be the glory and the honor and the praise.

1 Samuel 3:9

Therefore Eli said to Samuel, "Go, lie down, and if he calls you, you shall say, 'Speak, LORD, for your servant hears.'"

1. The Lord speaks to His people through His Word, yet many people do not know the voice of God. They look at Scripture as a piece of literature written on parchment, no different from any other document on the planet.

2. But Scripture is unlike any other writing. We must first acknowledge that all Scripture is God breathed and is profitable for teaching, reproof, correction, and training in righteousness.[709]

3. When we approach the Word of God, we must first present ourselves to the Lord. We must acknowledge it is the very Word of God, and apart from Him, we can understand and do nothing.[710]

4. God's Word is always active. When approached in a way that glorifies and honors the Lord, it either teaches us, leads us to repentance, or hardens the hearts of those who hear it.[711] When we approach the Word of God, our response should be, "Speak Lord, for Your servant hears." We must deny self-lordship and approach the throne of grace as servants of Christ and Christ alone.

---

[709] 2 Timothy 3:16, [710] John 15:5, [711] Isaiah 6:8–13

Father, Your Word is true. You have ordained what I am to read today. You have created this day and are mindful of those things before me. You are working all things together for Your glory and my good. I praise You! Oh Lord, guard my heart from words that tickle my ears. Words that lead me into self-idolatry. Grant me, Your servant, to hear Your voice by Your grace in Your Word, that I may praise You. Lead me on level ground according to Your Word.[712] In Christ's name I ask this.

Acts 4:19

But Peter and John answered them, "Whether it is right in the sight of God to listen to you rather than to God, you must judge."

1. The aim of God's people is not to be right or good based upon the standards of a culture. Our measurement is not the measurements of man but the standard of God. For we are to be holy as God is holy.[713]

2. Our every move, thought, action, word, and deed are done before a holy God, and it is His standard, His ways, we are to honor and to glorify. We are to test our thoughts and be mindful of them, not according to man's standard but God's standard, which is Christ the Word of God reflected in His Word, for His Word is truth.[714]

3. Each person is accountable for their actions before a holy God. If we fashion a god from our own imagination, we allow ourselves to justify all our actions according to how we feel or what we desire.

4. Let us judge against Christ. Let us choose this day whom we will serve. Either the gods of the people of the world, who conjure up their ideas according to their emotions and worldly standards, or the God and Father of our Lord Jesus Christ. As for me and my house, we will serve the Lord.[715]

---

[713]Leviticus 19:2, [714]John 17:17, [715]Joshua 24:15

Father, You are holy! Christ is exalted, and it is Christ and Christ alone who is to be my aim. Forgive me for the many times I have measured my deeds and thoughts against the world rather than in Christ alone. I forget so easily and fall into unbelief so quickly apart from Your grace. Grant me to know Christ, think on Christ, pursue Christ, bow my knee to Christ, trust Christ, for Christ's sake and His glory.

Hebrews 3:12–13

Take care, brothers, lest there be in any of you an evil, unbelieving heart, leading you to fall away from the living God. But exhort one another every day, as long as it is called "today," that none of you may be hardened by the deceitfulness of sin.

1. What is the greatest evil of the heart of man? It is unbelief, for unbelief is what hardens the heart to not know the Lordship of Christ and causes us to fall away from the truth of a living God.

2. It is unbelief that keeps us from resting and knowing the living God. Unbelief is subtle, for it tends to creep in through the cracks of our lives. We must test everything in our lives and hold fast to that which is good, abstaining from every form of evil.[716]

3. Sin is deceptive, for it allows our hearts to proclaim the Lordship of Christ on Sunday mornings but then hardens our hearts to all other aspects. We are deceived by practical burdens of the day; we are tempted to keep Christ from entering our speech with friends to save us from embarrassment. We are pragmatic with our children. All of these come from an unbelief and hardening of the heart.

4. Let us not quench the Spirit![717] We must give thanks to God in all aspects of our lives. We are to exhort each other and encourage each other in the Lordship of Christ, and we are to do it for as long as today is called today. To the extent we do not do this in every and all spheres of our lives, our hearts will be as hardened as stone.

---

[716] 1 Thessalonians 5:21, [717] 1 Thessalonians 5:19

Father, You have sent Your Son into the world to establish Your Kingdom! How glorious! Your Kingdom is over all areas and spheres of our lives, yet how we easily relegate You to Sunday mornings and harden our hearts to the rest of our lives. Forgive us, Lord. Loosen our tongues to sing Your praises in all spheres and every aspect of our lives. Draw Your church to Yourself that we may proclaim the excellence of Him who has called us out of darkness and into His marvelous light. In Christ's name.

Psalm 4:7

*YOU HAVE PUT MORE JOY IN MY HEART THAN
THEY HAVE WHEN THEIR GRAIN AND WINE ABOUND.*

1. At the fall, in the garden of Eden, our walk with God was completely taken away because of our sin. Since that exact moment, after our separation from God, our lives have been spent attempting to refill our hearts with what our sin took away.

2. Our flesh seeks joy, and apart from the grace of God, we seek to fulfill this longing with the things of earth: relationships, money, food, stuff; but nothing satisfies, nothing gives our hearts satisfaction. Nothing can satisfy our depraved hearts' yearning apart from Christ.

3. But the mercy of our Father radiates forth! Our Father knows our frame; He remembers we are dust![718] He has sent Christ, His only Son, to conquer death,[719] and in Christ alone our joy is complete![720]

4. In this truth, we are to seek first the Kingdom of God, and all these things shall be added to us.[721] The Lord promises to satisfy us according to His wisdom in Christ Jesus. The joy of the Lord is our strength,[722] and in Christ and Christ alone we have all we will ever need.

---

[718]Psalm 103:14, [719]1 Corinthians 15:54–55, [720]Romans 5:11, [721]Matthew 6:33, [722]Nehemiah 8:10

Father, thank You for Christ! What does it mean to seek first the Kingdom of God, and all these things will be added to me? When I think of this promise, I realize it is so opposite of the world and all it declares that I do. I am so easily tempted to think I need what the world says I need. Will You please help me to seek Your Kingdom and trust in Your goodness and grace? Will You allow me to know the joy of my salvation? Please lead me in Your way. In Jesus' name.

Exodus 23:2–3

You shall not fall in with the many to do evil, nor shall you bear witness in a lawsuit, siding with the many, so as to pervert justice, nor shall you be partial to a poor man in his lawsuit.

1. We must remember two things. First, neither majority nor circumstance ever defines what truth is. Second, truth and justice are found in the Person, Christ Jesus, and is witnessed by His Word.

2. God has given us His Word. His Word is truth[723] and it does not falter. It is infallible, and it is authority. It is never wrong nor does it err. We must be careful and wise, for even though Scripture never errs, those who read it are fallible and are sinful. So we must never trust in man or in our leaders, but we must trust only in the Lord.[724] We must never trust our own word but trust the Word of God.[725] The masses do not define truth but only the Word of God.

3. God ordains the circumstances of every person. "In the day of prosperity be joyful, and in the day of adversity consider: God has made the one as well as the other, so that man may not find out anything that will be after him."[726] We must never define truth by someone else's circumstances. We must never define truth by what we feel. Truth is objectively true because it is only found in one Person.

4. God's Word is truth, and the Word of God became flesh and dwelt among us.[727] Truth and justice are embodied in only one Person. He does not show partiality; He is not compromising; He is settled. He is our Lord and Savior. Truth came into the world, and Truth was crucified. He was buried and was raised on the third day and has conquered death. In Christ we stand. We need nothing more, nor do we define truth by anyone else.

---

[723] John 17:17, [724] Psalm 118:8–9, [725] Proverbs 3:7, [726] Ecclesiastes 7:14, [727] John 1:14

Father, thank You for Christ! Thank You for Your Word! Father, I have so many times lost sight of Christ, denied Your Word, defined myself by things other than the finished work of Christ. Forgive me. Grant me to have a more glorious view of Your Son, a clearer knowledge of His glory and preeminence, and grant me a boldness to humbly serve Him. Thank You for Jesus.

Mark 10:15

Truly, I say to you, whoever does not receive the kingdom of God like a child shall not enter it."

1. The faith of a child is bold and unapologetic. The bravery is unparalleled in any way. This is how the Lord desires for us to know and follow Him.

2. When the foolishness of the world tempts and deceives us, we begin to act like practical atheists in all our thoughts, words, actions, and deeds. We have a fear of man rather than the fear of the Lord. For the fear of man lays a snare, but whoever trusts in the Lord is safe.[728]

3. We, in our self-proclaimed wisdom, conjure up lies and deceive ourselves with possibilities that never occur. We sin against God's Word and lean on our own understanding.[729] The evil in our hearts makes us wise in our own eyes,[730] and we fear what others think of us rather than resting in the truth of God's Word.

4. Not so a child. A child's heart trusts with reckless abandon the truth of God. It emboldens him, assures him, it affirms him, it defines him. He cannot defend it, but he need not worry because truth will defend itself.

---

[728]Psalm 29:25, [729]Proverbs 3:5, [730]Proverbs 3:7

Father, Your Word is truth. I am so easily manipulated by emotions and by what others think and say. Forgive me. Will You embolden and strengthen my heart according to Your Word? Help me to have a childlike faith, guard my heart from practical atheism, and help me to boldly rest in Your Word. In Jesus' name.

Amen

Psalm 1:2-3

BUT HIS DELIGHT IS IN THE LAW OF THE LORD, AND ON HIS LAW HE MEDITATES DAY AND NIGHT. HE IS LIKE A TREE PLANTED BY STREAMS OF WATER THAT YIELDS ITS FRUIT IN ITS SEASON, AND ITS LEAF DOES NOT WITHER. IN ALL THAT HE DOES, HE PROSPERS.

1. What do you delight in? On what do you meditate? Do you meditate on your emotions, on what you see in the world, on the wars and rumors of wars you hear about? Or do you meditate on the truth of God's Word?

2. Those who look to the Word of God and trust His Word, the Lord promises He will sustain. He will sustain Him in the same way He sustains all of creation. His Word will be a stream that refreshes your soul for what the Lord has for you in this very day. Every event the Lord has ordained, He has also given His Word to lead you in and through that time.

3. We must also be aware and mindful that His way is opposite of the world. When our hope is not in the world, the world will persecute us because the world does not understand. When our strength is not in our circumstances but in the Word of God, we will be scorned and mocked because it will be opposite of all the world knows.

4. But is this not what happened to our Lord, and He conquered death! For He was pierced for our transgressions; He was crushed for our iniquities; upon Him was the chastisement that brought us peace, and with His wounds we are healed.[731]

---

[731] Isaiah 53:5

Father, Your Word is glorious!
Will You bring to my mind Your Word?
Will You reveal the truth of Your
Word to me? Will You convict my
heart with Your Word? Will You
embolden my heart with Your Word?
Thank You for Your Word!
In Jesus' name.

Amen

Haggai 1:13-14

THEN HAGGAI, THE MESSENGER OF THE LORD, SPOKE TO THE PEOPLE WITH THE LORD'S MESSAGE, "I AM WITH YOU, DECLARES THE LORD." AND THE LORD STIRRED UP THE SPIRIT OF ZERUBBABEL THE SON OF SHEALTIEL, GOVERNOR OF JUDAH.

1. When the Lord calls His people to action, He never leaves us to do what He asks on their own. He comes in the midst of them.[732] He leads us through the deepest trials, and He promises that nothing will consume us.[733] He commands His church to be bold and courageous, not terrified or dismayed. For the Lord our God is with us wherever we go![734]

2. Our aim is not to worry but to so abide in Christ, and Christ in us, that we long to do His will in all things,[735] regardless of the cost.[736] We are to look to the Lord and pray, "Your Kingdom come, Your will be done on earth as it is in heaven."[737]

3. Many times, though, we cease to walk by faith and instead walk by what we see. We allow our emotions and frail humanity to tell us what to believe rather than looking to Christ. Our hearts, apart from the Holy Spirit, attempt in every way to deceive us and make us think Christ is not sitting on His throne, that His calling is too great for us, and the circumstances too dire for us to live in a way that glorifies Him.

4. Let us not be deceived by what the world says or what our hearts say; let our souls abide in the truth of God's Word, for by it all else is bound.[738] Let us look to Christ, who has all authority in heaven above and on earth below. Let us go out and make disciples, baptize them, and teach them all Christ has commanded, abiding in the truth that Christ is with us from now to the end of the age.[739]

---

[732]Deuteronomy 23:14, [733]Isaiah 43:2, [734]Joshua 1:9, [735]John 15:4, [736]Matthew 16:24, [737]Matthew 6:10, [738]John 17:17, [739]Matthew 28:19-20

Father, how easily I am swayed from Your Word. You show me day after day my frailty and humanity. Forgive me for my faithlessness, and increase my faith. Guard me from a gnostic view of You, and help me to walk in the reality of the Lordship of Christ regardless of what I see, but rooted in the truth of who You are. In Christ's name.

1 John 4:1

*BELOVED, DO NOT BELIEVE EVERY SPIRIT,
BUT TEST THE SPIRITS TO SEE WHETHER THEY ARE FROM GOD,
FOR MANY FALSE PROPHETS HAVE GONE OUT INTO THE WORLD.*

1. Words are powerful. They can make peace, and they can start wars. Words have the power to stir up dissension, and they have the power to comfort. Spoken word is what created the world, for God said, "Let there be light, and there was light,"[740] and God's Word became flesh and dwelt among us, and we have seen His glory, the glory of the One and only.[741]

2. But not all words are truth. Even though we have the ability to speak, many words are false. Words are many times reflective of the serpent in the garden of Eden, when Satan said, "Did God really say…"[742] to cast doubt in our hearts and make us feel as fools in the eyes of the world.

3. We are told the Word of God is a good book about great intentions, a set of ideals, but that we are to be "wise" when reading it and not take it too literally. We are told to be religious but not practical with it, for only a fool would take it too seriously. The prophets of science, pragmatism, culture, entertainment, and moralism thump their chests and attempt to make us doubt the very Word of God.

4. But we are to test each of these against the Word of God. We must trust and act upon any word given to us that comes under the acknowledgment and submission of the Lordship of Christ. We must flee any words that do not, for they are the spirit of the antichrist.[743] God will lead us and guide us by His Word, and He has promised He will draw near to those who are humble and contrite in spirit and to those who tremble at His Word and His Word alone.[744]

---

[740]Genesis 1:3, [741]John 1:14, [742]Genesis 3:1, [743]1 John 4:2–3, [744]Isaiah 66:2

Father, Your Word is true, and it shall never be shaken or moved. It is rooted in truth, for You are truth. I confess the many times when I feel lost and alone. I am tempted to doubt Your Word, or I seem lost as to what to think, act, be, or do. The unbelief of sin crouches at my door at all times, and I am indecisive and weak. Oh Lord, help me to bask in the greatness of who You are and to abide in Your Word. Strengthen my heart, my mind, my soul, and my hands with Your Word, that I may do Your will, for Your glory and the good of others. In Christ's name.

Revelation 12:17

Then the dragon became furious with the woman and went off to make war on the rest of her offspring, on those who keep the commandments of God and hold to the testimony of Jesus. And he stood on the sand of the sea.

1. Those who hold fast to the truth of God's Law and the proclamation of the Lordship of Christ are under attack at every moment. The world and our flesh are at enmity with God. To love God is to declare war against Satan and the kingdom of darkness. For we do not wrestle against flesh and blood, but against the rulers and authorities and the cosmic power of this present darkness.[745]

2. The war that Satan wages against God's people is to make us doubt the truth and certainty of God's Word. He tempts us to take our eyes off of the truth of who God is, and, in turn, tempts us to trust our own thoughts and feelings. For in the garden of Eden he asked Eve, "Did God really say…"[746] Later in Scripture, Satan tempted Christ to doubt the promises of God and to put His Father to the test.[747]

3. The most subtle of all Satan's tactics is to tempt our hearts to, instead of holding fast the truth of God's Word in all places of life, desire peace with the world. But peace with the world is enmity with God. It is not the world that is holy, but God. It is not the world that is truth, but God. It is not the world that is the aim and goal of our lives but knowing God.

4. Christ came to earth to pay the penalty for our sins and to free His church from the clutches of Satan. Christ did not come to bring peace but to bring a sword of truth.[748] Truth divides, separates, and conflicts with all things that are not truth. Truth is a Person. He became flesh and dwelt among us, and He is the One whom we look to for all things.[749] He has won, and we are to walk in the truth of the victory of the finished work of Christ for His glory.

[745]Ephesians 6:12, [746]Genesis 3:1, [747]Matthew 4:1–11, [748]Matthew 10:34, [749]John 1:14

Father, You have won all things. You are victorious. You do not need anyone because You have sent Your Son into the world to bring people to Yourself. Help our hearts realize, Lord, that this side of glory we are in a battle. Do not let our hearts become lazy and to justify our unbelief based upon a false sense of peace. Root our hearts in the truth of Your Word, and give us courage and joy to boldly proclaim Your truth to all nations, for Your glory and the exaltation of Christ. In His name I pray.

Amen

Matthew 24:12

AND BECAUSE LAWLESSNESS WILL BE INCREASED, THE LOVE OF MANY WILL GROW COLD.

1. What is to compel the believer to do all that he does for God is the knowledge of God's love for him, and in turn, reciprocating that love back to God for His glory and the good of others.[750] This love is seen first and foremost in the Father sending His only Son to come and live the perfect life, to be crucified, buried, resurrected on the third day, and now sitting at the right hand of God until all of his enemies are placed under His feet.[751]

2. But many times, instead of looking to Christ for our hope, we, in turn, look at the sin and the chaos in the world and define hope, or the lack of hope, upon what we see with our eyes and not what God tells us in His Word. The Lord tests our hearts to see if the love that we proclaim for Christ is true love or if it will fade away when we see the world.

3. Many hearts grow cold to the Lord when their view of God is defined by the world rather than God's Word. Many a person who claims to be a Christian realizes they are to depart from the church, for Christ will say, "I never knew you; depart from me, you workers of lawlessness."[752]

4. Let us look to what God says, and let us not grow weary of doing good![753] Let us take God at His Word, His promises, His truth, and let us not grow weary of doing good, for He has said that we will reap in due season if we do not grow weary of doing good.[754] Let us put our hope in the truth and the reality of God's Word rather than in the world, knowing that our King will bring all things to His perfect purpose.

---

[750]1 John 3:1, [751]1 Corinthians 15:25, [752]Matthew 7:23, [753]2 Thessalonians 3:13, [754]Galatians 6:9

Father, I praise You for Your Word. For it radiates all the more, the more clearly that we see it, and the truer that it discerns the hearts and evil intentions of the world. Forgive me for basing my joy and hope on temporal things rather than Your Word. Fan my love for You more and more into flame, and guard my heart from growing cold. In Christ's name I ask this.

Amen

Genesis 20:11

Abraham said, "I did it because I thought, 'There is no fear of God at all in this place, and they will kill me because of my wife.'"

1. Once again, Abraham told Sarah to lie to the people of the land and to tell them she was his sister rather than his wife.[755]

2. Abimelech took Sarah to make her his wife, but the Lord mercifully stopped the king from sinning against God and against Abraham.[756]

3. Notice Abraham's response to Abimelech. "I did it because I thought..." How easily we deceive ourselves when we do not go to the Lord in prayer. We trust our own minds and thought processes; we become wise in our own eyes. We are never to lean on our own understanding without first trusting in the Word of God![757] When we become wise in our own eyes, we cease to fear the Lord and therefore sin against Him.[758]

4. What causes us to do this? We listen to the devil when he whispers, "Did God actually say…?"[759] We fear the man more than we fear the Lord. We walk by sight rather than by faith in Almighty God. We deny the Lordship of Christ and place ourselves on the throne. We must stop and seek the Lord, trusting His Word and acting in accordance with all He has done and is doing.

---

[755]Genesis 20:1–2, [756]Genesis 20:6, [757]Proverbs 3:5, [758]Proverbs 3:7, [759]Genesis 3:1

Father, we come to You and thank You for Your Word, for Your Word is truth![760] Lord, help me to know Your Word. Help my heart and mind to soften and to adore Your Word and trust it, and to walk by grace in it. Forgive me for how many times I doubt and walk in unbelief. Lead me in Your way everlasting! In Jesus' name.

[760] John 17:17

2 *John* 6

And this is love, that we walk according to his commandments; this is the commandment, just as you have heard from the beginning, so that you should walk in it.

1. *Love* is a word the world desires to define apart from *truth*. This word has been ripped from truth and become synonymous with *desires*. But when we change a word's definition and relegate it individually, the word becomes subjective, based upon the context of that person. By redefining a word, we actually live a lie.

2. So, what does God's Word say about love? We show love when we honor Him who called us out of darkness and into His marvelous light.[761] When we walk holy, as He is holy, we radiate our love for him.[762] The lack of following His Law and commandments is sin and leads to utter depravity.[763]

3. The Law of God is perfect and revives one's soul.[764] His precepts are right, making the heart rejoice, and His commandments are pure, giving us wisdom to do His will![765] His rules are true and absolute, regardless of how the world views them, and they are righteous altogether.[766]

4. Christ promises to abide with us if we keep His commands.[767] He promises to never leave us nor forsake us.[768] So let us love the Lord with all our hearts, souls, and minds.[769] Let us follow His commands and not define ourselves by the world's standards. Let our standard be the very Word of God. For He who did not spare His own Son but gave Him up for us all, how will He not give us all that we need and desire?[770]

---

[761]1 Peter 2:9, [762]Leviticus 11:44, [763]1 John 3:4, [764]Psalm 19:7, [765]Psalm 19:8, [766]Psalm 19:9, [767]John 15:10, [768]Hebrews 13:5, [769]Deuteronomy 6:5, [770]Romans 8:32

Father, You defined love by sending Your Son to us. You defined mercy and grace by giving us Your Law and saving us from the death we deserve. Lord, I confess how I easily change the definitions of words based upon convenience or my human inclinations. Forgive me. Help me to walk in a way that You are glorified, magnified, and made much of. Help me to walk faithfully before You, that others may see my good work and praise You in heaven. In Christ's name!

1 John 4:6

WE ARE FROM GOD. WHOEVER KNOWS GOD LISTENS TO US; WHOEVER IS NOT FROM GOD DOES NOT LISTEN TO US. BY THIS WE KNOW THE SPIRIT OF TRUTH AND THE SPIRIT OF ERROR.

1. There is such a thing as absolute truth, and it is rooted in an absolute Person. Those who are not in that Person are not from that Person.

2. The reason why the world does not know us is that it does not know Him.[771]

3. The focus, however, is not on the other person. Our focus should be on the Person who we know to be the way, and the truth, and the light.[772]

4. Man judges the outward (the fruit), but God judges the heart.[773]

5. Our goal, our object, our aim, is to know Christ and Christ alone. Christ is our test, Christ is our objective, Christ is our hope, Christ is our aim, Christ is our all in all. Let Christ be our test. Some people are not in Christ, and not everyone who says, "Lord, Lord," knows Christ.[774] This is terrifying and just. This is convicting and hopeful. Lord, have mercy.

---

[771] 1 John 3:1, [772] John 14:6, [773] 1 Samuel 16:7, [774] Matthew 7:21

Jesus, I praise You, for You are King of kings and Lord of lords. Forgive me for looking at my own humanity, my own moralism, as the measuring stick of my self-righteousness. Thank You for saving me and bringing me into Your Kingdom. Jesus, guard my heart from laziness and legalism. Guard my heart from mysticism and intellectualism; guard my heart from moralism and antinomianism; and help me to walk, think, seek, talk, and do all for Your glory. Please guard my mind and to help me to walk in all righteousness, for Your glory.

Psalm 53:1

The fool says in his heart, "There is no God."
They are corrupt, doing abominable iniquity;
there is none who does good.

1. Remember, it's not the wise person or the smart person who says there is no God, but the fool. The person who scoffs at a holy God is the One who is the biggest fool of all.

2. The fool's basis of truth is himself, a depraved individual, who as soon as he claims to know truth apart from God, actually denies absolute truth. All truth based on an individual is relative and ceases to be absolute. This is true of every person who has ever existed, except One, Jesus Christ.

3. The root sin of the fool is unbelief in a holy God. An unbelief of His promises, His covenant, His sovereignty, His omniscience, His omnipresence, His holiness, His Word, His Son.

4. Every time I act contrary to the Word of God and act in a way that contradicts His will, I am the fool, and I commit the sin of unbelief.

5. The only Person who ever was absolute truth and walked on the earth is Christ Jesus. For, in the beginning He was God, He was with God, and He was God; He was with God in the beginning.[775]

6. No one can know truth apart from knowing Christ and Christ alone, for Christ Himself said, "I am the way, and the truth, and the life; no one comes to the Father except through me."[776]

[775]John 1:1, [776]John 14:6

Father, You are so merciful. You are truth, and Your Word is truth.[777] I confess, Father, the many times when I, in my pride, scoff at those who are in unbelief, and then I recognize I am the fool many times. I deny Your Lordship, I deny Your sovereignty, I deny Your love for me so many times. Forgive me and have mercy on me. Help me to walk in the truth of Christ, by the power of the Holy Spirit, to the glory of God. Thank You for truth; thank You for Christ. In Jesus' name.

Amen

---

[777] John 17:17

Judges 2:10

And all that generation also were gathered to their fathers. And there arose another generation after them who did not know the Lord or the work that he had done for Israel.

1. Every child is a gift from the Lord. The Word of God states that He is a blessed man who has many children.[778] Yet with each child, God has called the parents to teach them to love the Lord.

2. We are to teach our children diligently of all the Lord does. We are to discuss it when we sit down and when we rise, when we walk by the way, and when we lie down.[779]

3. We are to train up our children in the way they should go, so when they are old they will not depart from it.[780] Our knowledge and our worship of God is only one generation from ceasing to know the Lord.

4. The responsibility begins with fathers teaching about the work and the commands of God. Mothers are to help fathers in training up their children in the Lord, and they will be held accountable before Him. We are to share with our children what the Lord is doing in our lives, how He is working, and how He is bringing His Kingdom to the world. This is not a moralism or a legalism, but a reality that God has commanded His people to do for His glory, and for the good of generations to come.

---

[778]Psalm 127:5, [779]Deuteronomy 6:7, [780]Proverbs 22:6

Father, You are good and Your steadfast love endures forever. Thank You for our children. Thank You for bringing us to this moment and for allowing us to know You and train up our children. Forgive me for not speaking of Your deeds, for instead speaking pridefully and pragmatically in front of my children. Open my heart and my mind to speak of Your great deeds in our family's life, that they may see Your great work and praise and serve You, our Father in heaven.
In Christ's name I ask this.

Amen

Deuteronomy 26:11

And you shall rejoice in all the good that the Lord your God has given to you and to your house, you, and the Levite, and the sojourner who is among you.

1. All things come from the Lord, and all are for His glory and our good. We must be mindful of the gifts of God, lest we deceive ourselves and think we ourselves are the provider and sustainer of our lives.

2. As John Calvin wrote, our hearts are "idol factories." We constantly attempt to affirm our greatness in what we have, and our flesh desperately tries to deny the Lord.

3. So we must exhort each other and be mindful to praise the Lord and thank Him for all things. For in the same way that God looked upon His creation, and said, "It is good,"[781] we must stop, pause, and reflect to see the goodness of God.

4. Lastly, our wealth is not for ourselves alone, but it is for those whom God has placed in our lives. For in the same way that God so richly blesses us, we are to bless others. We are to bless the Bride of Christ—the church—with our tithes and offerings. We are to bless missionaries with the blessings God has given us. Lastly, we are to bless those whom the Lord sends across our path every day. The sojourner, who is our neighbor, our coworker, the people around us who are in need. We are called to bless others and reflect God's blessing to us.

---

[781] Genesis 1:10

Father, I thank You and praise You for being in our midst. I praise You for You have created all things, and You have so richly blessed our family. There are times I feel fear and frustration, and it's in those moments when I forget Your sovereignty and that all things come from You. Forgive my pride. Work in my life and in our family a heart of thanksgiving and joy at Your providence, and open opportunities for us to give in a way that reflects Your abundance to those in need. In Jesus' name.

Psalm 37:1-2

FRET NOT YOURSELF BECAUSE OF EVILDOERS; BE NOT ENVIOUS OF WRONGDOERS! FOR THEY WILL SOON FADE LIKE THE GRASS AND WITHER LIKE THE GREEN HERB.

1. As people of God, we are not to worry about what others do or how they prosper. We are not to look to those who lie, steal, and cheat for selfish gain and attempt to build towers of Babel in the same way.

2. For it is God who rules overall and supplies our every need. We are to focus on knowing God and making Him known. We are to love the Lord with all our hearts, with all our souls, and with all our might.[782]

3. We are not to be anxious about anything, but in every prayer and petition and with thanksgiving, we present our requests to God. And the God of all peace will guard our hearts and our minds![783]

4. The intimacy of God abounds in the hearts of His people. The Lord inhabits the praises of His people![784] Let God's people seek the Lord, thank the Lord, and trust the Lord in all the acts He sets before us.

---

[782]Deuteronomy 6:5, [783]Philippians 4:6–7, [784]Psalm 22:3

Oh Father, You are great and glorious and You know me! Forgive me for comparing myself to others. Forgive me for envying the wicked. Forgive my pragmatic and atheistic heart and for erecting idols in my heart and mind that do not honor You. Thank You for all You have done and are doing, and help me to walk in Your way, with a heart of thanksgiving for Christ and for Your glory! In Jesus' name!

Psalm 37:3

TRUST IN THE LORD, AND DO GOOD;
DWELL IN THE LAND AND BEFRIEND FAITHFULNESS.

1. We are to trust the Lord in all circumstances and in every situation. For our God is sovereign over all things and He is working all things together for His glory and our good.

2. In trusting Him, though, we are not to sit around and be lazy like the servant who buried his talent in the field.[785] We are to have an active obedience. An obedience that reflects the attributes of God.

3. Our God is never not good in all His ways. He is a covenantal God and is faithful to us. He makes the sun rise every morning and sustains us through all things. We, in turn, are to reflect His attributes back to Him as an act of worship.

4. Our trust and obedience are to be active—doing good and loving our neighbor as ourselves[786] and being faithful in the same way God is faithful to us. We are to leave all the results to Him and, in turn, trust Him as we pursue His glory and our good.

---

[785]Matthew 25:25, [786]Matthew 22:39

Father, You provide and do all things together in Your perfect way. How easily I forget Your sovereignty and Your goodness. I preconceive the answers I desire rather than Your will. Forgive me! Help me and strengthen me to do good to those You bring along my path. Help me to be faithful in all I do. Grant me the freedom and the joy to faithfully serve You all my days! Thank You, Father, for Jesus. With praise and adoration!

Philippians 1:6

And I am sure of this, that he who began a good work in you will bring it to completion at the day of Jesus Christ.

1. The believer's foundation and the believer's hope is not in himself but in God. For it is God who saves, it is God who calls, and it is God who works all things together for His glory and our good.[787]

2. It is an atheistic thought that drives into our hearts a hopelessness of the future. For in this moment, instead of beginning with the truth of God, we replace God as sovereign and worry about what is ahead of us. In that exact moment, our humanity bears witness to our frailty and we lose all hope.

3. Let us never start with ourselves, but with God only. Let us never attempt to be "like God,"[788] but let us humbly bow our knees to Him, denying ourselves, taking up our cross, and following Christ.[789]

4. Regardless of what the world says, the Lord is making all things new.[790] He is orchestrating all things and there is no government, no power, and no authority not under His sovereignty.[791] Let us then wait for the Lord; be strong, let your heart take courage, and wait for the Lord.[792]

---

[787]Romans 8:28, [788]Genesis 3:5, [789]Matthew 16:24, [790]Revelation 21:5, [791]Colossians 1:15–20, [792]Psalm 27:14

Father, in You is hope. This is so antithetical to what the world says. The world says our hope should be in our strength, in our efforts, and in the things of this world. When we see things are not good, we despair. But, You have called us to keep our eyes on You, to hold fast to the things You are revealing about Yourself, and look to Christ. Lord, guard my heart against unbelief and help me to walk humbly before You. In Jesus' name.

Amen

Philippians 2:3-4

Do nothing from selfish ambition or conceit, but in humility count others more significant than yourselves. Let each of you look not only to his own interests, but also to the interests of others.

1. "Do nothing from selfish ambition." What an antithetical statement to the heart of man. The unregenerate man does not know the Lord, so every morning he wakes with the weight of having to defend himself, needing to build himself, and has no one to look to, except himself.

2. Yet the believer looks to Christ. He does not need anything, for all he has is in Christ. We do not serve ourselves but serve Christ. We humbly look to Christ, "who, though he was in the form of God, did not count equality with God a thing to be grasped, but emptied himself, by taking the form of a servant, being born in the likeness of men. And being found in human form, he humbled himself by becoming obedient to the point of death, even death on a cross."[793]

3. Our hearts, apart from the work of the Holy Spirit, fight against this. We question and fear it. For the devil and the world tickle our ears, whispering that God does not really know what He is doing and that He isn't with us. But oh, believer, do not listen. Look to the Word of God and rest upon His promises. Ask the Lord to help you see Christ and to humbly serve Him with boldness, for His glory and your good, trusting Him with all your heart, and leaning not on your own understanding![794]

4. This can only happen in true love of one another, and the only way we can truly love others is if we know the love of the Father. How do we know the love of the Father? Look to Christ! The Father sent His Son because He loves us. Christ is the key to all things, to the glory of the Father.

[793]Philippians 2:6-8, [794]Proverbs 3:5

Father, I have not rested in Your love. I confess I don't know how to rest in Your love. In my heart I struggle with love because I have many times defined love by the standards of the world rather than in Christ. Help me to know Your love for me. Help me to know Your love, that I may reflect it in a way that glorifies You. Guard my heart against selfish ambition and conceit, and help me to love, trusting Your sovereignty. In Jesus' name I ask this.

Amen

Exodus 16:4

Then the Lord said to Moses, "Behold, I am about to rain bread from heaven for you, and the people shall go out and gather a day's portion every day, that I may test them, whether they will walk in my law or not."

1. The Lord showed the people of Israel His mighty power by delivering them from Egypt and leading them through the Red Sea. But, when in the middle of the wilderness, instead of going to the Lord and petitioning Him to provide for them, they grumbled at Him.[795]

2. In turn, the Lord promised to give the Israelites bread from heaven. This was to provide for them but also to test their hearts.

3. None of the Lord's providences are without sanctification. Each and every one leads us to Him. The blessing of the Lord many times reveals the idols in our hearts and, as we seek Him, can many times lead us to repentance.

4. This also is the first Law the Lord gave the Israelites outside of the land of Egypt. Would they obey the Word of the Lord and only gather food for six days, or would they ignore His Law and gather more out of practicality? Would they be lazy and not gather enough food on the sixth day, or would they be glutenous and gather more than they need? This required the Israelites to search their hearts while they worked. They were not to judge their neighbor but were held accountable by the living God.

5. How often do we look at the dispensations of life the Lord sends us through in light of His Word? Let us be mindful of our hearts. Let us be mindful of the motivations and justifications of our actions. For man looks at the outward appearance, but God looks at the heart.[796]

---

[795] Genesis 16:2, [796] 1 Samuel 16:7

Father, Your Word is truth.[797] How easily I justify my actions by what others do or don't do, rather than looking to Christ. Lord, You are ever near, for in You we live and move and have our being![798] Oh Lord, search my heart and know me. Help me to walk in repentance and humble dependence on Your Word and on the finished work of Christ and Christ alone!

Amen

[797] John 17:17, [798] Acts 17:28

Exodus 16:8

And Moses said, "When the LORD gives you in the evening meat to eat and in the morning bread to the full, because the LORD has heard your grumbling that you grumble against him—what are we? Your grumbling is not against us but against the LORD."

1. All that we say and do, the Lord Most High sees, for in Him we live and move and have our being.[799] When we grumble, we deny the Lord's sovereignty—that He is orchestrating all things for His glory. We claim Him as *deistic*, rather than *theistic*, over all things.

2. Grumbling is a sin against God, for we are to do all things without grumbling![800] What a glorious command; what a convicting command. For so many times we attempt to justify our grumbling for what we deem to be our right.

3. Our hearts grumble when we think God is holding back something good. We cease to remember all things that come from God are good, and we look at and envy what others have and decide we have the right to it too. We forget the promises of God; we cease to acknowledge His love and His providence, and grumbling is the seed in which we cease waiting on the Lord and take matters into our own hearts instead.

4. The less we know who God is, and the less we rest in the finished work of Christ, the more we will grumble. For we cease to know we have a Great High Priest who goes before the throne of grace on our behalf! We do not walk forward in the assurance of faith in Christ but in justifying our own actions.[801]

5. Let us encourage one another and consider how to stir up one another to love God, serving our neighbor![802] May we as the church not be a people of grumbling, but let us be a people who know God and make God known in all of our thoughts, words, actions, and deeds, for God's glory and our good.

[799]Acts 17:28, [800]Philippians 2:14, [801]Hebrews 10:19–22, [802]Hebrews 10:24

Father, how easily I grumble! How easily I gossip and forget Your goodness, justifying my actions against other people's and denying the finished work of Christ. Forgive me. Grant me the joy of Your salvation. Help me to walk by grace through faith in the finished work of Christ. Use me for Your glory. In Jesus' name.

Exodus 20:1

And God spoke all these words, saying,

1. This is the first verse of the Ten Commandments. All the Israelites came to Mount Sinai, not to build or construct a law but to receive the Law from the Lord.

2. The Ten Commandments are not a human construct. They are not the work of philosophers or those with legal backgrounds. These words are not induced by a concoction of chemicals colliding in our hearts and minds. These words were spoken by God and God alone, given by God and God alone to His people.

3. All other laws reflect these laws, regardless of how they're acknowledged by society. Since the beginning of time, all societies have, in some way, shape, or form, been created to reflect these laws. They are still ordained by God, but sin has distorted them in a grotesque way.

4. Not only did God speak this Law and give it to the people of Israel, but the Law of God is still written on each person's heart. Our consciences are in conflict with our human nature because God has written His Law on our hearts.[803] What mercy! What grace! This, in turn, shows the mercy of God, for why should we have morals? Why does a child struggle with guilt the first time he lies, steals, or cheats? If the Law of God was not real or not true, we would not feel any guilt; but the Lord has given us this mercy to keep us from our depravity.

---

[803] Romans 2:15

Father, You are so merciful. You did not have to give us the Law, and You did not have to save us from our sin and depravity, but You have. Bless You, Father, for Your goodness. Father, I confess I have many times I've denied Your Law. I have looked at it as though Christ abolished it. I have had such confusion about this, but I see that Your Law is good and I am to delight in it! Grant my heart to know and cherish Your Law. Open my eyes to see my sin, that I may repent and turn to You, and You alone. In Jesus' name.

Exodus 22:28

You shall not revile God,
nor curse a ruler of your people.

1. The word revile means to *curse* or *despise* the Lord. For He is God, and His steadfast love endures forever.

2. The Lord is good. This is not because of what He has done—though all dispensations of God are good—but it is because He is good; it's His very essence.[804] Regardless of our circumstances, regardless of the goings-on in our lives, God's goodness does not diminish in any way, shape, or form.

3. So, to revile or curse God would be to tell Him that what He has ordained for you is not fair. But who are you, O man, to answer back to God? Will what is molded say to its molder, "Why have you made me like this?"[805] Our God is in the heavens; He does whatever He pleases![806]

4. Our thoughts, actions, prayers, hopes, and dreams should always start with a right view of God and then a right view of ourselves, not the other way around. When we define ourselves by the circumstances of our lives, we deny the goodness, sovereignty, and holiness of God.

5. This concept is the same for all forms of leadership, governments, and people of power whom the Lord has established. Let every person be subject to the governing authorities. For there is no authority except from God, and those who exist have been instituted by God.[807]

6. So let us humbly go to God, seek His will, and submit ourselves to His sovereignty and Lordship. Let us repent of our pride and ask for the grace to worship and serve our God, who is good in all circumstances.

[804]Mark 10:18, [805]Romans 9:20, [806]Psalm 115:3, [807]Romans 13:1

Father, You are never not good. You are perfect in all Your ways. Forgive me for the many times I base Your goodness on what I see and what I receive from You rather than who You are. I begin to erect the blessings from You as idols in my heart. Forgive me and have mercy on me. Open my eyes to see You. Open my eyes to see and to know Your goodness; let me see it more fully in Your love for me through Christ Jesus. In Jesus' name.

Exodus 30:37–38

And the incense that you shall make according to its composition, you shall not make for yourselves. It shall be for you holy to the Lord. Whoever makes any like it to use as perfume shall be cut off from his people.

1. The worship of God is not an emotive act, though emotions are stirred. The worship of God is not a human construct, though all of creation declares the glory of God.[808] The worship of God is holy, and we must be mindful of who we are and who God is.

2. We are to have no other gods before Him.[809] This pertains to every part of life. Our hearts before God must be total and complete. We are to trust in the Lord always and never in man. We are to seek first the Kingdom of God and His righteousness, and all these things will be added to us.

3. Our aim is Christ—to know Christ, love Christ, and adore Christ, for it is in Christ alone we can approach the throne of grace. He is the perfume, the incense that is ours given to us by the Father! There are no works, no prayers, no desires, no emotions, no law, but only God's grace, through the redemption of our souls, rooted in Christ, that brings us before God the Father.

4. Christ is not a playing card to become healthy, wealthy, and wise. Christ came to save men for the glory of the Father. To use Christ in any other way is to cut ourselves off from God, for God will not be mocked.[810]

---

[808]Psalm 19:1, [809]Exodus 20:3, [810]Galatians 6:7

Father, You are holy. That word "holy" is so many times spoken in a matter-of-fact way rather than in mindfulness. Father, so many times I attempt to use Christ for my earthly good, rather than trusting Him and coming before the throne of grace. Forgive me. Will You please grant me a heart and mind that adores and walks in truth for Your glory? Grant me to be mindful of Your holiness, of who You are, and of who I am. Thank You for Christ. In Jesus' name.

Psalm 114:7-8

Tremble, O earth, at the presence of the Lord, at the presence of the God of Jacob, who turns the rock into a pool of water, the flint into a spring of water.

1. We are to tremble before the Lord. We are to know and be mindful of the awesome power of our God. For His power turns even the rock into a pool of water, the flint into a spring of water.

2. Our hearts are stone apart from the grace of God, who removes the heart of stone and gives us a heart of flesh.[811]

3. Our hearts will not flow forth living water until the Lord changes them. We cannot change our hearts with good deeds or perceived right motives, any more than a person can change the color of their skin, or the leopard change his spots.[812]

4. Let those who hear and those whom the Holy Spirit gives understanding humble themselves before the Lord God, their Maker. Seek the Lord while He may be found; call upon Him while He is near![813] For everyone, all who call upon the name of the Lord shall be saved![814] For the Lord is near to the brokenhearted and saves the crushed in spirit.[815]

---

[811]Ezekiel 11:19, [812]Jeremiah 13:23, [813]Isaiah 55:6, [814]Romans 10:13, [815]Psalm 34:18

Father, what does it mean to tremble before You? I ask this humbly. So many things cause me to tremble, and many times, none of those things are Your awesome power but the things of this world. The things this world tell me I should fear many times are the things that steal my heart from You. Forgive me. Help me to tremble in fear of the Lord. Guard my heart from man-centered thinking, from selfish ambition. Grant me the strength, conviction, and joy to do Your will, for Your Kingdom, for Your glory. In Jesus' name.

Amen

Psalm 109:21

But you, O God my Lord,
deal on my behalf for your name's sake;
because your steadfast love is good, deliver me!

1. The psalmist, after declaring all that had unjustly occurred against him, refrained from seeking vengeance and looked to God instead. He did not take matters into his own hands but trusted in the Lord.

2. The actions we take in every moment of every day reflect our view of who God is. If we take actions to praise ourselves, we do not trust the Lord to work all things according to His purpose. If we seek vengeance on the injustice in our lives, then we do not truly see that the promise of God when He says, "Vengeance is mine, I will repay,"[816] is true.

3. Our thoughts, words, actions, and deeds, in every moment and in every circumstance, reflect our trust and hope in God. We must prayerfully seek the Lord, trust His sovereignty, press forward, and leave everything in His hands. The Lord reigns, and regardless of what others think, say, or do, we can trust in this. "The Lord is not slow to fulfill his promise as some count slowness, but is patient toward you, not wishing that any should perish, but that all should reach repentance."[817]

4. So let us lay before the Lord our worries and anxieties; let us trust Him in all things. Let us seek Him in wisdom and trust His providences. Let us be careful with our judgments and entrust all things to His hand.

---

[816] Romans 12:19, [817] 2 Peter 3:9

Thank You, Father, for listening to my prayer. Thank You for knowing me. Father, guard my heart from selfish ambition. Forgive me for my prideful and large view of myself and small view of You. I confess that when I am honest and look at everything happening around me, all of it is in Your hands. All of it is ordained by You and held together by You. Silence my mouth in self-exaltation, and open my lips for worship and praise and adoration of all that You do. In Jesus' name.

Amen

Psalm 90:12

*SO TEACH US TO NUMBER OUR DAYS THAT
WE MAY GET A HEART OF WISDOM.*

1. Wisdom is accepting that which God gives us and fearing Him over anything else.[818]

2. Since sin entered the world, death and decay have been a part of our lives. Creation was subjected to it unwillingly but because of our sin and He who subjected it.[819] We know that *"all of Creation itself will be set free from its bondage to corruption and obtain the freedom of the glory of the children of God. For we know that the whole creation has been groaning together in the pains of childbirth until now"* because of sin, and sin alone.[820]

3. To be mindful of our age, to be mindful of the Lord's leading, to be mindful of where the Lord has brought us and where He is leading us to conform us to the image of Christ, is the beginning of a heart of wisdom. We recognize that we are but a breath and then gone.[821] When we attempt to deceive ourselves and make ourselves think we are immortal and will live forever, we are attempting to build our Tower of Babel;[822] we are attempting to be like God rather than serving Him.[823]

4. So let us come to the Lord and ask Him to make known His glory. Let us be mindful of our limited time on earth and strive with every bit of His strength to do His will. Let us confess our laziness and our idleness, and let us run the race for God's glory with every fiber of our beings.

[818]Proverbs 1:7, [819]Romans 8:21, [820]Romans 8:21–22, [821]Psalm 90:10, [822]Genesis 11:1–9, [823]Genesis 3:5

Father, teach me to number my days, that I may know who You are and my need for You. Teach me, that I may have wisdom to declare the excellencies of Your greatness, Your strength, Your power, and Your might. Help me to be mindful of Your sovereignty and Your strength. Give me a fervor and the means to do Your will, with Your joy, in Your strength, for Your glory, and my good. In the name of Your Son I ask this.

Amen

Psalm 90:17

*Let the favor of the Lord our God be upon us,
and establish the work of our hands upon us;
yes, establish the work of our hands!*

1. Everything we have is the Lord's, and there is nothing we have that did not come from Him.

2. In our hearts and minds, let us check ourselves for selfish ambition, for allowing our hearts to desire anything other than His Kingdom come, and His will be done. But let us also guard ourselves against a lethargic and atheistic mindset, in which we do not seek the Lord but instead carry a victim mentality.

3. Let us seek the favor of the Lord in all our actions. Let us strive for His glory and our good; let Him establish the work of our hands as we stand on His promises. Let us not look to ourselves but boldly come before the throne of grace and ask the Lord to use us for His glory. Let us rest in whatever He ordains.

4. The life of the believer is not to be lived mindlessly, but we should come to the Lord and ask for His mercy to give us His plans, His guidance, His purpose, and His will, that we may serve Him all our days, with every bit of the strength He gives us, and to seek Him to establish our work for His eternal Kingdom.

Father, let Your favor rest upon me. What is it like to knowingly be in Your favor? How do I strive under Your favor? Do not forsake the work You have done in my life. Do not forsake the work of Your hands. Please give me wisdom and lead me by Your hand to do Your will. Keep from my heart selfish ambition and man-centered fear. Help me to be joyfully content in striving to do Your will. Make Your way straight before me, and go before me, for Your glory. Give me a heart of praise and courage to proclaim Your excellencies. In Jesus' name I ask this.

Amen

Genesis 27:5

Now Rebekah was listening when Isaac spoke to his son Esau.

1. Rebekah heard Isaac speak to Esau and immediately acted swiftly to help Jacob receive the blessing from Isaac. God promised her this blessing when she gave birth to Jacob and Esau.[824]

2. Rebekah planned and put into motion a strategy to get Jacob the blessing and attempted to work out everything God had promised her.

3. Yet, Rebekah did not go to the Lord. She didn't trust His promises and decided to "help" God accomplish His ways. She told Jacob what she would fix for Isaac's favorite meal,[825] then she instructed Jacob to cover himself with goat hair so he would feel like Esau.[826] Rebekah did all this so Jacob would receive Esau's blessing.

4. Notice the subtleness and deception of sin. We perceive the righteous thing to do, and instead of seeking the Lord and trusting His promises and timing, we seek to manipulate and bring God's plans to fruition ourselves. We become practical atheists. We deny the power of God, and we diminish in our hearts His Word, His truth, His love, and instead sin against the Lord our God.

5. We are to trust the Lord with all of our hearts and lean not on our own understanding.[827] Let us wait for the Lord, be strong and let our hearts take courage, and wait for the Lord.[828]

---

[824]Genesis 25:23, [825]Genesis 27:9, [826]Genesis 27:16, [827]Proverbs 3:5, [828]Psalm 27:14

Father, Your ways are perfect, but I confess the many times that instead of praying, seeking You, and trusting You by faith in Your promises, I act self-righteously. My heart hardens at Your Word, and I act as an atheist, a person who denies You. Forgive me. Help me to walk by faith and not by sight in accordance with Your plan. Help my heart to rest and find its boldness in Your sovereign plan. Help me to cast all my cares on You and to find comfort and courage in Your will. In Jesus' name.

Amen

Genesis 21:19

Then God opened her eyes, and she saw a well of water. And she went and filled the skin with water and gave the boy a drink.

1. Many of our struggles and temptations in life are caused by our unbelief in the promises of God. God had made a promise to Abraham to make Ishmael a great nation.[829] This promise is firm and true because God is the One who made it.

2. Even though God makes promises, this does not mean He will not bring us through trials and tests to refine us and to grow our faith in who He is. The trials we go through help bring to life the sins of unbelief, selfishness, and pride rooted deep within our souls. Hagar, having received a promise from God, still doubted and placed Ishmael under a tree and walked away so as to not presumably watch the child pass.[830]

3. After this, she lifted her voice and wept. She lifted her heart to the Lord. We must do the same in every moment, on every day, in every circumstance. We are to stand on the promises of God and lift our hearts to Him in service to Christ, trusting Him to work all things for the good of those who love Him and are called according to His purpose.[831]

4. Notice it was "then" when the Lord opened her eyes. He did not stop her temptation, and he did not stop the trial through the valley of the shadow of death. Whatever the Lord ordains is right! The Lord did not allow death to befall her. The Lord will always answer. He is always present, "The Lord is near to all that call on him, to all who call on him in truth."[832]

5. When Hagar humbled herself and called on God, He opened her eyes to His providence and rested her in His promises. The water had been there all along, but all things come from God, and all that we need is in Christ, as we call on Him. Christ is the living water; it is He who will make you thirst no more.[833]

[829]Genesis 21:13, [830]Genesis 21:16, [831]Romans 8:28, [832]Psalm 145:18, [833]John 4:10

Father, You hear me when I call.
I am humbled that You know my voice.
Oh Lord, how many times I keep silent
in my work. How I keep to myself and
don't acknowledge You; forgive me.
Help me to joyfully call upon You.
Remove my skepticism, and soften
my heart to call You and to know
Your voice. Help me to walk in Your
truth, for Your glory and my good.
In Jesus' name.

Genesis 19:16

BUT HE LINGERED. SO THE MEN SEIZED HIM AND HIS WIFE AND HIS TWO DAUGHTERS BY THE HAND, THE LORD BEING MERCIFUL TO HIM, AND THEY BROUGHT HIM OUT AND SET HIM OUTSIDE THE CITY.

1. "But he lingered." Lot had been instructed to leave Sodom, for destruction was coming for the city.[834] Two angels told him to move his family rapidly; but instead of moving quickly, Lot lingered.

2. Many times, the things of this world cause us to pause and linger, to stare at and weigh the price of obeying the Word of God. What price could even come close to the price God paid in sending His only Son? When the Holy Spirit convicts us of sin and works in our hearts to repent, we must thank Him. We must act, lest we quench the Spirit[835] and He leaves us to our flesh.

3. All the Lord does is a mercy, and there is nothing we receive from Him that we deserve. God extended His mercy beyond Lot and to his family! How merciful![836] Do not test the Lord; do not presume upon His mercy; do not linger. You and your family pursue the Lord!

---

[834]Genesis 19:12–14, [835]1 Thessalonians 5:19, [836]Genesis 19:14

Father, You are so merciful. I have read this passage so many times, yet I had not realized how merciful You were to Lot and His entire family. Who are we to receive such mercy? Forgive my lingering; help me to know those things from which I am to flee, and give me the courage and strength to act, with thanksgiving, to do Your will. In Jesus' name.

Mark 6:52

FOR THEY DID NOT UNDERSTAND ABOUT THE LOAVES, BUT THEIR HEARTS WERE HARDENED.

1. God's glory, His power, and His strength are on full display. There is nothing that can thwart Him. There is nothing that can prevail against Him. All things are subject to Him, and through the finished work of Christ, all the promises of God find their amen.[837]

2. Why, then, do we not understand? Why do we not perceive? Because our hearts are hardened. Take this verse, for instance. The disciples had just watched Jesus perform the miracle of feeding five thousand people with only a few loaves of bread and some fish. Because of their unbelief and hardness of heart, they did not understand.

3. This is so hard for us with a worldview that celebrates the "self-made" man. We celebrate the intellectual and the One who can do everything, and so we think we can change our hearts and open the eyes of our hearts to see and know and to believe and trust in God. But this is not true, for Christ quoted Isaiah the prophet saying, "They may indeed see but not perceive, and may indeed hear but not understand, lest they should turn and be forgiven."[838]

4. So how do we surrender our hearts? We seek the grace of God. We pray, "I believe; help my unbelief!"[839] Cease to look at the mountain and look instead to the Creator of the mountain. Cease to tremble at the valley and look instead to the Lord of the valley. Call upon Christ, and walk humbly and with boldness before the throne of grace, that we may receive mercy and find grace to help in time of need.[840]

[837]2 Corinthians 1:20, [838]Mark 4:12, [839]Mark 9:24, [840]Hebrews 4:16

Father, I believe; help my unbelief. Give me strength by Your grace and mercy. Give me hope in Christ. Help me to walk by grace, through faith, in all You would have for me. Guard my heart from unbelief and practical atheism, and help me to boldly live, as Your servant, for Your glory, in Your Kingdom, for Christ's sake.

Genesis 16:2

And Abram listened to the voice of Sarai.

1. Many people along our lives' paths will try to make us doubt the Word of God. They will tempt us to believe what they say is wise and is validated by what we perceive. In this instance, Abram listened to the voice of Sarai, and rather than trusting the Word of God, he decided to circumvent the Lord's promises. In doing this, Abram conceived a child with Hagar, Sarah's maidservant, and she bore a son named Ishmael. Ishmael is the father of the Arabic world, and Isaac and Ishmael have been in conflict ever since.

2. The sin of unbelief is a pervasive and subtle sin. It creeps into our hearts and minds when the Lord does not work according to man's wisdom but is perfect in His own timing.

3. Regardless of who speaks to us, we must always take what someone says and hold it against the Word of God. We must take every thought captive to obey Christ and Christ alone.[841] There is only one objective truth, and that is the Word of God. For Christ has declared, "Your Word is truth!"[842]

4. Society's worldview is constantly competing in telling us what is true or acceptable, but the only One who matters in what we do moment by moment, day upon day, is the very Word of God. The reformers referred to this as *Sola Scriptura*, Scripture alone. When it comes to receiving advice or being wise in our own eyes, we know "the grass withers, and the flowers fade, but the Word of our God will stand forever."[843] Everything should be held against the Word of God.

---

[841] 2 Corinthians 10:5, [842] John 15:5, [843] Isaiah 40:8

Father, Your Word is true. Oh, how easily I am tempted to believe my emotions, my perception, my mind, and to fall into the sin of unbelief. I instead deny Your promises and goodness. I deny Your Lordship and justify it based upon what I feel. Forgive me. Help me to know Your Word and to rest in Your Word. Strengthen my heart and mind to walk according to Your Word. Thank You for Christ Jesus.

Psalm 148:5

LET THEM PRAISE THE NAME OF THE LORD!
FOR HE COMMANDED AND THEY WERE CREATED.

1. The entire Psalm is a call out to everything we experience, see, observe—and even those things we don't (angels and hosts in verse 2) to praise the Lord!

2. All created things were created by the very Word of God,[844] and all He has said will not pass away unless He declares them to be final.

3. There is nothing that can defeat or thwart God. Even that which corrupts the things of God is still held at bay and can only act in accordance with the will of God.[845] Nothing occurs by luck, chance, or circumstance.

4. What should this lead us to? Praise and adoration! In the midst of a trial, praise the Lord! In the midst of heartache and loss, praise the Lord! In the midst of exhaustion, praise the Lord! In the midst of abounding joy for His providence, Praise the Lord!

5. Everything and all things are to praise the Lord, for they exist from His voice of command.

[844]Psalm 148:6, [845]Job 1

Father, we praise You, for what else can we do? Even the ability to feel joy is a means of grace commanded by You. Not only have You commanded it, but You sustain it in each and every moment. Nothing we see or experience is not held together by You, and there is no event outside of Your sovereignty. Even fire and hail, snow and mist, and stormy wind fulfill Your word![846] Forgive us for our unbelief. Open our eyes and strengthen us to sing Your praise for all You do. In Jesus' name.

[846]Psalm 143:8

Genesis 14:22-24

But Abram said to the king of Sodom, "I have lifted my hand to the LORD, God Most High, Possessor of heaven and earth, that I would not take a thread or a sandal strap or anything that is yours, lest you should say, 'I have made Abram rich.' I will take nothing but what the young men have eaten, and the share of the men who went with me. Let Aner, Eshcol, and Mamre take their share."

1. Abraham had just won a great victory against the kings of the land and rescued his nephew Lot. In doing this, the king of Sodom attempted to give him some of the spoils of war to help his wealth grow.

2. We must be mindful of how Abraham responded. First, we see that Abraham already knows the heart of Sodom is wicked, for the Word states, "Now the men of Sodom were wicked, great sinners against the LORD."[847] We must be mindful of who we associate with; are these people in Christ, or are they outside of Christ?

3. We must never act out of selfish ambition or vain conceit[848] but must seek the Lord in all things. Abraham's biggest concern was that the king of Sodom would receive the glory for the victory and wealth Abraham had, rather than God.

4. Be mindful with whom you associate; be mindful of their ways with the Lord; be mindful of your own heart and the temptation of the flesh. For all that is in the world, the lust of the flesh, the lust of the eyes, and the pride of life are not from the Father but from the world.[849]

---

[847]Genesis 13:13, [848]Philippians 2:3, [849]1 John 2:16

Father, You are the possessor of heaven and earth,[850] and all things are Yours. Lord, so many times we are tempted to associate with the world for help rather than come to You and call upon Your name. We desire immediate gratification and desire to fix our problems on our own, rather than seeking You. Forgive us for our pride. Help us to call upon You and be mindful of our thoughts, words, and deeds, turning from every evil. Help us to see the glory of Christ and our sufficiency in His providence. Strengthen us to trust in Your providence and to steward Your blessings for Your glory, and not the glory of man. In Jesus' name.

[850]Genesis 14:19

1 Peter 3:17–18

You therefore, beloved, knowing this beforehand, take care that you are not carried away with the error of lawless people and lose your own stability. But grow in the grace and knowledge of our Lord and Savior Jesus Christ. To him be the glory both now and to the day of eternity. Amen.

1. Many thoughts and ideas consume the heart of man, and apart from the Word of God they are nothing. Only God is holy, and we must measure everything against the Word of God.

2. Many people, myself included, have put others on a pedestal and worshiped their words or the intellect they reflect, but none of these are holy; only the Word of God is holy. All our thoughts must be taken captive,[851] and we are to hold fast to the truth and despise every kind of evil.[852]

3. So what is our aim? If it's not intellectual superiority or a loftiness of ideas or a strength in an argument, what is it? Our aim is knowing, abiding, dwelling with, and growing more in intimacy with Christ and Christ alone. We are to grow in the grace and knowledge of our Lord and Savior Jesus Christ, and all things are to His glory, from now and into all eternity.

---

[851] 2 Corinthians 10:5, [852] 1 Thessalonians 5:21–22

Jesus, help me to know You. Help me to grow in the grace and knowledge of You in all things, and to see all things for Your glory. Many times I have walked in accordance with what I see rather than in the truth and grace of You by faith.[853] Save me; have mercy on me and help me to walk in accordance with You, for Your glory.

Amen

Genesis 9:6

Whoever sheds the blood of man, by man shall his blood be shed, for God made man in his own image.

1. The only creature made in the image of God is mankind. There is no other creature in the entire universe that received this blessing.

2. Many ramifications occur if we do not have a right view of God. First, without a right view of God, we diminish the honor of bearing God's image and raise other creation to that same honor. For instance, in our society are animals elevated to the status of humans? Is the same honor, the same care, the same love bestowed on certain animals as there are with humans? We can look at this as just society and just life, or we can recognize this as a lack of relationship with the Creator of the universe.

3. Without a right view of God, we do not have a right view of the sanctity of life. We devalue God's command to "be fruitful, and multiply, and fill the earth."[854] We look at unborn children, not as people conceived in the image of God, but as tiny cells without a soul. What horror!

4. Our view of God has ramifications in all aspects of life, the greatest of which is how we view each other. There are the consequences of not honoring the Lord. But God sent his Son into the world to pay the price we sinners deserve. The judgment we deserve as image bearers of the Most High God Jesus Christ took upon Himself that we may have fellowship with God for all eternity.

---

[854] Genesis 9:1

Father, You are holy, and You have created all of humanity in Your image. Who are we? Forgive me for my pride and for not recognizing that all of humanity is created in Your image. Help me to reflect Christ's love to all around me and to know Christ more fully and more deeply in those relationships You bring into my life, for Your glory. In Jesus' name.

Genesis 8:20–22

Then Noah built an altar to the Lord and took some of every clean animal and some of every clean bird and offered burnt offerings on the altar. And when the Lord smelled the pleasing aroma, the Lord said in his heart, "I will never again curse the ground because of man, for the intention of man's heart is evil from his youth. Neither will I ever again strike down every living creature as I have done. While the earth remains, seedtime and harvest, cold and heat, summer and winter, day and night, shall not cease."

1. Here we have the Noahic covenant, which God made with Noah when he left the ark after the flood. A covenant is a binding promise and is held to the standard of the one making the covenant. God said, "I establish my covenant with you, that never again shall all flesh be cut off by the waters of the flood, and never again shall there be a flood to destroy the earth."[855]

2. This covenant promised God would never again curse the ground because of man. It also declared that God would never kill all creatures and that He would hold seedtime and harvest, cold and heat, summer and winter, day and night, promising they would not cease.

3. Yet how would this covenant affect the mind of a human—someone created in the image of God—if this person did not know this covenant? He would fear constantly that the world would destroy itself. If the standard you measure against is humanity, then almost everything is to be feared.

4. *But Christ.* Let those words ring in your hearts and minds. For those who are hidden in Christ, "I am sure that neither death nor life, nor angels nor rulers, nor things present nor things to come, nor powers, nor height nor depth, nor anything else in all creation, will be able to separate us from the love of God in Christ Jesus our Lord."[856] We can be bold; we can remain rooted in confidence that the Lord reigns because in Christ, the Noahic covenant is ours to rest in.

[855]Genesis 9:11, [856]Romans 8:38

*Father, how glorious You are!
You hold all things in Your hand.
There is not a sparrow that falls to
the ground that You do not ordain.[857]
Yet forgive us, Lord, for we conjure
up things in our hearts and minds;
we listen to things that tickle our
ears and make us believe You are not
Lord, and our hearts are deceived.
Open our eyes and ears to see You
in the most minute details, holding
all creation and orchestrating it
for Your glory and our good!
In Jesus' name, I ask this!*

[857]Matthew 10:29

Matthew 28:9

And behold, Jesus met them and said, "Greetings!"
And they came up and took hold of his feet and worshiped him.

1. When the disciples went to the tomb and found it empty, they ran back to Galilee because the angels told them Christ was going to see His disciples. When they saw Jesus, they grabbed hold of His feet and worshiped Him. The definition of worship is to express in attitude or gesture one's complete dependence on or submission to a high authority figure, [fall down and] worship.[858] The disciples worshiped Christ Jesus, not as a moralism or a good person, but as God in flesh.

2. Today, the church sees Christ as a good person rather than God. We respect Him as someone we are thankful for and who we try to emulate, but we have ceased to look at Him as King. He has become an ideal rather than the object of our worship.

3. The object of our worship has become politics, sports, and entertainment. Our perception of who God is has diminished to such stupidity that we worship a person who does good according to the world rather than the One who holds the world together. The love of the world has filled our hearts rather than the love of the Father.[859]

4. So, who is Christ, and why should we worship Him alone? *He is the image of the invisible God, the firstborn of all creation. For by him all things were created, in heaven and on earth, visible and invisible, whether thrones or dominions or rulers or authorities—all things were created through him and for him. And he is before all things, and in him all things hold together. And he is the head of the body, the church. He is the beginning, the firstborn from the dead, that in everything he might be preeminent. For in him all the fullness of God was pleased to dwell, and through him to reconcile to himself all things, whether on earth or in heaven, making peace by the blood of his cross.*[860]

---

[858]Arndt, W., Danker, F. W., Bauer, W., & Gingrich, F. W. (2000). A Greek-English lexicon of the New Testament and other early Christian literature (3rd ed., p. 882). Chicago: University of Chicago Press. [859]1 John 2:15, [860]Colossians 1:15–20

Father, thank You for Christ. He is God; He holds all things together, and from Him, through Him, and to Him all things are made.[861] How easily I forget. How easily I worship myself rather than Christ. Forgive me, and help me to know Christ, to worship Him more by faith every day. Thank You, Jesus, for saving me.

Amen

---

[861] Romans 11:36

Esther 4:14

AND WHO KNOWS WHETHER YOU HAVE NOT COME TO THE KINGDOM FOR SUCH A TIME AS THIS?

1. The Lord is over all things in our lives. He has formed every person's days, and all of them are written in the Book of Life from beginning to end.[862] God chose each of our parents; He chose our ethnicity, our geographical location, and He orchestrated every event that will occur in our lifetimes, both the mundane and the fantastic, and He did it perfectly.

2. Each Christian must recognize that as we go through life, we are tempted to believe that if we lived in another time period or in other circumstances, our lives would be easier. We idolize nostalgia and the "good ole days" and deny God's perfect timing. We reduce our role in the world to a set of circumstances rather than God's sovereignty. We think atheistically and deny the intention of our Creator in every aspect of our lives.

3. Our God orchestrates everything, and He does whatever He pleases.[863] He purposefully created you for this time and for this moment. He orchestrated who your neighbors are, your spouse, your children, your friends, and even your singleness. God purposefully, intentionally, and with exact precision ordained every infinitesimal detail of our lives for His glory and the good of others.

4. In light of this truth, we should walk both humbly and boldly, asking the Lord what He would have us do as we journey through life. In the same way Mordecai told Queen Esther that she was "created for such a time as this," we must also remember the Lord created each of us "for such a time as this." In times of peace and war, in circumstances of joy and heartache, we were created to fully live in a way that others may see our good work and praise our God in heaven for such a time as this.[864]

[862]Psalm 139:16, [863]Psalm 135:6; Psalm 115:3, [864]Matthew 5:16

Oh Father, I praise You for who You are. I praise You for Your intentionality and mindfulness in creating me and placing me in the world for Your glory. Father, I confess the many times I take my eyes off You and deny Your intentionality in creating me for such a time as this. Please give me wisdom to steward every moment of every day, that I may live a life fully for Your glory. I praise You, Father, in Christ's name.

Ezra 7:10

For Ezra had set his heart to study the Law of the Lord, and to do it and to teach his statutes and rules in Israel.

1. Ezra went to Jerusalem to help rebuild all that had been destroyed when Babylon took Israel into exile. He had been sent by Artaxerxes to rebuild and was given all the materials to begin working. This was done because the good hand of the Lord was on him and worked all of these together.[865]

2. But as the Lord worked in Ezra's life, Ezra did not set his heart and aim on what was being built, but instead on studying the Law of God. God's Word is the foundation of all that we do. Regardless of what is before, we are to be like the psalmist who wrote, "but his delight is in the Law of the Lord, and on His Law he meditates day and night."[866]

3. We must trust God with the circumstances of our lives—with the blessings, the disciplines, and the desires, and lay those before His throne, and then spend our lives growing to know Him. To know His character, His Laws, and His Kingdom should be the aim of our life.

4. As we grow in the knowledge and wisdom of God, we are then to go out and share His Word with whomever God places in our lives. Just as Ezra pursued the Lord, he then went and taught God's statutes and rules to the people in Israel. Christ has commanded us to do the same. We also are to go and make disciples of all nations, baptizing them in the name of the Father, and the Son, and the Holy Spirit, and teach all Christ has commanded us to do in His Word.[867]

---

[865]Ezra 7:6, 9, [866]Psalm 1:2, [867]Matthew 28:19–20

Father, You are perfect in every way. There is nothing in who You are that needs me in any way; yet in love, You have called me to know You, that I may make You known. I confess, Lord, the many times I take my eyes off Your Word and cast them fearfully on all that needs to be done. I so easily think it is my effort, rather than Your grace, that provides. Forgive me. Please help me to know You more intimately and give me a passion and direction to share with those whom You place in my life the reality and the calling You have given Your people. For Christ's sake, I ask this.

Ephesians 4:15

RATHER, SPEAKING THE TRUTH IN LOVE, WE ARE TO GROW UP IN EVERY WAY INTO HIM WHO IS THE HEAD, INTO CHRIST.

1. The aim of the heart apart from Christ is to be equal with God.[868] Our hearts desire autonomy, self-direction, becoming better and greater versions of ourselves, and to be like God. In our natural state, our focus, our aim, and our direction are to the glory of ourselves in all things and in all circumstances.

2. But once a person is called, by God's grace through faith,[869] our entire aim shifts from ourselves to Christ. We are to fall more deeply in love with Christ, to reflect Christ, to show Christ. We must no longer walk according to the flesh but according to the Spirit.[870]

3. So then the life of the Christian is to seek, know, meditate on, and reflect Christ, who is our King, Lord, and Savior in all circumstances. The true Christian is to deny himself, pick up his cross, and follow Christ.[871]

4. We are to empty ourselves in the same way Christ did, for even Christ, though He is God, did not count equality with God something to be grasped. Christ emptied Himself and descended to earth to walk a perfect life, and He humbled Himself by becoming obedient to the point of death, even death on a cross.[872]

5. How does one grow in the likeness of Christ? First, ask Him to open your eyes to know Him. Christ is not an ideal or philosophy. He is God. He will send His Spirit to those who call upon Him, and He has promised to save them![873]

6. Then, as we grow in relationship with Christ, and as He bears more and more fruit in our lives, we are to seek Him in all things—dying to ourselves and coming alive in Christ for the glory of God and the good of His people.

---

[868]Genesis 3:5, [869]Ephesians 2:8, [870]Romans 8:9, [871]Matthew 16:24, [872]Philippians 2:6–8, [873]Romans 10:13

Father, I thank You for Your Son. Who am I that You would send Your only Son into the world to die for me? I confess the many times I have focused on myself and on being a bigger, better version of myself that I have ceased to look at Christ. Forgive me. Open my eyes and my heart to grow in love, adoration, and to reflect Christ in all things. In Christ's name I ask this, and for His glory.

Romans 2:5

But because of your hard and impenitent heart you are storing up wrath for yourself on the day of wrath when God's righteous judgment will be revealed.

1. All of creation bears witness to the Lord, for the heavens declare the glory of God, and the skies above declare His handiwork.[874] Every good and perfect gift we receive in every infinitesimal moment of our lives comes from the Father,[875] and His kindness leads us to our repentance and the glory of Himself.[876]

2. But our thoughts and our hearts look only to that which is created, rather than going beyond to the Creator, who upholds all things.[877] We begin to worship that which is created rather than the Creator, and in doing that, we steal the worship, adoration, glory, and joy that all belong to Christ.[878]

3. The more we focus on something created rather than God the Creator, our minds become darkened and futile.[879] In every instance that we cease to acknowledge God as the ultimate and the One deserving all worship and praise, His wrath is aimed at that in which He does not receive glory.[880] In our pride and our unbelief, we claim we are wise by denying God and worshiping ourselves. Instead, we become the very fools we think we are avoiding becoming.

4. Let us go to the Lord and not harden our hearts against God's promises and His Word. As long as it is today, let us turn and repent so our hearts may not be hardened by the deceitfulness of sin![881] For the Lord is a jealous God,[882] and though His anger is for a moment against our sin, His favor is for a lifetime for those who love Him and keep His commandments.

[874]Psalm 19:1, [875]James 1:17, [876]Romans 2:4, [877]Colossians 1:16, [878]Romans 1:22, [879]Romans 1:21, [880]Romans 1:18, [881]Hebrews 3:13, [882]Exodus 34:14

Oh Father, how glorious You are and how perfect are Your ways. All things are from You, and through You, and to You, and to You be the glory. I see, Lord, how many times I turn Your blessings into idols. I harden my heart to praise You, and so many times I cease to worship You because of my feelings and perceptions rather than the truth of Your Word. Soften my heart and open my mouth to praise You in all things and in everything. Help me to recognize Christ as King and Lord over all, that I may praise Him all the more. In Christ's name.

2 *Corinthians* 1:20

For all the promises of God find their Yes in him. That is why it is through him that we utter our Amen to God for his glory.

1. All hope and assurance the believer has is found in Christ and Christ alone. All of Scripture, from the beginning of Genesis to the end of Revelation, points toward Christ and Christ alone, and in Christ alone we are boldly brought near to the throne of grace to receive mercy and find grace in time of need.[883]

2. It is Christ who brings us into the fellowship of God. It is Christ who has gone before us and stands before the Father on our behalf to reconcile us as a people before God.[884] In this truth, we have confidence.

3. Confidence in the promises of God, that for those who love Him, all things work together for good.[885] To know the Lord is my helper[886] and I will not fear, for what can flesh do to me?[887] The Lord is my protector;[888] I shall not fear armies that stand against me.[889] If I should walk in the midst of the shadow of death,[890] I will not cease to have good hope.[891]

4. We must meditate on these promises day and night,[892] and they are to be applied in every aspect of life in which the Lord leads us. Every moment of every day is ordained by our Heavenly Father, and trusting His promises grows our faith in Him and our desire to obey Him, and not according to our intellect, but according to His Word. May we walk in the truth of His Word according to His promises.

---

[883]Hebrews 4:16, [884]Hebrews 9:24, [885]Romans 8:28, [886]Psalm 118:6; Psalm 117:6, [887]Psalm 56:4; 55:5, [888]Psalm 27:1; 26:1, [889]Psalm 27:3, [890]Psalm 23:4, [891]Psalm 56:5; 55:4; 71:14; 70:14, [892]Psalm 1:2

Jesus, in You, all Your promises come true. You are good, and perfect, and true. There is not one promise in all of Scripture that is not for Your glory and my benefit. Your Word is true in every aspect of life, and You have called me to walk according to Your Word! Forgive me for not walking according to Your Word so many times. Help me to walk in Your Way, that I may know Your joy and see You glorified and magnified in all things. In Christ's name.

Amen

Psalm 57:1

Be merciful to me, O God, be merciful to me,
for in you my soul takes refuge;
in the shadow of your wings I will take refuge,
till the storms of destruction pass by.

1. It is in God alone we are to take refuge, and none other. When trials and troubles arise and we are tempted to leave the battle and flee to somewhere we can hide,[893] that is when we are to go to God.

2. We are to preach the Word to ourselves, in season and out of season.[894] With the Lord's strength, let us pull ourselves from the abyss of our sinful thoughts, worries, and fears and let us cry out to God, who listens to our prayers. We do not deserve His comfort, but His mercies are new to us every morning.[895]

3. The world tempts us to find its pleasures within or to drown our worries and sadness in things other than God.[896] But the Lord will stand beside you and will give you strength.[897] We are to ask Him to fill our minds with His Words and His truth. We are to walk according to His truth, knowing that the testing of our faith produces steadfastness and that steadfastness will have its full effect, making us complete and lacking in nothing through Christ.[898]

4. All our resolve, hope, and strength must be found in Christ and Christ alone. For Christ resisted temptation, even to the point of bleeding.[899] Christ's aim was to do the will of the Father and to accomplish His work on earth,[900] regardless of how He felt. We, in turn, are to do the same, but we are not alone in doing it. We are to look to Christ. We are to call out to Him for mercy, trusting by faith that He will bring us through to advance and proclaim the gospel to a dying world—all for the joy set before us, trusting God's perfect protection and providence in all circumstances.

[893]Psalm 55:6, [894]2 Timothy 4:24, [895]Lamentations 3:22–23, [896]Proverbs 31:3–5, [897]2 Timothy 4:17 [898]James 1:2–4, [899]Hebrews 12:4, [900]John 6:38

Oh Lord, how merciful You are! I praise You, for You have made known to us Your mercies in all things. I confess how I am so easily tempted to worry, fear, doubt, and not trust You. Forgive my unbelief and help me to walk according to Your Word. Fill my heart and mind with the truth of Your Word, and lead me according to Your will and way. In Christ's name.

Isaiah 30:15

For thus said the Lord GOD, the Holy One of Israel,
"In returning and rest you shall be saved;
in quietness and in trust shall be your strength."
But you were unwilling.

1. The Lord rules over all situations in our lives. He promises in His Word that He will withhold nothing that is for our own good.[901] This means all our trials and tests, joys and sorrows, are in His hands. He has ordained each one to test the righteous[902] and to see if there are any who seek Him.[903]

2. Man, in his hardness of heart, will many times turn inward for solutions when placed in difficult situations. Apart from the work of the Holy Spirit, he will attempt everything he can to fix his own problems and to place himself as the center of his circumstances. He will play the fool and say in his own heart, "There is no God!"[904]

3. But those who are in Christ realize that since the Lord is sovereign over all things, we can declare with the psalmist, "It is good that I was afflicted, that I might learn Your statutes."[905] The Lord many times lets His arrows pierce us, and He will place His hand upon us to lead us to repentance.[906] It is only through repentance and belief in Jesus Christ and His Lordship we are saved.[907]

4. Regardless of our circumstances, we are to live lives of repentance,[908] turning to walk in a way that glorifies the Lord and leave our old ways behind. Christ promises that if we repent, He will bring us into quietness and trust in Him, in the strength of His promises, and in the saving knowledge of His Lordship over all things, for His glory and our good.

[901]Psalm 84:11, [902]Psalm 11:5, [903]Psalm 14:2, [904]Psalm 14:1, [905]Psalm 119:71
[906]Psalm 38:2, [907]Acts 16:31, [908]Luke 3:8

OH LORD, HOW EASILY I FORGET YOUR WORD AND HOW EASILY I SLIP INTO TRYING TO FIX MY LIFE RATHER THAN REPENTING AND TURNING TO YOU. SO MANY TIMES I TRUST MY OWN EYES RATHER THAN YOUR WORD. SO MANY TIMES I MURMUR AND GRUMBLE AGAINST YOU RATHER THAN REPENT AND TRUST IN YOU. FORGIVE ME. FILL MY HEART AND MIND WITH THE TRUTH OF YOUR WORD, AND LEAD ME IN THE JOY OF REPENTANCE AND STRENGTH IN CHRIST ALONE. IN CHRIST'S NAME I PRAY.

2 Timothy 4:2

Preach the word; be ready in season and out of season; reprove, rebuke, and exhort, with complete patience and teaching.

1. The man of God is to preach the Word at all times and in every situation. He is to meditate on it day and night so he is like a tree planted by streams of water that yields its fruit in season and whose leaf does not wither. In everything he does he prospers.[909]

2. The first person the man of God is to preach to is himself. He must first examine his own heart before he examines another.[910] He must look to Scripture for all decisions, regardless of the circumstances. In every season, his mind must be ready to give an answer with Scripture. For the Word of God is complete in every way for all of life.

3. The world will often try to make us think "logically" and "pragmatically," doing all it can to keep us from seeking the Lord. Our ears are tempted to "itch" with the passions of the day and lead us toward myths of deception in every aspect of life.[911] But we must avoid all such silly babble. We must be a people of the Word in all ways.

4. Look to God's Word in all things. Just as David, when he was depressed from his circumstances, preached to himself and asked, "Why are you cast down, O my soul, and why are you in turmoil within me? Hope in God; for I shall again praise him, my salvation and my God."[912] We are to take the Word of God, which is the sword of the Spirit,[913] and to take captive every thought. For man does not live by bread alone but by every word that comes from the mouth of God.[914]

---

[909]Psalm 1:2–3, [910]Matthew 7:5, [911]2 Timothy 4:3–4, [912]Psalm 42:5–6, [913]Psalm 6:17, [914]Matthew 4:4

Oh Lord, Your Word is true and glorious. My mind is always tempted to diminish the truth and authority of Your Word in my life. So many times I justify my thoughts or experiences based upon the standard of the world rather than what Your Word commands us. Forgive me. Help me to know, to live, to rejoice, to trust, and to hope in Your Word in all times and in all situations, for Your glory. In Christ's name.

Psalm 77:2

IN THE DAY OF MY TROUBLE I SEEK THE LORD;
IN THE NIGHT MY HAND IS STRETCHED OUT WITHOUT WEARYING;
MY SOUL REFUSES TO BE COMFORTED.

1. In the day of trouble, where do you turn? To whom do you run? Do you define your life by that which you observe in the day-to-day happenings, or is your life rooted in the truth of God's Word? Do your emotions fluctuate with the news of the day or with the images that catch your eyes? Or do you stand firm on the promises of God?

2. In the midst of everything God is sovereign over, the Lord tests us to see if our hearts and minds truly look to Him and Him alone. David writes in Psalm 119, "It is good that I was afflicted that I might learn your statutes."[915]

3. We are to trust the Lord always and seek Him in all circumstances. We are to ask Him for wisdom, never doubting that He will provide it. For if we doubt, we are a "double-minded way, unstable in all our ways."[916] We must not expect to receive anything from the Lord unless we fully put our hope in Him.

4. Let us not be fearful of man, who attempts to make himself God and tries to tell us the secrets of God, those things only God knows. When man tells us to fear, let us respond that the only One we are to fear is the Lord, for He is the root of all true wisdom![917] Let us look to the Lord, who holds all our days in His hands.[918] Let us stretch out our hands to Him and only seek true comfort in His Word, defining the times not by what we see but by faith in His Word and His Word alone.[919]

---

[915]Psalm 119:71, [916]James 1:8, [917]Proverbs 1:7, [918]Psalm 31:15, [919]2 Corinthians 5:7

Oh Lord, You are good, and I lift my hands to You and You alone. Forgive me, Lord, for the many times I've attempted to define my days by what I see, in the same way the world does. I am so easily manipulated by the fears of the world and so quickly look to the world rather than You, Lord. Fill my heart with Your Word and make me walk in Your ways. For You are my God, and for You, I wait all the day long. In Christ's name.

James 3:1

NOT MANY OF YOU SHOULD BECOME TEACHERS, MY BROTHERS, FOR YOU KNOW THAT WE WHO TEACH WILL BE JUDGED WITH GREATER STRICTNESS.

1. The responsibility of a teacher of God's Word is to only speak the Word of God, and His Word alone.[920] For God's Word is breathed out by God alone, and is useful for teaching, for reproof, for correction, and for training in righteousness, so that the man of God may be complete, equipped to do every good work.[921]

2. But the one who teaches must also be careful to handle the Word of God in accordance with the fear of the Lord, for he will be held accountable for every falsehood he speaks or writes before the Lord, and the Lord will repay him according to his deeds.[922] For Christ Himself cursed the Pharisees and Scribes for not handling the Word of God correctly.[923] They, in their foolishness and pride, had shut the Kingdom of God to those who listened to them and through their teaching were those who were going to hell.[924]

3. So, first let the teacher of the Word seek the Lord and recognize that apart from Christ, he can do nothing.[925] Let him recognize that the fear of the Lord is the beginning of wisdom,[926] and that each word that comes from his mouth must be weighed in line with God's Holy Word. Let him meditate on it day and night,[927] then let him proclaim the Word of God boldly and with courage, honoring the Lord with each word, teaching the repentance of sins and glory in Christ.

---

[920]Deuteronomy 12:32, [921]2 Timothy 3:16–17, [922]2 Timothy 4:14, [923]Matthew 22:29, [924]Matthew 23:15, [925]John 15:5, [926]Proverbs 1:7, [927]Psalm 1:2

Oh Lord, how beautiful and wonderful is Your Word. The more You place Your Word in my heart, the more I rejoice and see my complete need for Christ. Forgive me for any of my words that contradict Your Word. Help me to speak the truth in love, with courage and gentleness to all those whom You put in my path. For Christ's sake.

Amen

Psalm 55:22

Cast your burden on the Lord, and he will sustain you;
he will never permit the righteous to be moved.

1. What an incredible command and incredible promise. God has commanded us to place before Him all our burdens. Everything that minimizes our joy in Christ must be given to Him, and in that command He promises that in the toughest of times, those who are in Christ will not be moved.

2. All circumstances must be brought before the Lord in this. Circumstances of our enemies who desire to crush us,[928] every instance and every circumstance that causes our heart anguish, fear, trembling, and the possibility of death and utter destruction—the Lord wants us to pray and present these to Him.[929] We can even share with Him how we long to flee from the battle. Pour out your hearts to Him, for He hears when you are so afraid that all you want to do is pull away from everything![930]

3. These are not only those things that are circumstantial, but even those in which our friends and family hurt,[931] for the Lord is near to the brokenhearted.[932] In all these things we are called to call upon Him. We are commanded to place all our burdens before Him, and He will bring us through them in His perfect plan. He can hear our complaints, our sorrows, and our hurts.[933] Let us not complain about God, but let us take everything that attempts to steal our joy in Christ and approach the throne of grace with confidence![934]

4. Lastly, those things we do not bring to God are those we do not deem Him Lord over. When we do not cast our burdens on the Lord, we make those burdens our idols and attempt to erect our own strength. This is a deceptive scheme of the devil. Guard your heart against it, and hold fast to God. For His Word is true, and He will sustain all He leads you through.

---

[928]Psalm 55:3, [929]Psalm 55:4-5, [930]Psalm 55:6-8, [931]Psalm 55:12-15, [932]Psalm 34:18, [933]Psalm 55:16-19, [934]Hebrews 4:16

Oh Lord, so many things weigh my heart down, things I have made bigger than You. Forgive me. Help me to see You as Lord over all my life. Soften my heart to come to Christ and to lay these burdens down before the throne of grace and show Yourself glorious. Help me to see Christ's Lordship and His love and purpose for me. Strengthen me, Lord, for apart from You I am nothing. In Christ's name.

Deuteronomy 2:7

For the Lord your God has blessed you in all the work of your hands. He knows you're going through this great wilderness. These forty years the Lord your God has been with you. You have lacked nothing.

1. The Lord is the One who blesses and gives all things. His means of grace is to use our hands and our efforts with the strength He has given us. Everything in our lives is from Him, yet He is the One who strengthens us to live and move and to have our being.[935]

2. As we trudge through the wilderness and experience difficult times, we are to look to the Lord. We are not to look at the wilderness and define ourselves by what we see, but in turn, we are to instead look to the Word of God. We are to let the Word of God define the truth and the reality of what we see happening in the Word[936] rather than by the circumstantial evidence we perceive.

3. This is not only antithetical to the world but also to the majority of those who call themselves Christians. God's promises are to be the anchoring of our hearts and minds in all things and in all circumstances. This does not mean we are to be cavalier and stupid, but it also does not mean we should be mindless and dumb. We are to assess the situation by faith and then act accordingly. We are to root the plumbline of our soul[937] in Christ and His Word alone.

4. God is not only God of those things that flourish, but He is God over the wilderness. For there are times He leads us through the valley of the shadow of death,[938] just as He led His own Son into the wilderness.[939] His promises still remain, and we will lack nothing we need.[940] He will never leave us nor forsake us.[941] We are to walk in the truth of that promise.

---

[935]Acts 17:28, [936]John 17:7, [937]Isaiah 28:17, [938]Psalm 23:4, [939]Mark 1:12, [940]Psalm 34:10, [941]Hebrews 13:5

Oh Lord, You are true and good, and Your Word never fails. There is no circumstance You are not Lord over. How easily I define Your nearness by my circumstances rather than by Your Word. Forgive me, and fill my mind with the truth of Your Word, and may it permeate every area of life by grace and through faith. In Christ's name.

Job 36:15

> *HE DELIVERS THE AFFLICTED BY THEIR AFFLICTION AND OPENS THEIR EAR BY ADVERSITY.*

1. Every circumstance the Lord leads us through is purposeful and intentional. In this we can know that both blessings and afflictions are used by God to grow us "into him who is the head, into Christ."[942] Both His blessing and discipline come from His perfect love, to draw us to Himself.

2. Many times we measure our afflictions and trials according to the world, but not according to God's Word. What the world means for evil, God means for good in all and in every situation.[943] We are to lift our eyes from the dispensations the Lord brings us through and lift our eyes to the Lord, knowing that for those who love the Lord, all things work together for good, who are called according to His purpose.[944]

3. We can say with the psalmist that it is good I was afflicted that I may learn the Lord's statutes.[945] Every affliction is ordained by the Lord; the Lord leads us to better know Him and trust Him. The Lord disciplines those He loves, as a father would discipline the son in whom he delights.[946]

4. It's in these truths where the Lord saves the afflicted by their afflictions. We can know there is no such thing as luck, chance, or circumstance, for these are all human constructs created to deny our Lord's sovereignty. Love and rest in knowing there is purpose and intentionality in every moment. And let us then respond with thanksgiving; "Let us praise the Lord that he does not deal with us according to our sins, nor does he repay us according to our iniquity."[947]

---

[942]Ephesians 4:15, [943]Genesis 50:20, [944]Romans 8:28, [945]Psalm 119:71, [946]Hebrews 12:6–7, [947]Psalm 103:10

Father, You order every moment, and You never waste a moment in time. All things are working for Your glory and our good, and we are to rest in the truth of this. Even Your discipline is a loving kindness in helping us to know You more and to learn to rest in Your grace. Forgive me for murmuring against You. Forgive me for making the circumstances You have ordained be void of thinking on You. Help me to have a more assured, more joyful, more true view of You and Your Lordship over all things. For the sake of Christ I ask this.

Luke 14:33

So therefore, any one of you who does not renounce all that he has cannot be my disciple.

1. Christ is King over all things,[948] and there is nothing we have that is not at His disposal. With every aspect in our lives, we submit to someone or something to rule over us in that moment, yet God has told us we shall have no other gods before Him.[949]

2. The idols in our lives are those things that if the Lord removed them from us, our lives would be meaningless and would carry less value. Christ said we should be willing to leave father, and mother, and wife, and children, and brother and sister, and even our own lives for the sake of Christ.

3. Yet many times when it comes to Christ, we diminish the cost and magnify the comfort in our lives. We do not take Christ at His Word and trust that He is sufficient in all things. We strive to be like God rather than to submit to His Word.[950]

4. To the world that is perishing, the cross of Christ is foolishness; but to those who are saved, it is the power of God unto salvation![951] All our boasting and purpose must be in Christ and Christ alone.[952] The more we seek Christ and follow Him, the more the world and all its riches fade away. The more we see the glory and the reality of Christ over all things, the more we recognize that everything is rubbish in comparison to Christ.[953] To count the cost of Christ is to see the richness of Christ over all things.

---

[948]Hebrews 1:2–3, [949]Exodus 20:3, [950]Genesis 3:5, [951]1 Corinthians 1:18, [952]1 Corinthians 1:31, [953]Philippians 3:8

Lord, You are the radiance of the glory of God and the exact imprint of His nature. You hold together everything by Your power, and there is nothing created that You did not first speak into existence. How easy it is for me to diminish the truth of who You are. Open my eyes to the idols I have placed in my heart instead of bowing to Your Lordship. Lead me and guide me as Your servant in all things. In Christ's name.

Revelation 22:18-19

I WARN EVERYONE WHO HEARS THE WORDS OF THE PROPHECY OF THIS BOOK: IF ANYONE ADDS TO THEM, GOD WILL ADD TO HIM THE PLAGUES DESCRIBED IN THIS BOOK, AND IF ANYONE TAKES AWAY FROM THE WORDS OF THE BOOK OF THIS PROPHECY, GOD WILL TAKE AWAY HIS SHARE IN THE TREE OF LIFE AND IN THE HOLY CITY, WHICH ARE DESCRIBED IN THIS BOOK.

1. This warning should cause every believer to pause before speaking about the Word of God. For the Lord states that we are to never add to or take away from His Word. The Word of the Lord is objectively truth;[954] it transcends all of time and never diminishes in its power, for it is living and active and sharper than any two-edged sword.[955]

2. We must hide God's Word in our hearts, that we might not sin against Him. We are to meditate on Scripture day and night and prayerfully and humbly come before God's Word, allowing it to reach us and lead to repentance and freedom in Christ.

3. When our pastors, teachers, and leaders twist Scripture to advance their own personal agendas or self-help talk, they corrupt it and diminish the power of the gospel. Rather than looking to the Word of God, they preach to tickle the ears of the congregation, focused on numbers and growth rather than honoring God.

4. The Christian must guard his heart, for whoever adds to or takes away from Scripture is cursed. This is not an idea or an empty threat; this is a promise. This is a promise of eternal ramification, a promise from a Holy God, and we are to seek Him with all our hearts, and souls, and might.

[954]John 17:17, [955]Hebrews 4:12

Father, Your Word is true. Your Word terrifies me many times because I long to know it and not to speak in error. I long to live according to Your Word. Thank You for not sending Your Word apart from the Holy Spirit, who gives us wisdom and knowledge in knowing You. Guard my heart from prideful and selfish ambition, and help me to walk humbly before You, according to Your Word. May the words of my mouth and the meditations of my heart be acceptable in Your sight, Oh Lord, my Rock and my Redeemer.

Revelation 22:8–9

I, John, am the one who heard and saw these things. And when I heard and saw them, I fell down to worship at the feet of the angel who showed them to me, but he said to me, "You must not do that! I am a fellow servant with you and your brothers the prophets, and with those who keep the words of this book. Worship God."

1. God and God alone is worthy of worship and adoration. The Lord God of heaven and earth is the Creator of all things and is eternal. There was a time that was for all eternity. There were no angels, no heaven, no devil, no hell—nothing but God—and God was infinitely and completely satisfied in His perfection. He and He alone is the only one who deserves our worship.

2. There is no angel or saint or anything created that should ever be worshiped. "For by him all things were created, in heaven and on earth, visible and invisible, whether thrones or dominions or rulers or authorities—all things were created through him and for him."[957]

3. All things are to keep the Word of the Lord, and all are held together by the Word of the Lord. So our command is to worship God and God alone with full adoration. We are to be mindful of Him and to give thanks in all circumstances.[958] The psalmist says, "Bless the Lord, O my soul, and all that is within me, bless his holy name!"[959]

4. Let us take notice how at the end of these verses, after the angel admonishes John for worshiping him, he does not leave John without direction for His worship. He commands John to "Worship God." In the sight of the angel, John is moved to worship what he, at that time, believes is glorious; but the angel's glory pales in comparison with the glory of God. Let our hearts take heed of this command and let us all "Worship God," who alone is worthy of our praise.

---

[957]Colossians 1:16, [958]1 Thessalonians 5:18, [959]Psalm 103:1

Father, You are to be worshiped and praised. You and You alone are to be adored and honored. All things are from You, and through You, and to You. To You be the glory forever and ever.[960]

[960]Romans 11:36

2 *Chronicles* 36:22–23

Now in the first year of Cyrus king of Persia, that the word of the Lord by the mouth of Jeremiah might be fulfilled, the Lord stirred up the spirit of Cyrus king of Persia, so that he made a proclamation throughout all his kingdom and also put it in writing: "Thus says Cyrus king of Persia, 'The Lord, the God of heaven, has given me all the kingdoms of the earth, and he has charged me to build him a house at Jerusalem, which is in Judah. Whoever is among you of all his people, may the Lord his God be with him. Let him go up.'"

1. Cyrus is not a Jew but the king of Persia. He was not raised with the knowledge of the Lord, nor did he follow the Lord for most of his life. But the Lord has declared, "The king's heart is a stream of water in the hands of the Lord; he turns it wherever he will."[961] This is true of Cyrus, and this is true of anyone in leadership.

2. Notice also that Jeremiah spoke the Word of the Lord. Nothing could ever inhibit the Word of the Lord. That is why believers are to meditate on the promises and commands of God. We are to be mindful and trust in God at His Word and believe He will fulfill His purposes in His perfect timing.[962]

3. The hope this gives the believer is unparalleled. Israel had been in captivity for seventy years without any hope or assurance, except the promises of God. In the minds of anyone who knew the situation, there would never be a house of the Lord ever again. Yet God is never far, and He is never not at work. We can know that, "God works all things for the good of those who love Him and are called according to His purpose."[963]

4. This should encourage us believers and make our aim and our comfort only ever in the Lord and to meditate on the Law day and night, for it is like a stream planted by streams of water that yields its fruit in season and its leaf does not wither. All that He does prospers, and His Word never returns void.[964]

---

[961]Proverbs 21:1, [962]Psalm 138:8, [963]Romans 8:28, [964]Psalm 1:3

Father, all Your plans and all Your ways prosper. They never fail. I confess the many times I cease to be thankful. I cease to remember Your goodness, Your mercy, Your providence, Your sovereignty. Help me to rest in You and to do Your will. Guard my heart against man-centered thinking that denies Your sovereignty and purposes. Let my heart be thankful for all You do. Praise You, Lord. In Jesus' name.

Malachi 3:7

From the days of your fathers you have turned aside from my statutes and have not kept them. "Return to me, and I will return to you," says the LORD of hosts. But you say, "How shall we return?"

1. God has given us His Word for our lives, and we are to live all of life under the direction of and submission to His Word. We are to direct our lives in accordance with the Lord's commands and statutes of God and flee from being wise in our own eyes.[965]

2. Many times we relegate God to formulas, to Sunday mornings and quiet times, and deny Him in every other aspect of our lives. We rest upon moralism and philosophy and tell God we are good people rather than allowing God's Word to direct our lives. We attempt to build our own little kingdoms and ask Him to bless our desires rather than seeking His desire.

3. In doing this, we turn from the Lord. We leave the Lord. We deny the Lord. We begin comparing ourselves to society around us. We turn from the objective truth of God's Word and justify our actions by our emotions. We leave God.

4. Yet, the Lord is slow to anger and abounding in steadfast love and mercy. Even in the midst of all of this, He commands us to "return to Him," and then immediately He promises, "I will return to you." This is a promise. This is a glorious promise we must ponder and take to heart by faith. Whatever thoughts bombard our mind to say that we do not deserve God returning to us, the truth is that God Almighty, the Creator of heaven and earth, has made a covenant with His people and He will return.

5. So, the question remains, "How shall we return?" Repent; ask the Lord to forgive you. Ask Him to help you walk in accordance with His ways, for the joy of Christ. Humble yourself; ask Him to change your heart, to enable you to walk by His paths. And His promise is, He will do it.

---

[965] Proverbs 3:7

Father, so many times I've been lost and have gone contrary to Your Word. In those moments as well, instead of stopping and calling upon You, I fight. I attempt some form of pragmatism to work my way back to You and instead fall deeper and deeper into the bog. Forgive me, have mercy on me, strengthen me, and open my heart and mind to know Christ. Help me to come near to You and to know that You are near. Have mercy on me, Lord. In Jesus' name I ask this.

Malachi 2:15

DID HE NOT MAKE THEM ONE, WITH A PORTION OF THE SPIRIT IN THEIR UNION? AND WHAT WAS THE ONE GOD SEEKING? GODLY OFFSPRING. SO GUARD YOURSELVES IN YOUR SPIRIT, AND LET NONE OF YOU BE FAITHLESS TO THE WIFE OF YOUR YOUTH.

1. Marriage is not a human construct but a covenant among three people: the husband, the wife, together under the authority of God. The marriage is triune in nature and is a beautiful reflection of our great God.

2. Yet since we live in a fallen world, sin corrupts every marriage. When husbands and wives do not fear the Lord, that lack of gratitude to the Lord quenches the very Spirit[966] that holds the bonds of marriage together.

3. Godly marriage is a means of grace, as well as that which the Lord uses to lead His people to flourish, for they are to raise godly offspring.

4. Children are to be raised up in the fear of the Lord, that the Lord may be proclaimed to all generations! The Lord uses godly families to subdue the world for His glory for generation after generation.

5. The unity of marriage is contrary to what the world would have us believe and is not for the sake of emotions but for His glory. God ordained marriage that man would not be alone and that he would have a helper to do the will of God. Emotions can be beautiful in marriage, but the aim of marriage is not created for happiness. Marriage is created by God to glorify God and to reflect Christ's love for the church, and to raise children up in the fear of the Lord.

6. All other thoughts are to be guarded against. Guarded against because it's just not right to think other thoughts? No! All other thoughts go contrary to God's revealed Word.

---

[966] 1 Thessalonians 5:19

Father, thank You for ordaining and creating marriage. Thank You for placing Your Spirit in the bonds of marriage and for sending Your Son and reflecting marriage to us in Christ's love for His people. Father, help me to love my bride as Christ loves the church, to lead her in a way that honors You, and to raise my children up in the fear of the Lord. I ask this in Jesus' name.

2 *Chronicles* 34:15

Then Hilkiah answered and said to Shaphan the secretary, "I have found the Book of the Law in the house of the Lord." And Hilkiah gave the book to Shaphan.

1. Josiah became king at the age of eight, and by the age of twelve, began a massive reform in the kingdom.

2. People had been worshiping Baal, Molech, and Ashera and had abandoned the Lord their God. It is quite reflective of the book of Judges, which says, "And everyone did what was right in their own eyes."[967]

3. Regardless of how perilous the times are, observed by our human eyes, we must know that God's Word is eternal, regardless of what we say or do. The prophet Isaiah declares, "The grass withers, the flowers fade, but the Word of our God stands forever."[968] In this truth our faith must take hold.

4. How providential and merciful that the Lord allowed them to find the book of the Law of Moses, and at the right time—when the land was being brought back to its last reformation. The Lord is always merciful, He always hears, and He never despises those who come near with a broken and contrite heart.[969] Was this a coincidence? Was this by chance? No! This is the Lord's incredible mercy at His specific time!

5. God is never far from those who repent to and seek Him. He will always give us His Word. For in the beginning was the Word, and the Word was with God, and the Word was God. He was with God in the beginning.[970] Jesus Christ is the Word made flesh and is bringing all His people to be part of His Kingdom. Draw near to God, and He will draw near to you.[971]

---

[967] Judges 21:25, [968] Isaiah 40:8, [969] Psalm 51:17, [970] John 1:1–2, [971] James 4:8

Father, thank You for Your Word. There is nothing sweeter, nothing more glorious, nothing more beautiful than Your Word. So many times I diminish Your Word or am not mindful of it. Please, Lord, help me to be mindful, captivated, hopeful, and refreshed by Your Word. Lead me to walk in accordance with Your Word.

Amen

2 Chronicles 33:23

And he did not humble himself before the Lord, as Manasseh his father had humbled himself, but this Amon incurred guilt more and more.

1. How does one humble himself before God? To do so is antithetical to a culture that magnifies humanity.

2. To humble one's self is to answer the question, *Who do I serve?* Or, *Who is Lord over my life?* Is it my thoughts, my desires, or is it the Lord Jesus Christ? Those things the Holy Spirit reveals to us we are to repent of and turn to Christ.

3. The Lord has told us what is good, and what does the Lord require of us? But to do justly, to love mercy, and to walk humbly with our God.[972]

4. This is not a sentimental walk or one that occurs only on Sunday morning or even in our daily quiet times. This is a life fully submitted to the authority of the Word of God and a pursuit of Him by grace through faith. This is a life that is bearing fruit with repentance.[973]

5. The Lordship of Christ is to pervade every and all aspects of our lives, and to the extent that we do not humble ourselves before the Lord, we incur the wrath of God and guilt before the Lord God. We must remember it is a terrifying thing to fall into the hands of the living God.[974]

---

[972]Micah 6:8, [973]Matthew 3:8, [974]Hebrews 10:31

Father, I confess the many times I do not walk humbly before You. The unbelief in my heart is so pervasive, and the self-serving pragmatism so deceiving, that I do not seek nor do I walk under Your Lordship as I ought to. Help me to know You. Help me to know what it means to walk in accordance with Your will. Help my unbelief.[975] I ask this in Jesus' name.

2 Chronicles 32:19

And they spoke of the God of Jerusalem as they spoke of the gods of the peoples of the earth, which are the work of men's hands.

1. Those who do not know God, who have not known Christ as their Lord and Savior, view life through a lens that is incompatible with a Christian mindset. The world presupposes that since all other "gods" act in a certain way, all "gods" act in the exact same way.

2. That is false, for there is only one God, and He alone rules and reigns over all things. To Him be the glory forever and ever.

3. So what are the "gods" idolized in today's time, in a time when people pride themselves on their intellect? Pragmatism, self-help, man-centeredness, evolution, and man-centered science. All these things are used as a way to suppress the truth and place confidence in anything other than the true God.

4. This idolatrous faith is a faith unbelievers cling to. Though they attempt to proclaim their words as fact, their confidence has no grounding or support. All men have faith in something in which they place their confidence.

5. Only God and God alone deserves our faith, hope, and trust. Put your trust in God and in His living Word. Trust in the Lord with all your heart and lean not on your own understanding.[976]

---

[976] Proverbs 3:5

Father, You are sovereign over all things. There is none like You. I confess the many times I come to You with a view of life and reality contrary to Your Word. Forgive me! Help me to rest and to know Your Word, that I may walk in accordance with Your Word, and that You may receive all the praise, glory and honor! In Jesus' name I ask this.

2 *Chronicles* 32:7-8

"BE STRONG AND COURAGEOUS. DO NOT BE AFRAID OR DISMAYED BEFORE THE KING OF ASSYRIA AND ALL THE HORDE THAT IS WITH HIM, FOR THERE ARE MORE WITH US THAN WITH HIM. WITH HIM IS AN ARM OF FLESH, BUT WITH US IS THE LORD OUR GOD, TO HELP US AND TO FIGHT OUR BATTLES." AND THE PEOPLE TOOK CONFIDENCE FROM THE WORDS OF HEZEKIAH KING OF JUDAH.

1. Even though a vast army formed against Judah, King Hezekiah did not look to the arm of man but to God, in whom he trusts to save him from the approaching enemy.

2. Our emotions are led by our knowledge of God. If we have a small view of God, then when trials come, they engulf us with fear and doubt. On the other hand, if we have a correct view of God, one in which He is Lord over all things, then when trials come, we can be strong, knowing God is our refuge and strength, a very present help in trouble.[977]

3. So how do we have a right view of God? Study and meditate on who God is and how He reveals Himself in Holy Scripture. Take every preconception of who God is and align it with Scripture to know what is true and what is good and what is beautiful.

4. The Lord has given us two offensive weapons, and only two: Scripture[978] and prayer,[979] and then we are to walk by faith in who God is, and not by the sight that is before us, for His glory and our good.[980]

---

[977]Psalm 46:1, [978]Ephesians 6:17, [979]Ephesians 6:18, [980]2 Corinthians 5:7

Father, as I read this today, I realize how many times I view my circumstances rather than who You are. For what are circumstances, except God-ordained, God-authored moments to glorify You. I confess the many times I don't act in a way that reflects You, because I look at myself rather than at You. Please open my eyes and help my heart to know You and to walk by faith for Your glory and my good, according to Your will. In Jesus' name I ask this.

Revelation 17:8

The beast that you saw was, and is not, and is about to rise from the bottomless pit and go to destruction. And the dwellers on earth whose names have not been written in the book of life from the foundation of the world will marvel to see the beast, because it was and is not and is to come.

1. Salvation is from God, and He has sovereignly decreed those whom He will bring to Himself. This we see as we observe the Book of Life, in which is written the names of those who are His! When was this book written? Was it written on a day-to-day basis, was it written as time unfolds? No! It was written from the foundation of the world; this book was written in eternity past, before time was created.

2. It is a singular book with a beginning and an end. This book has written in it the names of people before they were even born! What glory! What praise and adoration!

3. How should this encourage the reader? In that there is nothing that can separate him from the love of God in Christ Jesus![981] How should this lead the unbeliever? That if today you hear His voice, cry out for mercy and trust the Lord, affirming that your name is with Christ! Then let us walk in boldness, knowing Christ's work is finished and that we have been grafted into the promises of our great God.[982]

---

[981] Romans 8:39, [982] John 19:30; Romans 11:17–23

Father, Your plans are perfect, and there is nothing that can impede them. Those who are Yours are completely Yours, and You have known them in eternity past. What mercy, what grace, what love, what hope. Father, in this, please use me to make known Your grace and to proclaim to the lost Your Truth, that those who are Yours may come to a saving and beautiful knowledge of You. I ask this in Jesus' name.

2 *Chronicles* 31:20–21

Thus Hezekiah did throughout all Judah, and he did what was good and right and faithful before the Lord his God. And every work that he undertook in the service of the house of God and in accordance with the law and the commandments, seeking his God, he did with all his heart, and prospered.

1. Guard your heart in reading this against two evils that can prevail against you. First is the evil and deception that whoever follows the Lord receives prosperity. This is not true, and for anyone who reads history, this is a heresy. On the other hand, we must also guard our hearts from a nihilistic or pietistic theology declaring God does not bless us nor makes us prosper but wants us to reflect poverty. Both of these ideas are sinful and heretical against the Word of God.

2. So should then our aim be something else? Our aim should be that which is good, right, and faithful before God, and whatever the Lord ordains is right.

3. God's will always prospers, the Lord always wins, and the gates of hell will never prevail against Him.[983] But we also must remember that God's thoughts and God's ways are not our thoughts and our ways.[984]

4. Look to Christ; look to the finished work of Christ, acknowledge your need for Him, and acknowledge His defeat of sin, and then step forward by faith in doing what the Lord has called you to do. Trust that God's plan—not yours—will prosper according to His purposes, and be thankful He has chosen you for His purposes, for His glory, and your good.

[983]Matthew 16:18, [984]Isaiah 55:8

Oh Father, how beautiful are Your plans and how perfect are Your ways. Father, I confess I have looked at my words, my thoughts, and my desires rather than Your Word. I have not been faithful and have doubted many times. Forgive me. Help me to see and to walk by grace through faith in accordance with Your will. And may all I do according to Your will and strength prosper in a way that magnifies Christ. All to Christ, for the glory of Christ. In Christ's name I ask this.

Amen

Revelation 16:8–11

THE FOURTH ANGEL POURED OUT HIS BOWL ON THE SUN, AND IT WAS ALLOWED TO SCORCH PEOPLE WITH FIRE. THEY WERE SCORCHED BY THE FIERCE HEAT, AND THEY CURSED THE NAME OF GOD WHO HAD POWER OVER THESE PLAGUES. THEY DID NOT REPENT AND GIVE HIM GLORY. THE FIFTH ANGEL POURED OUT HIS BOWL ON THE THRONE OF THE BEAST, AND ITS KINGDOM WAS PLUNGED INTO DARKNESS. PEOPLE GNAWED THEIR TONGUES IN ANGUISH AND CURSED THE GOD OF HEAVEN FOR THEIR PAIN AND SORES. THEY DID NOT REPENT OF THEIR DEEDS.

1. The world is not run by natural laws, systems, processes, or evolving time. What happens in weather patterns or climate changes or plagues are not laws autonomous from the sovereign control of God but are completely and directly under the sovereign control of our God.

2. Deism is a heretical mindset brought into light by the philosopher Immanuel Kant. This mindset believes God created the world and then stepped back and let the world run itself, like a watchmaker winding up a watch and then stepping back to let the watch run.

3. Nowhere is this in Holy Scripture. God is sovereign over all things, and He works all things for His glory and our good. The greatest good is to know God, and the way we know God is through repentance and surrendering our lives to Him.

4. In this passage, the Lord ordained fire, plagues, and darkness to reveal Himself to those who denied Him. Yet even in the Lord revealing Himself, they will not repent or glorify God.

5. Those who are cast for all eternity into hell will know God exists and who He is, but even in the midst of damnation, their hearts will never glorify God or repent and turn from their wicked ways.

Father, You are merciful and gracious, slow to anger and abounding in steadfast love and mercy. It is only by Your grace that we are aware of our depravity and glorify You. Forgive me for my selfish ambition and pride and those things that keep me from a fuller knowledge of who You are. Open my eyes to what keeps me from You, the sin that so easily entangles me, that I may turn in full repentance and glorify You in adoring praise and adoration, through the redemption of Your Son. In Jesus' name.

2 Chronicles 30:9

FOR IF YOU RETURN TO THE LORD, YOUR BROTHERS AND YOUR CHILDREN WILL FIND COMPASSION WITH THEIR CAPTORS AND RETURN TO THIS LAND. FOR THE LORD YOUR GOD IS GRACIOUS AND MERCIFUL AND WILL NOT TURN AWAY HIS FACE FROM YOU, IF YOU RETURN TO HIM.

1. What a glorious promise the Lord has given to us in His Word. What the Lord has called us to is a return to God.

2. In the day of Israel at that time, polytheism was rampant. People worshiped Baal and other idols. The idea was that they would have to do certain things to get the idols' attention, to do enough work or put in enough effort to warrant any material blessing from those idols.

3. We can scoff at them today; except we do the very same thing. We believe in the idols of pragmatism and self-help to help us get what we want. We measure our success, our worth, our "goodness" by the numbers of people who follow us on social media, or our incomes, or who likes us.

4. All of this is meaningless before a holy God. There is only one thing God requires of us, and that is to repent. We are to repent and seek the Lord and to love the Lord with all of our hearts, souls, and with all of our might.[985] The beauty of this verse, though, is the *If*. "If" we repent and trust the Lord, He will be gracious and merciful and will not turn His face away from us.

5. There is no act that can bind the Lord, for what do you have that has not been given to you by God?[986] Repent; trust the Lord with all of your heart.[987] Walk humbly with Him,[988] and He will lead you perfectly, according to His will.

---

[985]Deuteronomy 6:5, [986]1 Corinthians 4:7, [987]Proverbs 3:5, [988]Micah 6:8

Father, Your thoughts and Your ways are not my thoughts and my ways, for You are holy, and I am not. I confess the many times I am tempted to think I can build, do, manipulate, or even bind You to get what I think I want, yet who am I? You love me more than I can imagine, and yet I deny that love and play the fool. Forgive me, Lord. Help me to know Your love for me. Help me to rest in that love, strive in that love, be patient in that love, and glorify You in all things. Thank You, Jesus.

Amen

2 *Chronicles* 1:1

Solomon the son of David established himself in his kingdom, and the Lord his God was with him and made him exceedingly great.

1. The Lord is with Solomon.

2. Nothing in Solomon, of Solomon, or anything he did made him great.

3. The Lord chooses whom He chooses. The Lord has mercy on whom He will have mercy, and He will have compassion on whom He will have compassion.[989]

4. This is all done by the providence of God.

5. I am to seek the Lord and His presence continually.[990]

---

[989]Romans 9:15, [990]1 Chronicles 16:11

Father, as I read Your Word, I see how nothing can thwart You. I also see in my own heart how success, achievement, and accolades can become idols. Help me to see You, Father, as You are. Help me to walk in the fear of the Lord, to walk humbly before You at all times.

Genesis 13:9

Is not the whole land before you? Separate yourself from me. If you take the left hand, then I will go to the right, or if you take the right hand, then I will go to the left."

1. Abraham approached Lot and placed a choice before him. Lot could have the land on the left or the land that was on the right. Abraham left the decision completely in the hands of Lot. When Lot looked at the land, he measured everything by what he could see: "And Lot lifted up his eyes and saw that the Jordan Valley was well watered everywhere like the garden of the LORD, like the land of Egypt, in the direction of Zoar."[991]

2. At a cursory glance, this is logical to the mind of man. Lot saw with his eyes and chose the better land, but we must ask ourselves, how did Abram look at the situation? Abram looked at the entire situation through the eyes of faith in God. He knew God had brought him from the land of Ur.[992] Abraham acted upon the promises of God, that the Lord would make him a great blessing among the nations and that He would bless Abraham. In light of these promises from God, Abraham trusted God knowing that, "The heart of man plans his way, but the LORD establishes his steps."[993]

3. Our faith and assurance grow and are measured by that which our faith rests in. Christ is the radiance of the glory of God, and all things hold together by the word of His power.[994] All angels and all of creation do His bidding,[995] and His rule has no end.[996] Lastly, He not only rules over all, but He calls us brothers and knows all our temptations and sorrows.[997]

4. Our confidence rests in Christ and what He has done, for in the same way that Abraham believed and trusted in the promises of God in all things, we are to look to Christ and believe and trust His Word and act in such a way that honors, glorifies, and reflects His Lordship and love for us in all that we seek for His glory.

[991]Genesis 13:10, [992]Genesis 12:1, [993]Proverbs 16:9, [994]Hebrews 1:3, [995]Hebrews 1:7, [996]Hebrews 1:12, [997]Hebrews 1:12

Lord, I praise You. You are great and glorious and yet You know me. You know my name, You have called me by name, and I am Yours. Lord, so many things seem impossible to me. My hope vanishes at the thought, and they are many times greater in my mind than You are. Forgive me. Help me to have a greater and more sure and true view of You, and give me strength to walk boldly by faith to do Your will in all things. In Your name I ask this.

Zephaniah 3:1-2

WOE TO HER WHO IS REBELLIOUS AND DEFILED, THE OPPRESSING CITY! SHE LISTENS TO NO VOICE; SHE ACCEPTS NO CORRECTION. SHE DOES NOT TRUST IN THE LORD; SHE DOES NOT DRAW NEAR TO HER GOD.

1. God is the One who stated this was a "woe," that it was something terrible. He is the One who declared the goings-on as sin and must be punished.

2. What was this sin? What was the sin so rebellious and defiled? Israel did not listen to the voice of God, the correction of God. She did not trust the Lord; she did not draw near to her God!

3. The heart is never neutral. Israel was drawing near to someone, or something. In fact, what she might have drawn near to was wise in the eyes of the world but did not seek the Lord.

4. We are to seek the Lord and His strength; we are to seek His presence continually.[998] We are to be joyful always, pray continuously, and give thanks in all circumstances, for this is the will of God in Christ Jesus.[999] When do I seek the Lord? In all things, or in dire straits? In things I deem spiritual or too great for my mind? Or at all times? Do I seek the Lord and His strength?

---

[998] 1 Chronicles 16:11, [999] 1 Thessalonians 5:14–17

Father, You are great and mighty! Help me to seek You and rejoice in You. For You are the God of my salvation! Forgive me for thinking that rest is my salvation, or things of this world are my salvation! Forgive me for thinking that being a human is a reason to have an excuse rather than trusting Your providence. Give me wisdom, Lord. Help me to walk in accordance with Your will! I thank You, Jesus.

Revelation 14:1–5

Then I looked, and behold, on Mount Zion stood the Lamb, and with him 144,000 who had his name and his Father's name written on their foreheads. And I heard a voice from heaven like the roar of many waters and like the sound of loud thunder. The voice I heard was like the sound of harpists playing on their harps, and they were singing a new song before the throne and before the four living creatures and before the elders. No one could learn that song except the 144,000 who had been redeemed from the earth. It is these who have not defiled themselves with women, for they are virgins. It is these who follow the Lamb wherever he goes. These have been redeemed from mankind as firstfruits for God and the Lamb, and in their mouth no lie was found, for they are blameless.

1. The 144,000 is the total, the whole of all whom God has called and is bringing to Himself. This is not a literal number, but a number that reflects completion and that none are left behind. This is the invisible church. The church that Christ knows, calls, brings to Himself, who have a regenerated heart, and are made new in Christ.

2. How encouraging that we need not live with regret or worry that any of Christ's sheep will be lost. They will all come to Him, in all of time, and the Lord will tarry until that number is fully complete.

3. Let us also see the beauty as well that those who are His are pure. They are pure as virgins because of the blood of the Lamb, who paid the price for all the sins, all the stains of sin.

4. The total of the invisible church, those who are His, follow the Lamb. They do not follow idle traditions, they do not follow a man-made philosophy, they follow a Person, they follow the Lamb. This perfect, this is true objective beauty, this is our King, and we say with all of creation, "Come, Lord Jesus, come!"

Jesus, You are King of kings and Lord of lords! You alone are worthy of all praise and adoration! Lord, lead me in Your way everlasting. Forgive me for following those things contrary to Your Word, and help me to walk in Your truth. Your Word is truth! Thank You, Jesus.

2 *Chronicles* 27:6

So Jotham became mighty, because he ordered his ways before the Lord his God.

1. Notice how Jotham became mighty, but that is secondary to his focus. It is not by self-help or pragmatism or the way of the world that he was attributed might. The Lord blessed Jotham accordingly because Jotham's focus was to order his ways, to order his life before the Lord.

2. In the same way, we are to present our lives as a living sacrifice, holy and acceptable before God, which is our spiritual worship.[1000]

3. Our entire aim, our entire thought, our entire focus, is to know God and to make Him known in every aspect of our lives. Leave all the selfish ambition behind, search your heart, and be still. Let the prayer of your heart be, "Not my will but yours be done."[1001]

4. The Lord has promised He will never withhold any good from you.[1002] Whatever He blesses is more than we deserve, for He has given us everything in Christ and Christ alone. So let us trust Him, look to His Word, and pray that He guides us in that which He has called us to.

[1000]Romans 12:1, [1001]Luke 22:42, [1002]Psalm 84:11

Father, help me to order my days before You. Forgive me for making my own plans in my sinful nature and not ordering them or seeking You first. You are my joy, You are my hope, You are the longing of my heart. You have done all this by the power of Your Holy Spirit! Please lead me in Your way everlasting. In Jesus' name.

Revelation 13:4

*And they worshiped the dragon,
for he had given his authority to the beast,
and they worshiped the beast, saying,
"Who is like the beast, and who can fight against it?"*

1. Our view of God affects how we look at every and all aspects of life.

2. If our view of God is small, if it is limited to Sunday morning or a bumper sticker, then when things in life seem too big to comprehend, we deny the worship of God and instead worship the very thing that seems so big!

3. The people in this verse looked at the beast, looked at the size of the beast and asked, "Who can fight against it?" Yet, they never have a standard of measurement to measure against. There is no aspect of truth to substantiate even the thought.

4. When the world tells us we should be scared, when news reports say we should fear, when lust and temptation say we should envy, what is our standard of measurement we are measuring against? God or man?

5. Let God be our focus and our standard. Make God the focus and aim, and know Him. Ask the Lord and He will draw you to Himself. How? By His grace. In what way? In the perfect way He deems is best for His glory and your good. At what pace? His perfect timing. When? Now!

Father, save me from my sin. Oh, how deceitful is this sin that borrows, tucks, and finds its ways to deceive me. There are so many things I deem "big," "awesome," and "terrifying," yet they are never measured against You, only against themselves. What a fool I am! Please, Lord, help me to know You, that I may make You known. In Jesus' name.

2 Chronicles 26:16

But when he was strong, he grew proud, to his destruction. For he was unfaithful to the Lord his God and entered the temple of the Lord to burn incense on the altar of incense.

1. The Lord is always near, and so is our sin.

2. The Lord searches the heart and tests the mind to give to every man according to his ways, according to the fruit of his deeds.[1003] The blessings we receive from God are not apart from God. They are given to us for His glory, but the Lord also gives them to test the heart of man.

3. This testing is what reveals to us our utter depravity and sin. We must be mindful of our hearts and what they tempt us to believe. Do we fall back on our intellect? Do we run from fear? Are we wise in our own eyes? Or do we seek the Lord while He may be found?[1004]

4. Many people do not like wealth and prosperity because they show the corruption of the heart. But they also fear themselves and the sin in their hearts rather than pressing in and seeking the Lord, coming to Him in repentance and trusting Him.

5. There is nothing evil whatsoever with material blessing, but the Lord uses it to test the heart and reveal to us if He is God, or that which He has blessed us with.

[1003]Jeremiah 17:10, [1004]Isaiah 55:6

Father, all things are from You, and through You, and to You! So many things in my life I have sought with my internal wisdom or my perceived intellect, rather than coming to You. I have been strategic rather than prayerful. Forgive me. You are good, and everything that comes from You is good. Help me to walk in accordance with Your will and Your providence. Open my eyes to behold Your glory, and lead me in Your way everlasting. In Jesus' name.

Zechariah 8:9

Thus says the LORD of hosts: "Let your hands be strong, you who in these days have been hearing these words from the mouth of the prophets who were present on the day that the foundation of the house of the LORD of hosts was laid, that the temple might be built."

1. The Lord is strong, and there is nothing that takes away from or deters His strength. So, in that which the Lord calls to, our eyes should never look to ourselves but only to the Lord, seeking His strength. To not seek the Lord is to be wise in our own eyes and to deceive ourselves into thinking we do not need God in every aspect of our lives.

2. As we see the world move further and further from God, we see that the heart of man realizes the fragility of humanity. When we remove a right view of God, our minds and emotions become nihilistic and we are unable to hope for a redemption to come. We are to let our hands be strong—strong in the Lord.

3. Christ has said that apart from Him, we can do nothing.[1005] This truth is not grounded in a religious act or just a gathering on Sunday but covers all aspects of life. In Christ, all the promises of God are fulfilled, so we are to walk with assurance and in boldness in those things the Lord has called us.[1006]

4. Throughout Scripture, the Lord promises He will never leave us nor forsake us.[1007] So, we are to walk by faith in accordance with His word. We are to trust the Lord's providence, calling upon Him continually for His strength,[1008] and thanking him with every step, every moment, every second for His strength.

[1005]John 15:5, [1006]2 Corinthians 1:20, [1007]Hebrews 13:5; Joshua 1:5, [1008]1 Thessalonians 5:15–18

Father, there is none like You. So many times I look at my strength, and my ability, and my humanity, and I am filled with fear, for I realize I am nothing. This, in turn, causes my unbelief in You and in Your calling and in Your Word. Forgive me, Father.

2 Chronicles 25:2

And he did what was right in the eyes of the Lord, *yet not with a whole heart.*

1. God has called us to love the Lord our God with all of our hearts, and with all of our souls, and with all of our might. The aspect of *all* is an impossible command apart from the power of the Holy Spirit. Anything less than all is a diminishment of God's command and thus is sin.

2. Man always attempts to be moral apart from God. We construct ideas of moralism and legalism and deny the power of God, thus taking the name of the Lord in vain. We measure our thoughts, words, and deeds based upon sinful man rather than on Christ Jesus, who is our standard.

3. So instead of looking to ourselves, let us look to Christ and call upon His name. He has said that apart from Him we have nothing.[1009] But in Him we have life, and joy, and peace. The Holy Spirit opens our hearts to our utter dependency on Christ and shows us those things in which we are to repent and seek Christ!

4. So let us each repent and ask the Lord to reveal to us the areas in which we are not living all unto the Lord. Let us trust Him to reveal those things to us in His perfect timing, and let us boldly move forward for His glory.

[1009] John 15:5

Father, You have created all things, and there is nothing that did not first come from You. Forgive me, because in my pride, I believe I am the only one who knows about so many things, or that I am the only one who sees my thoughts and my actions—but that is not true. You are God, and I am not! Please help me to follow You with my whole heart. Show me the idols in my heart, and help me to follow You all the days of my life. In Jesus' name,

Amen

2 *Chronicles* 24:20

Then the Spirit of God clothed Zechariah the son of Jehoiada the priest, and he stood above the people, and said to them, "Thus says God, 'Why do you break the commandments of the Lord, so that you cannot prosper? Because you have forsaken the Lord, he has forsaken you.'"

1. We must be very careful when we read this, for if we read it in one way, we will think the prosperity gospel is the core of Scripture. On the other hand, if we read it stoically and in a way that denies the providence of God, we will not see the beauty of who God is.

2. Those who follow God are still led through trials and tribulations ordained by God to lead us to a right view of Him. We see in the book of Job a man who followed God and was more "righteous" than anyone else, and the Lord still led him through difficult times.

3. In chapter four of the gospel of Matthew, the Holy Spirit led Jesus into the wilderness to be tempted by Satan. Even in those instances, though not pleasant, the Lord was working.

4. The point is, God is never impeded, nor are His plans thwarted in any time or circumstance. All His plans prosper in His perfect timing. This may not be done in the same way man measures success, but our measuring is not done by human standards; it is entrusted to the sovereign hand of God.

5. There is a warning, though, that if we do not pursue the Lord, He might give us what we want, but He will remove Himself from it, and the wrath of God will be poured out. We will no longer be in relationship with the Lord Most High, and the blessing becomes a curse as the blessing becomes an idol. The Lord is a holy God, and He will not be part of anything that does not glorify Him.

Father, You are holy, and You are never thwarted. Oh, how easily I forget that. I so easily think what I am doing is the "right" thing to do, and I cease to seek You. I grow cold in my prayers; I neglect Your Word. Forgive me. Help me to prosper in accordance with Your will, for Your glory, and guard my heart from selfish ambition. Thank You, Jesus. I ask this in Your precious name.

2 *Chronicles* 24:17–19

NOW AFTER THE DEATH OF JEHOIADA THE PRINCES OF JUDAH CAME AND PAID HOMAGE TO THE KING. THEN THE KING LISTENED TO THEM. AND THEY ABANDONED THE HOUSE OF THE LORD, THE GOD OF THEIR FATHERS, AND SERVED THE ASHERIM AND THE IDOLS. AND WRATH CAME UPON JUDAH AND JERUSALEM FOR THIS GUILT OF THEIRS. YET HE SENT PROPHETS AMONG THEM TO BRING THEM BACK TO THE LORD. THESE TESTIFIED AGAINST THEM, BUT THEY WOULD NOT PAY ATTENTION.

1. Every relationship we entertain bears consequences. Relationships are never not spiritual in relationship. The people you hang around, and the people you listen to, have a dramatic effect on your relationship with God.

2. Developing deep relationships with those who are older and wiser than you, and not with fools the same age as you, can save a man from an eternity in hell. For how can one who has never experienced the same things you have ever give you advice on things you don't know about? This is why the Proverbs say a companion of fools always suffers harm.[1010]

3. Let all advice be subjective, and hold fast to the objective Word of God. Let the Word of the Lord dwell richly in you.[1011]

4. Be selective with what you listen to, and never let your mind be idle. Guard your heart and take every thought captive, measuring it against the Word of God for the glory of our Lord Jesus Christ.[1012]

5. For Jesus is a jealous God, and He will share His glory with no man.[1013] He will fulfill all His promises. He will curse those who hate Him to the third and fourth generation but show steady love to thousands of those who seek Him and keep His commandments.[1014]

[1010]Proverbs 13:20, [1011]Colossians 3:16, [1012]2 Corinthians 10:5, [1013]Exodus 34:14, [1014]Exodus 20:5

Father, I praise You for Your Word. I praise You that You have brought me to You, and that You have revealed Your Son to me. Who am I? Father, many times I have not thought about the people and the relationships in my life. I have reacted emotionally and not been wise. Forgive me, and lead me in Your way everlasting. Give me wisdom, and surround me with people who help me to know You more. Guard my heart and my mind, and keep me from fools who tempt me to have a low and sinful view of You. In Jesus' name.

Zechariah 6:15

"And those who are far off shall come and help to build the temple of the Lord. And you shall know that the Lord of hosts has sent me to you. And this shall come to pass, if you will diligently obey the voice of the Lord your God."

1. The Lord never calls His people to something without also providing the means in which to accomplish it.

2. We are to call on the Lord for wisdom in all things, and we are to, by faith, trust in His perfect providence, without doubt, taking every step He lays before us.[1015]

3. As God's people, we are to cast all our anxieties on Him because He cares for us. As we move forward, we are not to measure our ability based upon what we perceive or what we have measured, but on the promises of God. God is always working, and He is always orchestrating all things for His good and our glory.

4. So we are called to seek the Lord, pray, and trust that He will lead us the way we should go—be it vocationally, personally, or within marriage and other relationships. We are not to be wise in our own eyes, but to be wise seeking the Lord and pressing forward.[1016]

5. Let us remember that unless the Lord builds the house, those who build it labor in vain. And unless the Lord watches over the city, the watchmen stay awake in vain.[1017] In this truth let us find confidence in Christ, looking at all things He has placed before us under His sovereign and blessed hand.

[1015] James 1:5–8, [1016] Proverbs 3:5–8, [1017] Psalm 127:1

Father, You are perfect, and there is nothing impossible for You. For You are the Alpha and the Omega, the beginning and the end. Forgive me, Lord, for not seeking You in all things and in all circumstances. Forgive me for presupposing Your answers, or Your will, without coming to You first. Please lead me in what You would have me do in Your Kingdom, for Your glory. In Jesus' name.

2 *Chronicles* 22:3–6

He also walked in the ways of the house of Ahab, for his mother was his counselor in doing wickedly. He did what was evil in the sight of the Lord, as the house of Ahab had done. For after the death of his father they were his counselors, to his undoing. He even followed their counsel and went with Jehoram the son of Ahab king of Israel to make war against Hazael king of Syria at Ramoth-gilead. And the Syrians wounded Joram, and he returned to be healed in Jezreel of the wounds that he had received at Ramah, when he fought against Hazael king of Syria. And Ahaziah the son of Jehoram king of Judah went down to see Joram the son of Ahab in Jezreel, because he was wounded.

1. Each of us walk in accordance with those to whom are closest. No person is totally and utterly autonomous but is in turn affected tremendously by those whom we spend time with.

2. Among the greatest teachers the Lord has ordained for our lives are our parents. They are the first ones called to show us a reflection of who God is. They are image bearers of God to the children they raise. If parents have a low view of God, their children, apart from God's grace, will have a low view of God.

3. Our sentimentality must not blind us to who God is. Regardless of how much we love and care for those around us, we must always look at them through the lens of truth, through the lens of Holy Scripture.

4. As we grow in the wisdom and knowledge of the Lord, we must be ready to pursue Christ at all costs, for in the cost we find the ultimate fulfillment. For Christ said, "Jesus said, "Truly, I say to you, there is no one who has left house or brothers or sisters or mother or father or children or lands, for my sake and for the gospel, who will not receive a hundredfold now in this time, houses and brothers and sisters and mothers and children and lands, with persecutions, and in the age to come eternal life. But many who are first will be last, and the last first."[1018]

[1018] Mark 10:29–31

Father, You are my Father in Christ. To You I should look for my every thought, word, action, and deed. Forgive me for looking to things, to people, to circumstances as my way of truth, rather than looking to Your Word. Open my eyes to behold You, and lead me in Your way everlasting. In Jesus' name.

Amen

Revelation 9:20-21

The rest of mankind, who were not killed by these plagues, did not repent of the works of their hands nor give up worshiping demons and idols of gold and silver and bronze and stone and wood, which cannot see or hear or walk, nor did they repent of their murders or their sorceries or their sexual immorality or their thefts.

1. In today's society, people believe that mankind is good. The truthfulness of total depravity is denied. Science becomes god, and only *matter* and *energy* exist in the minds of man—nothing more. The God of the universe is denied to the same degree, and we in our minds make ourselves God.

2. This leads back to Genesis 3, when the serpent in the garden of Eden asked Eve, *"Did God really say..."* Humanity scoffs at repentance. We will not seek God, we will not trust God, we will not love God if we deny His very existence and suppress the truth of God's Word.

3. In denial of God's existence, we worship demons, silver, gold, bronze, stone, and wood, all which cannot hear or talk. We justify our actions and fall into sexual sin and the murder of other human beings.

4. One of the most prevalent ways we see this in today's society is in a non-God-glorifying view of sex. We view it as a right rather than part of a covenant. In doing this, we justify the murder of hundreds of thousands of lives in abortions mills and live a life deranged and that leads to death.

5. It is Christ and Christ alone who can save us from ourselves. It is Christ and Christ alone who can free us from our depravity and lead us to life and freedom in Christ. Let us call upon Him and repent and turn from our wicked ways, trusting His saving grace for all our lives.

Father, have mercy on us. Our sin is ever before us, and we do not deserve to come before You now and to seek You with all our hearts, souls, and minds, to ask You to bring us to You. But I ask You to bring us to You. Please revive and renew our hearts with a passion for Your glory and Your renown. Reveal to me the idols in my heart, that I may turn from them and seek You with all my heart, soul, and strength. In Jesus' name.

2 *Chronicles* 21:4

When Jehoram had ascended the throne of his father and was established, he killed all his brothers with the sword, and also some of the princes of Israel.

1. Jehoram did what was pragmatically strategic to keep the kingdom. Each of his actions showed he had an incorrect view of God and actually reflected the idolatrous nations that surrounded Israel.

2. Our God is sovereign over all things and holds all things in His hands. All rulers come to power only by the providence of God, so we can trust Him and look to Him as He leads us and guides us. As the Lord establishes His people, He also defends His people—if we look to Him and seek Him.

3. Jehoram does not heed this, nor does he know that God directs the hearts of man like a water course, so that he need not fear his brothers, for God controls all things.

4. Yet instead of resting, trusting, and calling out to God, he breaks the Law of God and sins against Him, his brothers, their families, and the children of Israel.

5. Let us be more prayerful than strategic. Let us not reflect the pragmatism and self-dependence of Jehoram. Let us trust the Lord to fulfill His Word and reflect to the world a dependence upon His grace, trusting that whatever the Lord ordains is right.

FATHER, THANK YOU FOR YOUR WORD! FORGIVE ME FOR ALL THE TIMES I AM PRAGMATIC OR DO NOT TRUST YOUR WORD, LIVING ANXIOUSLY AND WALKING IN UNBELIEF. HELP ME TO WALK IN A WAY THAT BRINGS YOU GLORY AND HONOR, TO WALK IN A WAY THAT OTHERS MAY SEE MY GOOD WORKS AND PRAISE MY FATHER WHO IS IN HEAVEN.[1019]

2 *Chronicles* 19:6–7

Consider what you do, for you judge not for man but for the Lord. He is with you in giving judgment. Now then, let the fear of the Lord be upon you. Be careful what you do, for there is no injustice with the Lord our God, or partiality or taking bribes.

1. All vocations are from the Lord, and they are a grace given by Him to be used for His glory.[1020]

2. As Christians, we are here to work for the Lord and not for man. We are to seek the Lord and His strength,[1021] His wisdom,[1022] His grace and have no fear of man in whatever we do.[1023]

3. Our judgment is not to be our subject experiences but the Word of God. We are to be mindful of what we do and measure what we see purposefully and carefully, taking every thought captive to Christ. As we recognize how all our emotions apart from the grace of God are held captive by our sinful nature, let us go to Christ, allowing the very Word of God to bind our every thought, word, action, and deed.[1024]

4. We are to recognize that God never is less than Himself. There is no injustice, no partiality, no taking bribes. God is not empathetic to any status in life, but in turn, He is holy and true. We are to reflect this in our actions, being slow to anger, and abounding in steadfast love and mercy.[1025] Judging not by our humanity, lest we be judged by others' humanity, but in turn before the holy Word of God.

[1020] 1 Corinthians 7:17, [1021] 1 Corinthians 16:11, [1022] James 1:5–8, [1023] Psalm 146:3–5, [1024] 2 Corinthians 10:5, [1025] Psalm 145:8

Father, thank You for revealing to us Your holiness, and mercy. Thank You for giving us Your Word. Forgive me for so many times being mindless, for thinking I can act good apart from You. For apart from You I can do nothing.[1026] Father, please give me wisdom in all You have set before me today. Help me to recognize Your wisdom, Your strength, and Your presence, that I may be humbled and worship You. Forgive my hardness of heart, and lead me in Your way everlasting. In Jesus' name.

[1026] John 15:5

2 *Chronicles* 19:1–3

Jehoshaphat the king of Judah returned in safety to his house in Jerusalem. But Jehu the son of Hanani the seer went out to meet him and said to King Jehoshaphat, "Should you help the wicked and love those who hate the Lord? Because of this, wrath has gone out against you from the Lord. Nevertheless, some good is found in you, for you destroyed the Asheroth out of the land, and have set your heart to seek God."

1. In the previous chapter of 2 Chronicles, Jehoshaphat went to war with Ahab. He acted in a way that he already had his mind made up, rather than seeking the Lord.

2. In this way, the wrath of God came against Jehoshaphat.

3. The wrath of God is a terrifying thing. God's wrath is not a heated furnace or terrifying yelling. The wrath of God is God giving us over to our own desires and not allowing His presence to be felt or near.[1027]

4. When the Lord reveals this to us, we are to repent. When the Lord reveals the sin and wickedness in our hearts, we must repent. Realize that the only reason you recognize the sin in your heart is not because of your intellect but because of the work of the Holy Spirit. We are to seek the Lord and to seek His presence continually.[1028]

5. As the Holy Spirit conforms us more and more to the image of Christ, let us pray continually and give thanks in all circumstances, for this is the will of God in Christ Jesus for us.[1029] Let us seek the Lord and trust the Word of God, as He reveals it to us by the power of the Holy Spirit, for it is truth.[1030]

[1027]Romans 1:18–32, [1028]1 Chronicles 16:11, [1029]1 Thessalonians 5:14–17, [1030]John 17:17

Father, You are holy and perfect. You are wise in all Your ways. There is no error or lack in any of Your thoughts, words, actions, deeds, or being. Father, forgive me, for I have sought the wisdom of the world more than I have sought You. Forgive me, and have mercy on me. How do I speak to You in the day to day, and how do You speak back to me in the moment by moment? Forgive my unbelief, and have mercy on me. Lead me in Your way everlasting, for You are my God! Help me to seek You. Help me to seek You not only in my young years, but my entire life, for the glory of Christ, and help me to know Your voice. In Christ's name I ask this.

Zechariah 1:3

Jehoshaphat the king of Judah returned in safety to his Therefore say to them, Thus declares the LORD of hosts: Return to me, says the LORD of hosts, and I will return to you, says the LORD of hosts.

1. What a beautiful command, and what a beautiful promise.

2. How does one return to God? By following His commands and worshiping Him and seeking the Lord. We do not have to conjure up the Lord, but instead, we are to seek Him and trust Him in all we do.

3. If we seek the Lord, we will find Him. This command is not abstract or without the fulfillment of the command. The Lord promises to return.

4. One must seek the Lord. One must repent and trust in the Lord. He is to seek the Lord with all his heart and cry out to Him.

Father, You are a good Father. You are pure and holy. I confess I am sinful in all my thoughts, words, actions, and deeds. I have spoken in ways that do not glorify You. I have pragmatically sought solutions. I have not looked to You or trusted You in the way I should. Forgive me. How do I take a step in Your strength? How do I walk by the joy of faith? Help me to walk in the peace of God that transcends all understanding. Thank You, Jesus.

Amen

2 Chronicles 16:7-9

AT THAT TIME HANANI THE SEER CAME TO ASA KING OF JUDAH AND SAID TO HIM, "BECAUSE YOU RELIED ON THE KING OF SYRIA, AND DID NOT RELY ON THE LORD YOUR GOD, THE ARMY OF THE KING OF SYRIA HAS ESCAPED YOU. WERE NOT THE ETHIOPIANS AND THE LIBYANS A HUGE ARMY WITH VERY MANY CHARIOTS AND HORSEMEN? YET BECAUSE YOU RELIED ON THE LORD, HE GAVE THEM INTO YOUR HAND. FOR THE EYES OF THE LORD RUN TO AND FRO THROUGHOUT THE WHOLE EARTH, TO GIVE STRONG SUPPORT TO THOSE WHOSE HEART IS BLAMELESS TOWARD HIM. YOU HAVE DONE FOOLISHLY IN THIS, FOR FROM NOW ON YOU WILL HAVE WARS."

1. In the very first book, Hanani pointed out that Asa did not rely and depend upon the Lord. Instead, he depended upon the king of Syria.

2. He pointed out how the Lord had faithfully supplied the needs of Asa in the battle against the Ethiopians and Libyans (2 Chronicles 13:18). In fact, the armies of the Ethiopians and the Libyans were twice the size of Israel, and the Lord delivered them into Israel's hands.

3. "The eyes of the Lord run to and fro." There is nothing the Lord does not see. He does not look to and fro for help, but to give help and to work all things together for good for those who love God and are called according to His purpose.[1031]

4. One of the most terrifying things, though, is that the Lord does not only look for those whom He can give strong support, but He also looks at the heart of the person. Is this person blameless toward Him? Is this person reflecting God's holiness?

5. Unfortunately, Asa did not repent. He did not seek the forgiveness of God but instead hardened his heart.

[1031] Romans 8:28

Father, I am so prone to act in a way that does not acknowledge You. I am so prone to trust in what I see rather than in Your Word. Forgive me. What arrogance and pride to trust in my sight rather than in Your Word. Forgive me, and thank You for Your Word. Help me to trust, and to rest, and to seek You. Help my assurance in You to overflow with joy. How do I rest in Your grace through the day to day? How do I put my hope in You? How does my assurance abide in You? Is it in every and all circumstances? Please help me, Jesus. I thank You.

2 Chronicles 14:6

He built fortified cities in Judah, for the land had rest. He had no war in those years, for the LORD gave him peace.

1. God is sovereign over all things, but that does not remove the responsibility from us to strive and to work. Asa built fortified cities in Judah to protect against any war that might break out against Judah. The underlying factor, though, is that the Lord gave them peace.

2. The Lord uses all types of means to work out His will and His plan for His people. Apart from Christ we can do absolutely nothing.[1032]

3. This is also reflective of Psalm 127:1, which states, *"Unless the Lord build the house, those who build it labor in vain. Unless the Lord watches over the city, the watchmen stay awake in vain."* There are both watchmen and laborers, and both are needed to do their jobs, but it is the Lord who works all things for His glory.

[1032] John 15:5

Father, You give all things and You take all things. You are the One who gives peace, and You are the One who brings discipline. Lord, I confess that I am so leery of the prosperity gospel that at times I deny Your blessing and try to think nihilistically. Forgive my unbelief. Will You help me to know how to look at You in way that glorifies You, with Your providence and Your goodness? Help me to understand Your Lordship over all! In Jesus' name.

Amen

2 *Chronicles* 13:18

Thus the men of Israel were subdued at that time, and the men of Judah prevailed, because they relied on the Lord, the God of their fathers.

1. Jeroboam had 800,000 valiant men, and Abijah had 400,000.

2. According to those numbers, Jeroboam should have won. There was no practical reason why Judah should prevail over the people of Israel.

3. What Abijah did not do, however, was talk about the strength, the might, the genius, the fortitude, the power, and the covenant of man. He talked about the covenant of God. He proclaimed the truth of who God is, the sovereignty and the promises of God.

4. Abijah did not know what the outcome would be, but he did know God and left all results in the hands of the Lord.

5. How often do I trust in my own knowledge and am wise in my own eyes rather than walking by faith in accordance with who God is?

6. Do I put my eyes on the Lord, or on circumstances, probabilities, and even measure my own self-worth subjectively, based upon how I feel? Do I look to Jesus, the author and perfecter of my faith?[1033]

[1033] Hebrews 12:2

Father, thank You for this verse today. What a timely reminder to keep my eyes on You rather than on my circumstances. I confess the many times in the day to day I become self-absorbed and pragmatic rather than keeping my eyes on Christ and walking by faith and not by sight. I admit I am scared to ask You to help me walk in accordance with who You are rather than by sight because I fear You will take me through difficult times. More heartache, more removal… But Lord, I would much rather see You and know You and walk with You. Strengthen me to walk in accordance with who You are and who I am in Christ to You. Help me to rely on Your power and not to rely on my own. Thank You, Jesus.

2 *Chronicles* 12:1

When the rule of Rehoboam was established and he was strong, he abandoned the law of the Lord, and all Israel with him.

1. Rehoboam was "established and he was strong." We must remember those measurements in the eyes of God are subjective, for the Lord is the One who upholds us.

2. In having a wrong and evil view of self-worth, Rehoboam abandoned the law of the Lord. Pride and arrogance, the selfishness of thinking that we are "like God" is what sends us to evil. In fact, this is the exact same situation as in Genesis 3. Our hearts are abhorrently evil apart from the grace of God.

3. A leader is held to a higher standard than those not in leadership. This is because if the heart of the leader abandons the Law of the Lord, so do those who follow. Notice how Rehoboam abandoned the Law—and all of Israel did as well.

4. This leadership is not a corporate kind or what the world perceives as leadership. But within the family, I am to lead my wife by following Christ. I am to lead my sons by following Christ. I am to walk and to seek the Lord among clients, and my team, and all people.

Father, forgive me. I am overwhelmed because right now, I see how I have not sought You. How even in what feels justified in a way the world deems right, I have not sought You. Forgive me, Lord, and have mercy on me. Will You lead me in Your way? Will You affirm my step and open my mind to know You? Will You strengthen, protect, and bless me to know You and Your will? Thank You, Father. I ask this humbly for Your glory and for the glory of Christ.

Amen

Revelation 1:12–16

Then I turned to see the voice that was speaking to me, and on turning I saw seven golden lampstands, and in the midst of the lampstands one like a son of man, clothed with a long robe and with a golden sash around his chest. The hairs of his head were white, like white wool, like snow. His eyes were like a flame of fire, his feet were like burnished bronze, refined in a furnace, and his voice was like the roar of many waters. In his right hand he held seven stars, from his mouth came a sharp two-edged sword, and his face was like the sun shining in full strength.

1. This is Jesus Christ. This is the Son of God.

2. Jesus is not weak in any way, shape, or form. There are no powers over Him; there is nothing that stops His control of all things; there is nothing out of His control. He is King of kings and Lord of lords, and even though those of the world might talk about the world in a way the world seems "lost," we have the ability to look to Jesus and declare that all things are working together for good for those who love God and are called according to His purpose.[1034]

3. From His mouth comes a sword: the Word of God. It is inerrant and full of authority. Nothing can conquer it or come against it.

[1034] Romans 8:28

Jesus, You are great and awesome. As I read this beautiful chapter in Your Word, I see how John even trembled at Your presence. How glorious! Yet, Lord, forgive me, for I have had a liberal, deistic, atheistic view of You. I have held a view that You are not in control. I have believed the voices, the pundits, the fools of the world who have declared You are not Lord over all things. Forgive me, and thank You for opening my eyes. Help me to see You as the Sovereign, as the King, and help me to run in the assurance of Your glory, by faith.

Amen

Luke 23:13–16

Pilate then called together the chief priests and the rulers and the people, and said to them, "You brought me this man as one who was misleading the people. And after examining him before you, behold, I did not find this man guilty of any of your charges against him. Neither did Herod, for he sent him back to us. Look, nothing deserving death has been done by him. I will therefore punish and release him."

1. The King of Glory stood before Pontius Pilate, and yet Pilate could not see. Pilate, who has been placed in leadership by God the Father as a ruler, and is deemed to have the "IQ" and the "wisdom" to rule, was blind to who stood before him.

2. Pilate did not seek the Lord. He did not go back and lay before the Lord the choices before him at that very time. How very unlike the King of kings, for Christ many times rose early and went away to pray to the Father.[1035]

3. Here is God, fully God and fully man, and to whom someday, every knee shall bow, and every tongue confess that Jesus is Lord, and give an account for this very moment, but Pilate did not see it.[1036]

[1035]Mark 1:35, [1036]Romans 14:11–12

Oh Father, You sent Your Son and we denied Him. Forgive me for how often I deny seeking You in the day-to-day. Have mercy on me, and lead me in Your way everlasting. In Jesus' name.

Amen

Zephaniah 1:12

*At that time I will search Jerusalem with lamps,
and I will punish the men who are complacent,
those who say in their hearts,
"The LORD will not do good, nor will he do ill."*

1. God is not complacent, nor is He ever not actively working and searching the heart of man.

2. Nothing is ever morally neutral. For even the complacent heart will be punished by God. We are to do all things for the glory of God and to trust His work and His timing.

3. God is always working. The Lord is testing the hearts of man! He will come and discipline and pour His wrath out on those who do not think He is working, sanctifying, molding, and conforming people either to the likeness of His Son or in their own likeness and depravity.

Father, it is a terrifying thing to fall into the hands of a living God.[1037] Forgive me for not seeking You, for not coming to You. There are no instances when I am not to seek You, when I am not to pour my heart out to You. Even now, at this exact moment, Father, I am so tempted to have a secular and sacred divide in my heart and not trust You with the desires of my heart. Please forgive me and lead me in Your way everlasting. Help me to see the goodness of the Lord in the land of the living! In Jesus' name.

[1037] Hebrews 10:31

2 Chronicles 9:23

And all the kings of the earth sought the presence of Solomon to hear his wisdom, which God had put into his mind.

1. Wisdom is not brain mass, nor is it a chemical. Wisdom is not something you autonomously create, or build, or intrinsically have within your DNA. Wisdom and truth are outside of you. They are absolute and they are precious. They are given as a gift from the Lord God.

2. Wisdom cries aloud in the street for all who will listen, and she freely gives herself to those who want to learn and desire to grow in wisdom.[1038]

3. The fear of the Lord Most High is the beginning of wisdom,[1039] and apart from the work of the Holy Spirit, we cannot know and rest in wisdom.

4. Whoever lacks wisdom can ask God, and He will give generously to all without hesitation. But he must ask in faith, with no doubting. For the one who doubts is like a wave of the sea that is tossed about by the wind. That man believes he doesn't receive from the Lord.[1040]

[1038]Proverbs 1:20, [1039]Proverbs 1:7, [1040]James 1:5–8

Father, You are full of wisdom and grace. There is nothing You lack in knowledge and wisdom. For who can discern Your thoughts, or who has ever given You counsel? Yet, many times, Lord, that is how I have walked. I have walked around wanting to be like God rather than looking to You. Forgive me. Lord, if it be Your will, give me wisdom to walk in accordance with Your way, that I may know You and make You known. In Jesus' name.

2 Chronicles 9:8

Blessed be the LORD your God, who has delighted in you and set you on his throne as king for the LORD your God! Because your God loved Israel and would establish them forever, he has made you king over them, that you may execute justice and righteousness.

1. The Queen of Sheba, who was not one of God's chosen people, saw all that happened in Solomon's life and bore witness that all of it was because of the Lord. In fact, she blessed the Lord for what happened in Solomon's life.

2. God is not a far-off God. It is God who gives, and it is God who takes away; the name of the Lord be praised.[1041]

3. God's blessing of His people is because of His love and His covenant with His people. God is a relational and covenantal God.

4. It was not Solomon who made himself king, or anything he did, for he knew that unless the Lord builds the house, those who build it labor in vain, and unless the Lord watches over the city, the watchmen stay awake in vain.[1042]

5. What Solomon was to do, in all things and in everything, was to seek the Lord.

[1041]Job 1:21, [1042]Psalm 127:1

Father, I come to You, for You do all things, and give all things according to Your perfect plan. I confess that my pride and unbelief have made me look at You deistically rather than as a close Heavenly Father. I have not trusted You, nor have I sought You as I ought to. I have told You my plans, what I will create, and I have demanded You build my Babel. Forgive me and have mercy on me. Thank You for Jesus. Help me to know what it is to reside in His finished work. May the joy of the Lord be my strength, and use me in accordance with Your will. In Jesus' name.

3 John 9

I HAVE WRITTEN SOMETHING TO THE CHURCH, BUT DIOTREPHES, WHO LIKES TO PUT HIMSELF FIRST, DOES NOT ACKNOWLEDGE OUR AUTHORITY.

1. Christ is first. God is the Alpha and the Omega, the beginning and the end.[1043]

2. In today's culture, we hear, "If you aren't first, you're last." What a prideful mindset. The motivation behind it is something in which that person attempts to motivate winning, but for the wrong reasons. This promotes two things: self-glory and an unbelief in the Lord.

3. The fear of man makes a man want to be first. It makes him desire credit because he presupposes if he does not accomplish this, he will fail.

4. This mindset presupposes that God does not see him, and only he sees himself—and that is all he has. It rules out the truth of a personal God in charge of all things.

5. This mindset presupposes unbelief, which hardens the heart of the believer and makes the believer focus only on himself. He does not rest in the sovereignty of God. He does not pray and seek the Lord. Instead, he naval gazes and ignores Christ.

[1043]Revelation 1:8

Oh Father, forgive me, for this is a reflection of my entire life—all I have strived for and all I have been scared about. The seduction of success, or just the seduction of wanting to accomplish something and be something, and the lust of power is blinding. To be honest, the weight of this sin makes me want to be and act defeated—to just stop and give up. Help me to know Christ. Help me to rest and trust and walk according to Christ. In Jesus' name I ask this.

2 Chronicles 8:1-2

At the end of twenty years, in which Solomon had built the house of the Lord and his own house, Solomon rebuilt the cities that Hiram had given to him, and settled the people of Israel in them.

1. In this chapter, we see everything Solomon built: all the cities, all the glory, all the prestige he brought back to Israel.

2. We see he married the daughter of the Egyptian pharaoh, and he made people in his land slaves. Then he placed Israelites as guards of the slaves. This is a complete reversal of when the Israelites were in Egypt.

3. What this chapter doesn't mention is that Solomon had many wives from many nationalities. The power he achieved became a temptation. But everything he accomplished was because of the power of God.

4. Nothing can be done apart from Christ,[1044] and yet we focus on so much self-help, self-righteousness, and self-worth, that we forget how everything is accomplished through the power of God, and that every good and perfect gift comes down from the Father of Lights.[1045]

5. This chapter did not talk about God at all, just the accomplishments of Solomon. What is startling is that this is also a reflection of Solomon's life. When God began to do a mighty work in Solomon's life, Solomon's fear of the Lord began to decrease, and the pride of life flourished. Lord have mercy on me.

[1044] John 15:5, [1045] James 1:17

Father, I come to You this morning, and I am overwhelmed with my sin. I have often asked, "What do You want to build or to do?" What a man-centered way to look at things, rather than declaring, "if the Lord wills." All things should be done for Your glory, looking only to You and trusting You as the Author and Finisher of my faith.[1046] Lord, will You please help me to know where I have strayed from You? Will You draw near to me and help me to walk in accordance with Your will? I am tempted to despair, and I am tempted to harden my heart in pride, both at the same time. Thank You for Jesus.

Amen

[1046] Hebrews 12:2

Habakkuk 1:16

THEREFORE HE SACRIFICES TO HIS NET AND MAKES OFFERINGS TO HIS DRAGNET; FOR BY THEM HE LIVES IN LUXURY, AND HIS FOOD IS RICH.

1. The Babylonians looked to the tools and physical items they used against their opponents as that which brought them victory. By doing this, they denied that the God of the universe is the only one who either builds or destroys.[1047]

2. Anything that does not find its foundation in God and in His providence is an idol.

3. John Calvin, in his institutes, writes, "Man's nature, so to speak, is a perpetual factory of idols."[1048]

4. Today, one of the biggest idols in a postmodern world is the idolatry of *self*. Our standard of truth, our law, is ourselves. Our praise is our intellect—that which is created has declared to our Creator that we are wise, just, and holy apart from Him.

[1047]Job 12:23, [1048](Vol. 1, p. 108)

Father, have mercy on us. My sin is ever before me, and my need for Jesus is ever more true. Yet, my flesh is at constant war within my heart and mind, and Satan tempts me to despair. Show me Your glory, Father. Thank You for Jesus, and help me to walk in Your ways everlasting!

Amen

2 Chronicles 6:30–31

Then hear from heaven your dwelling place and forgive and render to each whose heart you know, according to all his ways, for you, you only, know the hearts of the children of mankind, that they may fear you and walk in your ways all the days that they live in the land that you gave to our fathers.

1. One of the greatest things in the world is to be known. Known completely. For everyone who walks the earth, regardless of acknowledging God or not, is fully known by Him.

2. There is no human, spouse, child, sibling, or friend who knows you as God knows you.

3. God knitted you together in your mother's womb.[1049] He knows what words you will say to anyone, including Him, before they even leave your mouth![1050]

4. God is not impersonal; He not only knows—He hears as well. He hears the groaning and the hurt; he hears the pain and the rejoicing. He hears all things.

5. The greatest thing that can ever happen is to know God and to make God known. He does all he does so that we, His people, may fear Him and walk in His ways and live in His presence continually.

[1049]Psalm 139:13, [1050]Psalm 139:4

Father, You are perfect in all Your ways. You not only formed me, but You know me completely. You know me better than I know myself. So many times I act, think, and do in a way that does not glorify You but attempts to steal that glory from You. Have mercy on me and forgive me, and lead me in Your way everlasting. Thank You, Jesus.

2 Chronicles 6:18

But will God indeed dwell with man on the earth? Behold, heaven and the highest heaven cannot contain you, how much less this house that I have built!

1. Nothing can contain God, for God is omniscient and omnipresent. There is nothing that cannot be seen by Him. There is nowhere you can go from His presence.[1051]

2. Nothing can contain the Lord, not even our prayers. The Lord uses our prayers and commands us to pray,[1052] but our prayers do not bind God.

3. The Lord God is in the heavens, and He does whatever He pleases.[1053]

4. There is nothing we can build, do, dream, think upon, hope for, or imagine that is bigger than or can contain God.

5. Our aim is to know, to glorify, and to pursue God with all our hearts, souls, and minds.

6. Yet Christ—Christ, who is fully God and fully man, walked with us on earth. God came in the likeness of sinful man and dwelled among us.

[1051]Psalm 139:7, [1052]Romans 12:12; 1 Thessalonians 5:17, [1053]Psalm 115:3

Father, You are awesome! Nothing can hinder You or keep You from doing Your will, for Your will is perfect in all and in every way. Forgive me for my unbelief and for having such a small and humanistic view of You. Help me to see You working all things for Your glory. In the midst of "breaking news," and in the midst of "unparalleled times," what are these things man declares, in comparison to You? Yet for anyone who does not know You, even an anthill seems large. Show us Your glory. In Jesus' name I ask.

Amen

2 Chronicles 6:8–9

But the Lord said to David my father, "Whereas it was in your heart to build a house for my name, you did well that it was in your heart. Nevertheless, it is not you who shall build the house, but your son who shall be born to you shall build the house for my name."

1. The Lord reigns, and there is nothing that goes against His will. All that God desires He does, and He does it for His glory.

2. David was not lazy. He desired to build a house for the Lord. This motivation to do something great for the Lord is good, and God indeed declared, *"You did well that it was in your heart."* But this was not the plan of God. Our hearts should always, continually, and at every moment seek the Lord. No matter how good our intentions, the result is not the most important; the will of God is.

3. We see this in the garden of Gethsemane, where Christ, as He prays to the Father, says, "Father, if you are willing, remove this cup from me. Nevertheless, not my will, but yours be done."[1054] Christ is tempted at that moment, but at the moment all temptations must come before the throne of grace and be handed over to the living God.

4. God will fulfill His purposes in His way.

[1054] Luke 22:42

FATHER, NOTHING CAN BE DONE APART FROM YOU,[1055] FOR FROM YOU AND THROUGH YOU, AND TO YOU ARE ALL THINGS.[1056] SO MANY TIMES I HAVE SAID IN MY HEART AND MY MIND THAT, "I AM GOING TO BUILD THIS" OR "I AM GOING TO DO THAT." ALL THIS IS PRIDE. THIS IS A WALKING IN THE FAITH IN MY OWN MIND RATHER THAN ACCORDING TO YOUR WILL. FORGIVE ME, AND THANK YOU FOR CHRIST. MAY YOUR KINGDOM COME, AND MAY YOUR WILL BE DONE ON EARTH AS IT IS IN HEAVEN.

[1055] John 15:5, [1056] Romans 11:36

1 *John* 3:1

See what kind of love the Father has given to us, that we should be called children of God; and so we are. The reason why the world does not know us is that it did not know him.

1. The knowledge of God is giving to us a true and saving knowledge of God and is a gift of grace and mercy by the Holy Spirit. None of this comes from our intellect, or our IQ, or our ability to think and pass a standardized test. It is not because of geographical location.

2. This love of God, and the knowledge and beauty of His love, is not because of a prayer or an emotional experience, but it's because of the knowledge of a Person—that Person being Jesus Christ, the Son of the Most High God.

3. The reason why the world does not understand, cannot comprehend, is they believe God is a philosophy. But He is a Person. This goes beyond all comparison.

4. Paul's conversion came not because of intellect, or because he was smarter than anyone else, but because he met a Person, he was called by a Person, and he was sent by a Person.[1057] That Person is the Person of Jesus Christ.

[1057] Acts 9

Jesus, You are more precious than anyone or anything. You are glorious and high and lifted up. I have not understood or known You. In my pride, I have thought it was because of myself that I accomplished something. Forgive me. Jesus, You have placed me in front of so many leaders, so many people who do not know You. I ask that You open doors, in whatever way You desire, to be able to declare the mystery of You.[1058] There are many people who would look at me as weird, which I am ok with, but You have placed me in study groups. You have opened doors many people of influence. Please use me in whatever way, if it be, for them to know You. Bless me, that others may see my good works and glorify You.

[1058] Colossians 4:3

Nahum 1:12-13

Thus says the Lord, "Though they are at full strength and many, they will be cut down and pass away. Though I have afflicted you, I will afflict you no more. And now I will break his yoke from off you and will burst your bonds apart."

1. No number comes close to touching an infinite God. He is high and lifted up, and He is seated on His throne forever. "Full Strength" in light of who God is nothing. "Many" in the sight of who God is, is meaningless.

2. When I begin to use language that magnifies the bigness of man and the smallness of God, this says I have more fear of man rather than fear of the Lord Almighty.

3. In this verse, even though he brought to mind how the bigness and the grandness of their enemies were quantified in this way, it was the Lord who caused the affliction. It was the Lord alone who allowed this to happen to His people—for His glory and their good. God sovereignly ordains all things, and we are to rest in that knowledge. So, even though these were enemies of the people of Israel, they were ordained by God to afflict Israel and lead them to repentance—not to moralism, but to their knowledge and understanding of the need for God and His mercy.

4. God sovereignly orchestrates all things. In this verse, it was God who would break their yoke and burst their bonds.

Oh Lord, You are good, and You are mighty. Forgive me for looking at money, or title, or certifications, or wealth, as something bigger than You. I have had a small view of You in my heart and mind, and I have not sought You. Forgive me, and make me to walk in Your way. Father, You have afflicted me this year, many times to lead me to repentance. Yet many times, instead of repenting, I've shaken my hands at You. Forgive me, Lord, and have mercy on me. Will You burst the bonds and break the yoke of those things that keep me from resting in You? Would You help me to build a thriving business that promotes love and the gospel to those in need of knowing You, which models justice in making things right and is faithful in its calling? Magnify Yourself, for Your glory.

2 *Chronicles* 2:5

The house that I am to build will be great,
for our God is greater than all gods.

1. Solomon prepared to build a temple, a house for the Lord Almighty. In doing this, he built it in accordance with who God is. He built it "greatly" because God is greater than all things.

2. We should aspire to do great things in line with the knowledge of who God is. Dan Doriani states in his book, *Work: Its Purpose, Dignity, and Transformation,* that it is not enough to say we are doing things that are for God's glory, but that we should reflect God's attributes back to Him, because of who He is.[1059]

3. If we do not know God, how can we reflect back to one whom we do not know? If we do not know Him, we cannot reflect any of His attributes and character back to Him.

4. Doriani states three attributes for us to be mindful of to reflect back to God. Although there are more, he references God's Love, God's Justice, and God's Faithfulness.

5. I am to repent of all humanistic and small views of God, and I am to reflect the greatness of God, which is reflected most beautifully in His Son Jesus Christ, who came to earth, paid the price for my sin, was raised on the third day, and is now seated at the right hand of the Father.

[1059]Doriani, Daniel, Work: Its Purpose, Dignity, and Transformation. (pp 48). Phillipsburg: P&R Publishing, 2019

Oh Lord, You are high and holy and lifted up. You are King of all kings. Forgive me for having such a small and human view of You. Please help me to do Your will, and to reflect Your character, and to trust, by grace through faith, with thanksgiving, Your providence. Let the peace of Your Son, which passes all understanding, flood my heart and soul to do Your will and rest in You.

2 *Chronicles* 1:10

Give me now wisdom and knowledge to go out and come in before this people, for who can govern this people of yours, which is so great?

1. Solomon acknowledged the need for God to give him wisdom. He did not have the capacity to lead or do anything apart from the wisdom of God.

2. In doing this, he also acknowledged this wisdom was to help lead and serve others, and to also acknowledge that he looked to God for that wisdom, for apart from God, he had nothing.[1060]

3. Solomon began with prayer. He began his reign with prayer to the Lord, seeking the Lord. He did not consult his mind, his intellect, or his self-help books; he went to the Lord in prayer.

4. Solomon reflected James 1:5-8, in which James says if anyone lacks wisdom, he should ask the Lord, who gives generously and without reproach.

5. What are the things in which I do not seek the Lord? If I am not seeking the Lord in something, am I approaching it in pride and arrogance? Am I saying to the Lord that I believe what I am doing is not big enough for Him to bother?

6. What areas in my life am I not bringing before the Lord and seeking Him?

[1060] John 15:5

Father, You are wisdom. You know all things, and all things are held together by Your sovereign grace. Lord, I feel overwhelmed with being a husband, father, layman, advisor, friend. I feel inadequate to "go out and come in" in front of the people You have placed in my life. But Christ is perfect. Christ is all wisdom, all hope, all assurance, all goodness. Christ leads perfectly. Help me to reflect Christ in all things. Help me to have Christ's wisdom in studying. Help me to grow in wisdom and in stature for Your glory.

2 Peter 3:17–18

You therefore, beloved, knowing this beforehand, take care that you are not carried away with the error of lawless people and lose your own stability. But grow in the grace and knowledge of our Lord and Savior Jesus Christ. To him be the glory both now and to the day of eternity. Amen.

1. Many thoughts and ideas occupy the heart of man, and apart from the Word of God they are nothing. Only God is holy, and our only form of measurement is the Word of God.

2. Many people, myself included, put others on a pedestal and worship their words or intellect. But none of these are holy; only the Word of God is holy. All thoughts must be taken captive,[1061] and we are to hold fast to the truth and despise every kind of evil.[1062]

3. So what is our aim? If the aim is not intellectual superiority, or a loftiness of ideas, or strength in an argument, what is it? Our aim is knowing, abiding in, dwelling with, and growing in more intimacy with Christ and Christ alone. We are to grow in the grace and knowledge of our Lord and Savior Jesus Christ, and all things are to His glory, from now and into all eternity.

[1061] 2 Corinthians 10:5, [1062] 1 Thessalonians 5:21–22

Jesus, help me to know You. Help me to grow in the grace and knowledge of You in all things and to see all things for Your glory. Many times I have walked in accordance with what I see rather than in the truth and grace of You by faith.[1063] Save me, have mercy on me, and help me to walk in accordance with You and for Your glory.

Amen

[1063] 2 Corinthians 5:7

Job 8:13–15

Such are the paths of all who forget God; the hope of the godless shall perish. His confidence is severed, and his trust is a spider's web. He leans against his house, but it does not stand; he lays hold of it, but it does not endure.

1. Who or what we put our confidence in is reflected in how we live our lives moment by moment. Every step we take, every word we utter, every moment we live reflects strength and the assurance of our hope and faith. Every person places his or her faith in someone or something.

2. For those who do not put their trust in the Lord, their confidence shifts moment by moment, based on their experiences. Their faith and confidence are rooted in what they perceive to be true within their current circumstance. They don't know God because they deny Him and harden their hearts, and all confidence is gone. With each moment their hearts continue to harden, and they are wrapped in unbelief, fear, and doubt, as though caught in a spider's web. In their own strength, they are unable to be free of it.

3. In our own strength and might, we are unable to free ourselves from the deception of our hearts.[1064] Apart from the work of God, we are doomed to death.[1065] Let those caught in this web cease to fight on their own, and in turn, cry to the Lord for mercy.[1066]

4. But for those who put their trust in God, they endure all trials the Lord mercifully leads them through. Their hope is in God and not in their circumstances. The true believer is not afraid of bad news, for his heart is firm, trusting in the Lord. His heart is steady, not be afraid until he looks in triumph on his adversaries.[1067]

[1064]Ephesians 2:5, [1065]Ephesians 2:1, [1066]Romans 10:13, [1067]Psalm 112:7–8

Father, I thank You that You have made Yourself known and are sovereign over all things. Nothing that occurs is outside of Your sovereign grace. Forgive me, Lord, for making idols out of people and circumstances. Open my eyes and give my heart and mind wisdom to walk humbly with boldness in Christ, for Your glory. In Christ's name.

Amen

Malachi 1:13

"But you say, 'What a weariness this is,' and you snort at it," says the Lord of hosts. "You bring what has been taken by violence or is lame or sick, and this you bring as your offering! Shall I accept that from your hand?" says the Lord.

1. Every means of grace the Lord has given His church is a grace to remind the believer of the reality of Christ over all things and our pursuit of Christ. From the gathering of the saints, which we are not to neglect,[1068] to the Lord's Supper,[1069] each is given to us by God.

2. Our hearts deceive us[1070] and have a higher view of our dependency on ourselves rather than acknowledging our utter need for Christ. We look at the things going on in our lives, and our hearts become weary and hardened to the things of God. We begin to compare ourselves to the morality of our neighbors rather than the holiness of God.

3. We bring excuses and offer them to God and do not give our whole hearts over to the Lord because we perceive that God is merciful and that His ways do not apply to us. We become proud in our hearts and lose the fear of the Lord in every aspect of our lives.[1071]

4. But let us remind ourselves of the deceit of sin and note both the kindness and severity of God. For God has in His mercy and kindness given us these means of grace to remind us of His love toward us. These are not man-made institutions or habits created in the mind of man, but instead in the mind of God for our good. Let us humble ourselves, lest He cut us off from Himself, and let us walk in a manner that is worthy to bear the name of His Son.[1072]

[1068]Hebrews 10:25, [1069]1 Corinthians 11:23–25, [1070]Jeremiah 17:9, [1071]Romans 11:20, [1072]Romans 11:20–22

Father, thank You for the gift of grace You have given to Your Church. Thank You for Your Word and for Your Holy Spirit, who is working to bring Your people to Yourself. Forgive me for having such a low view of the means of grace You have given Your Church. Help me to have a deeper love and a deeper passion for the things You have given Your Church, for Your glory. In Christ's name.

Matthew 1:17

So all the generations from Abraham to David were fourteen generations, and from David to the deportation to Babylon fourteen generations, and from the deportation to Babylon to the Christ fourteen generations.

1. All of time is under the sovereign rule of God. In the beginning there was no time, for God the Father, God the Son, and God the Holy Spirit lived together for all eternity, fully and completely without want or need or desire in any way.

2. Then God, in His love and grace, spoke time into existence.[1073] Before God created time, there was eternity, which is the absence of time. When God spoke, He spoke and created things out of love, for His glory and for the good of those He created, and in that moment, time began.

3. God created Adam from the dust in the ground and Eve from Adam's rib, and then He breathed life into them.[1074] God placed them in the garden to work and to keep the garden for His glory and the good of mankind.[1075]

4. Then Adam and Eve sinned against God. When they sinned against Him, He cursed them[1076] and threw them out of the garden.[1077] But in that moment as well, He revealed His sovereign plan of redemption through His Son.[1078]

5. God revealed through His Son that there is no time outside of His control and Lordship. Though sin entered the world through Adam, God made a covenant through Abraham, and through over forty-two generations, God perfectly orchestrated the redemption of His people and has brought together His Church to reflect His Kingdom to all mankind.

6. In light of these truths, we need not fear the time before us. We can look at the faithfulness of our God and know that just as He has perfectly orchestrated His creation and His sovereign plan since all eternity, that He who began a good work in us will bring it to completion at the day of Jesus Christ.[1079]

[1073]Genesis 1:3–5, [1074]Genesis 2:7, [1075]Genesis 2:15, [1076]Genesis 3:14–19, [1077]Genesis 3:23, [1078]Genesis 3:15, [1079]Philippians 1:6

Oh Father, how perfect You are in all things. You are Lord over all time, and You orchestrate all things according to Your sovereign plan. Forgive me, Lord, for the many times I doubt Your sovereignty. I look at the present times and I am tempted to not believe You care, that You are Lord, that You are working all things. Give me boldness, strength, and joy to live and to serve You all my days, for Christ's sake and His glory alone.

Matthew 8:5–6

When he had entered Capernaum, a centurion came forward to him, appealing to him, "Lord, my servant is lying paralyzed at home, suffering terribly."

1. Look at the faith of the centurion. The centurion came before the One who holds all things in the universe by the word of His power[1080] and shared with Him that his servant was sick. He recognized Christ as the Son of God and faithfully placed His request before the Lord.

2. Let us examine our own hearts as our daily circumstances ebb and flow, and let us be honest with ourselves about how many times we act faithfully or how many times we act out of a practical, atheistic heart.

3. We are to cast all our burdens on the Lord, trusting that He will sustain us in all and every circumstance.[1081] To not cast our burdens on the Lord is to make an idol out of that which we fear. It is to look at the circumstance the Lord is taking us through and to have a small and distrusting view of God.

4. When we faithfully go to God with each of our desires, we show Him that we trust Him in every circumstance in our lives. The centurion did not know how Christ would answer his request, but he knew Christ could do all things, and he trusted Him to do what was best.

5. Christ marveled at the faith of the centurion.[1082] The word *marvel* means to be astonished or in awe. Is the Lord in awe of how much you trust Him with the details of your life? Does He marvel at how you look to Him for all things? Do you go to the Lord with an obligatory acknowledgment, or do you humbly approach Him in all things, knowing the same mouth that spoke the world into creation is the same mouth that ordains all things that we go through?

[1080]Hebrews 1:2–3, [1081]Psalm 55:22, [1082]Matthew 8:10

Oh Lord, how glorious You are! You speak all things, You declare all things, and You allow us to approach You in all things. Lord, soften my heart to bring my burdens, my cares, my hopes, and my dreams before You. Help me to walk in such a way that You rejoice and are magnified. I am not worthy to bring You glory. I am not worthy for You to even look at me, but use my life in such a way that You are magnified in all details. In Christ's name.

Matthew 3:9

And do not presume to say to yourselves, "We have Abraham as our father," for I tell you, God is able from these stones to raise up children for Abraham.

1. The temptation of the heart in every aspect of our lives is to be like God.[1083] The heart desires to look at the parameters of the world and to believe that not only man but God Himself is bound by someone or something other than who He is, which is God. In our modern minds, we attempt to make God a creation rather than Creator.

2. We are to look at all of life, not by what the world decides is true, or good, or beautiful, but we are to look at all of life in the reality of who God is. His Word proves true, and everything He says we can rest in because of who He is.[1084]

3. For God's people, our hope is in Christ, our future is in Christ, and our days are in Christ's hands. Regardless of what the world tells us, God is able to even make children for Himself out of stones. Nothing can deter God's perfect plans, so we can rest assured that all things work together for good for those who love Him and are called according to His purpose.[1085]

4. Let us be mindful of what humanistic things we relegate the workings of God to. Let us place our hope in God's goodness and repent of making God like man. For God's thoughts and God's ways are not our thoughts or our ways.[1086] Let us meditate on His promises, striving to see Him, and trust that His plans are perfect. Even the Lord's disciplines are good, for He only disciplines those He loves, as a father disciplines the son in whom he delights.[1087]

[1083]Genesis 3:5, [1084]Proverbs 30:5, [1085]Romans 8:28, [1086]Isaiah 55:8, [1087]Proverbs 3:12

Lord, I thank You for Your Word. I thank You that it is truth and that You have given us truth. Forgive me for the many circumstances I've denied Your Lordship or projected on You what I thought truth was rather than taking You at Your Word. Help me to see life as Christ sees all things unto the glory of the Father. Help me to walk in the hope and truth of who You are, by faith, and with wisdom—for Your glory in all circumstances. In Christ's name.

Job 32:2

Then Elihu the son of Barachel the Buzite, of the family of Ram, burned with anger. He burned with anger at Job because he justified himself rather than God.

1. God's Word commands us to be angry and yet not sin.[1088] This leads many to think about what we should be angry about and what not to be angry about. Elihu, in the book of Job, showed us what righteous anger is.

2. All our aim in life is to be about the glory of God.[1089] When we begin to justify ourselves rather than God, we cease to serve and acknowledge God's sovereignty over our lives. We tell God how we have a better idea of how our lives should be constructed rather than trusting His sovereignty. We break the first commandment by placing another god before God, which is usually ourselves.[1090]

3. God's thoughts and God's ways are not our thoughts and our ways.[1091] We are to trust our Heavenly Father in whatever He allows in our lives. The Lord disciplines those He loves, as a father the son in whom he delights.[1092] When we murmur in our hearts against God and justify our actions, we stir up the anger of the Lord in the same way the children of Israel murmured against God.[1093]

4. God's anger poured out against the children of Israel in the desert because they did not trust Him. In turn, God's wrath turns against us, and His Spirit is quenched when we murmur and grumble against Him.[1094] What angers God should anger His people. Let us not justify ourselves before God, but in turn, acknowledge that He is working all things together perfectly for those who love Him and are called according to His purpose.[1095]

[1088]Ephesians 4:26; Psalm 4:4, [1089]1 Corinthians 10:31, [1090]Exodus 20:2, [1091]Isaiah 55:8, [1092]Hebrews 12:6, [1093]Psalm 78:19, [1094]1 Thessalonians 5:19, [1095]Romans 8:28

Father, how great and awesome You are and how much I need You. Forgive me for my lack of faith and unbelief that drives away my joy in You and hardens my heart. Let the joy of You be my strength. Let the hope in Christ fan into flames the thanksgiving of my heart to proclaim Your excellencies to all You bring into my life. For Your glory, and for Christ. In His name I pray.

1 Corinthians 2:14

THE NATURAL PERSON DOES NOT ACCEPT THE THINGS OF THE SPIRIT OF GOD, FOR THEY ARE FOLLY TO HIM, AND HE IS NOT ABLE TO UNDERSTAND THEM BECAUSE THEY ARE SPIRITUALLY DISCERNED.

1. There are two people groups in the world today, and their distinction is the Lordship of Christ. Those who are in Christ know Him and are known by Him. Those who are of the world are those Christ has never known.[1096]

2. Those who are in Christ are to be in the world, but not of the world.[1097] Our aim is not to please man but to please God. For it is God who takes us through all our circumstances to test us and make us more into the image of His Son.[1098]

3. But as we walk more and more in the light of Christ, depending upon the promises of God in all things and looking to God's Word to be our standard, we look foolish in the eyes of the world. We are not to look wise in the things of the world but foolish in the eyes of those who deny Christ![1099] We are to never be wise in our own eyes but to fear the Lord and turn from all evil.[1100]

4. For we know the mind that is set on the flesh is hostile to God, for it does not submit to God's Law; indeed, it cannot![1101] But if we are alive in Christ, the Spirit of God who raised Him from the dead dwells richly in us.[1102] While we walk in Christ and walk opposite of the world, this is what makes the church a shining light, a city on a hill.[1103] Let us walk in such a way that others see our good works and praise our Father in heaven.[1104]

[1096]Matthew 7:21–23, [1097]John 15:18–19, [1098]1 Thessalonians 2:4, [1099]1 Corinthians 3:18, [1100]Proverbs 3:7, [1101]Romans 8:7, [1102]Romans 8:11, [1103]Matthew 5:14, [1104]Matthew 5:17

Lord, I thank You for Your Word. It is true and perfect and right in all things. Lord, I confess the many things that make me desire to be liked by the world rather than to follow You. Forgive me. Change my heart and mind in such a way that all that I do brings You glory and praise. Give me wisdom to not walk according to the world but according to Christ. May I be foolish to the world and wise in Christ. In His name.

Job 12:10

IN HIS HAND IS THE LIFE OF EVERY LIVING THING AND THE BREATH OF ALL MANKIND.

1. All of life is in the hand of God. Every heartbeat, every breath, every movement, every aspect of life is held together by the hand of God. This is a truth that should both comfort the believer, and at the same time, lead us to the fear of the Lord and repentance for our unbelief.

2. Every day of our lives is written in the Lord's book of life. In fact, each day was formed specifically for us.[1105] This was done before we were even conceived; before the foundations of the earth we were intentionally thought of, loved, and known.

3. This is not just for humanity though but for all creation. The birds of the air, the creatures on the earth, and the fish of the sea are all held together intentionally by the hand of God. He holds all the universe by the power of His Word,[1106] and in Him, all of creation and all of the heavens live and move and have our being.[1107]

4. So, how are we to respond to such high and lofty and ultimate truths? We are to respond in worship and fear of the Lord. For who then can know the mind of the Lord, or who can discern His ways? If He is the ultimate over everything, and His hands are the life of all things, then from Him, and through Him, and to Him are all things. To Him be the glory forever and ever![1108]

5. We are to live a life of only the fear of the Lord. No fear is to grip our hearts, for our hearts are in the hands of the Lord. No enemy or threat should make us timid because it is the Lord who defends us,[1109] and it is the Lord who gives and takes away. The name of the Lord is to be both feared and blessed.[1110]

[1105]Psalm 139:16, [1106]Hebrews 1:2–3, [1107]Acts 17:28, [1108]Romans 11:33–36, [1109]Proverbs 91:10, [1110]Job 1:21

Lord, You are perfect in all Your ways. You hold all of life in the palm of Your hand. Even as I am here before You, the only reason my heart beats is because of Your grace and mercy. Lord, do not let my thoughts sink to a low view of You. Forgive me for the many times I have denied Your supremacy in my life. Lift my eyes, lift my heart, lift my mind to be mindful of who You are, and lead me in Your way everlasting! In Christ's name I ask this.

Romans 15:4

For whatever was written in former days was written for our instruction, that through endurance and through the encouragement of the Scriptures we might have hope.

1. God's Word was written that it might be an encouragement in and throughout the days of the believer. It is to point us to God throughout all of redemptive time, and to give us the assurance that we may endure and be faithful to the end.

2. Our hope and the aim of our focus is to be in Christ, who is the Word made Flesh,[1111] and to see how from Adam to Christ to the present, God is working out all things for His glory and our good. But this is not accomplished through "self-talk" or "wishful thinking" on our part. This can only be rooted in truth, and God's Word is objectively true in all circumstances.[1112]

3. All of Scripture is God-breathed and is profitable for teaching, for reproof, for correction, and for training in righteousness, that the man of God may be completely equipped for every good work.[1113] We are to meditate on God's Word day and night;[1114] it is to be a lamp unto our feet and a light unto our path.[1115]

4. As we focus on His Word, it gives us hope to endure to the end. It points us to who God is, and gives us assurance in God's redemptive work. We can say with Joseph, "What you [the world] meant for evil, God meant for good!"[1116] Our assurance and hope are not in our circumstances, but in the One who is over all things, who orchestrates all things, and the One the Scriptures instruct and encourage us to follow with endurance to the very end.

[1111]John 1:14, [1112]John 17:17, [1113]2 Timothy 3:16–17, [1114]Psalm 1:2, [1115]Psalm 119:105, [1116]Genesis 50:20

Lord, Your Word is perfect and complete. It feeds the soul and strengthens the heart to continue to press on to the end. I confess the many things my heart seeks to find its identity other than You. I read the news, I listen to what's going on in these times, and I am tempted to doubt You. Forgive me. Give me wisdom and strength to remove that which does not glorify You, and lead me in Your truth alone. In Christ's name.

2 Timothy 1:7

*FOR GOD GAVE US A SPIRIT NOT OF FEAR
BUT OF POWER AND LOVE AND SELF-CONTROL.*

1. For those who are in Christ Jesus, we must recognize that we are the sons of God. For all who are led by the Spirit of God are sons of God through Christ Jesus.[1117] In light of this truth, we must be mindful of who we are in Christ and the fruit that bears witness in our lives to the reality of who we are.

2. Our hearts and minds are to reflect the truth of Christ's Lordship over all things in our lives. The only One we must ever fear is God alone, for He is the Creator and sustainer of all things. He gives us the strength to do that which He has called us to, equipping us to do His will,[1118] prepared in advance for us to do it.[1119]

3. In light of the truth of who God is, and who we are in Christ, we are to be strong and courageous. Our confidence is hidden with Christ and in the truth of the power of His resurrection and Lordship over all things. We are to live our lives in boldness for Christ and fearing only the Lord and none other.

4. This is opposite of the world, which lies and deceives to control us and cause us to deny the Lord. That which we worship is that which we fear. We either fear the world or God Most High, and we act on the reality of that fear. Those who fear the Lord walk in power, love, and self-control in the truth of the Lord's reign over all things, and that in Him and Him alone we live and move and have our being.[1120]

[1117]Romans 8:14, [1118]Hebrews 13:20–21, [1119]Ephesians 2:10, [1120]Acts 17:28

Oh Lord, I praise You, for You are Lord over all things. Those who are in You are to fear none other than You. I confess the many times I am tempted to fear and doubt and not walk in the spirit and truth of who You are. My eyes are ever tempted to look at the world rather than Your Word. Make me to know Your ways, Oh Lord, and teach me Your paths. Lead me in truth and teach me, for You are the God of my salvation, and for You I wait all the day long![1121]

[1121] Psalm 25:4–5

Psalm 31:24

Be strong, and let your heart take courage, all you who wait for the Lord!

1. Those who are in Christ must take courage in all circumstances. For we must remember that God did not give us a spirit of fear but one of power, love, and self-control.[1122]

2. The fear of our hearts arises when instead of seeing the Lord working all things together for His good, we begin to believe that someone or something is greater than God. This happens when we begin to believe our friends and neighbors dislike us,[1123] or when we think we have been forgotten by everyone,[1124] or when we hear the whispers of those saying evil and wrong things about us.[1125] We begin to believe the world rather than the Word of our God.

3. But we must remember that our trust in every aspect of our lives is in God and God alone.[1126] Every aspect of our lives is in His hands; all our days are numbered and are held purposefully and intentionally for His glory and our good.[1127] We must turn to prayer rather than to the world; we must rejoice that our God reigns and turn to the Lord, asking Him to help us go forward in all He has called us to.[1128]

4. So in all circumstances, let us look to the One who is over all things. Let us remind ourselves who God is, that the Lord never sleeps nor slumbers,[1129] and that He keeps us in His hands. Let us be strong in the Lord's strength. Let us take courage that all our time is in His hands, and let us wait expectantly, knowing that in His time He will perfectly do all He has sovereignly ordained for us.

[1122]2 Timothy 1:7, [1123]Psalm 30:11, [1124]Psalm 30:12, [1125]Psalm 30:13, [1126]Psalm 30:14, [1127]Psalm 30:15, [1128]Psalm 30:3, [1129]Psalm 121:4

Oh Lord, how glorious and mighty You are, and how easily I am discouraged. I so easily forget Your majesty; I so easily get lost in my mind, rather than trusting in You and You alone. Forgive me. Give me vision in You, hope in You, assurance in You, and strengthen me to do Your will. I thank You, Lord, for Your mercy and grace. In Christ's name I pray.

Amen

Proverbs 29:25

THE FEAR OF MAN LAYS A SNARE,
BUT WHOEVER TRUSTS IN THE LORD IS SAFE.

1. That whom we fear the most is the One who rules over us. Every aspect of our lives is about observing what causes the least amount of fear, thus rooting all our choices in fear.

2. To fear man is to set a snare for our feet, for we deny God and His working in every moment of our lives. We cease to look at His Word and to trust His promises and instead trust our thoughts, feelings, and emotions. We conjure up ideas and scenarios that do not exist, and in the moment of analyzing our imagination, we get caught up in things that do not exist. We scream, "There is a lion in the street! I shall be killed!" and cease to trust in the Lord and do that which He has called us to.

3. But our hope is in Christ alone, and Christ is faithful over God's house as a Son. All those in the house of God are to put all boasting and confidence in Christ.[1130] In Christ, we have a Kingdom that cannot be shaken, and we are to at all times worship, praise, and adore Him and Him alone![1131]

4. Our God is a consuming fire.[1132] He is our Rock, our Deliverer, our shield, the horn of our salvation, our stronghold.[1133] Every moment of our lives is to be rooted in the truth of who God is, trusting in the promises of His Word and taking direct action in those things He has prepared in advance for us to do.[1134] When we do this, we honor the Lord and can trust that whatever befalls us, we are safe in Christ for all eternity.

[1130]Hebrews 3:6, [1131]Hebrews 12:28, [1132]Hebrews 12:29, [1133]Psalm 18:1-2, [1134]Ephesians 2:10

Father, I praise You for Your Son. I praise You that You have brought me into the life of Christ. I confess the many times I have looked at this world and have trusted my emotions rather than trusting in You. I have acted in a way to trust and build myself up rather than walking boldly in honoring and trusting Christ. Forgive me, Lord. Show me Your ways and give me strength and hope to do Your will. In Christ's name I ask this, and for His glory.

Proverbs 2:5

THEN YOU WILL UNDERSTAND THE FEAR OF THE LORD
AND FIND THE KNOWLEDGE OF GOD.

1. This is a glorious promise that follows instruction from the author of the book of Proverbs. Before we think through what the Lord instructs us, we must remember the beauty God Himself promised to understand the fear of the Lord and find knowledge of Him. Who are we that He would give us such a glorious promise?

2. First, though, we must store His Word in our hearts. We are to listen to what God has said to us in His Word and follow His commands, walking in accordance with Him in every aspect of life.[1135] When we incline our ears rather than our mouths, we acknowledge that we do not have wisdom and know the One who speaks has all wisdom.

3. We are to call out for insight and to ask our loving Heavenly Father for wisdom. It is a fool who believes he knows how things should go and doesn't call out to God. For only a fool would think he knows the plans of even the next millisecond. Only a fool would elevate himself to "be like God." All such boasting is evil in the sight of the Lord.[1136]

4. Seek the Lord while He may be found, and let us call upon Him while He is near.[1137] For this is the person the Lord will look to: "He who is humble and contrite in heart, and trembles at His Word."[1138] It is this person who, by faith, seeks the Lord with all His heart, the Lord draws near to. It is this person who seeks Christ with His whole heart, the Lord grants to know Him. Regardless of our past sins, as we seek God humbly, to know and to praise Him, He will make Himself known and great in our lives.

[1135]Proverbs 2:1, [1136]James 4:16, [1137]Isaiah 55:6, [1138]Isaiah 66:2

Oh Lord, how beautiful are Your promises. How glorious is Your Word! I confess the many times I have attempted to conjure You up intellectually rather than trusting Your amazing grace. Please give me wisdom and direction to seek You as a husband, father, businessman, and child of God, and to know You and to make You known in all things. In Christ's name.

John 17:14

I HAVE GIVEN THEM YOUR WORD, AND THE WORLD HAS HATED THEM BECAUSE THEY ARE NOT OF THE WORLD, JUST AS I AM NOT OF THE WORLD.

1. The Word of the Lord is to dwell in our hearts richly,[1139] to encourage, strengthen, and fill our hearts with the joy of Christ in all things.[1140] In every aspect of our lives, we are to abide in Christ, and apart from Him we can do nothing.[1141]

2. The litmus test to see if the lives we live actually do bear fruit is that the world will hate us. The more we reflect Christ, who is not of this world, the more the world will hate us with a vengeance and a passion.

3. This is why our Lord said, "Blessed are you when others revile you and persecute you and utter all kinds of evil against you falsely on my account. Rejoice and be glad, for your reward is great in heaven, for so they persecuted the prophets who were before you."[1142] The wisdom and power of God is foolishness to the hearts and minds of man, for they cannot understand it apart from the work of the Holy Spirit.[1143]

4. Those who abide in Christ have the joy of Christ in all things.[1144] The joy of the Lord is our strength,[1145] and we are to be "joyful always, pray continuously and give thanks in all circumstances, for this is God's will for us in Christ Jesus!"[1146] We, the people of God, regardless of what the world says, are to have the peace of God which transcends all understanding, and He has promised that He Himself will guard our hearts and minds in Himself.[1147]

5. The Christ-exalting joy of our Lord Jesus Christ, and the reality of His Lordship, places us at enmity with the world.[1148] The more we love Christ, the more the world will hate us. Our aim should not be to be beloved to the world but to be faithful to Christ and to trust that whatever He ordains is right.

[1139]Colossians 3:16, [1140]John 17:13, [1141]John 15:4–5, [1142]Matthew 5:11–12, [1143]1 Corinthians 1:18, [1144]John 17:13, [1145]Nehemiah 8:10, [1146]1 Thessalonians 5:16–18, [1147]Philippians 4:7, [1148]James 4:4

Oh Lord, You are truth and light, and You are above all things. In You is joy and truth, and yet the world desires to crucify the reality of You. I confess, Lord, the many times I have desired a friendship with the world rather than be persecuted for acknowledging Your Lordship over my life. Fill me with Your joy and Your strength, and make me to walk in Your ways for Your glory. In Christ's name.

John 9:41

JESUS SAID TO THEM, "IF YOU WERE BLIND, YOU
WOULD HAVE NO GUILT; BUT NOW THAT YOU SAY,
'WE SEE,' YOUR GUILT REMAINS."

1. The world lives shamelessly because they do not know Christ. When the light is denied, then darkness is not considered dark because there is nothing to contrast it. Darkness is just what it is when not juxtaposed alongside light.

2. But the light has come into the world, and the world has run away from it because the world is dark, and the works of all darkness are evil.[1149] Darkness can never overcome light, for the only reason that darkness is dark is because of the truth and reality of light. But in Christ, the light shines in the darkness, and the darkness has not, and will not, overcome it.[1150]

3. For even in my sin, when I attempt to deny God or hide from Him and think surely the darkness shall cover me, and I shall be hidden from the light of truth,[1151] our evil is not hidden from God. There is nowhere we can hide from Him, for darkness is as light to Him.[1152]

4. We must be mindful that God, who being rich in mercy and because of the great love with which He loved us,[1153] has called us by name out of the darkness and into His marvelous light.[1154] We see our guilt, but this is only by His grace because our guilt is made known in seeing Christ. When we truly see Christ and the guilt of our depravity, we can leave our guilt behind because of the grace of Christ's atoning work on the cross, and recognize that in His resurrection, our guilt is finished.[1155]

[1149]John 3:19, [1150]John 1:5, [1151]Psalm 139:11, [1152]Psalm 139:12, [1153]Ephesians 2:4, [1154]1 Peter 2:9, [1155]John 19:30

Lord, what freedom we have in Christ! Your light blinds my heart with joy and humbles me to my very core. Who am I that You would make Yourself known to me? The darkness of my heart is too dark for anyone to save me—except one Person—You, the light of life, Christ and Christ alone. Forgive me for the times I forget Your glory and the light and truth of who You are. Let Your light shine even deeper and brighter in my soul, that I may praise You all the more! In Christ's name.

Amen

2 Timothy 3:7

ALWAYS LEARNING AND NEVER ABLE TO ARRIVE AT A KNOWLEDGE OF THE TRUTH.

1. The Word of God is not only for growing in knowledge but must be applied throughout every aspect of our lives. It is "profitable for teaching, for reproof, for correction, and for training in righteousness, that the man of God may be complete, equipped for every good work."[1156]

2. There is no other book like it in all the world, for it was not created by man but breathed out by God. It was revealed to man by God, and is meant for all facets of our lives. We are not to grow fat in knowledge, for even the devil knows the Word of God, as he used it against our Lord when he tempted Him in the wilderness.[1157]

3. The difference between the devil and the man of God is the man of God must apply all of Scripture to all of life. God's Word is a lamp unto our feet and a light unto our paths.[1158] We are to meditate on it day and night, careful to do all it says, for then God has promised we will be profitable and will succeed in all God has called us to.[1159]

4. Let us not add to or take away from God's Word,[1160] but let us seek God's truth. Let us hold fast to that which He has given us in spirit and in truth,[1161] praying and seeking His will in all things and applying His Word in every domain of our lives by His grace. His Word is true,[1162] and in this we find rest and assurance and hope.

[1156]2 Timothy 3:16–17, [1157]Matthew 4:1–11, [1158]Psalm 119:105, [1159]Joshua 1:8, [1160]Deuteronomy 12:32, [1161]John 4:24, [1162]John 17:7

Oh Lord, I praise You for Your Word. I praise You for its efficiency and its completion. Lord, in so many areas of my life, I have not applied Your Word. I have not applied Your truth and instead created things from my sinful imagination. Forgive me. Help me to walk according to Your Word in all areas of my life. Open my eyes to Your truth, and may Your Holy Spirit lead me according to Your will. In Christ's name I ask this.

Isaiah 7:9

IF YOU ARE NOT FIRM IN FAITH, YOU WILL NOT BE FIRM AT ALL.

1. Everything we do must be rooted in the truth of who Christ is and must be lived out by faith in all circumstances of our lives. God's Word promises that those things not firm in our faith are those things not firm at all.

2. Christ is the solid Rock on which we are grounded, and not even the gates of hell can overcome or even withstand this truth.[1163] We are to preach this to ourselves and to our brothers and sisters in Christ every day. The devil attempts to deceive our sinful flesh and to make us diminish the reality of our Lord in many aspects of life. We are tempted to place our faith in our circumstances, status, family, and even the information we receive in our times rather than the truth of God's Word.

3. Let us approach the throne of grace with confidence, knowing that our Lord desires for us to repent of our fears and doubts. Let us be mindful that anything else we root our trust in is sinking sand![1164] When we look at the floods rising, when we struggle through the storms, we are to look to Christ and Christ alone. The joy of the Lord is our strength![1165]

4. Let us remember when Peter, in the middle of the storm, walked on water. But when he took His eyes off Christ, he began to drown in the rising waves. Let us heed the Word of our Lord when He admonished Peter and said, "O you of little faith."[1166] Let us confess those idols that attempt to steal our faith, and let us walk with boldness in our King, knowing that from Him and through Him, and to Him are all things![1167]

[1163]Matthew 16:18, [1164]Matthew 7:26, [1165]Nehemiah 8:10, [1166]Matthew 14:31, [1167]Romans 11:36

Oh Father, how glorious is Christ and His Lordship over all things. How easily I forget this, Lord. Forgive me for denying His Lordship over all things. Forgive me for being fearful of anything but You and You alone. Help me to see Christ over all and give me wisdom and strength to joyfully do Your will and Your command. In Christ's name.

Jeremiah 1:7-8

But the LORD said to me, "Do not say, 'I am only a youth;' for to all to whom I send you, you shall go, and whatever I command you, you shall speak. Do not be afraid of them, for I am with you to deliver you, declares the LORD."

1. In everything the Lord calls us to do, we must be confident in the sufficiency of who God is and in His sovereign grace. The person whose mind is not on the Lord will many times place before the Lord every man-made argument to justify his inability for the task. He will look at circumstances and pragmatic reasoning to justify his lack of doing the Lord's will.

2. But in everything we are to look to God. We are to meditate on the promises of the Lord and act in accordance with them. We are to press forward with the Lord's commands, and wherever He sends us, we are to go, trusting that He will take care of us. We are to know that even in situations that render us speechless, He will provide us perfectly the words and the wisdom to accomplish His will.[1168]

3. The aim of the believer is to trust in the Lord with all his heart and to lean not on his own understanding, knowing the Lord will make His paths straight before him.[1169] Our confidence and boasting are not to be in our flesh but in the truth of who Christ is and His Lordship over every aspect of our lives.[1170] It is the Lord who is our shepherd. He leads us beside still waters, and He leads us through the valley of the shadow of death—all for His namesake.[1171]

4. So, let us seek the Lord. Let us ask Him to make His way known to us, and let us trust that He will lead us. Let us deny ourselves and our perceptions of ourselves and instead take up our crosses and follow where our Lord leads. For He has said whoever will save his own life will lose it, but whoever loses his life for Christ's sake and the for the gospel will save it.

[1168]Mark 13:11, [1169]Proverbs 3:5–6, [1170]Philippians 3:3, [1171]Psalm 23

Oh Lord, how great and awesome You are! How glorious and wise and sovereign You are over all things! I confess the many times I look to my own heart and circumstances, and I deny Your Lordship and sovereignty. Forgive me. Lead me to wherever You would use me to bring glory to Your name. Give me vision and strength to accomplish Your will. Help me to recognize any self-centered or man-centered ideas so that I may repent and follow You. Be glorified in every aspect of my life. In Christ's name.

Isaiah 45:5

I AM THE LORD, AND THERE IS NO OTHER, BESIDES ME THERE IS NO GOD; I EQUIP YOU, THOUGH YOU DO NOT KNOW ME.

1. In every instance of our lives, the Lord is molding us and making us into the image of His Son.[1172] He is growing us and leading us to do the work He has prepared for us to do before the foundation of the world.[1173]

2. As we plan and look to the future, with everything we do, we are to remind ourselves that even though we plan our steps, it is the Lord who brings them to fruition.[1174] In light of this truth, we can know that each moment and each step we take are from the Lord. We cannot know the reason behind every step, but we can know the One who ordains these steps and know they are all purposeful for His glory.[1175]

3. Let us then meditate on His Word day in and day out, seeking to do His will and trusting Him with every detail. For He has promised that if we seek Him and follow Him, He will make our way prosperous according to His good pleasure and will give us success to do His will and His will alone.[1176]

4. In trusting Him with every detail, we can know that even though He may lead us through the valley of the shadow of death, He is with us. His rod and His staff, they will comfort us.[1177] In trusting Him, we are to seek Him and to look to Him, trusting that He will equip us with every good thing to do His will, that we might please Him and glorify Christ our King and Lord over all![1178]

[1172]Ephesians 4:15, [1173]Ephesians 2:10, [1174]Proverbs 16:9, [1175]Proverbs 20:24, [1176]Joshua 1:8, [1177]Psalm 23:4, [1178]Hebrews 13:21

Oh Father, how great and awesome You are. Every detail of my life You hold in Your hand and You equip me in Your perfect timing and perfect way to do Your will. Lord, I confess the many times I feel inadequate to the task. I worry I am unable to do what You have called me to. Forgive me, and open my eyes. Strengthen me and give me wisdom. Grant me to do Your will, that I may glorify Christ and Christ alone in what He has called me to do for His glory and the good of others. In Christ's name.

Amen

Isaiah 51:7

"Listen to me, you who know righteousness, the people in whose heart is my law; fear not the reproach of man, nor be dismayed at their revilings."

1. God has commanded that we are to listen to Him in all things and in every situation, applying the Word of God to every aspect of our lives. "For all Scripture is breathed out by God and is useful for teaching, for reproof, for corrections, and for training in righteousness, so that the man of God may be thoroughly equipped for every good work."[1179]

2. We are to meditate on God's Law day and night,[1180] to think on and praise Him in all circumstances,[1181] knowing by faith He is working together all things in our lives for the good of those who love Him and keep His commandments.[1182] By looking to the Lord and trusting His Word above all things, this is what brings His Kingdom on earth as it is in heaven.[1183]

3. Those who are righteous are mindful of the truth and reign of Christ over every aspect of their lives. Even when their family and friends ridicule them for their faith in Christ's Lordship, we are not to fear man nor be dismayed at their taunting. We are to seek the Lord, trust in His promises, and walk boldly with our Lord. For Christ has promised that we are blessed when others revile and persecute us and utter all kinds of evil against us for the sake of Christ.

4. The identity of the believer is not in the things of the world but in the Lordship of Christ. We are to trust Him regardless of what the world tells us, for He upholds the universe by the power of His Word. So let us run, seeking Him and depending upon Him in all things and in everything.

[1179]2 Timothy 3:16, [1180]Psalm 1:2, [1181]1 Thessalonians 5:18, [1182]Romans 8:28, [1183]Matthew 6:10, [1184]Hebrews 1:2–3

Oh Father, how glorious You are that You have given us Christ and that You have sent Your Son to pay the penalty for my sins. I so easily diminish the truth and of the Lordship of Christ over every aspect of my life. So many times I am tempted to worry about what others think of me rather than to trust in You. Forgive me, Lord, and fill my heart and mind with Your Word, that I may walk in Your truth. In Christ's name.

Psalm 119:1

BLESSED ARE THOSE WHOSE WAY IS BLAMELESS,
WHO WALK IN THE LAW OF THE LORD!

1. The Law of God is not a human construct, nor is it an act of man; it is a grace the Lord has given us that we should walk in them. All things are held together by God, and it is in Him and Him alone that we live and move and have our being.[1185]

2. Man, in his foolishness, many times believes there is such a thing as natural law. But all things are held together by God. The sun rises and falls and declares the glory of God because the Lord is the One who orchestrates it day after day.[1186] The world is established, and it cannot be moved because of the Lord's grace in keeping His Word.[1187] We need not fear ever again a global flood.[1188] God controls every raindrop and makes it to rain on the just and the unjust.[1189] All these things occur by the hand of God.

3. God has also given us His Law by which to live and by which to glorify Him. This Law He has written on the hearts of man, though man attempts in every way possible to suppress the truth in unrighteousness.[1190] The Law of God is good and true. He blesses His Law and promises that in His perfect timing, it will be successful and will make us prosper and flourish in the Lord's perfect timing.[1191]

4. We must go to the Lord daily and look to His Word, abiding in it day in and day out. We must acknowledge our need for a Savior and trust Him to lead us according to God's Word. Those who trust in the Lord will be blessed. They will know their God, and they will worship Him. Even when the Lord leads us through the valley of the shadow of death,[1192] we will rejoice, for we know we are His. Let us then meditate on His Law and abide in His grace in all aspects of our lives.

[1185]Acts 17:28, [1186]Psalm 19:1, [1187]Psalm 93:1, [1188]Genesis 9:11, [1189]Matthew 5:45, [1190]Romans 1:18, [1191]Joshua 1:8, [1192]Psalm 23:4

Lord, I praise You for Your Law, for Your commandments, for Your statutes, and for Your Word. For we do not deserve these graces. There is nothing we have done to earn the right to know You, but You, in Your grace, have made Yourself known. Forgive me for so many times denying Your Law and Your Word. Help me to be mindful of all that I say and do, that I may glorify You, and use my life for Your glory. In Christ's name.

Psalm 119:147

I RISE BEFORE DAWN AND CRY FOR HELP;
I HOPE IN YOUR WORDS.

1. Each morning let us arise from our sleep with the knowledge that it is the Lord Himself who has sustained us throughout the night. As we rise from bed, let our hearts and our minds be filled with thanksgiving for the Lord's watch over us in our sleep. We are not to seek our own dependency in our own humanity but to instead look to the Lord who has ordained every aspect of our days.[1193]

2. As we move forward in our days, let us bow to the Lord and let us seek Him in His Word. Let us ask the Lord and listen to His faithful love for His people, that we may walk in a way that honors Him in every moment. As we come to Him, we acknowledge our trust in Him. We acknowledge that there is nothing we can do apart from Him and that our full dependency is on Him in all things.[1194]

3. As we acknowledge our dependency on Him and confess our sinfulness and depravity, let us then look to Him for the way to go throughout the day.[1195] Let us meditate on the promises of God early in the morning, that we might have full dependency and full joy of life the Holy Spirit.[1196]

4. This is accomplished through faith.[1197] We must look to the Lord and His Word, and by faith act and walk throughout each moment. We are not to shrink back from the task at hand, but instead be watchful, stand firm in the faith, act like men, be strong, and let everything we do be in love for Christ and for His glory.[1198]

[1193]Ephesians 2:10, [1194]John 15:5, [1195]Psalm 143:8, [1196]Psalm 119:148, [1197]Hebrews 11, [1198]1 Corinthians 16:13–14

Oh Lord, You are awesome, and it is You alone who upholds the universe by the power of Your Word. You command the seconds, minutes, hours, days, months, and years of our lives, and each one serves You for Your glory. I confess how the hardness of my heart and the carelessness of my mind diminishes Your sovereignty over all of time, Lord. Forgive me, please, and fill my heart and mind with the truth of Your Word. Help me to walk boldly according to the promises You give me in the morning and a passion and zeal for You. In Christ's name, and for His glory.

Joshua 1:7

Only be strong and very courageous, being careful to do according to all the law that Moses my servant commanded you. Do not turn from it to the right hand or to the left, that you may have good success wherever you go.

1. The believer is called to be strong in the Lord and in the strength of His might in every situation and circumstance through which the Lord leads him.[1199] This is done first and foremost by knowing who God is at all times. We are to destroy every argument and lofty opinion raised against the knowledge of God and, in turn, take every thought captive to obey Christ.[1200]

2. The Word of God is true[1201] and is a lamp to our feet and a light to our path.[1202] In light of this, we are to be mindful that all we do reflects the truth of God's Word in our lives. We are to meditate on His Law day and night,[1203] trusting that His Word will prosper and succeed in all He leads us through.[1204]

3. This gives the believer an unwavering confidence, for even though the Lord might lead him through the valley of the shadow of death, He will have no fear. For He knows God is leading Him on all paths.[1205] We must be careful not to test the Lord,[1206] but to instead walk humbly with Him and trust Him in all situations and places the Lord has called us.[1207]

4. This confidence and courage is reflective of our King, the founder and perfector of this perfect and true and courageous faith, who for the joy that was set before Him endured the cross, and despised the shame of the world, and is now seated at the right hand of the Father![1208] We, in turn, are to boldly and joyfully submit our entire lives to this King and to do His will with courage and hope in all things.

[1199]Ephesians 6:10, [1200]2 Corinthians 10:5, [1201]John 17:17, [1202]Psalm 119:105, [1203]Psalm 1:2, [1204]Joshua 1:8; Psalm 1:3, [1205]Psalm 23:4, [1206]Deuteronomy 6:16, [1207]Micah 6:8, [1208]Hebrews 12:2

Oh Lord, how glorious is Your Word! For Christ has given us freedom to be courageous and bold in showing the world hope of His Lordship and His redemption of His people. Lord, my heart falters so easily. I am so easily discouraged and prone to fear when I look at the world. Forgive me, give me hope in Christ, and make Your way straight before me. Place Your Word deep in my heart that I may glorify You in all things. In Christ's name.

Isaiah 62:7

AND GIVE HIM NO REST UNTIL HE ESTABLISHES JERUSALEM AND MAKES IT A PRAISE IN THE EARTH.

1. In everything the Lord gives us to do, we are to seek Him. For it is the Lord who builds the house; it is the Lord who watches over and defends, and it is from the Lord that all things are from, and through, and to.[1209]

2. Yet, many times we are tempted to doubt the Lord, not wanting to trouble Him with the trifles of the world. We begin to think we should only go to the Lord about big things, but the seemingly small and mundane things we are to figure out on our own. Our gratitude and our hope in the Lord begin to diminish, and our pride begins to increase. We begin to quench the Spirit and His power within all aspects of our lives.[1210]

3. We must turn back to God. All authority in heaven and on earth has been given to Christ,[1211] and it is Him alone who upholds the universe by the power of His Word.[1212] So, in light of these truths, we are to go to Him in all things. Our aim must not be for the small things in our live, but for His goal, which is the saving of the world under His Lordship. We are to look at each small thing as a building block for His Kingdom. We are to pray for His Kingdom to come and His will to be done on earth as it is in heaven.[1213]

4. In every aspect of our lives, let us pray. Let us ask the Lord in every moment, giving Him no rest in our prayers to bless the work of our hands for His Kingdom. Pray for His wisdom, His blessing, His protection, His strength, to do His will, for His glory, and for our good in all things.

[1209]Romans 11:36, [1210]1 Thessalonians 5:19, [1211]Matthew 28:18, [1212]Hebrews 1:2–3, [1213]Matthew 6:10

Oh Lord, Your Kingdom come, Your will be done. We know Your Kingdom will be built because You have promised us so. You have brought us here for such time as this, in such a way as this, for this moment. Let us not waste one moment. Fill our hearts with prayer and petitions to do Your will for Your glory. Give us strength and hope in Christ to press on, trusting in Your sovereign grace for Your Kingdom and our glory. In Christ's name.

Isaiah 66:2

BUT THIS IS THE ONE TO WHOM I WILL LOOK: HE WHO IS HUMBLE AND CONTRITE IN SPIRIT AND TREMBLES AT MY WORD.

1. To whom will God look? With whom will God abide? To whom will God give wisdom? Is he the strongest, the mightiest, the best looking? All the measurements the world has to offer are meaningless before our God, for our God is the One who created all things, and commands all things, and who orchestrates all things according to His will.[1214]

2. Those who bow to the Lord, who meditate on His Word day and night,[1215] who look to the Lord and tremble at His Word—those are with whom the Lord will abide. The one who submits to God's command to do justly according to the commandments of God, who loves mercy in the way he has received mercy, and walks humbly before the Lord all of his days,[1216] this is the one to whom the Lord will look.

3. It is to the humble, and humble alone the Lord makes His ways known. He will teach those who submit to Him the way they should go.[1217] These are all glorious and merciful truths and promises the Lord gives us. Apart from the Holy Spirit working the truth of God's Word in our hearts and opening our eyes and ears to our depravity and need for Him, these are impossible to attain.

4. We must daily submit our lives to the Lord. We must look to Him and trust each moment, each day to His goodness, trusting that His steadfast love endures forever and that He is purposefully working all things together for the good of those who love Him and are called according to His purpose.[1218] It is in light of this truth that we can humbly say with confidence, if our God is for us, who can be against us?[1219]

[1214]Psalm 135:6–7, [1215]Psalm 1:2, [1216]Micah 6:8, [1217]Psalm 25:9, [1218]Romans 8:28, [1219]Romans 8:31

Oh Lord, how great are all Your deeds! You are high and lifted up, and yet You know me! Lord, I am so easily tempted to think I can do things apart from You. I am so prone to wander and to deny the truth of Your Word. Forgive me! Help me to walk with humble confidence in Christ, according to Your Word in every moment. Soften my heart and mind and plant Your Word deep into my heart, that I may serve You with my whole being. In Christ's name.

Isaiah 35:4

Say to those who have an anxious heart, "Be strong; fear not! Behold, your God will come with vengeance, with the recompense of God. He will come and save you."

1. We are to go to God in all things and cast all our anxieties on Him because He cares for us.[1220] There is nothing too great, nor too small, for the Lord, for all things come from Him. We are to look to Him and know He supplies all our needs.[1221]

2. As the Lord leads us through the mountains and the valleys, we are in turn to not define ourselves by our circumstances but to reflect upon God's providence and His mercies in sustaining us through all the trials and uncertainties of life.[1222]

3. Let us be careful not to murmur against the Lord or complain against the dispensations He carries us through. For to grumble against God is to think He does not know what He is doing or that He has failed in some way.[1223] The Lord is faithful, showing steadfast love to those who love Him and keep His commands.[1224]

4. So let us in every moment look to God, who so loved the world that He sent His only Son, that whoever believes in Him will not perish but have everlasting life.[1225] Let us be mindful that we are to be strong, take heart, and to wait on the Lord.[1226] Let us encourage each other, as long as it is today so that none of us become hardened in heart with sin.[1227] Let us know we are to be strong and not to fear, for our God is perfect, and He works for His people, for His glory and our good.

[1220]1 Peter 5:7, [1221]Romans 8:32, [1222]Deuteronomy 7:17–19, [1223]Deuteronomy 1:27, [1224]Exodus 20:6, [1225]John 3:16, [1226]Psalm 27:14, [1227]Hebrews 3:13

Oh Lord, how easily I take my eyes off You. You bring the sun up every morning and set it every evening. You keep all things working together, and You sustain all of life. Regardless of what the world says, You are King and You uphold all things by the power of Your Word. Yet, how easily I forget. How fickle and lazy is my heart. Help me to meditate on You and Your goodness. Strengthen me to be mindful of who You are, and help me to do Your will with joy in Christ and Christ alone. In His name I ask this.

Jeremiah 3:13

Only acknowledge your guilt, that you rebelled against the Lord your God and scattered your favors among foreigners under every green tree, and that you have not obeyed my voice, declares the Lord.

1. What is it that keeps the Lord at bay and causes our hearts to harden and walk in unbelief? An unrepentant heart. When we deny the Law of God, His statutes, His precepts, and His wisdom over all of life and only do that which feels good,[1228] we play the fool. We do not realize an unrepentant heart leads to death and the depths of hell.[1229]

2. But the Lord has commanded us to live a fruitful life in keeping with repentance.[1230] A life of repentance is a life that is truly humble before the Lord, turning from that which does not glorify Him and walking anew in light of His Word. We are to acknowledge our need and dependency on His sovereign grace and walk by faith in each moment. We need not attempt to justify ourselves before a watching world, for Christ is our justice. We need not attempt self-righteousness, for Christ is our righteousness.

3. The Lord is near to those who are brokenhearted and to those who are crushed in spirit.[1231] When we turn and look to the Lord, He will lead us. He will make His way known before us and will guide us according to His Word along the path life.[1232]

4. The eyes of the Lord look to and fro throughout the whole land to see if there are any who seek Him and Him alone.[1233] When we do not humble ourselves in repentance, the Lord sets Himself against us. When we demand our foolishly perceived rights, the Lord becomes our enemy. But for those who humbly call on Him, acknowledging our sin and total dependency on Him, He gives grace upon grace.[1234]

[1228]Proverbs 9:17, [1229]Proverbs 9:18, [1230]Matthew 3:8, [1231]Psalm 34:18, [1232]Psalm 119:105, [1233]Psalm 53:2, [1234]James 4:6; John 1:16

Oh Lord, how gracious You are. You have given us Your Son to pay the penalty for our sin. You have given us Your Word, by which we are to walk. You have given us Your church, with which to encourage and exhort each other as long as it is today to do Your will. But, so often I do not repent. Instead, I attempt to justify my sin before a holy God. How foolish and deserving of all justice. Lord, have mercy on me and help me to humbly walk a life of repentance, with boldness and assurance in Christ and Christ alone. In His name I pray.

Amen

Romans 1:17

For in it the righteousness of God is revealed from faith for faith, as it is written, "The righteous shall live by faith."

1. The good news of Jesus Christ has never been "plan B," but has been the purpose of God from the beginning of time. God the Father has called a people to Himself "before the foundations of the world,"[1235] and this has been written down by the very hand of God.[1236] In it, the world has seen the righteousness of God on full display.

2. We know in our hearts we need a Savior to reconcile ourselves to God, yet so many times, instead of bowing our knee to Christ in faith, we suppress this truth in unrighteousness.[1237] We in our sin want to establish our own rules, with subjective morality and things to fear other than God.

3. More than five hundred years ago, the church and culture of the time attempted in every way to place their own morality and humanistic laws to fit their narrative. But a German monk named Martin Luther could not get past the simple and powerful truth that, "the righteous shall live by faith."

4. It is this truth the world attempts in every way to suppress, and yet it is this very truth the world needs to know and God's people need to remind each other of daily.[1238] This truth will cause us persecution for the sake of Christ, for it denies the deceitful power and manipulation of the world and instead acknowledges the Lordship of Christ over all things.[1239] Why the persecution? Because those who know the gospel and walk by faith in it are free indeed to know God, to abide in Christ, and to live by faith in the reality of His true Lordship over all things.

[1235]Ephesians 1:4; 1 Peter 1:20, [1236]Revelation 13:8, [1237]Romans 1:18, [1238]Romans 1:12, [1239]Matthew 5:11-12

O Father, you are so glorious and your ways and thoughts are so far beyond anything I could possibly imagine. That you sent your Son to die for me is something beyond anything I could ever comprehend. Forgive me for the many times I deny the reality of the gospel. I feel the temptation to bind my conscience to the things of the world, rather than to serve Christ with all my heart. Have mercy on me, and help me to walk by faith in the finished work of Christ in all of life, for you glory and for the proclamation of the gospel. In Christ's name I pray.

ACKNOWLEDGMENTS

Writing this acknowledgments page has been the most difficult part of the entire book-writing process because the Lord has used so many people pouring into me over the years to complete this book. Anna Floit has managed, edited, and encouraged me through this entire process. The Lord brought her at the right time to help make this happen, and it could not have happened without her. Thank you to Caleb Faires, who designed the crest; Nicole Stalder on all things digital; Cheryl Casey, designer and formatter; and Ashley Hagan, publishing services. All four are gifted by God to take words and make them beautiful.

Thank you to all the mentors and brothers the Lord has placed in my life: Steve Craver, Michael Hampton, Clarence Risen, Corky Dawes, Mike Oates, Gene Lee, Dr. Steve Barnes, Stephen Barnes, and many more. Thank you to the pastors God has graciously placed in my life to preach the Word of God: Dr. George Grant and Scott Patty.

Thank you to my brother Abraham, who the Lord has brought to encourage and be in fellowship with Christ with as we move forward, pouring into my sons and to where the Lord leads us. To my great friend Keith Knell, who has loved me in Christ and whom Christ has used to help me know Him, love Him, and adore Him—I am eternally grateful; words do not suffice for how much you have poured into me and my family.

To my wife Katie, who always encourages me to press on toward Christ and to unapologetically and intentionally follow Him for His glory. To my sons Nolan, Micah, Titus, and Caleb, who are the arrows the Lord has given me to shoot forward into the generations to come. Ultimately to Christ, apart from whom I can do absolutely nothing.

AUTHOR BIO

Solomon Kafoure and his wife Katie raise their four boys in Middle Tennessee, where he owns a consulting / wealth planning / estate planning firm. The Kafoures attend Parish Presbyterian Church in Franklin, Tennessee.

www.ingramcontent.com/pod-product-compliance
Lightning Source LLC
Chambersburg PA
CBHW072339300426
44109CB00044B/1978